# Literary Culture in Jacobean England

# Literary Culture in Jacobean England

## Reading 1621

Paul Salzman

*Senior Lecturer*
*English Department*
*La Trobe University*
*Australia*

First published 2002 by
PALGRAVE MACMILLAN
Houndmills, Basingstoke, Hampshire RG21 6XS and
175 Fifth Avenue, New York, N.Y. 10010
Companies and representatives throughout the world

PALGRAVE MACMILLAN is the global academic imprint of the Palgrave
Macmillan division of St. Martin's Press, LLC and of Palgrave Macmillan Ltd.
Macmillan® is a registered trademark in the United States, United Kingdom
and other countries. Palgrave is a registered trademark in the European
Union and other countries.

ISBN 1–4039–0073–6

This book is printed on paper suitable for recycling and made from fully
managed and sustained forest sources.

A catalogue record for this book is available from the British Library.

Library of Congress Cataloging-in-Publication Data

Salzman, Paul.
    Literary culture in Jacobean England : reading 1621 / Paul Salzman.
        p. cm.
    Includes bibliographical references (p. ) and index.
    ISBN 1–4039–0073–6
    1. English literature—Early modern, 1500–1700—History and
    criticism.   2. Great Britain—History—James I, 1603–1625.
    3. England—Intellectual life—17th century.   I. Title: Reading 1621.
    II. Title.

    PR431 .S35 2002
    820. 9'003—dc21                                          2002072334

10   9   8   7   6   5   4   3   2   1
11   10   09   08   07   06   05   04   03   02

Printed and bound in Great Britain by
Antony Rowe Ltd, Chippenham and Eastbourne

*For Susan, Imogen, Joseph and Charles*

This publication has been supported by La Trobe University
*Internet: http://www.latrobe.edu.au*

# Contents

*List of Figures*                                                                x

*Acknowledgements*                                                              xi

*Timeline*                                                                     xiii

*Preface: 1621*                                                                 xv

**1 John Chamberlain Reads the Year**                                           1

**2 Selves**                                                                   13
  Subjectivity                                                                 13
    *Mortalities Memorandum*: a dream of the self                             15
    *The Anatomy of Melancholy*: 'Thou thy selfe art
        the subject of my Discourse'                                          17
  Sermons                                                                      31
    John Donne: 'alwayes preaching to himself'                                32
    Lancelot Andrewes: Noli me tangere                                         41
    Thomas Gataker's *Spark*                                                   52
    Samuel Ward: happiness in practice                                         54
    George Hakewill's advice to the prince                                     58

**3 Transformations of Romance**                                              64
  The publication of *Urania*: woman writer as 'hermaphrodite'                65
  *Arcadia* and the politics of romance in 1621                               67
  John Barclay's *Argenis*: the perfect glass of state                        75
  Transforming romance                                                        80

**4 Performances**                                                            82
  Thomas Middleton in 1621: performance and political
      critique                                                                85
  Islands, princesses and wild goose chases                                   92
  Massinger and the state                                                     97
  Double writing/double marriage                                             101
  The witch                                                                   104
  Masques                                                                     107
  Audiences                                                                   111

5  **Poetry**                                                              **113**
   'Pamphilia to Amphilanthus': freely expressing
      the captive self                                                      113
   George Wither: the poet in prison                                        117
   John Taylor: waterman/satirist                                           123
   Manuscript poetry: libels, lyrics and anthologies                        129
   John Ashmore and Joseph Martyn: translations,
      epigrams and satire                                                   133
   Elegy: Donne and the reprinting of mourning                              134
   *Envoi*: elegy for Hugh Atwell                                           138

6  **News**                                                                **140**
   News-paper: the coranto                                                  141
   Foreign correspondence                                                   143
   News from parliament                                                     146
   Ballads and broadsheets                                                  150
   Almanacs                                                                 154

7  **Instruction**                                                         **159**
   Religion                                                                 159
      The sermon as instruction                                            160
      Religious guides                                                     162
      Meditation                                                           167
      Maternal advice                                                      170
      Religious controversy                                               173
      Providence and punishment: *The Triumphs
         of God's Revenge*                                                 177
   History                                                                 181
      Ralegh: history and power                                           181
      Bacon: power and history                                            189
      Samuel Daniel: history and the English state                        191
      Heylyn's *Microcosmus*: historical/geographical/
         political/theological                                            194
      History as exemplary knowledge                                      195
   Secular instruction                                                      197
      Education                                                           197
      Practical arts                                                      198
      Economics                                                           199
      Psychology                                                          200
      Living                                                              201
      Knowledge on the market                                            202

**Conclusion** **204**

*Notes* 209

*Bibliography* 241

*Index* 260

# List of Figures

1. Title-page of Robert Burton, *Anatomy of Melancholy* (1621), by permission of The British Library, C.45.c.30.  19
2. Samuel Ward, Engraving 'To God', British Museum, BMC 41.  56
3. Title-page of *Wither's Motto* (1621), by permission of The British Library, 1076.c.19.  118
4. Title-page of *Taylor's Motto* (1621), The Huntington Library, San Marino, 69646.  124
5. Anatomical man from Daniel Browne, *Almanac* (1621), British Library, P.P. 2465.  156
6. Title-page of Walter Ralegh, *History of the World* (1614), British Library, C.38.i.10.  183
7. Frontispiece/title-page of Walter Ralegh, *History of the World* (1621), The Bodleian Library, Oxford University, Antiq.C.E.1621.1.  185

# Acknowledgements

My work on this book began when I was asked by Professor Howard Erskine-Hill to contribute a volume to the Cambridge University Press Eighteenth Century series. While my interests dragged the project back in time until I settled on 1621 as my year, I remained under the protective wing of CUP's editor Josie Dixon, who encouraged me over the many years that I spent working on the book. It is, therefore, fitting that the manuscript ended up following Josie to Palgrave Macmillan, and I am delighted that the book finally appears under her aegis.

Throughout this lengthy period of research I have been supported by my department and colleagues at La Trobe University. I was able to undertake a major part of my primary research while the recipient of two visiting fellowships during periods of study leave granted by the Faculty of Humanities and Social Sciences at La Trobe. In 1996 I was a visiting fellow at Clare Hall, Cambridge, and particularly benefited from the warm collegial atmosphere there. In 1999 a visiting research fellowship at Merton College, Oxford enabled me to spend a glorious six months residing with my family, so appropriately for someone working on the seventeenth century, in Anthony a Wood's house in Merton Street. I am extremely grateful to the Warden and Fellows of Merton, and especially to Richard McCabe, for making us so welcome.

The bulk of my primary research was conducted in the Cambridge University Library, British Library and Bodleian Library. I also owe a special debt to the tireless and cheerful interlibrary loan staff at the Borchardt Library, La Trobe University, especially in the late stages of my work, when they responded indefatigably to an avalanche of requests for microfilms.

Many individuals offered invaluable help at various stages of this project. Here I want especially to thank Tom Healy, Elaine Hobby, Harold Love, Richard McCabe, Andrew McRae, Michelle O'Callaghan, Susan Wiseman and a number of anonymous readers at both CUP and Palgrave Macmillan.

Several versions of Chapter 1 were presented as papers at the London Renaissance Seminar, the Clare Hall History Discussion Group, The Oxford Renaissance Seminar, The Society for the History of Authorship, Reading and Publishing conference at Cambridge, and the Victorian Universities Seventeenth Century Discussion Group. Some of the material in Chapter 3 formed part of a paper delivered at the London Renaissance Seminar and also part of my essay 'The Strange Constructions of Mary Wroth's *Urania*: Arcadian Romance and the Public Realm', in Neil Rhodes, ed., *English Renaissance Prose: History, Language and Politics* (Tempe, Medieval and Renaissance Texts and Studies, 1997).

The illustrations have been reproduced by the kind permission of the British Library (Figures 1, 3, 5 and 6), the British Museum (jacket illustration and Figure 2), The Huntington Library, San Marino (Figure 4), and the Bodleian Library, Oxford University (Figure 7).

My greatest debt is to my family: Susan Bye has lived with this project for many years and our three children were, so to speak, born into it. Without their cheerful support the book would never have been completed.

# Timeline

(For the purposes of this study, the year runs from 1 January to 31 December; in 1621 the year began on 25 March.)

**Prelude**

Anne of Denmark, James I's wife, died in 1619, and by 1621 King James's favourite, George Villiers, was at the height of his influence. Villiers was created Earl of Buckingham in 1617, Marquess in 1619, and was to be made Duke in 1623. James's daughter Elizabeth married Frederick, Elector Palatine in 1613. In August 1619, the Protestant Frederick was elected King of Bohemia, to the fury of the European Catholic powers, especially Spain. By 8 November 1620, Frederick and Elizabeth had been driven out of Bohemia after the Battle of White Mountain, then out of the Palatine, and were exiled in The Hague. There was enormous popular support and sympathy for Frederick and Elizabeth in England, but James, particularly under the influence of the Spanish ambassador Gondomar, was determined to keep England out of the European conflict. James was, however, under pressure to call a parliament by the end of 1620, as he needed to raise enough money to persuade Spain that he might at least consider supporting the Protestant cause with arms. James's last parliament was the so-called 'Addled Parliament' of 1614, which had been dissolved after nine weeks.

**5 December 1620** Burton dates the preface to *Anatomy of Melancholy*, which is published in Oxford early in 1621.

**1621**
**6 January** Ben Jonson's *Pan's Anniversary* performed at court.
**8 January** Essex House Masque performed for French ambassador, the Marquis de Cadenet.
**27 January** Francis Bacon, the Lord Chancellor, created Viscount St Albans.
**30 January** Parliament convened and begins to attack monopolies and Buckingham in its first session. Lancelot Andrewes preaches the opening sermon to Lords and Commons on Psalms 82.2.
**12 March** Committee for Courts of Justice moves against Francis Bacon accusing him of taking bribes.

**3 May** Bacon loses office, is fined and exiled from court.

**14 May** *Wither's Motto* entered in Stationers' Register.

**4 June** Parliament adjourned, pledging subsidies to support English engagement over the Palatine and the Protestant cause in Europe.

**26 July** James's reiteration of a 1620 proclamation against anyone speaking on matters of state.

**3 August** Ben Jonson's *The Gypsies Metamorphosed* performed at Burley, Buckingham's estate; performed again at Belvoir (home of Buckingham's father-in-law the Earl of Rutland) on 5 August and again at Windsor in September.

**29 September** Lord Mayor's Show: Thomas Middleton's *The Sun in Aries*.

**20 November** Parliament reconvened and dares to advise James on foreign policy. This leads ultimately to parliament's protestation of its liberties, which in turn leads to its dissolution.

**19 December** Parliament adjourned.

**25 December** Donne preaches at St Paul's on John 1.8.

**28 December** James dissolves parliament and tears the protestation from the Commons' Journal.

# Preface: 1621

'In speaking of the past, I point at the present.'
Walter Ralegh, *The History of the World*

## Writing 1621

Why write a literary and cultural history of 1621? The simple answer is that such a project offers the opportunity to solve some of the problems raised by the theoretically informed return to history in Renaissance/ early modern studies over the last fifteen years. The limitations of new historicism have been pointed out at such length now that I don't propose to dwell on them here.[1] I am particularly interested in the feminist argument that new historicism failed to deviate from a fairly limited and obvious canon of texts (however much those texts may have been juxtaposed against more unusual forms of writing), and in the critique from the left of new historicism's reliance on a determinist view of history and power. I want to see how far it is possible to play a certain elementary empiricism against the undeniable fact (almost always acknowledged by old historicists) that what we look at is *our* early modern period, not theirs.

This crude oversimplification is where I begin. As a number of scholars have been showing us recently, some form of micro-history yields results that cut through the theoretical impasse of new historicism. I'm thinking of such quite disparate projects as, for example, Leah Marcus's *Puzzling Shakespeare* and Annabel Patterson's *Reading Holinshed's Chronicles*.[2] The history of a year might run into the trouble of not seeing the wood for the trees, but at least I hope to avoid not seeing the trees for the wood. Within my demarcation lines, I can suddenly see what a difference a year makes; or a month, or even a day. Such an approach compels a political reading of all the material available, because suddenly the context closes down to such a sharp focus on particular events. (This procedure can run into trouble when individual works are of an uncertain date, but the methodology remains wholly inviting.) It also focuses attention on the interrelationship between writing of various kinds.

In particular, a look at what we now have access to that appeared in 1621 in manuscript and print certainly adds to the current rethinking of genre boundaries and the status of readers. It is quite clear that the

xv

traditional picture of firm barriers between genres and readers being put into place during the late 1610s and early 1620s is not accurate. This period was once seen as a time when clear demarcations were being established between reading groups (and viewing groups) which coincided with class or status distinctions. It now seems clear that the situation was in fact in a state of flux. Educated readers certainly still read a wide variety of so-called popular works, if we look at examples like Robert Burton (discussed in Chapter 2) or John Chamberlain (discussed in Chapter 1). And much recent work on manuscript publication indicates that, while still a higher status form of 'publication' than print, at least before 1640, manuscript distribution also crossed class or status barriers during the century.[3] I believe that the process that Nigel Smith terms 'generic agitation' in the civil war period is already discernible in 1621, although not in as radical or socially far-reaching a form.[4] Like Smith's cogent study of writing from 1640 to 1660, I want to attend particularly to the intersection between genre and its social context; like him, I have often found that 'in opposed but related texts (related by genre) are the fictions and traces of identity which were beginning to reshape the nature of political and religious life', even years before the civil war began.[5]

So, to sum up, looking at a year means shifting modern readers' perceptions of early modern writing, so that canonical texts resume their place alongside forgotten, neglected or hidden texts. It also involves a reassessment of who readers were and, of course, of who writers were. Where the methodological controversies of the last fifteen years remain crucial is at the level of *my* reading of 1621. This project is not a bibliography. When it becomes the *writing* of 1621, the year, of course, becomes mine, if not ours. I say that political readings of the writing of 1621 are compelling, but they are perhaps only compelling because of the kinds of questions we ask now. For example, I have a chapter on subjectivity because that is one of our questions. But I think that I ask our questions differently because of what circumstances forced me to read: Burton's *Anatomy of Melancholy* and Nicholas Coeffetau's *Table of Human Passions*; Mary Wroth's *Urania* and Dorothy Leigh's *A Mother's Blessing*; sermons by Donne and sermons by Thomas Gataker; *The Doctrine of the Bible* and *A Discourse of Trade*.

Indeed, the nature of the material encountered forced me to move between what might be called generically-based chapters or sections, and those arranged more thematically. For example, in Chapter 2, 'Selves', I begin by discussing subjectivity in relation to what are clearly works with an autobiographical focus (*Mortalities Memorandum* and *Anatomy of Melancholy*), but I then move on to sermons. This shift from one genre to another is generated by the way that a series of sermons written by Donne and Andrewes turn upon an examination of the self, but that self is seen in a political context, and this idea in turn leads me to examine the full range of sermons delivered and published in 1621, many of which relate directly to the political/religious crisis on the continent. In contrast, Chapter 3, 'Transformations of Romance', looks in detail at a genre which literary critics once saw as being moribund by the early seventeenth century, but which in fact was undergoing a series of realignments, specifically in relation to political concerns and, in the case of Mary Wroth's *Urania*, in relation to a woman writer's sense of how the genre might reflect her experiences in the world of the Jacobean court. Other chapters shift constantly between generic issues (such as the nature of drama and performance, addressed in Chapter 4, or poetry, addressed in Chapter 5), and an attempt to see how readers in 1621 addressed issues such as: what constitutes news (Chapter 6), or how does didactic writing operate in such a heterogeneous marketplace (Chapter 7).

But why 1621? To some degree the choice of a year is arbitrary, but 1621 was a parliamentary year, a year of intense political debate, especially in the area of foreign policy, and it was a year late in King James's reign when many literary and non-literary genres were in a state of flux. As I detail in Chapter 3 (see pp. 45ff below), James's vacillating foreign policy in 1621 led to a crisis in which parliament, having embarked upon an attack upon monopolies and the impeachment of Francis Bacon, was dissolved after daring to advise James on foreign policy (and defend its liberties). In this context, a great variety of writing in 1621 was weighted with either direct or oblique political commentary: sermons, poems, engravings, even advice manuals, commented on the political crisis. Popular opinion in London in particular opposed James's perceived support for the Catholic cause in Europe and agitated for greater English support for the Protestant cause in general, and for James's son-in-law Frederick in particular. The situation was also exacerbated by popular responses to James himself, who, by 1621, was in thrall to George Villiers (Buckingham), and tainted by a number of earlier scandals, including the Overbury affair which involved James's earlier favourite Robert Carr's marriage to Frances Devereux.[6]

On a personal level, 1621 has for much of my career been the year of Mary Wroth's *Urania*, and I started out, a long time ago, just wanting to know more about the context for the publication and reception of that particular, extraordinary work. As I wrote my history, I realised that the choice of year is both arbitrary and fortuitous, for it certainly dovetails with the period that has, of late, especially interested historians of various persuasions, as an era of transition, poised somewhere before the years that could be seen to be leading to the civil war.[7] I want my readers to see the particularity of 1621, but in the hope that such a viewing will explore some of the problems of any encounter with any past script.

## Reading 1621

One of these problems is the necessity to avoid asking our questions so loudly that we drown out the otherness, the strangeness, of 1621.[8] This strangeness is immediately apparent when, as a reader of 1621, I have to pay attention to all of its texts, not simply those that have risen to some sort of canonical status. Here my methodology differs from James Chandler's in his magisterial *England in 1819*, because my focus is on what was readable in 1621, not simply on what was written in 1621.[9] Accordingly, I look at works that were republished or recirculated or reperformed in 1621, as well as works that were first written in 1621. As a form of contextualisation, I have found it useful to see how the 1621 edition of Sir Walter Ralegh's *History of the World*, which acknowledged his authorship for the first time on its title-page, had a quite different context (especially a political one) from its first publication in 1614.[10] Similarly, I write about the 1621 *Anatomy of Melancholy* (the first edition), not the greatly enlarged *Anatomy*, product of five further editions, which most modern commentators write about.

However, drawing a map of what was read in 1621 becomes a complicated process, because the material is so varied that, at first sight, one might well feel that there is no relationship whatsoever between many of the individual items. I am not arguing that there inevitably was a relationship, although at least one reader in 1621, John Chamberlain, the subject of the next chapter, absorbed examples of pretty well all kinds of writing, seeing them as related through their ability to be processed as news.[11] Rather, I want to register the diversity of the writing, as well as the interconnections.[12] And indeed, in Chapter 4, it is necessary to deal with the fact that records of performances in 1621 allow one access to only a very limited number of surviving examples, in the form of play texts and records of performances of various kinds, so that my methodology has had to take on a certain self-conscious scrutiny in relation to not only diversity of writings, but also questions of representativeness.

The first thing that becomes apparent just from the bibliography of 1621 is that general guides to the output of the press in particular don't always correlate to a specific year. For example, H.S. Bennett's invaluable

*English Books and Readers 1603–1640* led me to expect to find about 50 or so published sermons for 1621.[13] In fact, there were almost twice that number, presumably in part because the connection between religious controversy and the crisis in Bohemia created a booming market for polemical sermons (fuelled, rather than quelled, by official attempts to suppress such controversy).[14] I was expecting to see more plays in print (there were only three). I wasn't expecting to see such a range of poetry, from George Wither's inflammatory *Wither's Motto* to Rachel Speght's meditative and autobiographical *Mortalities Memorandum*.

I have, of course, ranged well beyond what was in print, as this is not a history of what was published in 1621, but what was read, watched or heard in 1621. Manuscripts have presented some problems because dating manuscript miscellanies and anthologies is often very difficult (at least to within a single year), but it is possible to date many individual items (such as the poem by King James discussed in the next chapter).[15] I have not by any means confined myself to 'literary' manuscript material, but include letters, diaries, proceedings of various kinds preserved in the State Papers and other archives. This material again raises the question of audiences. Some manuscript material circulated almost as widely as printed material, such as the poetry miscellanies; other manuscript material was intended for a very restricted readership.

In all cases, just as I have not restricted myself to particular kinds of writing or performance, so I have not restricted myself to particular kinds of reading. I have looked at John Chamberlain reading; I have read for the politics of sermons but also for their dialogue with subjectivity; I have examined the reshaping of genres such as romance and pastoral, which in their reshaping are engaged with a sense of the intersection between the public and private spheres; I have tried to reconstruct what the performances of 1621 were like for a variety of viewers and participants; I have read, in I hope some of the spirit in which it was written, the mass of didactic material that was so popular, from the simple information of newsbooks to descriptions of marvels and transcriptions of 'God's judgements'. Throughout I have tried to maintain a balance between allowing what I have found to take me some way towards understanding a very different way of reading (and writing) from our own, and the necessary imposition of my own frame of reference in order to make a modern reading of such material possible.

# 1
# John Chamberlain Reads the Year

'I love not altogether ydle and empty letters.'
John Chamberlain to Dudley Carleton, 18 August 1621

'To know Chamberlain in and out, his comings and goings, his reports of what occurred and what was said, is to come close to living in his generation.'
Wallace Notestein, *Four Worthies* (1956)

In the forty-six years since Notestein wrote, scholars have become much less confident about coming anywhere close to living in another person's generation. However, the letters of John Chamberlain have been an alluring source for historians in particular, who have felt that he provides a window onto his age. Chamberlain's extensive correspondence, stretching from 1597 until 1626, and running to 479 letters collected by his editor, Norman McClure, is a particularly rich source for those interested in the minutiae of the court, especially the court of James I, because Chamberlain was, essentially, fascinated by gossip.[1] Most of his letters were sent to his friend Dudley Carleton, who served as an ambassador in Venice from 1610 to 1615, and in The Hague from 1616 to 1624.[2] In them, Chamberlain passed on information about everything that could be read as a sign of the times, from court scandals to speeches in parliament. He relayed accounts of court masques and copies of popular ballads; he informed Carleton about who was in favour and who was out of favour. Chamberlain was, in essence, an interpreter, a reader of all that came his way: of people, of places, of things, of fashion. For that reason, he stands, for me, as an example of how an individual within my chosen year might have read that year, but this is a very particular kind of reader: in early modern terms,

1

Chamberlain is a practised reader of information from a position both within a certain elite grouping (he was a gentleman), but outside the centre of court culture.

Chamberlain was born in 1554 and followed the usual career of a promising young man: he attended university (Cambridge), though left without taking a degree. He then went to Gray's Inn. While the Inns of Court were the training ground for lawyers, they also attracted those who wanted to be at the centre of artistic and intellectual life.[3] Chamberlain was not called to the bar and lived his whole life as a gentleman of modest but independent means – as, indeed, a 'looker on', to use Notestein's phrase,[4] rather than a direct participant. Few details are known of his life prior to his letter writing, but from his first extant letter, written to Dudley Carleton on 11 June 1597, we hear a great deal about his day-to-day activities. McClure notes how Chamberlain positioned himself at the centre of London's information trade by living near St Paul's Cathedral, where booksellers and gatherers of information of all sorts congregated (i. 5). Chamberlain also had a number of active and influential friends well placed to pass on news to him, the most notable being Ralph Winwood, Secretary of State from 1614 to 1617.

Chamberlain's first 1621 letter, written on 13 January, offers a good sense of his style and his concerns. I will quote the first half of the letter in full. It is a careful account of some events surrounding the visit of the Marquis de Cadenet from France at a time when King James wanted to convince the Spanish that he might possibly be reconsidering a French match for Prince Charles, during a particularly tense stage of the European conflict which had resulted in James's son-in-law Frederick being driven out of the Palatine after his ill-fated attempt to rule Bohemia. The central incident involves a banquet held for Cadenet by James Hay, Viscount Doncaster and Earl of Carlisle, who had acted as an ambassador for James in an attempt to negotiate a peaceful settlement to the Bohemian crisis. Carlisle had strong sympathies with the European Protestant cause and a genuine desire for a French, as opposed to a Spanish, match for Charles.[5] Characteristically, Chamberlain focuses on the way that Cadenet's visit involves a jostle for position and precedence, and a careful display of symbolic conspicuous consumption by James's court:

> My very goode Lord: I have heard of no messenger since Captain Goldwell went, though Dieston looke every day to be dispatcht, by whom you shall heare again yf here be ought worth the sending. The next day after the frenchmen were at Hampton Court they were feasted by the King in the upper house of parlement, both the ambassadors

at the Kings table, the rest in the court of requests; the Count d'Auvergne absented himself because he could not be admitted to eat with the King, alleaging that Quene Elizabeth did his father that honor, but yt was aunswered that his father was a kings sonne and yet living. Divers others went away from the Lords table because they might not have precedence (or at least were not offered) of the Lord Chauncellor, Lord Treasurer and Lord Privieseale, which neretheles sat all on one side. That night they had a bal at Whitehall, and on Twelfth Day were invited to the maske there, which was handsomly performed, but that there was a puritan brought in to be flowted and abused, which was somwhat unseemly and unseasonable, specially as matters stand now with those of the religion in Fraunce. On Monday they were intertained in seeing the Prince with sixe or seven noblemen more run at tilt, which the Prince performed very well and gracefully; that night they were feasted by the Lord of Doncaster at Essex House, with that sumptuous superfluitie, that the like hath not ben seene nor heard in these parts; whereof to geve you some taste, yt is to be understoode that there were more then a 100 cookes (wherof forty were masters) set on worke for eight dayes before: the whole service was but sixe messe furnished with 1600 dishes, which were neither light nor sleight, but twelve fesants in a dish, fowre and twentie patridges, twelve dosen of larkes, *et sic de caeteris*: and for fish all that could be found far and neere, whole fresh salmons served by two and three in a dish, besides sixe or seven Muscovie salmons wherof some were above sixe foot long. Yt were to no purpose to recken up the grosser meates as two swannes in a dish, two chines of beefe, two pigges and the like; but yt is doubted this excessive spoyle will make a dearth of the choisest dainties, when this one supper consumed twelve score fesants baked, boyled and rosted. After supper they had a banquet, then a maske, then a second banket, so that the sweet meats alone rising to 500li the whole charge is saide to be above 3000li, besides sixe pound weight of amber-gris spent in cookerie valued at 300li. The King and Prince were present with the ambassadors at a table that went crosse the upper end of the long table, so that the King sitting in the midst had the full view of the whole companie and service; they supt in a lower gallerie. The maske was in a large roome above. (ii.333–4)

Chamberlain clearly revels in this description, however much he may also intend to offer a judgement about ostentatious waste ('this excessive spoyle'). The feast – like the masque, the tilt, even the ordering of places – was intended to impress; it had, indeed, to be excessive in order to achieve this. Thus Chamberlain places value upon it over and over again: value that we can guess at by the amount and rarity of the dishes, and value in monetary terms that is specified down to the very subtotals. Amounts are what count here, rather than the specifics of any one dish: the number of dishes, indeed the number of cooks, conveys the magnitude of the occasion. The signs of prestige are always registered in Chamberlain's letters: 'Divers others went away from the Lords table because they might not have precedence.'

This passage also provides a context for the way a whole range of cultural events fit into a particular political/social context: the ball, the masque, the tilt. Much has been written in recent years about the role of these symbolic cultural forms in the Stuart and Caroline courts, particularly the function of the masque.[6] For Chamberlain, clearly, the Earl of Doncaster's feast is the most notable event in this series of shows to impress the ambassadors (and others). Indeed, Doncaster had, in his biographer's words, 'carved himself a unique and virtually unassailable position as a banquet master'.[7] He used such a symbolically weighted feast with a deliberation clearly understood by Chamberlain, who applies to it the appropriate analysis. (Unfortunately, the entire manoeuvre was spectacularly unsuccessful, as the Spanish ambassador, Gondomar, was able to induce James to offer a humiliating explanation that he had never intended to reopen negotiations for a French match for Charles.) The tilt is dealt with quite perfunctorily, but the masque receives a more substantial, and again critical, comment.

Recently, Martin Butler has established that the masque in question was Ben Jonson's *Pan's Anniversary*.[8] I will be discussing Jonson's two 1621 masques (the other was *The Gipsies Metamorphosed*) in detail in a later chapter, but in the present context it is important to register Chamberlain's sense of how the political implications of the masque might be read. Chamberlain's 'readings' of cultural events are quite unlike our own forms of interpretation, in so far as he tends to spend much less time than we would like him to on events we have ranked more highly than a dinner. Jonson's masque strikes an unintended sour note because, as Butler has so cogently explained, it was caught between a domestic resistance to Puritanism and the pressure King James was under to defend the interests of Protestants in Europe. Butler thus notes that 'Chamberlain's point is that satire on Protestant extremism is fine when it is designed to counter the growth of popular interest in politics at home, but when the context was the state of Protestantism in Europe generally the issue was far more sensitive'.[9] Chamberlain registers the reverberations of the masque within a particular political context, rather than commenting in any detail on its contents. But his letter makes it quite clear that there is no real dividing line between *Pan's Anniversary* and Doncaster's banquet: both are symbolic cultural forms designed for a particular set of effects, and in both cases, the response of an audience, onlooker or interpreter cannot be predicted nor made homogeneous. Thus Doncaster's banquet, like Jonson's masque, cannot guarantee a particular interpretation.

Because Chamberlain, in my view, is an inveterate interpreter of everything that comes his way, he underlines the continuing interaction of a multilayered and intersecting set of genres of writing which still, in 1621, cross over between a variety of readers. Chamberlain subscribes to a hierarchy of writing, as we will see, but he is an inclusive rather than exclusive reader, and wants to absorb everything that crosses his path. He is far from certain that the recipient of most of these letters, Dudley Carleton, clearly a more self-important and serious individual than Chamberlain, will feel the same way, and is therefore often apologetic about some of the more trivial items he sends along with his letters. For example, on 17 November 1621, he says to Carleton: 'Yf you have not seene this ydle pamflet before, yt is like to make you laugh though you had no list' (ii.408). Some irony lurks in this offhand phrase. 'Ydle' pamphlets, like 'ydle and empty letters', cannot easily be distinguished from their opposites within Chamberlain's method of interpretation. His news is always an admixture of what, to the partial reader, is trivia and what is a matter of importance. This is quite clear when one reads modern historians, who pillage Chamberlain for his comments on parliamentary proceedings, but never place what they would regard as his 'serious' political reportage in the context of an entire letter, where *all* information is, as we have already seen, subject to a constant level of interpretation, and it is difficult to set up an opposition between the serious and the trivial. The 'ydle pamphlet' will make Carleton laugh, even if he has no desire to do so; the idle letter is also always going to have an effect on its recipient.

There is one moment when Chamberlain feels that something really is beneath Carleton's attention: 'This inclosed ballet [i.e. ballad] came to my handes by great chaunce, and having scant reade yt I send yt to my Lady for her recreation though perhaps she take no great pleasure in such toyes but only to see the wanton witts of the time' (ii.373). It is hard to tell here whether Chamberlain feels that the ballad should go to Carleton's wife because of its genre or its content. Indeed, he wonders whether she might not take any pleasure at all in it, except as an example of wantonness (which may imply sexual licence, or merely 'idle' waste-fulness). 'Toys' remains a deceptive word in 1621, echoing the typical Renaissance nonchalant pretence that something quite significant is really of no importance at all; it is a word famously used by Philip Sidney to describe his literary endeavours.[10] It is clear that Chamberlain does take pleasure in such toys, and it is tempting even to speculate on the implications of a 'scant' reading of a ballad. Given that, to our eyes, ballads don't require much reading at all, Chamberlain clearly read a ballad with the same intent scrutiny that he used when reading a banquet, or a masque, or a proclamation, or reports of a day in parliament. Accordingly, we have to be careful about automatically interpreting this passage as an indication that ballads are toys fit only for ladies' eyes (again a claim made by Sidney for his *Arcadia*). Without any way of comparing the idle pamphlet sent to Carleton with the wanton ballad sent to his wife, we cannot be sure what form of discrimination is going on in Chamberlain's mind.[11] But it seems to me that he is acknowledging an area where Anne Carleton's taste may coincide with his own, rather than judging the status of ballads or of women readers.

Chamberlain worries about Dudley Carleton's sense of what might be trivial and unworthy of his attention in reference to another ballad: this time a song from the second of Jonson's 1621 masques: *The Gipsies Metamorphosed*. In this case, Chamberlain rather disingenuously states that the song is a substitute for hard news – I say disingenuously, because it comes at the end of a letter containing a fair quantity of news, including material once again often cited by modern historians as conveying the sense of economic crisis at this time, such as 'And withall I can assure you that monie goes here very low and scant and the opinion of our great wealth is well fallen' (ii.404). The Jonson song is included, Chamberlain says, because it attracted the praise of the court:

> For lacke of better newes here is likewise a ballet or song of Ben Jonson's in the play or shew at the Lord Marquis at Burly, and repeated again at Windsor, for which and other goode service there don, he hath his pension from a 100 marks increased to 200li per annum, besides the reversion of the mastership of the revells. There were other songs and devises of baser alay, but because this had the vogue and generall applause at court, I was willing to send yt. (ii.404–5)[12]

Much of this comment is concerned with Jonson's place, and therefore it is simply part of Chamberlain's general reporting of shifts in people's positions and offices. As well as Jonson's song, in this letter Chamberlain included 'a copie of the Kings letter to the commissioners in the Lord of Caunterburies cause' (ii.404), so that the notion that news is lacking seems particularly odd. I think that once again Chamberlain is a little defensive about how his interest in matters like songs might appear to Carleton (it is worth noting that in his own letters Carleton encloses gazettes – i.e. newsbooks – and serious political tracts). Again what is most notable about this comment of Chamberlain's is that it registers the *effects* of Jonson's masque (in this case, its favourable reception, in contrast to *Pan's Anniversary*), rather than offering any commentary on the contents. The song is included because of the court's praise, not because of Chamberlain's own admiration. This is a rather different situation from that concerning the idle pamphlet sent to Dudley Carleton and the ballad sent to Anne Carleton, clearly instances where Chamberlain's own response (however much expressed in a spirit of *sprezzatura*) is a motivating factor.

As a purveyor and interpreter of news, Chamberlain looks to a wide range of sources, for he is concerned to understand how news is processed by different members of society. He is acutely conscious of attempts to control news (and ideas), and notes the conflict caused (particularly in a year when parliament met) by the struggle over control of information. Here he comments on the response to James's proclamation which endeavoured to suppress, in essence, news of the very sort that pervades Chamberlain's letters:

> there is come out a new proclamation against lavish and licentious talking in matters of state, either at home or abrode, which the common people know not how to understand, nor how far matter of state may stretch or extend; for they continue to take no notice of yt, but print every weeke (at least) corantas with all manner of newes, and as strange stuffe as any we have from Amsterdam. (ii.396)

Chamberlain naturally sees himself as elevated far above the common people, but he, like they, deliberately promulgates news beyond the stretch of matters of state. Of course, the public dissemination of news is very different from Chamberlain's private letters to Carleton. Nevertheless, Chamberlain's letters are corantos of a sort: books of news, calculated to convey information, and, even more importantly, offered as interpretations, readings, of events. To be a true reader and reporter of news, Chamberlain needs to look up at the doings of the court and down at the common people's response to a royal proclamation. In both cases he finds a shared disingenuousness. The common people,

Chamberlain makes plain, do indeed know how to understand the proclamation: by pretending not to understand how far it may stretch or extend. The proclamation of 26 July 1621 referred back to the proclamation of 24 December 1620 'against excess of Lavish and Licentious Speech of Matters of State.' The earlier proclamation reinforces the connection between the liberties taken by both the highest and lowest members of society:

> it is come to Our eares, by common report, That there is at this time a more licentious passage of lavish discourse, and bold Censure in matters of State, then hath been heretofore, or is fit to be suffered, Wee have thought it necessary, by the advice of Our Privie Councell, to give forewarning unto Our loving Subjects, of this excess and presumption; And straitly to command them and every of them, from the highest to the lowest, to take heede, how they intermeddle by Penne or Speech, with causes of State, and secrets of Empire, either at home, or abroad, but containe themselves within that modest and reverent regard, of matters above their reach and calling, that to good a dutifull Subjects appertaineth.[13]

Chamberlain's own letters represent a deliberate setting aside of the implications of this proclamation, containing, as they do, and despite Chamberlain's occasional move towards circumspection, a considerable amount of lavish discourse on matters of state. Because of his insatiable appetite for news, Chamberlain's eye extends unusually far for a reader at any level of society in 1621.

Modern scholars have been disappointed by Chamberlain's lack of interest in the public theatre. Most of his references to it are concerned with its social impact, rather than with descriptions of individual plays. (With a few exceptions. Naturally he was interested in a phenomenon like Middleton's scandalous success of 1624, *A Game at Chess*.) In 1621 Chamberlain notes Gondomar, the Spanish ambassador's, visit to a play: 'growne so affable and familiar, that on Monday with his whole traine he went to a common play at the Fortune in Golding-lane, and the players (not to be overcome with curtesie) made him a banket when the play was don in the garden adjoyning' (ii.391). Chamberlain doesn't even mention what play Gondomar saw; what is important is the implication of the visit (and his reception), given the shifting tides of anti-Spanish feeling. The same theatre features a few letters later, in an event which many may well have seen as a fitting retribution for such a courteous reception to the much-hated ambassador:

On Sonday night here was a great fire at the Fortune in Golding-lane the fayrest play-house in this towne. Yt was quite burnt downe in two howres and all their apparell and play-bookes lost, wherby those poore companions are quite undon (ii.415)

Chamberlain is interested in the playhouse as an institution, rather than in particular plays; he is concerned with the events it precipitates.

The two moments, in the correspondence for 1621, when Chamberlain engages in something that more closely resembles what we might call literary interpretation, are really, once again, instances of political commentary. Both involve the King. The first relays a famous and much-quoted quip of James's about Bacon's *Novum Organum* (published in 1620): 'the King cannot forbeare somtimes in reading his last booke to say that yt is like the peace of God, that passeth all understanding' (ii.339). Chamberlain in an earlier letter of 28 October 1620 reported Bacon's presentation of *Novum Organum* to the King:

This weeke the Lord Chauncellor hath set foorth his new worke called Instauratio Magna, or a kind of new organum of all philosophie. In sending yt to the King he wrote that he wisht his Majestie might be as long in reading yt as he hath ben in composing and polishing yt, which is well neere thirtie yeares: I have read no more then the bare title, and am not greatly incouraged by Master Cuffes judgement, who having long since perused yt gave this censure, that a foole could not have written such a worke, and a wise man wold not. (ii.324)

Chamberlain is, as usual, more interested in conveying the jokes and general impressions made by Bacon's magnum opus than in offering anything that we would consider to be a reading of it. He is interested, if you like, in reading the readings of *Novum Organum* and in noting its effect on Bacon's – increasingly shaky – relationship with James.

The second more daring piece of 'interpretation' concerns a work by James himself, inspired by his visit to Burleigh, 'where there was great provision of playes, maskes and all maner of entertainment' (ii.396), including *The Gipsies Metamorphosed*:

The King was so pleased and taken with his entertainment at the Lord Marques [i.e. Buckingham] that he could not forbeare to expresses his contentment in certain verses he made there to this effect, that the ayre, the weather, (though yt were not so here) and every thing els, even the staggs and bucks in their fall did seeme to smile, so that there was hope of a smiling boy within a while, to which end he concluded with a wish or votum for the felicitie and fruitfulnes of that vertuous and blessed couple, and in way of Amen caused the bishop of London in his presence to geve them a benediction. (ii.397)

It is worth reproducing the whole of James's poem before discussing Chamberlain's description of it.

*Verses made by the Kinge, when hee was entertayned at Burly in Rutlandshire, by my L Marquesse of Buckingham.*
*August: 1621*

> The heauens that wept perpetually before,
> Since wee came hither show theyr smilinge cleere,
> This goodly house it smiles, and all this store
> Of huge prouision smiles vpon vs heere.
>     The Buckes & Stagges in fatt they seeme to smile:
>     God send a smilinge boy within a while.

> *Votum*
> *A Vow or Wish for the felicity & fertility of the owners of this house.*
> If euer in the Aprill of my dayes
> I satt vpon Parnassus forked hill:
> And there inflam'd with sacred fury still
> By pen proclaim'd our great Apollo's praise:
> Grant glistringe Phoebus with thy golden rayes
> My earnest wish which I present thee heere:
> Beholdinge of this blessed couple deere,
> Whose vertues pure no pen can duly blaze.
> Thow by whose heat the trees in fruit abound
> Blesse them with fruit delicious sweet & fayre,
> That may succeed them in theyr vertues rare.
> ffirm plant them in their natiue soyle & ground.
>     Thow Joue, that art the onely God indeed,
>     My prayer heare: sweet Jesu interceed.[14]

Buckingham married Catherine Manners in May 1620, and the couple produced their first child in 1622 – a daughter, not the smiling boy James wished for them. Chamberlain clearly registers the embarrassing nature of this poem, which is rather like a fertility charm. Keen as he was on hunting and on smiling boys, James envisages something of a solipsistic paradise in the opening stanza.[15] The eliding of the smiling bucks, stags and boy is unsettling – perhaps even more so if one prefers Chamberlain's reading of bucks and stags in 'fall', rather than in 'fat', which offers an image of them as willing sacrifices at the King's hand.[16] It is hard to determine how much more judgement is implied in Chamberlain's characterisation of James's inability to contain himself: 'could not forbeare to expresses his contentment in certain verses'. There is at least some implication in the form of expression used that James perhaps *should* have forborne to express this particular form of contentment. This implication seems more likely given the odd double take about the weather: 'though yt were not so here'. Chamberlain is surely not simply registering climatic differences between London and Rutland with this observation, but rather acknowledging the effect of James's public expression of his feelings for Buckingham.

This is, once again, a reading of some of the political implications of this poem; Chamberlain sees it as a piece of writing which confirms (as do so many of James's literary productions after Buckingham's ascendancy) the King's feelings for his favourite, and that favourite's place at court. This sense is made even stronger when one reads the comment on the poem in the context of a letter which Chamberlain sees as being written at a time of little news. It begins: 'The last week was so barren that I had no list to write, (for I love not altogether ydle and empty letters) and though this be not much better, yet because I looke ere long to make a step to Warepark to enjoy the fagge-end of this sommer, (which hitherto hath ben such a season as I thincke was never seen,) I would not leave you unsaluted, and withall let you know how we stand here' (ii.396–7). Then Chamberlain offers the comment on the King's poem, and this is followed by another list of places, positions and fortunes, beginning with 'The Lord of Arundells graunt of the corranes [ie. currants] goes not forward' (ii.397). So the reading of the poem is very much in the context of Chamberlain's usual reading of matters of social consequence, high and low.[17]

I noted at the beginning of this chapter that it is not possible to use Chamberlain as a necessarily representative reader in 1621: he is quite unique in the way he positions himself as outsider and insider and as a reader of particularly catholic taste. But I do want to use Chamberlain as a paradigm for the practice of reading 1621, because he points to the possibility of ranging between forms, modes, social and cultural productions, generally taken to be quite distinct both in their genre and in their audience. Only when immersed in the general flow of news, of social and cultural data, as Chamberlain was, is it possible to gain some sense of how information came to be processed as a totality. Chamberlain is in many respects a political reader rather like recent scholars who have reread early modern culture with the aim of restoring it to its political and social context. I see him as the exemplar of a method that will endeavour to allow nothing to pass unnoted. Such a method ensures that we do not read an already over-sifted canon of representative early modern texts, but rather allow ourselves a greater chance to read from within the boundaries of 1621 itself. The result can hardly be a sense of living in Chamberlain's generation, nor, as Stephen Greenblatt has dramatically put it, can we truly speak with the dead.[18] What I am aiming at here is a richer sense of where past texts come from and, in 1621, where they were going.

# 2
# Selves

'That world which I regard is my selfe'

Thomas Browne, *Religio Medici*

## Subjectivity

Over the last fifteen years, much work on the early modern period has been particularly interested in the nature of subjectivity. Perhaps the most influential new approach to this issue has been Stephen Greenblatt's now classic *Renaissance Self-Fashioning*, which points to the interconnected nature in the Renaissance of the self and the social: 'I perceived that fashioning oneself and being fashioned by cultural institutions – family, religion, state – were inseparably intertwined.'[1] In Francis Barker's much more complex (and controversial) argument about the construction of bourgeois subjectivity in the course of the seventeenth century, there is once again a focus on a 'pre-bourgeois' self as marked, not by the interiority that an older generation of critics projected onto canonical literary works like *Hamlet*, but rather (in Barker's admittedly somewhat tortuous, but none the less suggestive formulation): 'Pre-bourgeois subjection does not properly involve subjectivity at all, but a condition of dependent membership in which place and articulation are defined not by an interiorized self-recognition – complete or partial, percipient or unknowing, efficient or rebellious – (of none the less socially constituted subject-positions), but by incorporation in the body politic which is the king's body in its social form.'[2] An important counter to this approach to early modern subjectivity has come from Katherine Eisaman Maus, who has looked at drama in particular as involving a sense of unknowable inwardness, a concept which she connects to the forensic problems within English law of judging the truth (and sincerity) of individual acts and declarations. This also extends to the problem of determining inward truth in a culture of religious controversy and contestation. Accordingly, for Maus, 'Renaissance religious culture nurtures in a wide variety of ways habits of mind that encourage conceiving of human inwardness as simultaneously privileged and elusive, an absent presence "interpreted" to observers by ambiguous signs and tokens.'[1]

At the same time, the influence of feminist approaches to the whole early modern period has also allowed for the possibility of a less wholly determinist view of subjectivity, particularly as a body of previously ignored or elided texts by women in genres such as diary, letter, spiritual testimony/prophecy, has been restored to visibility by feminist scholars. A good example of this is the summarising book by Barbara Lewalski, *Writing Women in Jacobean England*, which argues for 'the importance of the textual gestures through which these Jacobean women claimed an authorial identity and manifested their resistance within their repressive culture'.[1] Through this redirecting of attention within feminist scholarship, it has, I believe, become quite clear that we need to look at questions of early modern subjectivity in the context of a range of texts, many of them excluded in various ways from the canon. I will be arguing throughout this chapter, and the next, that the whole question of Renaissance subjectivity constantly leads out from Maus's 'inwardness' to questions of a self interconnected with the social, but not in quite the determinist manner that critics like Barker argue for. I move between work that is self-evidently 'about' the issue of subjectivity and a series of sermons that take up the issue of subjectivity and indicate how intimately interconnected it is with, not just what we would call 'religious issues', but also with political issues. My early discussion of Burton also points to that interdependence.

As far as the shift in perspective induced by the increasing visibility of early modern women writers is concerned, it is unfortunate for my purposes that so many of the more interesting autobiographical texts by women that relate particularly to these issues don't cover 1621.[5] However, one interesting 1621 example relating to this whole issue is Rachel Speght's poem *Mortalities Memorandum*. This is a work which points to many of the issues I want to discuss in the course of this chapter; in particular, it illustrates the intersection between subjectivity, religion and the social.

## *Mortalities Memorandum*: a dream of the self

Rachel Speght took part in a seventeenth-century pamphlet war over the
nature of women, started by Joseph Swetnam's *Arraignment of Lewd, Idle,
Froward and Unconstant Women* (1615), which rehearsed a series of standard
misogynistic positions. Speght replied with *A Mouzell for Melastomus*
(Muzzle for Blackmouth) in 1617, a learned and restrained defence of
women.[6] Speght is prepared to enter the public arena in her own person
(Swetnam's tract was in fact published under a pseudonym, and Speght
reveals his true identity), and, as a woman, boldly takes on an almost
exclusively male realm of polemic. Barbara Lewalski notes that throughout
her tract, Speght attempts 'to make the prevailing Protestant discourse
yield a more expansive and equitable concept of gender'.[7] Speght does
this by reinterpreting the biblical texts that traditionally were used to
assign woman to a position of subjection.

In 1621 Speght published a volume containing two poems: *Mortalities
Memorandum, with A Dream Prefixed, Imaginary in Manner, Real in Matter*.
She begins with a provocative preface to her godmother, Mary Mound-
ford, which fiercely claims the right to a public self:

> Amongst diuersitie of motiues to induce the divulging of that to pub-
> lique view, which was devoted to priuate Contemplation, none is
> worthy to precede desire of common benefit. Corne kept close in
> a garner feeds not the hungry; A candle put vnder a bushell doth
> not illuminate an house; None but vnprofitable seruants knit vp
> Gods talent in a Napkin. (A2)[8]

Speght goes on to dispute those who denied her authorship of her
polemical tract, and she is anxious to assert the interconnection
between her private (female) identity and her right to a public self, her
right (a right scarcely recognised for women in the early seventeenth
century) not to hide her light under a bushel. Elaine Beilin succinctly
notes that Speght's works taken together reveal 'the growth of her consciousness as a woman artist'.[9] Speght says, in her preface, 'I am now, as
by a strong motiue induced (for my rights sake) to produce and divulge
this spring of my indeuour' (A2v); she clearly sees herself as having
an identity bound up in the public presentation of her self and her
thoughts.

The first poem in the book is a dream narrative which allegorically
recounts her struggle against ignorance – the lot of so many women
at the time when she wrote. Speght offers a spirited attack on the
notion that ignorance was natural for women; indeed, she argues

that the essence of the female subject is knowledge, just as much as the male:

> Both man and woman of three parts consist,
> Which *Paul* doth bodie, soule, and spirit call:
> And from the soule three faculties arise,
> The mind, the will, the power; then wherefore shall
> A woman haue her intellect in vaine,
> Or not endeuour *Knowledge* to attaine. (5)

The whole substance of the dream allegory is concerned with the endeavour to fashion an active female self. Again Elaine Beilin has noted how Speght summons up her knowledge of both biblical and classical exemplars: 'Speght clearly uses Vergil with Scripture to correct the exclusion of women from *both* the active and contemplative life'.[10] However, Speght intertwines this public endeavour with her personal circumstances: the dream ends with her mother's death, and that fact seems to provide the premise for the longer second poem, 'Mortalities Memorandum', which is essentially a meditation on death and its influence over our conception of life. For Speght, the private self, which suffers personally from an event like the death of a mother, must be seen in relation to a public self which is able to provide a Christian lesson for the reader from such an event. None of the ideas and images in 'Mortalities Memorandum' is particularly original or startling (life as a troublesome voyage and death as a haven; the body as a loathsome entrapment for the soul), but in the context of Speght's brief career as a woman writer, it achieves a remarkably poised, didactic tone, which could be seen as her deliberate attempt to transcend any limited social function for a female self. Speght sees mortality as a marker of the self's liminal status: poised between a universal yet private experience, between the personal (within which circumstances vary enormously) and the social:

> In iourney ieopardie doth vs attend,
> In marriage griefe and care oppresse the minde,
> The single life is solitarie, vaine;
> The rich can little ioy in riches finde;
> For hauing much, his care must watch his wealth,
> From secret pilfring, and from open stealth.
>
> If pouerty be our appointed lot,
> Our griefe is great, reliefe and comfort small,

We must endure oppression, suffer wrong,
The weake in wrestling goeth to the wall:
If we be bit, we cannot bite againe,
If rich men strike, we must their blow sustaine.

If we be eminent in place of note,
Then stand we as a marke for enuies dart,
Coniecture censures our defect of worth,
Inquirie doth anatomize each part,
And if our reputation be but small,
Contempt and scorne doth vs and ours befall.

The infant from the wombe into the world
Comes crying, by the which it doth presage
The paines, and perils, it must vndergoe,
In child-hood, man-hood, and decreped age,
He that most knowes this life, least doth it loue,
Except affliction may affection moue. (22)

These commonplaces take on a new resonance placed within the context of Speght's argument about how a female self may enter into the
public realm and offer universal advice and counsel. As we will see
shortly in relation to Robert Burton, few writers were able to deal with
any sense of self-analysis that transcended the misogyny inherent in
Jacobean notions of gender. It is in that context that Speght offers a brief
glimpse of an untrammelled female self: not in terms of any retreat into
a notion of the self as private and secret, but rather in the notion of the
lack of any real gender division when the self intersects with the social.

## *The Anatomy of Melancholy*: 'Thou thy selfe art the subject of my Discourse'

The most obviously canonical text discussed in this book is also, appropriately, the most eccentric. Indeed, Robert Burton's *Anatomy of Melancholy*
is the kind of canonical text that is read by fewer and fewer people,
even if scholarly discussion of it has revived after a lapse of interest in
the 1980s. It attains its true scholarly canonical status with the appearance
of a massive edition finally near completion.[11] This edition has had to take
into account the extraordinarily complex publishing history of a work
obsessively revised and expanded by its author through five editions
following its 1621 publication, in 1624, 1628, 1632, 1638 and 1651.[12]
The Oxford textual editors estimate that Burton's text grew by 40 per cent

from the first publication to the 1651 edition (the greatest expansion being between the first and second editions). Because modern commentators have relied on convenient volumes based on either the sixth or seventh editions of Burton's text, criticism has offered little clear sense of what the 1621 *Anatomy* was like.[13] Indeed, as the Oxford edition is (quite rightly) based on the 1631 edition, this situation is unlikely to change substantially, although now scholars will have a collation which will allow them to discriminate between the different versions of Burton's ever-changing book.

The 1621 *Anatomy of Melancholy* is, to begin with, a much more modest-looking book than it became in succeeding editions. It is a quarto volume, 880 pages long – therefore not as modest as many another less substantial quarto published at the time, but not as substantial looking as when it became a folio, in the second edition, by which time it had also grown by some 70,000 words.[14] By the third edition, the plain title-page had become an elaborately engraved affair, which included a portrait of Burton himself together with nine emblematic panels.[15] In 1621 the title-page offered a plainer description of the book itself:

> The Anatomy of melancholy, what it is, with all the kindes, cavses, symptoms, prognostickes, and severall cvres of it. In three maine partitions with their seuerall sections, members, and svbsections. Philosophically, medicinally, historically, opened and cvt vp. By Democritvs Iunior. With a Satyricall Preface, conducing to the following discourse. Macrob. Omne meum, Nihil meum.

This title-page does open up several important questions that Burton invites us to ask, beginning most obviously with 'Who is Democritus Junior?' The satirical preface, 'Democritvs Ivnior to the Reader', takes up the first 72 pages of the 1621 *Anatomy*, and begins by teasing us about our curiosity:

> Gentle Reader, I presume thou wilt be very inquisitiue to knowe what personate Actor this is, that so insolently intrudes vpon this common Theater, to the worlds view, arrogating another mans name, whence hee is, why he doth it, and what hee hath to say? (1)[16]

Teasing questions of identity are evident everywhere we look, including the seemingly paradoxical epigraph from Macrobius: 'Omne meum, nihil meum': everything is mine, nothing is mine. But questions of identity are very different in the 1621 edition compared to later editions,

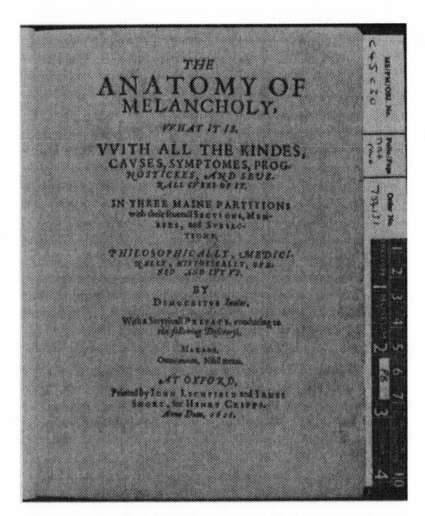

*Figure 1* Title-page of Robert Burton, *Anatomy of Melancholy* (1621), by permission of The British Library, C.45.c.30.

because the arch mask of Democritus Junior ('I would not willingly be known', p. 1) is suddenly, albeit with a flourish, removed at the end of the book in 'The Conclusion of the Author to the Reader', signed on the very last page 'From my studie in Christ Church Oxon. Decemb 5. 1620. ROBERT BVRTON' (Ddd3v). This signed conclusion disappeared from all later editions, though material from it was incorporated into the preface. Not that Burton did this in order truly to hide his identity, given that he inserted a portrait of himself on the engraved title-page. Rather, the game of authorial identity had a different set of rules for the 1621 reader. Devon Hodges has noted how 'In the first edition . . . the text seems to move from the veiled "I" of the preface to the unveiled "I" of the conclusion'.[17] In fact, the unveiled 'I' of the conclusion sounds, at times, quite craven, compared to the mocking voice of the satirical preface:

> I have annexed this Apologeticall *Appendix*, to craue pardon for that which is amisse. I doe suspect some precedent passages haue bin distastefull, as too satyricall & bitter; some againe as too Comicall, homely, broad, or lightly spoken. (Ddd1v)

In future editions, this apologetic tone is dissolved, as Burton maintains the mask of Democritus Junior consistently, though he plays bo-peep with the reader by strewing clues to his identity throughout the text. In what is still one of the most illuminating accounts of *The Anatomy of Melancholy* (and certainly the wittiest), Joan Webber notes how the authorial presence in the book is constantly being absorbed by the sense of ventriloquism imposed by the shifts in ideas, positions, voices – indeed, identities – necessitated by the omnivorous nature of the book: 'Though in one sense he can be himself only, in another he is all the parts he plays, because his book-personality becomes cosmic.'[18] From the very beginning, Burton is extremely self-conscious about the nature of his persona, or 'book-personality' in Webber's terms, in relation to the ubiquity of literary production, or at least its perceived ubiquity, at this period:

> You have had a reason of the Name, if the title or inscription offend your grauitie, were it a sufficient iustification to accuse others, I could produce many sober Treatises, euen Sermons themselues, which in their fronts carry more phantasticall names. Howsoeuer is is a kind of policy in these dayes, to prefixe a phantasticall title to a booke which is to be sold, for as larkes come downe to a day-net, many vaine Readers will tarry & stand gasing like silly passengers, at an Anticke picture in a painters shoppe that will not looke at a iudicious picture. (5)

Already Burton is moving towards a paradoxical position characteristic of so much of his book: what is written is unnecessary; too much is being written; yet, by implication at least, there is a need for this particular book to be written:

> *there is no end of writing of bookes*, as the wiseman found of old, in this scribling age, especially wherein *the number of bookes is without number, as a worthy man saith, Presses be oppressed*, and out of an itching humour, that euer man hath to show himselfe desirous of fame and honour, he will write no matter what, and scrape together it bootes not whence. *Bewitched with this desire of fame, etiam mediis in morbis*, to the disparagement of their health and scarce able to hold a penne, they must say something ... (7)[19]

We are disarmed because our worst criticisms are anticipated by the author himself (which may well be an indication that a certain craven quality is present even in the satirical preface):

> And for those other faults of Barbarisme *Doricke* dialecte, extemporanean stile, Tautologies, apish imitation, a rapsodie of seuerall rags gathered together from seuerall dunghills, & confusedly tumbled out: without art, inuention, iudgement, witte, learning, harsh, absurd, insolent, indiscreet, ill composed, vaine, scurrile, idle, dull and drie; I confesse all, thou canst not thinke worse of me then I do of my selfe. All I say is this, that I haue presidents for it, others as absurd, vaine, idle, illiterate; &c. we haue all our faults (9)

We are also disarmed because Burton's definition of melancholy expands to include us all: 'all the world is madde, that it is melancholy, dotes' (14). If everyone is subject to melancholy, then the reader cannot stand outside of the text and judge the author. This strategy allows Burton to move from the individual psyche to society in all its constituent parts. He uses the voice of Democritus initially to offer the satirist's view of general abuses in society, then in his own voice takes a view of his own world:

> If *Democritus* were aliue now, he should see strange alterations, a new company of counterfeit visards, whiflers, *Cumane* Asses, maskers, Mummers, painted puppets, outsides, phantasticke shadowes, Gulls, Butterflies, Monsters, giddy heads, &c. (26)

Burton moves through the folly of religion (specifically the 'extremes' of Popery and Protestant sects); of war, especially civil war such as obtained in France and in England during the Wars of the Roses; and particularly of corruption:

> A poore sheep-stealer is hanged for stealing victuals, compelled per-
> adventure by necessity of that inexorable cold, hunger and thirst, to
> saue himselfe from staruing: but a great man in office may securely rob
> whole prouinces, vndoe thousands, pill and pole, oppresse *ad libitum*,
> flea, grinde, tyrannize, inrich himselfe by spoyles of the commons,
> and be vncontrolable in all his actions, and after all bee recompenced
> with turgent titles, honoured for his good seruice, and no man dare
> find fault, or mutter at it. (30–1)

It is because, in Burton's view, melancholy/folly is universal that we end up inhabiting a blind and degraded society: 'So are wee fooles and ridiculous, absurd in all our actions, carriages, diet, apparell, customes, and consultations, and scoffe and point one at another, and in conclusion we are all fooles' (36–7). Since William Mueller stressed this aspect of *The Anatomy of Melancholy* as social critique in 1952, few commentators have been interested in the conjunction between the analysis of an individual malady and its political context.[20] This aspect of the *Anatomy* is certainly most evident in the preface, where Burton develops the notion of universal madness and a degraded society: 'Kingdomes, Prouinces, Families . . . Melancholy as well as men' (39). He is careful to tip his hat to the good fortune of England in having 'a wise, a learned, a religious King, another Numa, a second Augustus, a true Iosiah, most worthy Senators, a learned Cleargy, an obedient Commonalty, &c.' (52), but quickly goes on to say: 'Yet amongst many Roses some Thistles grow' (52). His account of England's economic woes multiplies the thistles considerably, taking in problems of depopulation outside of London, of general increases in poverty and in the economic downturn that was indeed evident in the early part of the seventeenth century.[21] This leads Burton to 'make an Utopia of mine owne' (56), which, especially through its account of improved administration, casts a very critical eye on current conditions in England.[22] Going into some detail, Burton glances at abuses that were to be taken up by the 1621 parliament; for example, the question of 'priuate Monopolies', an issue that was eventually to bring down Francis Bacon.[23] Throughout this discussion, Burton keeps in view the analogy between melancholy as an index to an individual self, and melancholy as a way of characterising a national or political situation: 'As it is in a mans body, if either head, heart, stomacke, liuer, spleane, or any one part bee misaffected, all the rest suffer with it, so it is with this Oeconomicall body' (62).

It is certainly true that when the reader reaches the first partition of *The Anatomy of Melancholy*, which deals with the causes and symptoms of melancholy, some of this social focus is lost. However, it returns in the second partition, which discusses cures, and is even more strongly present in the third, concluding partition, which is devoted to love melancholy. I say this with some confidence, but it is worth noting that few accounts of the fundamental nature of Burton's book are in agreement with each other, a situation which seems, for once, to have less to do with the business of modern criticism and its proliferating ideological battles and more to do with the complex nature of Burton's massive (and unstable) text. As we have seen, on the title-page Burton promises that melancholy will be 'philosophically, medicinally, historically, opened and cvt vp'. This is very much what we might understand the term anatomy to mean, in its medical as well as more general sense.[24] But for Burton, the cutting involves accretion, rather than paring away, and *The Anatomy of Melancholy* becomes an accumulation of citations, something like a giant commonplace book, leading to a situation aptly described by Lawrence Babb: 'Any subject of general interest among cultivated Jacobeans is likely to turn up somewhere in the *Anatomy*.'[25] For that reason, I think, critics have offered us a paradoxical *Anatomy* (Colie), versus a clear critique of society (Mueller); a highly ordered, intricately structured and consolatory *Anatomy* (Fox), versus an uncertainty-producing machine, or self-consuming artefact (Fish); a comforting sermon (Vicari), versus a dark struggle with Calvinism (Stachniewski); a mind in control (Lyons), versus a feather blown about by the material presented (Hodges).[26] And what might seem rather late in the piece, criticism has finally considered the issue of gender in the *Anatomy*, with an incisive account of Burton as representative of anxious masculinity in early modern England.[27]

This sense of instability when approaching the overall nature of *The Anatomy of Melancholy* reflects the difficult task Burton sets himself, for he offers an all-encompassing view of self and world (seeing the two as conjoined), without centring that view on a stable self. The effect of this has been described most pertinently by Joan Webber:

> man finds himself confronted by the problem of identity just because his personality is no longer stable and taken for granted, but, rather, needs to be continuously redefined. The sudden shifts in tone and

point of view, the leaps from character to character in Burton's book all illustrate the tendency of the age. The restlessness of the style is partly accounted for by Burton's habit of suddenly breaking off one discourse and turning to another, usually with the explanation that he does not know what he is talking about. The additive organization of the book confirms our sense of a personality that remakes itself from one moment to another.[28]

This also needs to be related to the cautious nature of Burton's social criticism, which similarly has a constantly shifting and often contradictory focus – a reflection of the fact that, in a discourse on melancholy, most things are both causes and cures.[29] Take hunting, for example. In the first partition, Burton warns of the dangers of 'those madde disports of Hauking and Hunting' (1.2.3.1, p. 158). He does carefully explain that he has in mind those for whom such pursuits are socially inappropriate ('honest recreations & fit disports for some great men, but not for every base inferiour person', ibid.), yet given King James's passion for such sport, Burton's tirade seems rather daring when he reaches his climax: 'Taxing the madnesse and folly of such vaine men that spend themselues in such idle sports, neglecting their businesse and necessary affaires' (1.2.3.1, p. 159) – this sounds rather like James. However, in the second partition, we find hawking and hunting amongst the cures for melancholy: 'they recreate Body and Mind' (2.2.4, p. 340). This apparent contradiction is perhaps best viewed as a particular kind of relativism; in Burton's terms, the simple fact is that everything has contrary properties depending upon the context. This includes both the self and the world at large, because Burton always shifts outwards from an account of general 'scientific' premises, to his own sense of himself, to, ultimately, the reader, captured in the portrait of melancholy being developed:

> You haue had at last the generall and particular causes of melancholy: now go & bragge of thy present happines whosoever thou art, bragge of thy temperature, and of thy good parts, insult, triumph, and boast? thou seest in what a brittle state thou art, how soone thou mai'st be deiected, how many severall waies, by bad diet, bad aire, a small losse, a little sorrow, or discontent, an ague, &c.: how many sudden accidents may procure thy ruine, what a small tenure of happynes thou hast in this life, how weake & silly a creature thou art. (1.2.5.4, p. 229)

The paradox emerging here, however, is the difficulty of accounting for a set of symptoms buried within the interior of the self, which may well be anatomised or cut open at one level in Burton's account, but which remains unique and, in the sufferer's mind, incommunicable: 'no man liuing can expresse the anguish and bitternes of our soules' (2.3.3, p. 405). Of course, Burton can even produce consolation from this solipsism, for he goes on to point out that one advantage of melancholy is that it is so inward it doesn't offend others, as diseases like leprosy do: 'In this malady, that which is, is wholly to themselues', and indeed there is even an advantage for the sufferer: 'solitarines makes them more apt to contemplate, suspition wary, which is a necessary humor in these times' (2.3.8, p. 429). Again, it is worth noting the constant transition between self and social context: Burton is always aware of how the self relates to 'these times'. This is most apparent in the third partition, which discusses love melancholy (under which Burton places religious melancholy).

In a particularly interesting account of charity early on in the third partition, Burton discusses how the individual desire for fame moves outwards into the world, turning it into a simulacrum of the vainglorious individual's rapacity:

> He that shall see so many law sutes, such endlesse contentions, such plotting, vndermining, so much mony spent with such egernesse of fury, euery man for himselfe his owne ends, the Diuell for all, so many distressed soules, such lamentable complaints, so many factions conspiracies, seditions, such grudging, repining, discontent, so much emulation, enuy, so many brawles, quarrels, monomachies, &c. where is charity? To see and read of such cruell warres, tumults, vproares, bloody battels, so many men slaine, so many citties ruinated & c. (3.1.3.1, p. 525)

War, destruction and a diseased society stem from, and contribute to, the disordered individual psyche:

> Tis no maruell then if being so vncharitable, hardhearted as we are, we haue so frequent and so many discontents, such melancholy fits, so many bitter pangs, mutuall discords, all in a combustion, often complaints, so common grieuances, generall mischiefes, so many plagues, warres, vproares, losses, deluges, fires, inundations, Gods vengeance, and all the plagues of Egypt come vpon vs since wee are so vncharitable one towards another ... (3.1.3.1, p. 526)

Love itself is, as one might expect, quite contradictory in its relationship to this situation. Burton acknowledges its contribution to civilisation, but is much more interested in its destructive effects:

> Loue indeed (I may not denie) first vnited Prouinces, built Citties, and by a perpetuall generation preserues mankind, propagates the Church, but if he rage, he is no more Loue, but burning lust, a disease, Frensie, Madnesse, Hell. (3.1.2.1, p. 536)

In this section, Burton's much remarked tolerance seems to break down, as his sense of the threat posed to the balance of both individual and psyche by love leads to a series of misogynistic tours de force that have gone largely unnoticed by critics prior to Mark Breitenberg's account of the *Anatomy* in relation to an early modern crisis in masculinity. Breitenberg points to Burton's account of melancholy as an exploration of the veiled threat of femininity to constructions of the masculine subject: 'Burton most closely follows Galen's version of negative melancholy, both in his inveterate misogyny and also in his portrait of the melancholic as in many ways feminine, or as potentially effeminised, as well as in the pervasive threat to masculine reason posed by melancholy excess.'[30] A good example is the astonishingly detailed and vituperative catalogue of female repulsiveness that is meant to demonstrate how love is blind, but that really seems to revel in the degradation of women:

> Euery louer admires his mistris, though she be very deformed of her self, ill fauoured, crooked, bald, goggle-eyed, or squint-eyed, sparrow mouthed, hookenosed, or haue a sharpe foxe nose, gubber-tuffed, rotten teeth, beetle-browed, her breath stinke all ouer the roome, her nose drop winter & summer with a Bauarian poke vnder her chin, laue eared, *her dugges like two double iugges*, bloodi-falne-fingers, scabbed wrists, a tanned skinne, a rotten carkase, crooked backe, lame, splea-footed, *as slender in the middle as a cowe in the waste*, goutie legges, her feet stinke, she breeds lice, a very monster, an aufe imperfect, her whole complection sauours, and to thy iudgement lookes like a marde in a lanthorne, whom thou couldst not fancy for a world, but hatest, lothest, & wouldest haue spit in her face, or blow thy nose in her bosome, *remedium amoris*, to another man a doudy, a slut, a nasty, filthy beastly queane, dishonest peradventure, obscene, base, beggerly, foolish, vntaught, if he loue her once he admires her for all this. (2.2.3.1, pp. 608–9)

Because the blindness of love is a symptom of love melancholy, this catalogue of loathing is proven by the back-handed remark that, to the lover, these vile attributes are admirable. One might say that such bravura performances of misogyny are merely an echo of further commonplaces, but I think that they need to be seen as part and parcel of the kind of self being conjured up within Burton's definitions of melancholy. This self is fundamentally vulnerable, and through its vulnerability, society is corrupted. Breitenberg links this to the fact that such a self is gendered masculine and its vulnerability stems from the threat of femininity: 'Burton utilises an age-old construction of woman as linked to base corporeality in order to purify masculinity from its own sexual desire and from its own consequent vulnerability.'[31] This results in passages such as the one where Burton suggests imagining the woman one desires naked: her very body will drive away desire: 'see her vndrest ... or suppose thou sawest her sick, pale, in a consumption, on her death bed, skin and bones, or now dead' (3.2.5.3, p. 641).

From this perspective, it is particularly interesting that the 1621 *Anatomy*, having begun with Burton 'clothed' in the figure of Democritus Junior, should end with a naked Burton who, like the figure of the threatening woman, will 'vnmaske and shew him as he is' (Ddd). Burton worries in the conclusion that he has anatomised himself, that he has been opened and cut up: 'I haue laid my selfe open (I know it) in this Treatise' (Ddd). There follows a typically contradictory series of submissive apologies and defiance, particularly over whether or not the book has been too satirical or too 'homely'. Then Burton does indeed seem to cross over into the role of naked body previously allotted to women: 'As Augusta Liuia sometimes said, *viros nudos castae feminae nihil a statuis distare*, A naked man to a modest woman, is no otherwise then a picture' (Dddv). When this transfer takes place, suddenly male nakedness, the self laid bare here at the very end, will present itself only as a simulacrum to the unmoved reader/viewer.[32]

This leads to the famous description by Burton of his style as being like a river, a description which was incorporated into the preface in the second edition, and therefore turned into a comment in the voice of the veiled self of Democritus Junior, rather than the naked Robert Burton.[33] In turning to this self-image, though, Burton is really returning again to a notion of the self/style as fluid and therefore ultimately indeterminable:

So that as a riuer runs precipitate & swift, & sometimes dull and slow; now direct, now *per ambages* about; now deep then shallow; now muddy, then cleere; now broad, then narrow doth my style

flowe, now more serious, then light, now more elaborate or remisse.
Comicall, Satyricall, as the present subiect requires, or as at that time
I was affected. (Ddd2)

This is as much as to say, 'You cannot pin me down', and at the end
of the 1621 *Anatomy* it might be read as a nervous counter to the laying
bare of Robert Burton as the author at the end of his treatise. In later
editions, Burton (who is, after all, actually depicted as a picture on the
title-page, and so perhaps not seen as truly naked by any modest
woman – or reader) plays a kind of striptease with us, strewing clues to
his identity through the text, but never quite coming out and saying
directly who he is. Nevertheless, the fact that the conclusion is signed
'Robert Burton' tells us who the author is, but doesn't exactly tell us
who Robert Burton is. Most readers are content to agree with Joan Webber
that Burton's self is his book.[34] That still leaves us with an unstable
sense of identity, given that there is such disagreement about the nature
of Burton's book. Another way to approach this question is to look more
closely at where the tone of the book shifts. If we begin with the teasing
satire of the preface, where Burton assumes the character of Democritus
Junior, then we move with the first partition into a much more severe,
scientific mode, as the discussion of the causes of melancholy involves
a great deal of detailed medical information. In the second partition,
which is devoted to cures for melancholy, Burton does suddenly provide
a great deal more personal information and indulges in some amazing
flights of fancy. The most remarked upon is the 'Digression of the Aire'
(2.2.3), which involves an imaginary flight from the study to the entire
universe:

> I may freely expatiate and exercise my selfe, for my recreation a while
> roue, and wander round about the world and mount aloft to those
> aetheriall orbes and celestiall spheres, and so descend to my former
> elements againe. (2.2.3, pp. 317–18)

It is in the course of this fantasy of total freedom, unbounded geographical scope, that Burton tells us his origins: '*Oldbury* in *Warwickeshire*,
where I haue often looked about me with great delight, and at the foot
of which Hill, |At Lindley in Lecestershire| I was borne' (2.2.3, p. 337).[35]
He returns to some of the details of his birth later in the partition, seemingly placing at the very centre of the *Anatomy* a sense of personal identity,
and also a mixture of mental freedom and confinement: we see Burton
both flying (in his imagination) through the air, but also confined to

his study like a man in prison, and in this partition the image of the prison is as powerful and significant as the image of the mind soaring like a hawk:

> We are all prisoners. What is our life but a prison? We are all imprisoned in an Iland. The world it selfe to some men is a prison, our narrow seas as so many ditches, & when they haue compassed the Globe of the earth, they would faine goe see what's done in the Moone. (2.3.4, p. 410)

The author's study is both prison and realm opening up the universe to the imagination; Burton imagines the unappreciated scholar as, indeed, a captive bird:

> But our patrons of learning are so farre now-a-dayes from respecting the *Muses*, and giuing that honour to Schollers, and reward which they deserue, and are allowed by these indulgent priviledges of many noble Princes, that after all their paines taken in the *Vniversities*, coste & charge, expences, irksome houres, laborious taskes, and wearisome dayes, dangers, hazards, barred *interim* from all pleasures, which other men haue, mewed vp like haukes all their liues, if they chance to wade through them, they shall in the end be reiected and contemned, and which is the greatest misery, driuen to their shifts, exposed to want, pouerty and beggery. (1.2.3.15, p. 172)

The scholar as the mewed up hawk accordingly looks inward upon himself (and is therefore, of course, subject to melancholy) and outward upon society – at least in the person of Robert Burton. Looking outward, what he sees (certainly in the 1621 *Anatomy* – he modified some of his expressions of discontent about lack of advancement in later editions)[36] is ignorance and a general lack of appreciation of the learning that makes up the entire project of *The Anatomy of Melancholy*:

> the major part [of the gentry] (& some again excepted, that are indifferent) are wholly bent for haukes and hounds, and carried away many times with intemperat lust, gaming, and drinking. If they read on a book at any time, t'is an English Chronicle, Sr *Huon of Burdeaux*, *Amadis de Gaul* &c. a play-book, or some pamphlet of Newes, & that at such times only when they cannot stir abroad, to driue away time, their sole discours is dogs, hawks and horses, and what newes? (1.2.3.15, p. 183)

Burton is clearly nervous about this attack, as can be seen from the
marginal note in the following quotation, but his energy is really
devoted to railing at those who cannot see the worth of the endeavours
of scholars like himself:

> There are amongst you I doe ingeniously confesse, many well deseruing
> Patrons, and true patriots of my knowledge, besides many hundreths
> which I neuer saw, no doubt, or heard of, Pillars of our commonwealth
> [I haue often met with my selfe, and conferred with diverse worthy
> Gentlemen in the Country, no whit inferiour, if not to be preferred
> for divers kind of learning to many of our Academicks], whose
> worth, bounty, learning, forwardnes, and true zeale in religion, and
> good esteem of all Schollars, ought to be consecrated to all posterity:
> but of your rank there are a deboshed, corrupt, covetous, illiterat crew
> again, a prophane pernitious company, irreligious, impudent and
> stupid, I know not what Epithets to giue them, enimies to Learning,
> confounders of the Church, and the ruine of a Common-wealth.
> (1.2.3.15, p. 183)

The reader who is a member of the gentry will naturally know in
which category he belongs. But as usual there is some disingenuousness
in Burton's attack. As a reader, Burton is an academic version of the
omnivorous John Chamberlain. He owned a considerable number of
books in the very categories on which scorned, foolish members of the
gentry wasted their time: English chronicles (Holinshed and many others);
not *Huon of Bourdeaux* and *Amadis de Gaule*, but the similar *Fortunatus*
and Henry Roberts's *Christian King of Denmark*; scores of playbooks by
Dekker, Heywood, Jonson, Shirley, Webster, Middleton; numerous
pamphlets of news; not to mention jestbooks and collections of wondrous
happenings.[17] Indeed, Nicolas Kiessling, in his account of the details of
Burton's library, points out how much more of it was devoted to secular
literature and ephemera, rather than to theology, compared to the
libraries of other fellows of Oxbridge colleges at the time.[38] *The Anatomy
of Melancholy* itself is a voracious consumer of books (though fewer of
them stem from the lighter reading in Burton's library, at least until the
third partition, which does offer a range of authors on love) and might
be seen as an image of the self and the self's relationship to society
transmitted through the book and the process of reading it.

Burton's great book has also been seen recently by Patricia Vicari as
something very like a gigantic sermon. While my account makes it clear
that I don't see the rather bland sort of consolatory sermon that Vicari

ultimately finds in the *Anatomy*, Burton clearly draws on the sermon form for some of the framework for his treatise. For my purposes, a more valuable crossover is evident when one considers how the sermon form, like *The Anatomy of Melancholy*, can be seen to participate in the intersection between an account of the self and a notion of the self as ultimately explicable only in social terms.

## Sermons

At first glance it may seem strange to discuss sermons in relation to these questions of subjectivity. The connections between Puritanism and spiritual autobiography and self-reflection have been exhaustively considered, but the sermon is not usually seen as related to this issue, particularly not as manifested by 'establishment' preachers like John Donne and Lancelot Andrewes. However, the sermon as practised in 1621 was certainly a form used for self-examination (whether of the preacher's self or the listener's). The other side to the sermon at this time is its engagement in matters of political moment. Patrick Collinson has noted how important printed sermons were at a time when many local churches outside of London and large towns often did not have a clergyman who preached, although the number of preaching ministers had increased greatly by 1621, in comparison to the Elizabethan Church.[39] Popular printed sermons were significant in terms of religious instruction, and that aspect of them is discussed in detail below in Chapter 7, where I note, as I do here, that there is no such thing as uncontroversial religious writing in 1621, and the most innocuous-seeming sermon may raise issues of religious doctrine that were fiercely debated, or take in political issues of equal importance.

In the sections below, I begin with the court preachers John Donne and Lancelot Andrewes, who participate in an activity and genre (the court sermon) that has been studied at length by Peter McCullough, who examines in particular how significant the court sermon became under King James. McCullough points to the political tensions between different aspects of court preaching, noting that the court might within a brief period move from a sermon by George Abbot to a sermon by William Laud, who were at opposite poles both in relation to church doctrine and in relation to James's foreign policy.[40] This conflict is also evident in court in relation to the situation of Prince Charles; I will be concluding my discussion by looking in particular at the case of Charles's chaplain George Hakewell, and the tensions over negotiations for Charles's Catholic marriage. But between these two discussions of court sermons and politics, I will be turning to the popular, polemical sermons, which in 1621 particularly concerned themselves with James's foreign policy, the crisis in Bohemia, and, by implication, the royal prerogative. As I shall show, during a year in which parliament debated James's apparent softening of laws against recusancy, and in which parliamentary members moved towards a daring intervention in foreign policy which touched on the royal prerogative, the sermon became a key genre for the expression of what can broadly be called political views – views which in recent years have attracted intense debate between political historians, who argue over how far Stuart discussions of monarchical power could be seen as a deeply rooted conflict over the constitution of the state, or whether they were merely differences of degree within an essentially consensual society.[41]

Both Court and popular preachers were caught up in controversies over the direction of the Church in England, controversies which I will look at in more detail in Chapter 7. But here it is worth noting that, just as political historians are not in agreement over the nature and extent of ideological conflict at this period, theological historians are also divided over the depth of division in the Church leading up to the period when, under Archbishop Laud, conflict became more overt (or, some historians argue, has simply been recognised to be so by some modern commentators). The very practice of sermons, as opposed to church ceremonies, formed a significant stalking horse for debates between those who saw preaching as essential, whether one calls them 'Puritan', or Calvinist, and those anti-Calvinists who wanted to stress prayer and ceremony over preaching.[42]

Sermons make up almost half the total number of 1621 texts which survive – there are about 95 examples extant, though of course many more sermons were preached than have survived in print. As a genre, the sermon can range from the intellectually taxing work of Andrewes or Donne to popular polemical writing as exemplified by Samuel Ward or Thomas Gataker (both discussed below). I have chosen examples for discussion here which underline the full range of styles and ideological debates manifest in the sermons of 1621.

### John Donne: 'alwayes preaching to himself'

By the end of 1621, John Donne was finally elevated to become Dean of St Paul's. Sermons survive from the whole range of his preaching activities in the course of the year: one preached to the Countess of Bedford; two preached to the court at Whitehall; a marriage sermon for Margaret Washington; possibly five sermons preached at Lincoln's Inn, though the dates for these are uncertain; and a Christmas Day sermon at St Paul's, the first sermon preached by Donne in his new post.[43] Throughout these sermons, Donne offers a characteristic depiction of a self (not necessarily an autobiographical self) under self-examination. This aspect of Donne was captured vividly, if a bit melodramatically, by Izaak Walton's famous description of him preaching:

> preaching the Word so, as shewed his own heart was possest with those very thoughts and joys that he laboured to distill into others: A Preacher in earnest; weeping sometimes for his Auditory, sometimes with them: always preaching to himself, like an Angel from a cloud, but in none.[44]

A standard modern example of this sense of Donne's preaching self is Joan Webber's:

> Other preachers extinguished themselves in their subjects. Donne is his own subject, becomes his own prose.[45]

Only recently has a move been made to reassess the political context for Donne's sermons.[46] It seems clear from the 1621 sermons that they can be approached both as examples of a self under examination and as events with a political context.[47] A good example is the sermon Donne preached to the Countess of Bedford on 7 January. Lucy Russell/Harrington, Countess of Bedford, was both a prominent figure in James's court in the early years of the century and a patron of writers like Drayton, Daniel, Jonson and Donne. She was the subject of a number of Donne's verse epistles, and wrote replies to them. Donne's biographer, R.C. Bald, notes that 'Donne responded to her admiration of the satires by telling her that her influence and example had caused him to renounce satire for religious verse'.[48] After an illness in 1612 she became noted for her piety, possibly under the influence of the Puritan divine Dr Burges. Donne's relationship with her cooled, perhaps owing more to his increasing dependence upon James's favourite Somerset, who was opposed by the Russells, than to any jealousy of Dr Burges.[49] By 1621, with George Villiers (Buckingham) having been safely installed as favourite for some time, that cause of tension was past (though the recent sale of Burley to Villiers by the impoverished Bedfords may have stung).[50] But Donne would still have been treading a delicate political balance, given the Harrington connection to James's daughter Elizabeth. She had been raised by the Harringtons, and Lucy's mother had

remained in Elizabeth's service in the Palatine after Elizabeth's marriage
to Frederick. I will be discussing the situation in Bohemia and the Palatine
at greater length below. To understand some of the reverberations of
Donne's sermon for Lucy Russell, one needs to bear in mind her interest
in the fortunes of Elizabeth and Frederick at a time when James was
seeking to curtail popular support for them.

The text for the sermon is Job 13.15: 'Loe, though he slay me, yet will
I trust in him.' Evelyn Simpson notes that this is a sermon with a 'melancholy tinge' (15), perhaps to suit the mood of its recipient. But it is
also a sermon typical of the kind of 'self' examination noted above as
characteristic of Donne. It begins with an arresting stress on mortality
and mutability, demanding that the Christian hearer:

> fixe his thoughts upon his *beginning*, and upon his *end*, and ever
> remember, that as a few years since, in his *Cradle*, he had no sense of
> that honour, those riches, those pleasures, which possess his time
> now, so, God knows how few days hence, in his *grave*, he shall have no
> sense, no memory of them. Our whole life is but a *parenthesis*, our
> *receiving* of our soule, and *delivering* it back againe, makes up the perfect
> sentence; Christ is our *Alpha* and *Omega*, and our *Alpha* and *Omega* is
> all we are to consider. (187–8)

The impecunious Russells were doubtless already well aware of the
fleeting nature of riches. What Donne stresses is the *experience* of this
mutability: 'This world then is but an *Occasionall* world, a world onely
to be us'd; and that but so, *as though we us'd it not*' (188). Therefore, as
the sermon proceeds, Donne offers an account of how the visible world
may give way to the invisible sense of God, using a series of concrete
examples of how such a process might work:

> When I expect a *friend*, I may go up to a window, and wish I might
> see a *Coach*, or up to a cliff, and wish I might see a *ship*, but it is
> because I hope, that that friend is in that Coach, or that ship: so I
> wish, and pray, and labour for temporall things, because I hope that
> my soule shall be edified, and my salvation established, and God
> glorified by my having them: And therefore every Christian hope
> being especially upon spirituall things, is properly, and purposely
> grounded, upon these stones; that it be *spes veniae*, a hope of *pardon*,
> for that which is past, and then *spes gratiae*, a hope of *Grace*, to estab-
> lish me in that state with God, in which, his pardon hath placed
> mee, and lastly *spes gloriae*, a hope that this *pardon*, and this *grace*,

shall lead me to that everlasting *glory*, which shall admit no night, no eclipse, no cloud. (196–7)

This is a fine example of Donne's preaching style. We are led through the concrete images to see the speaker standing in for us, examining the self that expects, wishes, hopes for a temporal thing that is in fact an image of a spiritual hope (bearing in mind that the sermon is moving through an explication of the 'trust' in God that is the essence of the text from Job). On the other hand, the sermon keeps returning to images of mutability, reminding us that we are mortal. Towards the end of the sermon this reaches its climax in a bravura passage using a concept familiar from much of Donne's religious imagery:

Looke upon the *water*, and we are as that, and as that spilt upon the ground: Looke to the *earth*, and we are not like that, but we are earth it self: At our Tables we feed upon the dead, and in the Temple we tread upon the dead: and when we meet in a Church, God hath made many *echoes*, many testimonies of our death, in the walls, and in the windowes, and he onely knowes, whether he will not make another testimony of our mortality, of the youngest amongst us, before we part, and make the very *place of our buriall*, our *deathbed*. (202)

This sense of mortality casts us down, but the sermon ends with the resurrection of the body: 'howsoever he lock us into our graves now, yet he hath the keys of hell, and death, and shall in his time extend that voyce to us all, *Lazare veni foras*, come forth of your putrefaction, to incorruptible glory' (205). Certainly this sermon could be seen as an attempt to reflect the Countess of Bedford's sombre disposition, as well as being a perfect example of Donne's examination of the self. Yet its theme also evokes the uncertainty in the air at the beginning of 1621, particularly for someone like the Countess of Bedford, with connections to support for the Protestant Cause in Europe in general, and for Elizabeth and Frederick in particular. Donne's message is 'trust in no earthly thing', but the events leading up to the eventual Thirty Years' War were an admixture of earthly and spiritual, as indeed all politics was in the period, given the significance of religious controversy.

Debora Kuller Shuger's notion that, in Donne, 'the inner and outer man are both constructed politically', is even more evident in the White Hall sermons.[51] I want to look at the one preached on 8 April, partly because it contains a particularly startling anatomical image of self-examination in the context of a sermon that could easily be seen to glance at a number of dangerous political issues. The rather curious text for this particularly virtuoso sermon (Evelyn Simpson feels it is too ingenious, p. 19) is Proverbs 25.16: 'Hast thou found honey? Eat so much as is sufficient for thee, lest thou be filled therewith, and vomit it.' The arresting opening sentence of this sermon raises the issue of temporal desire again, but in the context of this sermon, Donne is engaged in a more searching account of ambition which seems to glance directly at the court audience: 'There is a spirituall unsatiablenesse of riches, and there is a spirituall unsatiablenesse of sin' (225). While I am not suggesting that Donne would have dared (or desired) to direct such a critique at James's favourite, surely the court had some sense of Buckingham as the epitome of such 'unsatiablenesse' (not to mention other examples, such as Doncaster).[52]

Donne then offers a remarkable account of the consequences of insatiableness, joining together a desire for knowledge, colonial conquest, scientific speculation, and spiritual degeneration:

> As though this World were too little to satisfie man, men are come to discover or imagine new worlds, severall worlds in every Planet; and as though our Fathers heretofore, and we our selves too, had beene but dull and ignorant sinners, we thinke it belongs to us to perfect old inventions, and to sin in another height and excellency, then former times did, as though sin had had but a minority, and an infancy till now. (225)

This leads him to a consideration of the radically unknowable nature of the self. This is couched in religious terms: we cannot know if apparently conforming Christians harbour contrary religious principles (this is a dangerous notion, given that James was attempting to assure his subjects that Catholics who took the Oath of Allegiance could be trusted):

> so are the actions of men so ambiguous, as that we cannot conclude upon them; men come to our Prayers here, and pray in their hearts here in this place, that God would induce another manner of Prayer into this place; and so pray in the Congregation, that God would not heare the prayers of the Congregation; There hath alwaies been ambiguity and equivocation in words, but now in actions, and almost every action will admit a diverse sense. (226)

This is, when one considers it carefully, a deeply disturbing proposition to put before the court, which may *be* a place of dissimulation, but which never declares itself to be such a place. At a more abstract level, this enquiry also leads Donne to question just how knowable the self that is on display in the sermons (and elsewhere) might be. Such questions lead Donne to examine the problem of an individual's place in society, given that, in his interpretation, this text is concerned with the amount of 'honey' sufficient for a particular person's place: 'eat no more than is sufficient; And in that, let not the servant measure himselfe by his Master, nor the subject by the King' (226). That seems straightforward, but in this age of shifting appearances, can we be sure of people's places, sure that they know them and that they offer us the correct image of themselves so that we may easily place them:

> In which, we goe not about to condemne, or correct the civill manner of giving different titles, to different ranks of men; but to note the slipperiness of our times, where titles flow into one another, and lose their distinctions; when as the Elements are condensed into one another, ayre condensed into water, and that into earth, so an obsequious flatterer, shall condense a yeoman into a Worshipfull person, and the Worshipfull into an Honourable, and so that which duly was intended for distinction, shall occasion confusion. (227)

Only under the searching eye of the Holy Ghost can this abstract entity, undecidable by fellow humans, be assessed: 'the Holy Ghost in this collects Man, abridges Man, summes up Man in an unity, in the consideration of one, of himselfe' (227). At this stage of the sermon, Donne offers up the possibility that, if we cannot look into other souls clearly, at least we can look into our own: 'The direct looke is to looke inward upon thine own Conscience' (229). Such an inward look will ensure that we understand the temporary nature of material success: 'The things of this world we doe but finde, and of the things which we finde, we are but Stewards for others' (231). Similarly, there is something of a paradox in the central idea of what may be open to the sight of others, because if the image of honey takes in the idea of glory created for others' use, then we are to take up the example of the bees, who labour unseen, for the benefit of others: we should in that sense emulate 'the secresie of the Bee' (233).

When Donne comes to consider the question of sufficiency, he turns to another examination of the nature of the self's interior, in this instance, the interior of the body:

> Hee doth not say yet, lest thou bee satisfied; there is no great feare, nay there is no hope of that, that he will be satisfied. We know the receipt,

the capacity of the ventricle, the stomach of man, how much it can hold; and wee know the receipt of all the receptacles of blood, how much blood the body can have; so wee doe of all the other conduits and cisterns of the body; But this infinite Hive of honey, this insatiable whirlpoole of the covetous mind, no Anatomy, no dissection hath discovered to us. When I looke into the larders, and cellars, and vaults, into the vessels of our body for drink, for blood, for urine, they are pottles, and gallons; when I looke into the furnaces of our spirits, the ventricles of the heart and of the braine, they are not thimbles; for spirituall things, the things of the next world, we have no roome; for temporall things, the things of this world, we have no bounds. (235–6)

This passage has been discussed by Jonathan Sawday in *The Body Emblazoned*, his splendid account of dissection and the human body in Renaissance culture. Not only does this image of the body's interior offer yet another example (in the context of the sermon) of deceptive appearances, as the body's capacity expands infinitely to take more and more of the things of this world, but it also points to a subterranean world of what Sawday calls 'service chambers': 'It is as if the encounter with the body's interior has suddenly revealed a vista of an alternative (and dangerous) mode of existence in which the marginal, the low, the anti-rationalistic, reigns supreme'.[53] Indeed, as I have tried to show, the entire sermon puzzles over this split between the inner and outer self, particularly in relation to the question of degree, of how one can assess the self that is presented to society. Suddenly, the 'direct look' 'inward' seems impossible. This is because the covetous eater of honey has no room for a social 'look' outward:

The voyce of God whom he hath contemned, and wounded, The voyce of the Preacher whom he hath derided, and impoverished, The voyce of the poore, of the Widow, of the Orphans, of the prisoner, whom he hath oppressed, knocke at his doore, and would enter, but there is no roome for them, he is so full. (236–7)

And when such a person has vomited up the honey which was his worldliness: 'His honey was his soule, and that being vomited, he is now but a rotten and abhorred carkass' (237). The effect of this is, in another turn of the central image, to render him blind:

nothing weakens the eyes more then vomiting; when this worldly man hath lost his honey, he hath lost his sight; he was dimme sighted at the beginning, when he could see nothing but worldly things, things nearest to him, but when he hath vomited them, he hath lost his spectacles (238)

At the end of the sermon Donne offers the replacement of the honey of worldliness with the honey of the Gospel. This entails the replacement of the misleading self, misleading body, with religion, which must 'be as thy body' (239). He also offers the abnegation of the desire to know, to dispute, to categorise, as a way of shifting the self away from the centre of one's own attention:

Let humility be thy ballast, and necessary knowledge thy fraight: for there is an over-fulnesse of knowledge, which forces a vomit; a vomit of opprobrious and contumelious speeches, a belching and spitting of the name of Heretique and Schismatique, and a losse of charity for matters that are not of faith; and from this vomiting comes emptiness, The more disputing, the lesse beleeving. (240)

We end, therefore, with a self which must be purged of desire lest desire purge the self: 'Do not thinke thou wantest all, because thou hast not all' (240). Given the nature of Donne's sermons, there is some irony in the suggestion that there is a fundamental danger in intellectual dexterity. Indeed, this particular sermon is particularly ingenious, and Donne's ingenuity was clearly appreciated by his court audience. But careful consideration would surely have indicated to the court that this sermon does, if not undermine, at least call into question many of the values by which the court lived. It does this by taking apart and then putting back together differently the self that is both on display and invisible: the preacher's self is simultaneously examined and unknowable. Similarly, court values start to dissolve when all that is worldly is seen as part of self-deceit.

I want to conclude this brief account of Donne's sermons in 1621 by looking at the last he preached for the year: his inaugural Christmas day sermon at St Paul's on John 1.8: 'He was not that light, but was sent to bear witness of that light.' This sermon continues the consideration of impossible perception in the course of a wonderful meditation on the paradox of light:

In all Philosophy there is not so darke a thing as *light*; As the sunne, which is *fons lucis naturalis*, the beginning of naturall light, is the most evident thing to be seen, and yet the hardest to be looked upon, so is naturall light to our reason and understanding. Nothing clearer, for it is *clearnesse* it selfe, nothing darker, it is enwrapped in so many scruples. Nothing nearer, for it is round about us, nothing more remote, for wee know neither entrance, nor limits of it. Nothing more *easie*, for a child discerns it, nothing more *hard*, for no man understands it. It is apprehensible by *sense*, and not comprehensible by *reason*. If wee winke, wee cannot chuse but see it, if we stare, wee know it never the better. (256)

Despite this, Donne maintains that belief depends upon reason, or at least must satisfy reason – this is a standard rejoinder to Catholic notions of faith during the period – and he illustrates this through a startling image of how easily disbelief may topple the whole Christian edifice:

He that should come to a *Heathen man*, a meere naturall man, uncat-echized, uninstructed in the rudiments of the Christian Religion, and should at first, without any preparation, present him first with this necessitie; Thou shalt burn in fire and brimstone eternally, except thou believe *a Trinitie of Persons, in an unitie of one God*, Except thou believe the *Incarnation* of the second Person of the Trinitie, the Sonne of God, Except thou believe that *a Virgine had a Sonne*, and the same Sonne that God had, and that God was Man too, and being the imor-tall God, yet died, he should be so farre from working any spirituall cure upon this poore soule, as that he should rather bring Christian Mysteries into scorne, then *him* to a beliefe. For, that man, if you proceed so, Believe all, or you burne in Hell, would finde an easie, an obvious way to escape all; that is, first not to believe *Hell* it selfe, and then nothing could binde him to believe the rest. (357–8)

There is considerable tension between this account of the necessity to satisfy reason and the unsettling dismantling of certain knowledge in the account of what light is. Once again, Donne's purpose is to disarm those who trust implicitly in self-knowledge. The 'solution' to this crisis is the light of faith which follows on from the light of reason. Donne's ultimate vision is the solution to the opaque nature of mortal selves in the day of judgement, which is a denudation (that is, a laying bare of all things, including the true self):

This is that *Glorification* which we shall have at the last day, of which glory, we consider a great part to be in that *Denudation*, that manifest-ation of all to all; as, in this world, a great part of our inglorious servitude is in those disguises, and palliation, those colours, and pretenses of *pub-lique good*, with which men of power and authority apparell their oppressions of the poore; In this are we the more miserable, that we cannot see *their ends*, that there is none of this denudation, this laying open of our selves to one another, which shall accompany that state of glory, where we shall see one anothers *bodies*, and *soules*, *actions* and *thoughts*. (363)

This is an answer to the same problem posed in the White Hall sermon: if the presentation of the self to the world is untrustworthy, how can we have true knowledge of the selves we see around us, or indeed of our own self? Only out of this world can the disguises be penetrated; nevertheless, Donne posits a denudation of this world, whereby an individual, to attain glory, must at least reveal her or his sins. Through Christ, through a selflessness derived only from the light of Christ, selfhood will be simultaneously stripped and revealed as we receive 'a denudation and manifestation of your selves to your selves' (375).

Taken together, these three examples of Donne's preaching in 1621 offer an exemplary form of spiritual biography, if not autobiography. For Donne, the self can be seen only if it is seen through, and in order to achieve this knowledge, the preacher places his own identity under examination for the edification of his audience, and of himself. Each of these sermons is aimed at a particular audience and preached in a particularly resonant political context, while each is also focused inwards upon the speaker. This particularity becomes apparent as soon as we read a canonical author like Donne's 1621 sermons in the specific context of the year, rather than in isolation. Given this context, Donne's style can be contrasted with that of the other great metaphysical preacher of the period, Lancelot Andrewes.

## Lancelot Andrewes: Noli me tangere

Any discussion of Lancelot Andrewes has to bear in mind the warning in T.S. Eliot's famous essay on his favourite divine: 'His sermons are too well built to be readily quotable.'[54] Andrewes is a more forbidding preacher than Donne for the modern reader, but his allusive, learned style is arresting once one learns to pay it the fervent and close attention it requires. Again, few critics have bettered Eliot's description of Andrewes's method: 'Andrewes takes a word and derives the world from it; squeezing and squeezing the word until it yields a full juice of meaning which we should never have supposed any word to possess.'[55] Three sermons from 1621 are preserved: a sermon preached to the King and Lords at Westminster Abbey on the opening of parliament (30 January); an Ash

Wednesday sermon before King James at Whitehall (14 February); and an Easter sermon before King James at Whitehall (1 April). The Easter sermon is an excellent example of Andrewes at work. The text is John 20.17: 'Jesus saith unto her, Touch me Not/Dicit ei Jesus, Noli Me Tangere'. It is worth quoting the opening paragraph of this sermon in full, because it underlines the fact that Andrewes holds his audience not just through the bravura squeezing of words, but also through arresting and quite down to earth imagery:

> *Mary Magdalen*, because *she loved much*, and gave divers good proofes of it, had this morning divers favours vouchsafed her: To see a vision of *Angells*: To see Christ Himselfe: To see him before any other, first of all. He spake to her, Mary; she spake to him, *Rabboni*: Hitherto all was well. Now, heer, after all this love, after all these favours, even in the necke of them (as it were) comes an unkind word or two, a *Noli me tangere*, and marres all; turnes all out and in. Make the best of it, a *repulse* it is: but a cold salutation for an *Easter-day* morning. (543)[56]

If Donne's sermons centre on the preacher's self, then Andrewes's sermons centre on the hearer's self. The image of a spurned Mary Magdalene is brought home forcefully through a series of homely images which effect in the reader an identification with her emotions: 'turns all out and in'.[57] This is not to say that the sermon is a simple narrative. It is full of Andrewes' brilliant word-play and incisive intelligence: the whole sermon revolves around a series of paradoxical explications (Andrewes quickly moves from 'noli me tangere' to the contrasting earlier encounter of Mary with Christ expressed in the punning 'noli me plangere' – do not weep for me), but the hearer is carried along by the constant insertion into the narrative of her or his consciousness and response, underlined by Andrewes's characteristically staccato rhythms:

> Christ was not wont to be so dainty of it. Diverse times, and in diverse places, He suffered the rude *multitude* to *throng* and to thrust Him. What speake we of that? when, not three dayes since, He suffered other manner of *touches* and *twitches* both. Then, *Noli me tangere* would have come in good time; would have done well on *Good-Friday*. Why suffered He them then? why suffered He not her, now? She (I dare say for her) would have done Him no hurt, she. *Noli*, is to her: Not she: Not *Mary Magdalen*. She had touched Him before now; touched His *head*, touched His *feet; annoynted* them both: what was done, she might not, now? (544–5)

The sermon as a whole moves from the despair of rejection – as the hearer is left, initially, as puzzled as Mary about Christ's rejection – to the triumphant resolution of doubt, as Andrewes explains that Christ is teaching us to reject the physical touch for the spiritual:

> It was her error, this: She was all for the *corporall presence*; for the *touch* with the fingers. So, were His *Disciples*, all of them, too much addicted to it. From which they were now to be weined: That if they had, before, knowne Christ, or *touched* Him after the flesh: yet now from henceforth, they were to doe so no more, but to learne a new *touch*; to *touch* him, being now *ascended*. Such a *touching* there is; or els, His reason holds not: And, best *touching* Him, so; Better farre then this of hers, she was so eager on. (551)

Here where the argument of the sermon turns (from ignorance to knowledge; from doubt to faith) the hearer is still made to experience the shift in Mary's emotions, even while Andrewes attracts an intellectual admiration for the brilliance of his argument (and for the learning behind it). Andrewes was greatly admired by his court audience for his learning and for his intellectual dexterity in preaching, but also for his exemplary piety and ability to set some kind of moral example for the court by moving its members towards an imaginative identification with the hearing self projected by his sermons. As he moves the sermon towards its conclusion, the multifarious ramifications of touching are gathered together in a wonderful example of glancing anti-Catholic doctrine without any of the fierce polemic prevalent in the sermons which will be discussed in the concluding part of this chapter:

> Doe but aske the Church of *Rome*; Even, with them, it is not the *bodily touch*, in the *Sacrament*, that doth the good. Wicked men, very reprobates, have that touch, and remaine reprobates, as before. Nay, I will goe further. It is not that, that *toucheth* Christ at all. Example, *the multitude that thronged and thrust Him*; yet, for all that, as if none of them had *touched* Him, He askes, *Quis me tetigit?* So that, one may rudely thrust Him, and yet not *touch* Him, though: Not, to any purpose, so.
>
> Christ resolves the point, in that very place. The *flesh*, the *touching*, the eating it, *profits nothing. The words he spake, were spirit*: So, the *touching*, the eating, to be spirituall. (551–2)[58]

By this stage of the sermon we accede to the doctrine because we have had a sermonised self constructed for us through Andrewes' rhetorical dexterity, a self that has been through the process of standing in Mary's shoes, as it were, through Andrewes' rhetorical effects: '*Noli*, is to her: Not she: Not *Mary Magdalen*'. I say 'we' accede, and it does seem that James and his court did hear Andrewes' sermons in the way I have described. G.M. Story notes that Andrewes was 'one of the few persons in whose presence the coarseness of the King and the levity of the court was checked'.[59]

Of course, one could also see the whole of the sermon as glancing in some ways at the King as a figure who is himself hedged about with both divinity and prohibition. Andrewes' endorsement of the divine right of kings was clearly amenable to James, but Debora Kuller Shuger has argued that Andrewes is interested, not so much in reinforcing James' sense of his power in relation to the current political situation, as in asserting the suffusion of the spiritual in a society in danger of becoming secular: 'the defense of divine right belongs to a habitual sacramentalism that sees nature as infused with divinity and therefore explicitly rejects any secular grounding of power in a communal will or compact.'[60] Thus there is a curious allegiance between the King who, in 1621, was preaching religious tolerance (up to a point) alongside his sense of his own indisputable divinely bestowed power, and Andrewes' sense of the possibility of a kind of ecumenical moment, aptly summed up by Shuger: 'Andrewes' aversion to the political inclines him toward both religious toleration and mystification'.[61]

This complex position is expressed in fascinating terms in the sermon which Andrewes preached to the King and Lords at the opening of the 1621 parliament on January 30. The text is Psalm 82.2: 'God standeth in the Congregation of Princes: In the middst will He judge the Godds' (143). The sermon seems to begin with a simple, flattering assertion to the King, Peers and Bishops present: 'Of a *Congregation* of *Princes* is this *Psalme* (as you have heard.) And behold, heer, such a *Congregation* (And God, I trust, *standing* in it.)' (143). Andrewes actually reaches a point in the sermon where he seems to be endorsing a Divine Right of Lords:

> When we read, and weigh well with our selves, this high terme and title of *Godds*, given to them that are in *authoritie*, we learne, To hold them for *Godds*, to owe and to bear all reverend regard to their *Places* and *Persons*. And above all, highly to magnifie such *Assemblies* as this. (145)

With this thought before us it is hard to see why Paul Welsby, Andrewes's biographer, describes this as 'one of his more irritating and obscure sermons'.[62] Andrewes's main theme, which he takes from his interpretation of the psalm, is 'how to preserve harmonie in a *Congregation*' (144). At one point he uses the image of the body politic as a human body, a commonplace familiar to us through Menenius' speech in *Coriolanus*:

> Learn a parable of the *Naturall Body*. If there be no other cause, each *Member* is left to looke to it selfe; but if there be any danger toward the *whole body*, presently all the *parts* are summoned (as it were) to come togither, and every *Veine* sends his *bloud*, and every *sinnew* his *strength*, and every *arterie* his *spirits*, and all draw togither about the *heart* for a while, till the safety of the whole be provided for; and then returne back, every one to his place againe. So it is with the *Body Civill*, in case of *danger*, and never but in it.

The stress here is on the extraordinary circumstances which might necessitate the summoning of parliament – a view certainly shared by James, who had waited seven years before calling this one. When Andrewes goes on to explain what danger has led to this particular gathering of the body politic, we do encounter some of the obscurity levelled against the sermon by Welsby.

The parliament of 1621 looms large throughout this book, and at this point, having already touched on some of the political issues of 1621, I want to sketch in some of parliament's significance in relation to religious issues. James called his first parliament for seven years in response to the crisis in Europe that eventually resulted in the Thirty Years War. James throughout his reign saw himself as a monarch of peace, who would mediate between Catholic and Protestant interests in Europe. This involved a delicate balancing of competing interests, particularly in relation to the general feeling of anger in Protestant England about any alliance with Spain (such an alliance in fact for many years forming a cornerstone of James's policy). The balancing act became more precarious when James's son-in-law Frederick, Elector Palatine, accepted the crown of Bohemia from Protestant rebels, leading to an eventual Spanish response which pushed Frederick out of his own Palatinate as well as out of Bohemia, causing a wave of sympathy in England (amongst Protestants).

The stand-off with Spain led James to call a parliament because he needed to raise enough money at least to be able to convince Spain that he *might* go to war on Frederick's behalf.[63] At the same time, James was concerned to keep countering anti-Spanish feeling, and this included the Bishop of London's order to his clergy to cease preaching anti-Spanish sermons (an order that was defied, on the whole).[64] Robert Zaller

describes the mood of the country leading up to the convening of
parliament on 30 January 1621:

> The meeting of parliament in 1621 was bound up with the hopes
> and fears of the entire politically conscious public in England to an
> extent perhaps unique in the nation's history. The international situ-
> ation was the gravest of a century. England herself was not yet
> directly menaced, as in 1588, but the very existence of the Reformed
> faith seemed in dire jeopardy.[15]

As we will see below, the House of Commons had quite different
views from the King (and indeed from Andrewes) on the need to
uphold the Protestant cause in Europe through direct action. But
Andrewes certainly offers the image of a crisis to the Lords as a reason
for their gathering together, when he answers the question asked at the
end of the body politic image:

> But is there any *danger* then towards? There is, and that to both. To
> the *Synagogue* first, and that from a *twofold Synagogue*, and of *two
> sorts*. One continuall or *ordinarie*: The other not so, but speciall and
> upon *occasion*. The *danger*, this Psalme expresseth thus (*Ver.* V.) That
> *things are brought out of course, yea foundations and all.* Thus: there be
> (I may call them a *synagogue,* for they be many) of these same *mali
> mores*, that like *tabula terrae* shoot out dayly, no man knows whence,
> or how; never heard of before: These if they be suffered to grow, will
> bring *all out of course.* And grow they doe; for even of them, some
> that have *penalties* already set (I know not how) such a *head* they get,
> as they outgrow their *punishments*; that if this congregation grind not
> on a new & sharper *edge,* they will bring things yet further *out of
> Course.*
>   Besides, those that should keep all in course, the Lawes themselves
> are in danger too. There be a sort of men (I may well say, of the
> *Synagogue of Satan*) that give their waies, and bend their witts to nothing
> but even to devise how to fret through the Lawes as soon as they be
> made; as it were in scorn of this Congregation, and of all the Gods in it.

This seems to point to the crisis in the Protestant cause in Europe and
to the flouting of recusancy laws at home (although it is difficult to be
certain exactly who the *mali mores* accusation has in mind). If the laws
that need to be tightened to prevent men fretting through them are
indeed the recusancy laws, then Andrewes parts company with James,

who was attempting to balance some Protestant loyalty abroad with considerable tolerance at home. On the other hand, given Andrewes's usual religious toleration, it is possible that he is referring to secular laws and warning of the crisis over the administration of such things as patents of monopoly.

Where the sermon on 'Noli me tangere' creates, as it proceeds, a particular identity, even subjectivity, for the hearer which it projects, this more overtly political sermon gathers its hearers together into a body, a congregation, which Andrewes wishes to hold together in '*Concord and Vnitie*' (155) through a sense of the presence of God amongst them – through the inculcation of a desire, a longing, for that presence as the essence, the validation, of the assembly itself:

> if *he stand* not to us, we shall not *subsist*, we shall not *stand*, but fall before our *enemies*. This time is now, this danger is at hand. (158)

Shuger notes that, for Andrewes, 'The events of the Jacobean court belong to sacred history – not to the history of European power politics.'[66] I think that, in the case of this particular sermon, both the Jacobean court and European power politics are acknowledged and bound in with a sense of sacred history, as Andrewes clearly responds to a particular set of political circumstances.

Indeed, when sermons weren't concerned quite so overtly with self-examination and spiritual subjectivity (and often even when they were) they frequently carried a strong political charge. We need to recapture this sense of the political implications of forms of religious expression, nowhere more evident than in the numerous sermons of 1621, many of them deeply concerned with the religious conflict being worked out in Europe and in England during the course of the year. I want to begin this discussion by focusing on a relatively minor incident recounted in R.C. Bald's massive biography of John Donne. Donne was made Reader of Divinity at Lincoln's Inn in 1616, a little more than a year after he was ordained. (The young John Donne had been in residence at Lincoln's Inn in the early 1590s.) He was assisted in his duties at Lincoln's Inn (which included preaching virtually one sermon each week) by a chaplain, Edward May, who normally preached sermons on Sundays during the vacation. May seems to have been highly regarded until he preached a sermon which he then went on to publish some time in the middle of the year, entitled *A Sermon of the Communion of the Saints*.[67] After the summer vacation, the Council of Lincoln's Inn called for an investigation of 'the scandalles and indiscreet passages' in the sermon, 'conceaved to be taxacious and imputacious to some of this House'.[68] Punishment was decisive: 'by the generall voice of all the Masters of the Benche, noe man contradicting, [that] Mr Maye, who served the House as Chaplen there during pleasure, is amoved and absolutelie discharged of and from his said place.'[69]

The sermon attacks the Puritan members of Lincoln's Inn, who, in May's terms, 'grow old in affected-Ignorance, learned mis-interpretation, zealous malice, and in an holy contempt of all sacred and spirituall things' – the things are listed at length, including 'sacred orders; sacred offices; sacred ceremonies' (A3).[70] May preached on two texts that were rather contradictory, and they exemplify the somewhat ambiguous tone of the sermon. The first text, 1 Revelation 4.1, 'Try the Spirits whether they be of God or no', is in the contestatory spirit of separating out those who should not share the communion of the true Church. However, May's second text, Galatians 1.22.23, 'The fruit of the Spirit is charitie, joy, peace, long-suffering, gentlenesse, goodnesse, fayth, meek-nesse, temperance, &c.', seems quite conciliatory.

Bald wonders at the severity of May's punishment, considering the fairly tame criticism contained in the sermon: 'The attack is made in general terms, and even then does not seem to be very offensive, but it must have had a pertinence that can no longer be perceived.'[71] Wilfred Prest cautions against seeing this incident solely in terms of a Puritan society opposed to any other spiritual view: 'Although the benchers of Lincoln's Inn lost no time in dismissing the chaplain and vacation preacher Edward May, when he published in 1621 a high-flying sermon containing bitter attacks on certain unnamed puritan members of the society, they remained on the best of terms with May's contemporary John Donne, who was certainly no puritan'.[72] Bald does note that May printed his sermon with a mock dedication to a certain bishop, whose name was left enticingly blank: 'To the Right Reverent Father in God        by divine Providence, Lord Bishop of, &c.', and in the preface, May angrily denounces those who 'cut' him for delivering the sermon.

I think that there is a specific political context for May's sermon which helps to explain the angry reaction he provoked at Lincoln's Inn. In particular, we need to consider another sermon on the communion of saints, preached by Bishop James Ussher to the House of Commons on 18 February.[73] King James in his opening speech to parliament had held out his sense of a political and religious *via media* to his bishops, after stressing his need for money to the parliament as a whole: 'I mean not to compell men's consciences'.[74] This did not match the mood of the House of Commons, which, while happy to vote for the supply that

James needed, was also keen to address the 'questions of free speech and the flourishing of popery'.[75] The debate on what many in the Commons saw as the defiant flourishing of popery in England was detailed and heated. Thomas Shepherd, a young Lincoln's Inn lawyer, was expelled from the House for daring to suggest that the Commons should be as actively engaged in routing Puritans as Catholics.[76] (This would appear to indicate that Edward May was not without at least one supporter at Lincoln's Inn.) Parliament presented James with a petition strengthening the regulations against recusants on 17 February, which caused the King to reiterate Thomas Shepherd's argument and to reaffirm his resistance to any attempt to punish his 'loyal' Catholic subjects. It is worth noting that, despite this dispute, the Commons went on to vote two subsidies for the King (though clearly with the possibility of them leading to war with Spain in mind).

On 5 February, the Commons had been engaged in an interesting debate over collectively taking communion and hearing a sermon. According to the parliamentary diary of John Pym, Sir James Perrot offered a wonderful combination of idealistic and cynical reasons for such a ceremony:

> That wee might all receive the Comunion, gave these reasons. First, private reconcilliation was a good waye to agreement in generall busines. (2) It would be a meanes to knowe the faith of those of the Howse. (3) That this Parliament may have a Religious begining. Humane affaires doe best prosper when Gods service is ioyned with them.
> Hereuppon it was ordered That the Comunion should uppon Sondaie followeinge at the parish Church in Westminster, Doctor Usher to be requested to preache. Every man to deliver his name to fower gentlemen appoynted for that purpose. That soe they might be examined by the Clarkes booke.[77]

After some dispute over who, what and where with the Dean of Westminster and the King, the Commons had their communion service on Sunday, 18 February, including a sermon by 'Dr Usher'. James Ussher was Bishop of Meath and Professor of Divinity (he later became Archbishop of Armagh). His sermon was on the text 1 Corinthians 10.17: 'Wee being many, are one bread, and one body: for we are all partakers of that one bread.'[78] This sermon on 'the Communion of Saints' (2) might at first sight appear to have a certain air of tolerance and conformity with James's position:

If in some other things wee bee otherwise minded, than others of
our brethren are; let vs beare one with another, vntill God shall
reueale the same thing vnto us: and howsoeuer we may see cause
why we should dissent from other in matter of opinion; yet let vs
remember, that that is no cause why wee should breake the Kings
peace, and make a rent in the Church of God. (6–7)

But 'brethren' is a key word, and it certainly does not include Catholic
brethren, for all Ussher's rhetoric. This is emphasised when he stresses
(in accordance with the views of James Perrot) the need for a House
which is united in religious make-up:

Behold how good and pleasant a thing it is for brethren to dwell
together in vnity: what a goodly thing it is to behold such an
honourable Assembly as this is, to bee as a house that is *compact*
*together* in it selfe; holding fit correspondence with the other part of
this great body, and due subordination vnto their and our Head.
(8; emphasis in the original)

According to Ussher, Communion separates Protestants from those who
practise 'false worship' (26), particularly Catholics, who worship idols (30).
Ussher's extensive anti-Catholic message continues through to a reminder
of the Gunpowder Plot (47). The sermon, therefore, while ostensibly
thanking the House for being so complaisant and voting the King's subsidies 'in a time most seasonable' (10), sees those subsidies as directly
related to the fight against Papists, and fits the militant Protestant mood
of the Commons perfectly.

It is hard to know if John Chamberlain is representing the opinion of
members of the Commons in his account of Ussher's sermon: 'All the
nether house communicated on Sonday was sevenight at St. Margarets
where Dr. Usher (newly made bishop of Meath in Ireland) made as I hear
but a drie sermon and kept them so long, that yt was neere two a clocke
before they had all don.'[79] Certainly in its printed form Ussher's sermon
is on the long side. But it had clearly served its purpose of providing a
strict sense of religious conformity, as Pym drily notes: 'Noe man that
was absent at the Communion to be admitted into the Howse till he
had browght a Certificate that hee had received.'[80] We cannot be abso-
lutely certain that Edward May had Ussher in mind when he wrote his
preface, but May's sermon on the communion of the saints stands in
pointed contrast to Ussher's, particularly in relation to Catholicism.[81]
May and Ussher represent two poles in the fierce debate over foreign

policy in 1621 – a debate that was essentially argued out in religious terms. May's dismissal by the council of Lincoln's Inn reflected the highly charged atmosphere within which a sermon became a weapon in a war of words that many were certain would soon lead to England joining a European war for the cause of Protestantism. Sermons nearly always had such a political dimension, and even the choice of a text on which to preach is significant in terms of the general political situation.

Political historians disagree over whether this conflict over foreign policy reflects fundamental ideological differences. Glenn Burgess argues that 'for all the intensity of this sort of conflict, which fluctuated in response to perceptions of such things as the direction of royal policy and the general European situation, it should not be forgotten that it did not imply disagreement over such questions as the duty of subjects to be obedient, the sinfulness of resistance, or the nature of the royal prerogative'.[82] In direct contrast to Burgess, J.P. Sommerville maintains that these broader issues were indeed bound up in conflicts over particular policy directions, and that certain fundamental ideological disagreements over the nature of the prerogative can be traced through this period.[83] Sermons do not explicitly address the issues Sommerville traces through other forms of political commentary, but the very fact that so many different types of sermon addressed political issues in 1621 points to the general engagement with the foreign policy crisis, which combined religious issues (not just the defence of European Protestantism, but also conflict within the English Church) with issues that certainly touched on the royal prerogative, at least late in the parliamentary session, when James's sense of his prerogative and the Commons's defence of their privileges met head on.[84]

Indeed, this whole situation eventually led to James's 1622 'Directions to Preachers', set out in a letter to the Archbishop of Canterbury, which noted that 'at this present diverse young students, by reading of late writers and ungrounded divines, do broach many times unprofitable, unsound, seditious, and dangerous doctrines, to the scandal of the Church and disquiet of the State'.[85] The six directions, all attempting to constrain the commentary on issues directly relevant to state matters such as foreign policy which was characteristic of so many 1621 sermons, as well as those in the following year, included another attempt by James to reinforce even-handedness between attitudes towards Catholics and Puritans: 'That no preacher of what title or denomination soever shall presume causelessly (or without invitation from the text) to fall into bitter invectives and undecent railing speeches against the persons of either Papists or Puritans'.[86]

## Thomas Gataker's *Spark*

The truly polemical sermons of 1621 were much more direct in their political engagement than those of Edward May or James Ussher. A good example is Thomas Gataker's *A Spark Toward the Kindling of Sorrow For Sion*, entered in the Stationers' Register on 20 July. The apocalyptic tone is set in Gataker's preface, which notes, in the words of 1 Corinthians 10.11, 'wee are those on whom the ends of the world are fallen' (A).[87] Gataker takes, as his example of this apocalyptic moment, the indifference of England to the fate of Protestants in Europe:

> we are growne insensible of our own euils; and notwithstanding the ruefull and lamentable estate of the Church of God, in most parts at the present, and the insupportable afflictions that the Lords Faithfull Seruants, our Brethren, and fellow-members in Christ Iesu, doe by occasion of these hurly-burlies daily endure; yet the most regard it not, nor take any notice at all of it, saue as matter of newes and nouelty, to furnish discourse, or to feed their itching Athenian-like humours withall. (A3)

This despairing, indeed desperate tone is noted by Anthony Milton: 'Thomas Gataker's sermon . . . is often quoted as an example of a popular commitment to the cause of the continental Reformed Churches. It is worth emphasising, however, that (as the title implies) Gataker's sermon was prompted by a perceived *lack* of commitment to the international Calvinist cause.'[88]

Gataker's text is Amos 6.6: 'But they are not grieued for the affliction of Ioseph.' Partly because of its apocalyptic tone, Gataker's sermon soon has a quite threatening edge:

> That which may well serue for a warning to vs that liue in this land, whom God hath blessed abundantly with sundry speciall fauours aboue many round about vs, that wee take heed how we abuse this his goodnesse, and make this grace and fauour an occasion of wickednesse or wantonnesse: lest as he hath heaped vpon vs blessings extraordinarily aboue others, so he inflict also vpon vs iudgements extraordinarily aboue others; and as he hath made vs mirrors of his mercy vnto others, so he make vs spectacles also of his wrath. (6)

In the political context of the negotiations over England's position vis-à-vis the Palatine, the threat of divine judgement on a self-satisfied and passive country is provocative, to say the least. Gataker then implicitly criticises the effects of James's pacifist *via media* by offering action as the only course to be taken by the true Christian:

> There is a kinde of negatiue Diuinitie, and negatiue Christianity, that carrieth many away, grown rife among men: they are good Christians; and why so? they are neither *Papists*, nor *Puritans, Heretikes*, nor *Schismatikes*. They can easily tell what they are not; not so easily what they are. And so for life and conuersation; they thanke God, with *the Pharisie*, they are neither adulterers, nor drunkards, nor railers, nor back-biters, nor liers, nor swearers, nor oppressors, nor extortioners. And it were to be wished that some could say so much. All this is well: but this is nothing neere all. A man may truly say all this, and yet be farre enough from sinceritie. And vnlesse thou goe further then all this, thou art farre enough yet from that thou shouldest be, yea and professest to be, when thou makest profession of Christianitie. (10–11)

This seems to take a swipe at the very even-handedness (neither Papist or Puritan) that James publicly proclaimed to be the essence of his policy. Gataker also complains about excessive merriness, in a passage of the sermon that seems to glance at the indulgences of James's Court: 'What shall we say of those, that in a rebellious and preposterous manner, bend themselues to a cleane contrary course, then most of all giuing themselues to mirth and iollitie, when most cause is giuen of mourning and griefe?' (16–17). This image is driven home even more strongly early in the sermon through a tissue of quotations from Amos, Isaiah and Job:

> They lie stretching themselues on their Iuory beds; eat the fat lambes out of the fold, and calues out of the stall; vse all manner of varietie of musicke and melodie, inuenting daily new meanes of mirth; drinke their wine in deepe carousing cups; and anoint themselues with the principall and pretiousest ointments. (3)

Gataker goes on to link the spiritual state of England with the sufferings of fellow Protestants in Europe: 'And why may not the sinnes of our Nation also be in part the cause of those heauie disasters befallen our brethren in foraine parts?' (26). Quite specifically, the Protestant cause must be seen as one which connects England to those who may have been dismissed as both distant and foreign:

> Can all bee well with the right side, when there is a pleurisie in the left? Or all well with the head, I say not, when the whole body is heart-sick,

but when the heele or toe but, that is farthest off the head, is hurt? much more when there is a fracture in thigh or arme, or a rupture in some principall part of the body? Can we heare daily reports of our brethren in foraine parts, either assaulted, or distressed, or surprised by Popish forces, and a main breach made into the state of those that are by bonds, ciuill and sacred, so nearely knit to vs, and yet esteeme all as nothing, or thinke that we haue no iust cause to mourn and lament?

Neither let any man say; What is their affliction to vs? What are those parts to these? What is France or Germanie to England? (32–3)

James had been angry at Frederick's rash actions in accepting the crown of Bohemia (particularly given James's views on the evil nature of any rebellious usurpation of a throne), but his actions were seen by many in England as unnatural, given the eventual fate of his daughter and son-in-law and their children.[89] Thus Gataker stresses that the European Protestants in general are brethren, and that Frederick and Elizabeth in particular are bound by civil and sacred bonds to England. Again, this passage moves towards a threat: 'if the report of their calamities moue vs no more, then they haue done many hitherto, wee may iustly feare, lest, as God presently after threateneth this people, he cause the scourge to come in among vs' (33). Gataker evokes the curse of Meroz from Judges 5.23, a favourite text for sermons aiming at support for the Protestant cause: 'Curse ye, Meroz, said the angel of the Lord, curse ye bitterly the inhabitants thereof, because they came not to the help of the Lord, to the help of the Lord against the Mighty.' During the summer of 1621 James was still engaged in a quixotic endeavour for a negotiated peace over the Palatine; parliament was in recess, having ended its session on 4 June with a 'Public Protestation and Declaration', moved by James Perrot, 'That, if Religion and Right may not be restored by Treaty and peaceable Means, that then, upon our Return to Parliament (being thereunto required by his Majesty) we would be ready to adventure the Lives and estates of all that belong unto us, or wherein we have Interest, for the maintenance of the Cause of God, and of his Majesty's Royal Issue'[90] – the Protestant Cause was languishing at the moment when Gataker preached his incendiary sermon.

### Samuel Ward: happiness in practice

Choosing a representative polemical preacher from 1621 is difficult, given the large number of possible examples.[91] I have settled on Samuel Ward because he stretched across a number of genres, including the visual.

Samuel Ward of Ipswich is not to be confused with his more elevated cousin of the same name, the Samuel Ward who was Master of Sidney Sussex College, Cambridge. In his sermon, *The Happiness of Practice*, which was actually dedicated to the city of Ipswich, our Samuel Ward acknowledges the ubiquity of published sermons, as well as their transient nature: 'Sermons are as showres of Rain that water for the instant' (A3).[92] In the body of the sermon itself, Ward says 'words are but wind, and vanish into the winde, leauing no print or impression, more then a ship at sea, in comparison of actions which men take marke and notice of' (22). Perhaps this distrust of words led to a piece of visual polemic on Ward's part which gathers together many of the elements of anti-papist and anti-Spanish sentiment prominent in these sermons which argued for the Protestant Cause. As John Chamberlain describes it in a letter of 10 March 1621:

> We heare that Sir Robert Mansfeld and his fleet have don just nothing but negotiated with those of Argier for certain slaves and they complaine of theyre usage on the coast of Spaine that they are faine to buy theyre water, and could not be suffered to carrie aboard a thousand ducats they had taken up at Malaga, to provide fresh vitayles for their sicke and weake men, with a number of other discourtesies and indignities: so that yt seemes we have the same successe both by sea and land. But yt is not goode rubbing on that sore, for one Ward, a speciall preacher of Ipswich is but newly released out of prison (where he lay a good while) for having a picture of the Spanish fleet in 88 with the gun-powder treason, and some other additions of his owne invention and hand (having some delight and skill in limming) which his friends say had lien by him at least seven or eight yeares, and not looked into till now. (ii.350)

Ward's elaborate engraving juxtaposes two icons of anti-Catholic and anti-Spanish sentiment: the defeat of the Armada and the discovery of the Gunpowder Plot. The first is a harking back to what militant Jacobean Protestants saw as the heroic days under Elizabeth; the second, as we have seen, was a touchstone in so many sermons as the prime example of Catholic treason. Ward's engraving is entitled 'To God, In Memory of his Double deliverance From the Invincible navy and the Unmatchable Powder Treason'.[93] God is represented at the head of the engraving by the tetragrammaton (the four Hebrew letters representing the unnameable Jehovah), which quite literally sees the gunpowder plotters ('Video rideo: I see and smile'). God also presides over the dispersal of the Armada

*Figure 2*  Samuel Ward, Engraving 'To God', British Museum, BMC 41.

('I blow and scatter'). Most controversial of all in 1621 (regardless of how long the engraving may have 'lien by' Ward before its publication, if we can believe his friends), at the centre of the engraving we see a conference table with the Pope at the left head, the General of the Jesuits at the right head, the Devil in the centre (the whole tableau rather reminiscent of a parodic Last Supper scene), perhaps the King of Spain, and the figure of Gondomar, the Spanish ambassador to England, lurking behind the Pope's shoulder.[94] This central image clearly conveys the impression that current English negotiations with Spain ignore the precedents of 1588 and 1605.

At the end of the second edition of Ward's meditation *The Life of Faith*, the bookseller was actually advertising this engraving as an essential object of remembrance for every Christian household:

> Gentle reader, I pray thee take notis that Master Ward, hath lately published a Remarkable Monument, of the Inuincible Nauie of 88. & the unmatchable Powder Treason 1605. necessary to be had in the House of euery good Christian, to shew Gods louing and wonderfull prouidence, ouer this kingdome, when the papists twise sought their vtter ruine and subuersion.[95]

What the engraving endeavours to do is to make the conjunction between Spain, Papists and treachery seem normative and obvious. This tactic is also evident in *The Happiness of Practice*, where Ward tries the same trick, using rhetoric, rather than images:

> Men know nothing now adayes. It is become a disputable probleme, Whether the Pope be *Antichrist, Rome a good Church*; whether a man may worship God before pictures, play vpon any part of the Sabbath, as well as vpon the Weeke dayes; whether election be of foreseen faith; whether the True Beleeuer may Apostasize? Shortly, I thinke, whether there bee a God, or no? (30)

This strikes out at some of James's policies (such as the playing of sports on Sunday, officially sanctioned in the 1618 'Book of Sports' proclamation), as well as James's insistence that, although he thought the Pope was anti-Christ, this was a matter of opinion, not an essence of faith.[96] Like the engraving, *The Happiness of Practice* recommends an active, engaged Protestantism which asks the nation to question its spiritual (and, one assumes, political) neutrality: 'Bee not as little children, who while they are looking in the Glasse, thinke onely it is the babies face, and not thir owne' (37).

Ward had either a deliberately provocative or a particularly careless sense of timing. My final example of this is a sermon directed towards the duties of magistrates entitled *Jethro's Justice of the Peace*. When first published in 1618, this carried a dedication to Francis Bacon, not unaptly given his position as Lord Chancellor. But the whole dedication and sermon have a quite different impact when reissued in 1621 at the very time when Bacon was impeached by parliament for taking bribes.[97] Suddenly irony after irony pervades Ward's book, beginning with the dedication:

> The subject of the book is the principall obiect of your Office, to elect, direct and correct inferiour Magistracy. To which purposes, Nature, Literature and Grace haue inabled you, that if you should faile the worlds expectation, they will hardly trust any other in hast. (A4)[98]

The body of the text is full of references that must have amazed readers in 1621 with their unintended prescience: 'Oh root of all euill to Church and Commonwealth, when authorities and offices of Iustice shall be bought and solde' (11). One pithy comment in particular sums up what must have seemed like part of the case against Bacon, given his defence that he might have received gifts but they did not constitute bribes: 'if the right hand be full of bribes the left hand must be full of mischief' (48).

Ward even includes an attack on the Oath of Allegiance which was designed by James, as he explained to the 1621 parliament, to distinguish loyal from disloyal Catholics: 'A difference is to be made betwixt Papists . . . Those that Maynteyne the Oathe of Alleadgance, and such other Traytors as refuse it.'[99] Ward won't allow for this distinction:

> Why then, what are oathes for Atheists and Papists other than collers for monkies neckes, which slip them at their pleasure? Such neither are nor can be good subiects: much lesse good Magistrates. Papists will keep no faith with Protestants, let Protestants giue no trust to Papists though they swear vpon al the books in the World. (33–4)

Given this whole context, it is a wonder that Ward was only kept in prison for a short time!

### George Hakewill's advice to the prince

The clerical debate over the Protestant Cause and James's negotiations was not simply staged in the popular arena, but also much closer to James's home. Once again, John Chamberlain provides a useful summary of events which he discussed with Lancelot Andrewes:

I proceeded further about a treatise made and delivered the Prince by Dr. Hackwell his chaplain, wherein he dissuades him from marieng with one of a contrarie religion and an ydolater: and withall told his Lordship [i.e. Andrewes] that I heard he had maintained that papists were not idolaters. He told me that the King sending for him on a sodain, and shewing him some part of the booke, in the presence of Dr. Hackwell and two or three bishops, commaunded him to deliver his opinion. He answered that when he was younge he had seene and reade much of that argument, upon occasion of the late French kinges mariage with Henry the thirds sister, (whereunto Beza gave consent) and of the mariage of Madame his sister to the Duke of Lorrain: and for scripture we had the examples of Hester maried Ashuerus, of Salomon to Pharaus daughter, and of Moses to an Ethiopian: and that every papist was not an idolater, with a great deale more of that kind. (ii.393–4)

George Hakewill was made chaplain to Prince Charles in 1612, after the death of Charles's elder brother Prince Henry, supposedly in order to protect Charles from exposure to popery.[100] Hakewill is a fascinating if somewhat obscure figure. His first published work, *The Vanity of the Eye* (1608), written, according to the title-page, 'for the comfort of a gentlewoman bereaved of her sight', offers an elaborate series of arguments against the sense of sight, including an interesting notion of the self as constituted essentially by the other senses. Of particular interest, given the event described by Chamberlain, is the connection between sight and the idolatry associated with Catholicism, as in so much polemic (including, as we have seen, Ussher's sermon): 'Idolatry, which as it had his original form from the eye, so is it still nourished by the same' (14).[101] Accordingly, in Chapter 25, Hakewill argues 'That the Popish religion consists more in eye-service than the reformed' (127), and specifies a whole series of examples, including 'the daily elevation of their Idoll in the masse' (128). These are common polemical points made against Catholicism in the period, but the focus on the sinfulness of sight in general is original and arresting.

In 1621 Hakewill published a collection of twelve sermons expounding Psalm 101: *King David's Vow for Reformation of Himself his Family his Kingdom.* This volume is dedicated to Prince Charles and it is, at first sight, a very far cry from the polemical sermons I have been discussing. It contains a poised, meditative series of reflections, their impact enhanced by the prose style that, according to Boswell, attracted the attention of Dr Johnson as a model (along with Hooker, Bacon and Sanderson).[102]

But throughout, a clear message about papal allegiances is conveyed – one which reiterates some of the points made in *The Vanity of the Eye*:

> Nothing more different from Beliall than God, than Christ, than a glorified Saint; and yet than the representation of God, or of Christ, or of a Saint for religious use, nothing more a thing of Belial, be it never so cunningly wroght, never so artificially graven or carved, never so lively coloured, or richly attired: nay, be it of massie silver & gold, garnished with jewels and precious stones; yet beeing put to religious use, it is still a thing of Belial. (109–10)[103]

Hakewill begins the volume by stressing James's peaceful assumption of the throne of England, a thought which would have pleased James, but then sets up as a principle the unwavering establishment of the reformed church: 'Neither would hee, for the settling of his right, admit the toleration of any other religion, then that which hee heer found, and himselfe professed' (62). From this point on, *King David's Vow* veers between the expression of doctrine that James heartily endorsed and a fierce attack on Catholicism that, as we have seen, provoked James time and time again in 1621, and would do so all the more in this case, coming from the chaplain to the Prince who was designed for a peace-making marriage alliance with Spain. For example, Hakewill's notion of the King as father of the state is a commonplace of James's concept of patriarchal rule:

> Every house-holder is *parus Rex*, a little King in his owne Family: and the greatest Monarch, upon the matter, is but magnus *Pater-familias*, a great house-holder, or a common Father of the publique Family of the State. (94–5)

But over and over again, Hakewill returns to his discussion of verse 3 of the psalm: 'I will set no wicked thing before mine eyes', which he interprets as a prohibition against idolatry, as seen in the quotation about Belial above. But Hakewill also stresses that we should not associate with those who are idolaters – with, in his interpretation, Catholics:

> Now the best way for a man to keep himselfe free from this offence, is, to keep him free from the society, at least the domestick and familiar society, the inward bosom-acquaintance of those, who think it a main part of their religion, to set such things before their eyes. The Ark and Dagon will not stand together: neither can a Crucifix,

ordained to such an use, and Christ himselfe well dwell together under the same roof. (110)

Here is the published, public version of the advice set out at length in the manuscript tract against a Catholic marriage which Hakewill gave the Prince.[104] This whole event has been seen as an example of Charles's disloyalty: Hakewill asked Charles not to show the tract to James, but Charles did so within a matter of hours.[105] But this was always going to be a controversial and dangerous move on Hakewill's part, and he was clearly being offered advice by various officials, from Archbishop Abbot, who advised him to write the treatise, to the prescient Thomas Murray, Prince Charles's secretary, who offered a bit of *realpolitik* advice and suffered from not following it himself:

> Mr Sec. Murray hath bin commanded to his house at Barkehamsted since the beginning of the progresses vntill of late, vpon the occasion Mr Hackluite one of the Princes Chaplains was desierouse to present a tractate that he had made to the Prince against the match wth Spaine wherein he desiered to be furtherest for Mr Murray but Mr Murray when he vnderstood what it was refused to meddle with it & dissuaded him from going forward wth his intention assuring him that it would be both dangerous & fruitlesse, & that there was no liklyhood to alter resolutions of state by discourses. Mr Hackluite told him that he had considered of all this before, but yet neuerthelesse he thought himselfe obligde in conscience to deliuer the booke, wch he did, & after when the Prince gaue it to the K. & the K. understood that Murray knewe of it, he sent for him presentlie, & layd that constraint vpon him because he had not acquainted the K. wth the booke, though he did not make way for the deliuerie of it.[106]

Hakewill's tract was entitled *The Wedding Robe or A Treatise touching the unlawfullnes of Protestants marriages with Papists*. In the presentation copy to Charles, Hakewill, in a prefatory letter, begs Charles to 'cast a fauourable regard vpon that which springs from a loyal & well-wishing subject'.[107] Hakewill disingenuously tells Charles that 'I meddle not with busnes of state... but bound my selfe within the lists of mine owne profession, confining it to your Highnes priuatte vse'.[108] Hakewill painstakingly goes through all the biblical examples of what he interprets as forbidden marriages with idolaters (including the examples Andrewes mentions in Chamberlain's letter, and many others). Before doing so he clearly sets out an argument that uses a notion of the spiritual significance of marriage connected to a totally political view of the prince's self as an object which needs to be secured to the established church's dominance, in distinction to James's views, which were, of course, to use Charles's marriage to secure the state within a particular foreign policy of balanced alignments:

> As marriage is the groundworke wch prepares a body for the Commonwealth, soe Religion is the soule wch quickens and actuats this body; and as marriage is soe strong a band, that for this cause a man is bound to leaue father and mother and to cleaue to his wife, soe is the band of Religion stronger, in as much as for this cause a man is bound to leaue father and mother, and if need bee his wife too, and to cleaue to his Religion. (fol. 306)[100]

Hakewill returns to the notion of Catholics as idolaters and stresses how 'it is not vnfitt only, but vnlawfull for a professed member of the Church of England, but especially that of the highest ranke and most eminent degree, to contract marriage with any Idolater, and in speciall with a professed member of the Church of Rome' (fol. 306). This dangerous line of argument reaches a climax in a passage which again attacks James's attempt to strike a balance between loyalty and tolerance, when Hakewill points to the problems of a sovereign's spouse practising a different religion:

> Beesides the peaceable sufferance of the exercise of a different religion in the kings or princes hous cannot but in likelyhood quickly draw on a publique toleration of the same among inferior subiects: neither can that law bee duly executed in the Countrey whose edg is blunted in the Court. (fol. 313v)

Hakewill clearly tries to pander to some of James's fears of rebellion by stressing the impossibility of expecting loyalty from Catholics. Here, he (perhaps unconsciously) reiterates negatively his opening remarks about religious loyalty overriding all other considerations, as he points to the inherent rebellious nature of the Catholic subject:

> and beeing by them held lawfull that by the allowance of theyr ghostly Father, and for the good of the church a seruant may rise against his master, a souldier against his Captein, a subiect against his souereign a son against his father. I see no reason for the same good and by the same allowance a wife may as well rise and rebell

against her husband or if need bee dispatch him priuily, specially if shee bee set on by her confessors. (fol. 314v)

In *The Wedding Robe* we can see clearly the total intersection of religion, politics and the notion of how the self might be created, projected, shaped and examined. Unfortunately for Hakewill, the notion of a 'private' treatment of such questions, for the Prince's eyes only, could never be sustained, even if the Prince didn't turn disloyal quite so rapidly as Charles.

Throughout this chapter I have been trying to analyse how this intersection of public and private occurred in 1621, within a specific political context, using sermons and religious controversy in particular as a way of understanding how readers and listeners in 1621 understood that the self interconnected with the political. In the next chapter I want to turn to secular literature in order to look at two remarkable romances which continue this engagement with questions of how subjectivity is interconnected with the social.

# 3
# Transformations of Romance

Literary historians used to see the seventeenth century as a period of steady decline for the romance form. In recent years there has been an increasing realisation that a variety of important developments took place in the romance in the course of the seventeenth century.[1] Two of the most remarkable of these romances were published in 1621: Mary Wroth's huge, elaborate arcadian romance, *Urania*, and John Barclay's *Argenis*, a Latin political romance soon afterwards translated into English. Both romances, while very different in nature, share a complex interest in the intersection of the public and private spheres.

I noted at the beginning of the previous chapter how the feminist challenge to established literary canons has changed our view of early modern literature. Mary Wroth is perhaps the most significant of the women writers who have been (re)discovered thus far, given the scope and amount of her production in so many important genres. Her new stature is acknowledged by the editorial work of Josephine Roberts, and by a recent volume of essays dedicated solely to Wroth's *œuvre*.[2] In particular, Wroth's romance, *The Countess of Montgomery's Urania*, is at last becoming the object of the kind of intensive critical analysis formerly reserved for the *Arcadia*, the romance produced by her uncle, Sir Philip Sidney. Indeed, with the same kind of light being shed upon the writing of the Countess of Pembroke, and the editorial work on the poetry of Wroth's father, Robert Sidney, the Sidney family as a whole has been examined as a writing community, crossed and interconnected by a complex network of relations, including those of politics and gender.[3] In this context, *Urania* can be seen as a romance which enters into a dialogical relationship with the *Arcadia*, interrogating some of Sidney's assumptions about the nature of romance, particularly in relation to issues of gender and sexuality.[4]

### The publication of *Urania*: woman writer as 'hermaphrodite'

The publication of *Urania* in 1621 involved Wroth in much more than a familial dialogue. As is by now well known, the depiction in *Urania* of some actual scandals from the life of the Jacobean court provoked a sharp response, especially from the notoriously hot-tempered Edward Denny, who demanded the romance's withdrawal, and who produced a scurrilous poem about Wroth, attacking her for daring, as a woman, to enter the world of secular literature.[5] Denny's verse characterised Wroth as: 'Hermaphrodite in show, in deed a monster.'[6] It is significant that Denny sees Wroth as a hermaphrodite, a threatening figure of sexual ambiguity who has traversed the safe confines of gender boundaries.[7] He makes this even clearer in a letter which compares Wroth's activities to those of her aunt, the Countess of Pembroke:

> But lett your Ladyship take what course yt shall please you with me, this shall bee myne with you [*that*] to ever wish you well and pray that you may repent you of so many ill spent years of so vaine a booke and that you may redeeme the tym with writing as large a volume of heavenly layes and holy love as you have of lascivious tales and amorous toyes that at the last you may follow the rare, and pious example of your vertuous and learned Aunt, who translated many godly books and especially the holly psalmes of David.[8]

While the letter at least allows women the 'safe' and contained literary activity of pious translation, Denny's poem concludes on a note of total exclusion: 'Work o th' Workes leave idle books alone / For wise and worthyer women have writte none.'[9] There is a curious contradiction emerging within this couplet: how is an 'idle' book able to cause Denny so much distress? What are the implications of the *Urania*'s power to provoke such a response? (And Denny's response was evidently not unique, as a remark of John Chamberlain's makes plain: 'in her book of Urania she doth palpablie and grossely play upon him and his late daughter the Lady Hayes, besides many others she makes bold with, and they say takes great libertie to traduce whom she please, and thincks she daunces in a net.')[10] Wroth herself, in her poem responding to Denny's, takes the notion of hermaphrodite and turns it against him: 'Hirmaphrodite in sense in Art a monster.' (The whole notion of the monstrous becomes very important in the course of *Urania*. While there are a number of literal monsters in the narrative, the notion of the monstrous as implicated in gender issues emerges in the manuscript continuation, when Amphilanthus calls women 'monsters' (2.i.49v) as a response to his [mistaken] idea of Pamphilia's unfaithfulness, but then calls himself a monster in a typical moment of reversal in connection with such issues (2.i.51).[11] Philippa Berry cites Stubbs's reaction to gender disturbance in *The Anatomy of Abuses* [1583]: 'Hermaphroditi; that is, Monsters of bothe kindes, halfe women, halfe men.')[12] Wroth describes *Urania* as a 'harmless book'. At one level, this perhaps concedes the 'amorous toyes' allegation, in an ambivalence about the moral/immoral nature of literature which recalls Sidney's anxieties about the worth of his literary pursuits.[13] For the author to see *Urania* as a harmless book is a clear example of disingenuous argument, but this whole issue becomes more complex if we turn to Wroth's letter to Buckingham, written after the agitation of Denny clearly began to have some effect on court – and King James's – opinion of Wroth's actions.

Wroth's apologetic letter to Buckingham is dated 15 December 1621, and it addresses what she calls 'the strang constructions which are made of my book contrary to my imagination, and as far from my meaning as is possible for truth to bee from conjecture'.[14] By 'strang', Wroth presumably intends to mean 'strange', although there is a Bloomian felicity in the idea of '*strong* constructions' wresting a particular interpretation of her book from her intention. Again, the protestations about intention may be read as disingenuous, but a more interesting ambiguity is present in the revelation that Wroth, while protesting that she never intended *Urania* to be published ('which from the first were solde against my minde'), had sent Buckingham a presentation copy, which she now asks him to return in order to set a good example for *all* those who may refuse to surrender their copies: 'besides that your Lordship wilbe pleased to lett mee have that which I sent you, the example of which will without question make others the willinger to obay'.[15]

The whole episode of *Urania*'s publication, the response of its courtly readership, its withdrawal, and the subsequent manuscript continuation, which was never published, offers a significant paradigm for the complex issue of how an early modern woman writer like Wroth might negotiate the relationship between an enclosed sphere of allowable activity and the more dangerous entry into a public literary (and political) arena. Ostensibly seeking Buckingham's critical opinion of her work, Wroth was actually using the publication of *Urania* in 1621 as an intervention in the court world from which she had been excluded. One approach to this issue, which I believe casts some light on a complex series of questions about women's writing in early modern England, as well as answering some of the challenges thrown out by recent feminist and new historicist criticism of the period, is to examine what the implications of Arcadian romance were by 1621, when Wroth published *Urania*, and how Wroth is able to extend the genre to suit her own ends.

## *Arcadia* and the politics of romance in 1621

In the early years of the seventeenth century, Sidney and his work became associated with a nostalgia for Elizabethan heroic values, which were utilised in protest against King James, especially in relation to his policy of pacifism and religious neutrality in Europe. As Annabel Patterson states, 'Sidney's *Arcadia* . . . was constantly rewritten by later readers (as well as by Sidney himself) in the light of their own historical circumstances and ideological needs'.[16] The *Arcadia* was presented to the reading public as a printed text in two forms: the *New Arcadia*, offered in 1590 by Sidney's friend and biographer, Fulke Greville, as Sidney's revised but unfinished epic, and the composite version prepared under the direction of Sidney's sister and published in 1593. The composite text was the version reprinted during the seventeenth century, but this text offered considerable opportunities for continuations and completions, which duly followed.[17] Recently scholars alert to the political implications of Jacobean literature have pointed to the significance of pastoral poetry as a mode of protest, and this may also be linked to the role played by the *Arcadia* and the figure of Sidney. David Norbrook notes that 'The years 1613–14 saw a revival of pastoral poetry, and in adopting the persona of the plain-thinking shepherds the Spenserians were indicating their dissatisfaction with contemporary events.'[18] Mary Wroth herself was placed within a complex nexus of familial/political positions in relation to the Jacobean court. The Sidney/Herbert families did not form a simple or single political group, although they can be viewed as holding Protestant views which emerge most strongly in William Herbert's position at court.[19] Wroth's own position as Herbert's cousin and lover (she bore two illegitimate children by Herbert) must be taken into account, as well as her relationship to her husband, who was knighted by James in 1603, and whose father had served in the House of Commons since 1562/63.[20]

With the accession of James, Wroth took up a position in Queen Anne's court, which was established in 1606 (her father was appointed Anne's lord chamberlain).[21] In 1603 Anne had established what her biographer calls a 'lasting friendship' with William Herbert during her stay at Wilton, once again pointing to the intertwining of the Herbert/Sidney alliance with a court in some ways set up in opposition to James's.[22] Anne's court provided a female counter to James's male, not to say misogynistic, preserve.[23] The brief flowering of Prince Henry's court further emphasised this political alignment with the implications of the Sidney legend and the position of Arcadian romance. Henry set up a court which, like Anne's, could be seen as a counter to James's, but Henry's court was like his father's in its masculine (not to say macho) character. Roy Strong has emphasised how Henry deliberately associated himself and his court activities with Sidney, stressing a 'direct link between the new circle of the Prince and that centring in the previous reign on Sir Philip Sidney'.[24] Henry's love of the symbolic tilts reminiscent of those of Elizabeth's reign is evident in *Prince Henry's Barriers*, a masque of 1610 described by Strong as presenting 'the new court of St James's as the thinly veiled focus for a revival of the Elizabethan war party, fiercely Protestant and anti-Hapsburg', and in the 1610 Accession Day Tilt, at which William Herbert appeared dressed in 'two Caparisons of Peach-coloured velvet embroidered all over with oriental Pearls'.[25] It is notable that in *Urania* Wroth depicted versions of both the masque-centred court of Anne and James, and the tilt-centred world of Henry's court, as part of her examination of the interaction between female and male realms within a context of revived chivalric, as well as pastoral, romance motifs.[26]

Arcadian romance was available as, in some respects, a discourse already saturated with the criticism Sidney himself had directed against Elizabeth's policies.[27] The 1593 composite *Arcadia* itself was reprinted eleven times up until 1638, during the period when Fulke Greville helped to sharpen the political critique inherent in the *Arcadia*, commenting on how the romance shows the 'dark webs of effeminate Princes' in a state that declines as states do 'when Soveraign Princes, to play with their own visions, will put off publique action.'[28] Sidney's sister, whose 1593 edition of the *Arcadia* superseded Greville's, also played a role in the continuing Protestant aesthetic/political allegiance.[29]

The 1621 edition of *Arcadia* was published in Dublin but reissued in London.[30] Like all seventeenth-century editions, it was a composite joining together of the partly revised *New Arcadia* and part of the *Old Arcadia*. The 1621 edition included Sir William Alexander's thirty-page supplement, which helped to seal up the join between the two versions. This supplement includes a highly romanticised depiction of Sidney's death and it helps to emphasise that, by 1621, the *Arcadia* was being read as part of the heroicising of the Sidney legend and, implicitly, as a critique of James's policy of pacifism and his appeasement of the forces of European Catholicism.

When Wroth produced her romance, the homage to Sidney implied by the title (even if it may have been complicated by the nature of *Urania* itself) had, at least potentially, a serious political implication. *Urania*'s depiction of real events like those that enraged Denny can also be connected to the vogue for political romances, exemplified in John Barclay's *Argenis*, which will be discussed in the second part of this chapter. *Argenis*, with its detailed account of French political history within the mode of romance, offers an expansion of the possibilities of the genre, which in some ways can also be seen in Wroth's careful elaboration of the dynastic politics throughout the 'Europe' of *Urania*, as well as within the court society of England, which found itself caught and exposed in her narrative. Josephine Roberts notes in particular how *Urania* depicts a fantasy of a holy Roman Empire, with Amphilanthus as its ruler, as if Frederick had not only triumphed in Bohemia but united Catholic, as well as Protestant, Europe behind him.[31]

Wroth's act in producing *Urania* is rightly seen as a significant example of female intervention in the masculine world of secular literature. But her own strange constructions within *Urania* involve an even more unsettling critique directed at a series of distinctions within her society underpinning the exclusion of women from the public realm. A great deal of the ideological tension associated with the rule of Elizabeth failed to dissipate after the throne reverted to a male sovereign. As Leah Marcus has pointed out, in relation to the stage, 'The cultural memory for Elizabeth's mannerisms and characteristic strategies was longer than we are likely to find credible, and continued to exert a subtle shaping on stage depictions of female dominance – particularly those with a reformist bent – even decades after her death.'[32] In a discussion of the nature of female rule in *Urania*, Josephine Roberts suggests that Wroth depicts, particularly within the character of Pamphilia, a dilemma over the rival claims of the 'Queen's two bodies', offering 'a highly ambivalent view of female rule in which the central character struggles vainly to fulfil the dual nature of sovereignty'.[33]

However, while Wroth is certainly interested in the nature of sovereignty, both male and female, she is also able to overturn the opposition between public and private in relation to both the question of direct political power, and the issue of where female autonomy may be located. At present there is a debate emerging among critics over the nature of Wroth's 'intervention' in this area. In a provocative account of Wroth's sonnets, Jeff Masten sees them as an essentially private literary act, a withdrawal from the circulation of the market (which of course has more than literary implications for women): 'Wroth's texts ... do not merely reflect the emergence of a public/private distinction "in the culture," but also work to create that distinction', and he believes that *Urania* encapsulates 'the opposition of a public, male world and Pamphilia's withdrawal into a privatised locus of female poetic expression.'[34] This view may be directly contrasted with the position of Ann Rosalind Jones, who sees Pamphilia and her sonnets as examples of political power and intervention.[35] I believe that it is important to examine the whole public/private dichotomy much more carefully in order to determine how *Urania* may be read in such a context. At the most basic level, as commentators are increasingly emphasising, it is almost impossible to assign a fixed 'position' to *Urania*, because of Wroth's careful use of multivalent narratives, voices, characters, situations. (This aspect of *Urania* itself can be valuably read as an unfixing of the univocal nature of patriarchal discourse, and certainly as the questioning of any essentialised position on political or gender issues.)[36]

During the period when Wroth was writing she was moving between life inside the court of Queen Anne, and life outside it – albeit not unconnected with it, given, for example, the increasingly important position of the Herbert faction and of William Herbert himself under James and Charles. At that historical juncture, as I have noted in the previous chapter, the relationship between public and private was extremely problematic. In Jonathan Goldberg's succinct formulation, 'In the seventeenth century, privacy all but merged into the public'; or, to take a historian's less dramatic verdict, 'the dichotomy so familiar to us today between private and public is necessarily false when applied to the experience of early modern England'.[37] Wroth's intersection with the court may not seem to be an encounter with anything like a public sphere, but an event such as the presentation of *Urania* to Buckingham by a woman writer is an intervention in a public realm: a place outside the private, silent/pious, 'proper' place for an early modern woman.

Within *Urania*, this interconnection between the public and private is everywhere evident, particularly in the intersection between what might be formulated as the love of power and the power of love. Within Wroth's narrative, political sovereignty, be it male or female, is always challenged by the power of desire. In *Urania*, every court is subject to the menace of desire (like the Jacobean court Wroth knew so well, which was challenged by the intersection of desire and political calculation in incidents like the Overbury scandal). In the language of *Urania*, passion rules as (usually) a tyrant

Surpassing passion, excellent, still governe, how delicate is thy force?
How happie thy rule, that makes such excellent women thy subjects?
made so by thy gouernement, instructed by thy skill, taught by thy
learning, and indeed made by thee. (1.365)

In this context, it is worth returning for a moment to Denny's
response to Wroth's portrayal of his family scandal; a scandal both
personal and political. Denny can read *Urania* only as a product of a
(warped) desire which challenges assumptions about appropriate gender
roles in relation to writing; yet by replying with a poem ('How easy wer't
to pay thee with thine owne,'[38] he writes, apparently without irony),
Denny enters into the conjunction of the public and the private which
Wroth pursues throughout her romance.[39] This sovereignty is not simply
patriarchal rule over female subjects, even if the powerful central story
of Pamphilia is focused on female constancy set against male incon-
stancy (this very trait of Amphilanthus still proves him subject to the rule
of desire). The entire narrative of *Urania* is, after all, presided over by
a woman: Mellissea, a powerful enchantress, who (perhaps evoking the
memory of Elizabeth) rules alone, all-seeing, if not exactly all-powerful.
At the macrocosmic level in the romance, Mellissea's power is always
behind the multifarious narrative threads, the wanderings and crossings of
all the huge cast of characters. Mellissea is also responsible for reinforcing
the intersection between the apparently 'private' world of passion and
the public world of politics; each enchantment she sets up and then
allows the characters to solve has repercussions at the level of state politics
and at the level of dynastic (and therefore personal) attachments.

To take this interrogation of dichotomies such as public/private into
the realm of gender, Wroth engages in a complex account of the
relationship between female victims, and female power and solidarity.
Rather than see this as a clear, univocal statement in *Urania*, which has
led to a critical debate couched in either/or terms, I would prefer to read
the romance as a deliberately unsettled and unsettling strategy concerned to question the power of such categories.[40] One might start by
underlining the contrast between Pamphilia and Urania as a corrective to
a reading of the romance which insists on a unitary narrative with a single
pair of protagonists, namely Pamphilia and Amphilanthus. Urania's more
pragmatic view of love and its effects is contrasted to Pamphilia's
almost obsessive constancy. In terms of their political power, however,
their positions are reversed, as Pamphilia rules over her kingdom in her
own right, rather than through marriage (though she does inherit the
kingdom from her uncle). Josephine Roberts has argued that Pamphilia's

attachment to Amphilanthus has an adverse effect on her 'commitment
to the body politic', but she still wields the power in her state, and is
always conscious of the need for her good government: 'she lost not her
selfe; for her government continued iust and brave, like that Lady she
was, wherein she shewed her heart was not to be stirr'd, though her private
fortunes shooke round about her' (1.484).[41] At the same time, Urania
herself is praised by her husband Steriamus for her political perspicacity:
'how did her counsell rauish our eares, more Judiciall, more exquisite
then the whole great counsells of the greatest Monarchies' (2.i.57).

The most complex interrogation of such dichotomies occurs when
gender and genre interact in the *Urania*. At one level, Wroth has her
characters and also the narrator use conventional gender contrasts
between the weakness of women and the strength of men, to the degree
that the reader seems to be presented with essentialised traits. For example,
while we are given portraits of judicious women, able to offer counsel to
men, this very ability is seen in gendered terms: 'The lady, who had so
great a spiritt, as might be called masculine' (2.ii.57v). Displays of emotion
are frequently seen as 'womanish lamenting' (2.ii.58); and when a man
weeps he says that he 'playd the woman' (1.80). Even at the level of
writing, as has often been noted, the 'mad' overreaching Antissia as
female poet is contrasted to the modest, even secretive Pamphilia.[42]
Antissia strives beyond her scope, and this is seen in terms that seem to
emanate from an Edward Denny rather than a Mary Wroth: 'being
a dangerous thing att any time for a weake woman to studdy higher
matters than their cappasitie can reach to' (2.i.7). Yet this warning
stemming from Antissia's experiences is in complete contrast to the role
of a woman like Mellissea in the romance. Similarly, the notion of what
is truly 'masculine' shifts dangerously as well, and menaces the certainty
of such gender-based contrasts. Thus the chivalric virtues most evident
in the first part of *Urania* are frequently undermined in the second part,
when the heroes, having grown old, weaken, sicken, die, grow fat (a fate
reserved for Parselius) and become suddenly aware of the precarious
nature of the macho ideal: 'a dismall fate to all great ones, who neuer so
much adored, soe infinitely followed, assur'd, and as Gods on Earthe
glorified and magnified, lett their little small winde pipe bee butt stopt,
that the body falls, all due respect dyes with that, and the rising sun, is
then their only worship' (2.ii.57v).

This is seen most interestingly in relation to that supreme hero
Amphilanthus, who in the second part of *Urania* is subjected to a significant reversal of these apparently rigid sexual stereotypes. Amphilanthus's
response to the deception practised on him over Pamphilia's apparent

marriage is quite unlike her 'heroic' stoicism. He behaves 'not like Amphilanthus butt a puling lover' (2.i.51v). By book 2 he is behaving 'as if hee had bin bred in a ladys chamber' (2.ii.2); he faints at Pamphilia's feet (just before this we are told that he has 'hands of that delicasie for pure whiteness, delicate shape, and softnes, as noe lady could compare wth them', ibid.).[43]

It is worth noting that at this moment in the narrative, Wroth offers the reader a quite startling example of a male blazon, as Parselius gazes at Belario:

> hee was of stature tall, and soe proportionably shaped to his moderate stature [height], his lims of that excellent exactnes in euen proportion, and singular, as if nature wth art had fained to make him the onely true piece of sweetest excellencie, his haire of a light browne wch did naturally curle, and ly though carelessly (by him uncared for) as to womanish for his more high, and highest thoughts, yett in as due, and compleat order, as if tended wth all curiositie and daintiness could afford, his eyes inclining prettily to blackness, butt nott soe furious as som wch joye in causing perpetuall murder, butt his were of so sweet a commanding power, as to make hearts yt beheld them to confess an nessessitie of admiring them, then liking, then loving, and soe by the stealing inuasions of loue, to be seruants to such perfections, his lips like cherris red, and coule [?], still when shutting seeming to play one wth an other, as young folkes doe wth cherris, sporting wth one another, slender hee was, butt soe adorned wt excellent proportion, and sinewed strength, wch yett the pure whitness, and softnes of his skin, did butt as shew for excellency nott for force; yett was his strength and vallour such as often times itt had bin tried. (2.ii.3v)

This blazon complicates any notion of a male gaze directed solely at the female characters in the narrative, and it is perhaps most appropriate that we find it at this particular moment in *Urania*, when Amphilanthus is being used to unfix gender positions.[44]

This treatment of Amphilanthus forms part of Wroth's examination of a generic intersection with the public/private and male/female dichotomies I have been discussing: the contrast between chivalric and pastoral romance. If Sidney shifted the genre of the *Arcadia* from pastoral towards chivalric during his revisions, Wroth combines both forms in *Urania*.[45] The main chivalric literary influence on *Urania* is *Amadis de Gaule*, famously given a backhanded compliment by Sidney in the

*Defence of Poetry*: 'Truly I have known men that even with reading *Amadis de Gaule* (which God knoweth wanteth much of a perfect poesy) have found their hearts moved to the exercise of courtesy, liberality, and especially courage'.[46] Despite the not insignificant fact that *The Mirror of Knighthood* was translated by a woman, Margaret Tyler, who wrote an important defence of her role, *Amadis*, along with the other examples of chivalric romance, was associated with the public persona of the revival of ceremonial chivalry (both Elizabethan and Jacobean), and with the macho image of the questing knight.[47] This could be contrasted with the pastoral as a mode aligned with the private realm of contemplation (and therefore, to some degree, a realm either praised or disparaged for its potentially feminised character).[48] However, as I have noted earlier, Jacobean pastoral is also used as political critique, set against the repetition of the chivalric quest and the potentially tainted nature of what is described in *Urania* as 'a painfull court lyfe' (2.i.56) – a phrase that seems to reflect Wroth's experience of that state. The limitations of the chivalric stance and mode are most evident in the manuscript continuation of *Urania*, where Wroth depicts the necessary physical decline of the chivalric hero; but throughout the narrative, set against the undoubted relish with which chivalric encounters are described, is the paucity of any chivalric solution to the major problems which beset the characters.

Therefore, two genres with apparently opposed symbolic implications are used within *Urania* to interrogate each other's assumptions. This process ultimately involves a deferral of any final statement on the rival claims of either genre, just as the allied issues of gender are left undetermined (a situation certainly enhanced by the unfinished state of both the published *Urania* and the manuscript continuation).[49] Such a process is recapitulated in the nature of the publication of the *Urania* itself as an intervention in the masculine realm of letters: a shift, in Denny's terms, from the privatised piety of pastoral retreat to the public, political, perhaps even chivalric world of secular literature. The *roman à clef* element in *Urania* ensured that it interacted once again with the realm of the court, so that while Wroth herself had been marginalised (to a degree), *Urania* placed her in a quite different relationship to that particular centre, especially given the nature of the political context in 1621, and given her own allegiances within the Sidney/Herbert grouping at court. Wroth's act is interpreted by her as both private (she protests to Buckingham that her book is subject to strange constructions she never intended) and public (she sent Buckingham a presentation copy). While publication is to cease, and 'the books left to bee shut up',[50] as Wroth reassures Buckingham, the manuscript continuation of

*Urania* testifies to a much more complex notion of shutting up than perhaps Buckingham ever imagined, or than any oversimplified dichotomy between public and private might lead us to assume. Ultimately, this is because the strangest constructions are those practised by the narrative, rather than by the supposed impositions of false interpretation. Wroth's own strange constructions are evident if modern readers recognise that her romance has both an investment in heroism and an investment in its decline; an investment in the male quest (as opposed to female confinement) and an affirmation of endless lack at the heart of that quest; a sense of fulfilment within female containment as well as a sense of frustration; and, finally, a sense of female engagement (political and otherwise) as well as female detachment. Now that Wroth's book is moving from being mostly shut up to becoming more generally read and commented upon, it should be seen as a key example of how a woman writer in early modern England was able to question the boundaries between the public and the private, in an example that is of immense relevance to many current literary (and social) debates. Wroth was the most challenging of all 1621 authors.

## John Barclay's *Argenis*: the perfect glass of state

On 30 March 1622, John Chamberlain wrote to Dudley Carleton about a book that had taken Europe by storm:

> I had borrowed for a set time Barclaies Argenis (a booke somwhat rare yet, and hard to come by) I was so taken and caried away with yt that I could not geve over, (as indeed yt is the most delightfull fable that ever I met with). (ii.428)

John Barclay was born of mixed French and Scottish parentage. He lived in England from 1610 until 1616, leaving only after he failed to gain the preferment he hoped for from King James.[51] He wrote *Argenis* (in Latin) in Rome and died soon after its completion, in August 1621. The first edition was published in Paris in 1621; the first English edition was published in 1622. On 11 May 1622, Chamberlain continued his account of *Argenis'* growing fame in England, evidently responding to Carleton's difficulty in securing a copy in the Netherlands:

> I am sory you cannot meet with Barclayes Argenis which indeed are somwhat rare here beeing printed at Paris, and risen from five shillings they were sold at first to fowreteen, but I have taken order

to have one yf there were any to be had at Franckford mart: I heare
the King hath geven order to Ben: Johnson to translate yt, and that
yt is in goode forwardnes, but I am deceved yf he can reach the
language in the originall, or expresse himself in that manner, whatsoever he doth in the matter: besides there be many covert names
shadowed somtimes in Anagrams and sometimes otherwise, wherein
I had the fortune to discifer three or fower by meere chaunce, though
I be nothing goode at riddles, nor love not to trouble myself about
that is hard to finde. (ii.435–6)

Jonson's translation was entered in the Stationers' Register on 2 October
1623, but was among those works destroyed by the infamous fire of
November in the same year.[52] The first English translation was published by Kingesmill Long in 1625, followed in 1628 by a second translation 'published by his Maiesties Command', by Sir Robert Le Grys.
There were numerous European editions and translations in the seventeenth century, and English interest in *Argenis* was sustained through to
two new eighteenth-century translations.[53]

As Chamberlain's comment about anagrams makes clear, *Argenis* is in
fact, in Annabel Patterson's words, 'an encoded and fictionalised account
of European history in the late sixteenth century', under the guise of
romance.[54] Barclay's narrative centres on France under Henry III and
Henry IV, and indeed there are a number of direct correspondences
between the romance characters and real individuals through the medium
of anagrams and other allusions (for example, Usinulca = Calvinus).
Keys began to appear in later editions (in Latin in the *editio novissima* of
1627; in English in the second edition of Long's translation), although
commentators were quick to accede to Barclay's aim, stated through his
self-representation in *Argenis* as the poet Nicopompus, to write an indirect
and elusive allegory:

I will haue heere and there imaginary names, to signifie seuerall vices
and vertues; so that he may be as much deceiued, that would draw
all in my writing, as he that would nothing, to the truth of any late
or present passage of State. (109)[55]

Barclay (again through Nicopompus) declares his didactic purpose,
his intention to capture the reader:

While they reade, while they are affected with anger or fauour, as it
were against strangers, they shall meete with themselues; and finde

in the glasse held before them, the shew and merit of their owne fame. (109)

This idea is echoed by Long in the preface to his translation: 'I haue sometimes compared it to a greater Globe, wherein not only the World, but even the business of it is represented; it being (indeed) such a perfect Glasse of State' (A3). Therefore, *Argenis* encompasses both historically specific characters and events, and exemplary fictions which are intended to reform States. The narrative is always shifting between what is recognisable and what is transformed through the technique of romance. By setting the allegorical/historical layer of *Argenis* in the previous century, Barclay forces the reader to interpret the relevance of the events to present political situations. This clearly happened in the case of all of *Argenis*'s readers, from John Chamberlain to King James, but their interpretations were obviously quite different.

Barclay devotes a good deal of space to the civil dissension in sixteenth-century France caused by religious conflict. The followers of Calvin are clearly seen in the romance as the principal cause of social division (see p. 34), and while Barclay is always interested in staging debates that at least *appear* balanced over all issues, as a whole the romance offers a defence of Catholicism against the influences of Protestantism.[56] One can see how a sharp critique of religiously inspired civil war would have appealed to James in 1621 and 1622. If, as we have seen, James was attempting to negotiate a middle ground between the competing claims of Catholic power and Protestant cause, he could interpret *Argenis* as a test case for restraint in the midst of religious aggression. However Barclay intended *Argenis* to be read, the romance actually manifests the kind of openness that allows for exactly the kind of interpretation that James would certainly have desired.

Other aspects of *Argenis'* political analysis that would have appealed to James include an extensive discussion of the monarch's relationship with parliament.[57] This is accomplished through Barclay's depiction of Queen Elizabeth as Hyanisbe, who has a long discussion with Poliarchus about the necessary preparations to ward off the threat of Radirobanes (Philip of Spain). Here we are presented with a situation dear to James's heart: Hyanisbe says she is forced to call a parliament in order to increase her forces in preparation for war. Poliarchus wonders why that should be necessary:

Is therefore the sinewes of the Kingdome, that is, the Treasury, in the power of the people? Must they be Judge of all businesses, and Kings over their Kings, to rule by this custome all publique affaires, policies, and warlike provisions? Such truely are not absolute kings, neyther doth this agree with the title of free governement. (527)[58]

Hyanisbe begins by defending the custom, 'which I altogether adjudge honest and just' (528). She says that kings have their own great revenues for everyday use, but Poliarchus argues that taxation is both lawful and necessary (while noting that sometimes those who administer it may be corrupt). Kings should not have 'to please the multitude' (533) and surely a ruler's policies must be able to be kept secret, rather than having to be broadcast to the world through their airing in parliament. These speeches (surely music to James's ears) persuade Hyanisbe, who doesn't call a parliament, but instead simply demands funds from the city treasury.

The event behind this debate is Barclay's representation of the defeat of the Armada. I have discussed in the previous chapter how the Armada (together with the Gunpowder Plot) was a key symbol used to fuel anti-Spanish feeling in 1621. But Barclay dissolves the historical triumph over the Armada and its symbolic reverberations in the seventeenth century for English Protestants and refashions it within the romance. Not only does Hyanisbe capitulate to Poliarchus' arguments about the benefits of absolute monarchies, but the Elizabeth of heroic memory becomes instead a dependent woman, who allows Poliarchus to do battle for her. (The entire conflict is completely re-staged as a chivalric land battle, with Poliarchus eventually killing Radirobanes (Philip) in single combat.)

While Barclay was no longer courting James's favour when he wrote *Argenis* in 1621, this representation of Elizabeth would have been extremely appealing, particularly (as noted above) given her symbolic significance to those supporting active engagement for the Protestant cause. Hyanisbe actually says things like 'Wretched Woman that I am' (634) and at one stage, 'forgetting all Maiestie', casts herself at a character's feet (637). This may seem ludicrous, but in fact it represents a kind of counter-impulse to Wroth's linkage of the political possibilities of the romance form with a female perspective. Barclay, like James, offers a highly repressive view of feminine power, and rewrites Elizabeth's own skilfully managed self-portrayal into the cipher of a traditional, vulnerable female romance character. This not only defuses her threat as a female figure of power, but also as a potent symbol (in England by 1621) of Protestant militarism.

This section of *Argenis* can also be related to an earlier section in which characters discuss the ideal kind of monarchy. Unsurprisingly, the debate swings heavily towards establishing the favourable nature of an absolute monarchy. Part of the argument involves a critique of elected monarchies, and here Barclay glances at the Bohemian crisis by noting (through the character Dunalbius/Ubaldinus) Bohemia as an example of the chaos caused by an elected monarchy: 'what troubles arise from hence? What long and bloody warres have hence ensued' (95). This includes criticism of Dereficus (Frederick) as a usurper and principal cause of the conflict: 'Think you not these the greatest of mischiefs?' (96).

All this may have been seen by James as he looked into Barclay's glass. He undoubtedly failed to see himself in some of the other portraits painted in the romance, though others might have. For example, Meleander, who is essentially a portrait of Henry III, must also have brought James to mind for at least some English readers:

> He was a little too much given to hunting, in whose severall kindes he distinguished the seasons. He made friends rashly, and loved them violently: immoderate in bounty, impatient of businesse; which he oft committed to vntrustie seruants. (8)[59]

Barclay glances critically at the Overbury scandal in his account of 'the Phrygian couple ... who lately for Sorcery were condemned to dye, and taken from the Kings elbow, where they had been most powerfull but the King mindefull of his former affection, saued their liues, though condemned to perpetual prison' (16). The power of favourites is constantly criticised in *Argenis*, particularly in relation to their self-interest and potential corruption.

This critique can be related to Barclay's jaded account of the relationship of literary activity to the court. He satirises the hypocrisy of court poetry through an account of a series of elegies written to the memory of Aldina, Poliarchus' recently deceased bitch. We are even given an example by Hieroleander:

> Shee's dead. This beauteous Bitches obsequies
> Destroy'd by Fate untimely, solemnize.
> Erigones sad Dogge shall quench in teares
> His light, and fill th'amazed Starres with feares. (188)

This situation exposes the general hypocrisy of this kind of court, where such verses have to be commended 'for fashions sake' (189). In fact, it is this satirical moment which leads to Nicopompus' speeches about the difficulty of criticising princes, noting the many punishments to which writers who touch on the faults of princes have been subjected. For this reason, Nicopompus advocates indirection: 'I will circumvent them unawares, with such delightful circumstances, as even themselves shall be pleased, in being taxed under strange names' (192).

This is clever, but perhaps in the end too idealistic, as the example of James seems to indicate that the circumvention is indeed acceded to when it matches the prince's desires, but the taxing will go unrecognised. The potential danger of the whole process is perhaps registered in a curious comment of Chamberlain's in a letter of 1 July 1621:

> Touching Barclayes booke I ran yt over in haste three or fowre moneths ago, and never saw yt since for yt is yet but rare, whereupon our stationers are in hande to print yt here and we looke for yt to come foorth very shortly. Yet what I can remember to have observed then is here in a paper by yt self. (ii.445)

Why does Chamberlain now claim only to have *run* over a book he claimed three and a half months earlier he was unable to *give* over? Possibly he wants to ensure that Carleton won't expect too much from the summary he clearly asked Chamberlain to provide (once again, the paper containing Chamberlain's observations on *Argenis* has disappeared), but perhaps he is also reflecting the anxiety that Barclay's method will raise in everyone (except a king), in so far as interpretation is made such a crucial political issue in any reader's response to the romance.

## Transforming romance

Annabel Patterson has noted how the genre of romance shifted ground during the early seventeenth century: 'From being an attractive but untrustworthy alternative to the serious, romance itself came to be redefined as serious, as a way of perceiving history and even a means of influencing it'.[60] *Urania* and *Argenis* are both concerned with the intersection between the public and private spheres, but with important differences. Mary Wroth addresses the crisis of James's court through an intense focus on the position of women in an increasingly misogynistic society. She offers, as a critique, an enormous range of examples of female characters who raise, in a variety of ways, issues of female power and political instrumentality. This aspect of *Urania* is now particularly apparent in Josephine Roberts's edition, which stresses through the introduction, notes and indeed textual apparatus, just how much Wroth engages an entire social context.[61]

In contrast, Barclay seems intent on resisting Wroth's female perspective by reinforcing the very misogyny which Wroth critiques, particularly, as we have seen, through his reinterpretation of the character of Queen Elizabeth. Nevertheless, *Argenis* too is concerned with the way that the writer might, through holding up a glass, reflect the flaws of the State (even if the State's ruler ignores the picture). Barclay and Wroth are both interested in the role of the writer. For Wroth, the woman writer is embarking on a particularly dangerous path when she challenges social expectations of a proper female sphere. For Barclay, the challenge for the writer who skirts the court is to disguise, but not trivialise, his social critique. Both romances raise a series of controversial political issues. In the context of the religious conflict of 1621, they could be seen as taking up opposing positions (even if Barclay's careful balancing of opinions might have disguised the essentially Catholic nature of the ideal state in *Argenis*).

Similarly, both writers stretch a number of genres, not just romance. Wroth is particularly interested in contextualising poetry, and the published *Urania* ends with the sonnet sequence 'Pamphilia to Amphilanthus' (which I will discuss in detail in Chapter 5). Barclay also gives poetry a central role in *Argenis*, and one can see the figures of Nicopompus (in *Argenis*) and Pamphilia (in *Urania*) as parallel examples of self-exploration, as both characters are, in part, autobiographical. For Barclay, poetry is essentially public commentary; for Wroth, women's poetry moves uneasily between public and private, as a kind of liminal expression of the female self's position in Jacobean society. Both romances offer the reader the experience of a subtle estrangement of the romance genre. Such generic shifting can also be explored in the various performances of 1621, on the stage and elsewhere, which form the subject of the next chapter.

# 4
# Performances

'and for the stage / Fitted their humours'
commendatory poem to *Women Beware Women*

Where an older generation of theatre historians looked at the 1620s and saw a tradition in decline, recent work on the period has concentrated on the interaction between drama and the political ferment in the last years of James's reign.[1] The political tensions of 1621, in particular as outlined in Chapter 2 in relation to sermons, are similarly reflected in a number of plays, as well as in particular performances that took place outside the boundaries of the various playhouses.

A number of outdoor and indoor theatres were active in 1621.[2] The King's Men, the dominant company, used The Globe (rebuilt after a fire in 1614) for public performances and Blackfriars (from 1610) as an indoor playhouse. The Fortune, which burned down in 1621 (see the description by Chamberlain in Chapter 1, above), was used by the Palsgrave's Men, a company which had been Prince Henry's Men and became the Elector Palatine's Men after Henry's death in 1612. The Red Bull was, in 1621, occupied by The Company of the Revels (formerly Queen Anne's Men), and was regarded as a venue for popular and old-fashioned plays and performances. The second major indoor playhouse, after Blackfriars, was the Phoenix, also known as the Cockpit, built in 1616 and occupied, in 1621, by Prince Charles's Men. (There was a complicated relationship between the Red Bull and Cockpit at this time, both under the control of Christopher Beeston.) Plays were also performed at court: there are recorded performances of *The History of Abraham* (at the banqueting house), Massinger's *The Woman's Plot* (now lost); *The Woman is Too Hard for Him* (now lost); Fletcher's *The Island Princess*; *The Man in the*

*Moon Drinks Claret* (now lost); Rowley, Dekker and Ford's *The Witch of Edmonton*; and *Grammercy Wit* (now lost).[3]

Companies performed outside London as well; the extent of these performances is only just becoming evident with the publication of the Records of Early English Drama series, covering individual regions. A typical example of this type of regional touring is the arrival in Norwich of Lady Elizabeth's Men on 2 May, when they were refused permission to perform.[4] As well as touring London companies, various forms of local performance also took place.

University plays were also performed at Oxford and Cambridge. London dramatic companies visited the universities, but Oxford and Cambridge had their own dramatic tradition, largely based on college performances of original plays (many of them written in Latin). To take Cambridge as an example, by the beginning of the seventeenth century the professional drama companies stopped visiting, but a number of colleges had a strong history of performance, notably Trinity College, which used its grand new Hall as a venue.[5] James and other members of the royal family visited Oxford and Cambridge for particular performances. In Cambridge in 1621 records show performances at St John's, Trinity, and Corpus Christi colleges of one Latin and three English plays.[6]

Performance in 1621 was much more than theatrical production. Apart from plays, court masques and civic entertainments were major forms of performance. In Chapter 1, I discussed briefly John Chamberlain's responses to two Ben Jonson masques performed in various venues in 1621: *Pan's Anniversary* and *The Gypsies Metamorphosed*. Thomas Middleton was made Chronologer to the City of London in 1620 and was a notable producer of civic shows, which might be seen as the popular equivalent of court masques. Middleton's *The Sun in Aries* was the Lord Mayor's Show for 29 September 1621 and he also published a collection: *Honourable Entertainments*.

There is a major problem that has to be faced in this chapter: only a handful of plays can be ascribed to a performance in 1621 with any certainty.[7] However, this does provide the opportunity to interrogate many of the ideas underlying this entire project. I have, thus far, worked within a paradigm of completeness. As an approach to literary history, this has entailed narrowing my time scale to a single year in order to offer some sense of comprehensive coverage: within such a focus, I can offer a secure sense that all available data have been sifted and assimilated. This has (even in my own mind at the beginning of my research for this book) been reassuringly positivist. I believe that this method of constructing literary history pays dividends, particularly in its correction of the narrow selection of material that is the feature of so much work in the field. However, the material covered in this chapter underlines the contingent nature of even such a project as my own. All historical accounts of English Renaissance drama run into this problem: what we have available is merely the tip of the iceberg. This is not normally a problem because the tip consists of so many plays. But in this particular case, I am forced to rely on a handful of surviving plays and performance records to represent the hundreds that were available in 1621.

It would be easy to respond to this problem by claiming that contingency is the essence of historical understanding. To some extent, the contingent must be taken into account by all historians. In this book, the notion of assembling '1621' itself is presented as a heuristic device. But the rest of the book is at least devoted to a significant body of material that may be made to be representative, to at least some extent, of what is no longer available. In the case of performance, I can only claim a much less satisfying rationale of the arbitrarily representative. The frustration is exacerbated by the fact that we cannot know whether the repertoire system (which in essence gave most plays a run of three performances or fewer in a season) meant that the drama audience usually saw a large number of plays, or whether a larger number of people went to plays occasionally and weren't particularly concerned about what they saw (except for *causes célèbres* like *A Game At Chess*). The former case would mean that my miserly sample of 1621 plays represents nothing like the 1621 playgoer's experience. The latter case might mean that something more like a sample was available. One obvious answer is to place the 1621 plays in the context of the large number of plays from other years which, taken together, provide a fairly clear picture of the variety of possibilities. But I prefer to underline the arbitrariness of the whole procedure by taking what I have been given as a random sample. Plays now lost cannot be assumed to have been less significant (or even less popular) than those which have survived. Recoverable performances – and I am, of course, avoiding the whole issue of how far printed texts ever really represent performances – accordingly will be seen in this chapter as individual remnants of the year. Performances leave different traces from the material discussed elsewhere in this book, and given these traces, in the guise of reports, responses, and various records, alongside actual playtexts, it is at least possible to convey some of the experience of those who, in 1621, were surrounded by performances of various kinds at various levels of society. They will be seen as representative only in relation to the rest of the material examined in this book.

This does also involve some consideration of the not insignificant category of plays which cannot be dated 1621 with certainty. Three in particular will be discussed here: Massinger's *Duke of Milan* and *Maid of Honour* and Middleton's *Women Beware Women*. I will also consider the small group of plays published in 1621 and make some reference to those entered in the Stationers' Register for 1621. This sample group is, therefore, both an indication of what 1621 left behind, purely by chance, for posterity, as well as what we choose to see as related to the year because of references we desire to see as in some way pinning a play down – undatable plays, like plays without clearly identifiable authors, disturb critics, who are only just being guided by new bibliographical and textual theories towards the possibility that uncertainty may be preferable to the Romantic need to ascribe single, stable texts to single, stable authors.

## Thomas Middleton in 1621: performance and political critique

Thanks largely to the work of Margot Heinemann, Thomas Middleton has emerged in recent years as a key cultural figure of opposition to the court.[8] Attention has focused to a large extent on Middleton's *A Game at Chess*, the notorious (and immensely popular) anti-Spanish play of 1624.[9] Middleton's activities in 1621 are typically diverse: the civic entertainments noted above, the city comedy *Anything For A Quiet Life*, and (probably) *Women Beware Women*. All of Middleton's productions can, to some degree, be read in terms of Heinemann's characterisation of his political impact, but one needs to remain aware of the influence of generic and other expectations on individual examples. Neither *Women Beware Women* nor *Anything For A Quiet Life* seems, at first sight, to have the obvious political reverberations of *A Game at Chess*, or even the more subtle ones of *The Changeling*.

Margot Heinemann herself notes that *Women Beware Women* is far less concerned with the details of political intrigue than Webster's *The White Devil*, which is based on the same historical personages: 'the story is stripped down to its human and social essentials'.[10] The centre of *Women Beware Women* is a corrupt state personified in the Duke, who is so readily able to undermine the civic virtues of the factor Leantio's household. Heinemann stresses that the play is far from idealistic about the moral standing of any of its characters, but that ultimately it offers an indictment of 'the aristocratic social and economic code'.[11] Indeed, *Women Beware Women* is conjecturally dated 1621 because of a reference to the Duke's age being 55 – the same as King James in 1621.[12] It is hard to know just what point Middleton might be making if the Duke's age is indeed meant to remind the audience of James. A comparison between Duke and King could not be construed as a compliment, although a comparison so casually signalled might have been read merely as a nod to James's status, rather than a comment on his moral stature. If an audience did make the connection, the play would certainly appear as a strong attack on the morality of James's court, summed up aptly in the Cardinal's final speech:

> Two kings on one throne cannot sit together,
> But one must needs down, for his title's wrong;
> So where lust reigns, that prince cannot reign long. (167)[13]

In a particularly subtle and interesting political interpretation of the play, A.A. Bromham argues that Middleton specifically inserts a series of references to peace throughout *Women Beware Women*, having constantly in mind the difference between the 'false' peace pursued by James in 1621 and the only possible true peace – which would involve the fight for the Protestant cause in Europe.[14] For Bromham, the comparison between the Duke and James can be interpreted as genuinely complimentary if the Duke is seen, when he first appears, simply as a ruler of a certain age, like James, praised by Leantio's mother as being, at that age, 'best / For wisdom, and for judgement' (32). At this moment in the play, Bromham notes, we only know of the Duke as a wise ruler, not as a dissolute figure. Bromham argues that when the latter side of the Duke is revealed, an audience would be more likely to identify him with Buckingham than with James, prompted partly by Buckingham being a duke (although in 1621 Buckingham was a marquess – James elevated him to Duke in 1623), partly by the popular conception of Buckingham's licentiousness and abuse of power.

The Cardinal's speech quoted above might seem to be much more directly related to James's faults as the reigning prince, than to Buckingham. However, the image of two princes sitting on one throne might well evoke the association of Buckingham and James. Bromham's reading relates *Women Beware Women* to the crisis in 1621 over the Protestant cause, but this more overt political reading complements a more general sense of the play's resonances in 1621 (or thereabouts). These are also evident in the famous denouement, an especially complex and bloody masque in which most of the characters meet their deaths through such elaborate devices as flaming gold and poisoned smoke. One cannot draw too many conclusions from such a common device in Jacobean tragedy as the masque, but it is tempting to see the masque in *Women Beware Women* as an exemplar of the increasing attacks on the court's conspicuous consumption and moral laxity. This side of the play has been stressed by Albert Tricomi in the context of a whole genre of Jacobean and Caroline anti-court plays.[15] Tricomi also points out that the subplot of the play satirises the abuses of wardship, a contentious issue throughout the period and one particularly associated with the growing sense that James would never accede to suggestions for reform.

All this evidence of political reverberations must be seen in relation to other sides of the play which, while in some ways just as topical in or around 1621, remain topical and contribute to the modern success of *Women Beware Women* on the stage. Middleton's depiction of the four women in the play, Bianca, Livia, Isabella and Bianca's mother-in-law, can be seen in relation to heated early seventeenth-century debates about women's place and role.[16] The title of Middleton's play suggests that it offers a portrait of female nature directly related to the misogynistic pamphlets.[17] And at one level, the play can be interpreted as an exposure of the way that an immoral woman like Livia acts to corrupt Isabella and Bianca. However, the intersection of class and gender issues within the play complicates this simplistic moral reading. Bianca has left a wealthy family to marry Leantio. While this is initially seen as an example of love triumphing over social position, the play implies that Bianca's seduction represents, in part, social as well as sexual corruption. The Duke certainly suggests that resistance is useless ('I should be sorry the least force should lay / An unkind touch upon thee', he says menacingly, 64), but Bianca seems to be drawn naturally away from her lower social position with her husband towards the Duke's power. (She can also be seen to be reacting against her husband's attempts to keep her locked up in a manner rather like Celia in *Volpone*.) After the affair begins, her discontent with her material surroundings (scornfully saying 'Here's a house / For a young gentlewoman to be got with child in') provokes an outburst from her mother-in-law:

> What, cannot children be begot think you,
> Without gilt-casting bottles? Yes, and as sweet ones:
> The miller's daughter brings forth as white boys
> As she that bathes herself with milk and bean-flour.
> 'Tis an old saying, one may keep good cheer
> In a mean house; so may true love affect
> After the rate of princes, in a cottage. (75)

But Bianca's position is paralleled by her husband's, who, far from being depicted as a figure of middle-class virtue, is readily cast in a similar role to his wife; he is happy to become Livia's lover and to be kept by her as the Duke keeps Bianca. Self-interest is the overwhelming force driving the characters in the play. However one identifies the figure of the Duke, *Women Beware Women* offers a harsh view of a court *and* city world that must have seemed relatively familiar to its audience.

In contrast, Middleton's *Anything For A Quiet Life* is a city comedy which seems to offer a much more straightforward contrast of court and city values. This play also raises the question of authorship mentioned briefly above. *Anything For a Quiet Life* is generally seen as a collaboration between Middleton and Webster. It is typical of a large number of collaborative plays from the period. While I have already noted that recent textual and other criticism has stressed the need to move away from an older model of the 'author' of an early modern text, drama criticism has been reluctant to make any radical concessions to the joint or group authorship of plays like *Anything for a Quiet Life*. Ironically, the most accessible scholarly edition of the play is in F.L. Lucas's complete works of Webster, while scholars like Heinemann and Bromham and Bruzzi discuss it as if it is solely written by Middleton.[18] The question of authorship is interesting in so far as *Anything For a Quiet Life* is read as a political play by the 'Middleton' critics, who presumably do not want to consider Webster's contributions (seen as substantial by Lucas) because Webster is a less obviously 'oppositional' figure. I am not interested in debating the authorship of the play, but rather in noting how a true understanding of the experience of performance in 1621 requires some flexibility in relation to authors and texts. Again this is not necessarily a limitation on possible political readings of the play, but it might raise some doubts about a direct and absolute link between Middleton's general political position and the political meaning of *Anything For a Quiet Life*.

For Heinemann, the play represents a significant reworking of traditional city comedy themes to produce a comedy 'seen essentially from the moral point of view of the "middling sort of people"'.[19] In her view, the play as a whole offers 'a contrast of honest citizen thrift and industry against new-fangled court vices'.[20] Thus *Anything For a Quiet Life* can be contrasted with *Women Beware Women*, which refuses to locate any ideal virtue in the social milieu of the factor Leantio. Pursuing a more directly political, rather than social, approach, Bromham and Bruzzi offer a reading parallel in many ways to Bromham's reading of *Women Beware Women*, in which the references to peace and quiet are taken as signals of events in the play as (distantly) 'implicit warnings or criticisms of foreign policy' as well as 'criticisms of the effects of that policy at home, in England'.[21]

Both readings are alert to the large number of references to current events in the play (such as, 'a friend of his went over to the *Palatinate*', V.i p. 117); such references are common in city comedies. *Anything For a Quiet Life* also vividly depicts the second marriage of Sir Francis Cressingham to a much younger, grasping and materialist woman 'bred up i'th' Court' (I.i, p. 77). While many critics have pointed to the weakness of a plot device which reveals Lady Cressingham's actions as feigned so as to reform her husband, the bulk of the play is a lively, satirical account of an 'imbalanced' marriage in which a woman calls the shots and professes knowledge in advance of her husband. This is particularly the case in relation to financial schemes, and Lady Cressingham makes an interesting speech about her abilities (a kind of satirical version of Rachel Speght's positioning of herself in relation to patriarchal knowledge):

> Why my Father was a Lawyer, and died in the Commission, and may not I by a natural instinct, have a reaching that way? There are on mine own knowledge some Divines daughters infinitely affected with reading Controversies, and that, some think, has been a means to bring so many Suits into the Spiritual Court. Pray be advised, sell your Land, and purchase more ... (I.i, p. 85)

While we are clearly not meant to take Lady Cressingham seriously (especially after her about-face in the last act), she offers a challenge to the authority of husbands which is echoed in one of the subplots, the story of Sib, whose husband, Knaves-bee, tries to prostitute her to the dissolute Lord Beaufort. Sib's witty resistance involves an interesting class manoeuvre as well: she pretends to be in love with Lord Beaufort's page in exactly the same arbitrary, desire-driven way that Beaufort turns his attention to her:

> MRS KNA. I love your Page, sir.
> BEAU. Love him! for what?
> MRS KNA. Oh, the great wisdoms that
> Our Grandsires had! do you ask me reason for't?
> I love him, because I like him, sir.

Sib's challenging behaviour is licensed by her husband's immoral attitude towards her, but it is no less challenging for that. As is the case

with *Women Beware Women*, the women in the play may be read in relation to debates over the proper place for women which were current at
the time of its performance. In such a context, even a comparatively
unadventurous city comedy like *Anything For a Quiet Life* takes on a certain
edge, with its portrait of wives who flaunt their independence.

It is quite fascinating to compare Middleton's civic productions for
1621 with his plays. Middleton produced the 1621 Lord Mayor's Show
for the Draper's Company to honour Sir Edward Barkham. Middleton's
first Lord Mayor's Show was the grand and elaborate *Triumph of Truth* of
1613.[22] By 1621, Middleton had produced two more Shows, for 1617
and 1619. *The Sun in Aries*, the 1621 Show, is seen by David Bergeron as
being, like the two preceding Shows, competent but much less original
and exciting than *The Triumph of Truth*.[23] But Lawrence Manley has
pointed out that, from a social, rather than dramatic, point of view, the
Lord Mayor's Show was a sign, in its very elaborate nature, of the
increasing domination of the City by a few elite companies, the cultic
elevation of the Lord Mayor, and a widening gap between the leading
City merchants and the expanding body of middling shopkeepers, arti-
sans, journeymen and apprentices who constituted the great majority
in the citizen class.[24] For this reason, perhaps, Middleton is much less
inclined to move beyond simple flattery than he is in his plays. Manley
does note, though, that 'Middleton's pageants, sponsored by such
Puritan-dominated companies as the Grocers and the Skinners, were
especially frank in their allusions to contemporary vices threatening the
City's rulers'.[25] *The Sun in Aries* is, however, significantly attuned to the
whole issue of peace, which relates it to *Women Beware Women* and
*Anything For a Quiet Life*. James is praised as one who 'Vnites Kingdomes,
who encloses/All in the Armes of Loue, Malic't of None'. The final
speech in the Show, made by Fame, concludes by wishing peace to all:
'Triumph must cease/Ioy to thy Heart, to all a Blessed peace'. None of
the potential irony of the peace in the plays seems present here.

However, Middleton published a collection of ten civic entertainments
in 1621 in a volume evidently designed to flatter the variety of dignitaries
for whom the entertainments were devised. The collection indicates just
how varied Middleton's activities in this area could be, as well as indicating how, in London, ceremonial pageantry continued to be of great
importance in defining civic identity (for example, one piece is written
for the ceremonial visitation of the springs and conduit heads of the
city, which had been discontinued for seven years).[26]

The last two items in *Honourable Entertainments* describe receptions
for the Privy Council by the Mayor, on 5 April 1621 and by the sheriff

on 16 April. These entertainments form a direct response to James's annoyance with the city at this time. To some extent, the mayor and elite London guilds were on the defensive in 1621 against the attacks by parliament which indiscriminately projected hostility towards the city corporations.[27] However, the city was also the centre for hostility towards Spain and support for the Protestant Cause in Europe. On 29 March stones were thrown at Gondomar and when the perpetrator was ordered to be whipped as punishment, he was rescued by a mob.[28] Apprentices mounted another attack on 3 April. This resulted in a speech by James at the Guildhall admonishing the Mayor and Aldermen for not keeping the city under control, followed by a proclamation on 8 April 'for suppressing insolent abuses committed by people against persons of qualitie, aswell Strangers as others, in the Streets of the Citie and Suburbes of London'.[29] The proclamation is particularly tough on the civic authorities: 'there is just cause at this time to charge their chiefe Magistrates for negligent suffering, as to condemne the inferiour and baser sort of people for acting many Insolencies of rude & savage barbarisme, which dayly are committed in the Streets'.[30]

In this context, Middleton's entertainments for the Mayor and Sheriff take a tone hovering uneasily between hurt reassurance and rather aggressive defence. In a long speech, Flora begins by assuring the Council of the city's loyalty to the King: 'Not all the *Kingdomes* of the *Earth*, containe / A *Citty* freer to her *Soueraigne* / More faithfull and more carefull' (D7v). Yet this is a response to the King's admonition: 'Each reprehensiue word He did impart / Flewe and cleaude fast to their obedient Heart' (D8). The speech registers the uneasy relationship between James and the civic authorities in so far as they are co-opted into suppressing resistance:

> Twas fire within their bosome, could not rest,
> Till in some serious manner, they'de exprest
> Their duteous Care, with all speede put in *Act*
> Their *Soueraignes* sacred pleasire, to coact
> Where manners failde, and force, as with a Pill
> From *Humours* rude, the Venom of the Ill.
>
> (ibid.)

'Co-acting', 'forcing' and 'purging venom' are all images which reinforce the underlying sense of conflict between James's demands and the civic authorities' duties.

The last entertainment, at the house of the sheriff, is more circumspect. It begins with Flora again (whose precedence is disputed by her servants

Hyacinth and Adonis) who offers an apparently sincere (but in hindsight deeply ironic) paean to 'this high *Synode* of the *Parliament*; / Before whose faire, cleare, and *Vnbribed* Eyes. / (When it appeares) *Corruption* sincks and dies' (D2v). Taken together with the previous entertainment, this Easter celebration indicates how Middleton was able to continue some of the political critique characteristic of his drama within the more circumscribed genre and circumstance of civic pageantry and festival.

## Islands, princesses and wild goose chases

John Fletcher had two plays known to have been performed in 1621, *The Wild Goose Chase* and *The Island Princess*.[31] Recent work on Fletcher links him to a similar Puritan position to that exemplified by Middleton, and his plays can be seen in the same context of 'opposition drama'.[32] This has come about as critics have moved away from seeing 'Fletcher' as simply part of the Beaumont and Fletcher folio (and therefore invariably as a court phenomenon), to a more individual view of him as an author with a particular political position. Philip Finkelpearl interprets *The Island Princess* as a typical example of Fletcher's challenge to the corrupt court world, in this case through the figure of the idealistic and idealised Armusia. But the play is also a fascinating piece of the colonial jigsaw which has received so much attention in recent years.[33] The play's islands, Tidore and Ternata, are a representation of the Indies. The idealised Armusia offers a suitably idealising view of the play's locale, but with a typically colonial appropriative slant:

> We are arriv'd among the blessed Islands,
> Where every wind that rises blowes perfumes,
> And every breath of aire is like an Incence:
> The treasure of the Sun dwels here, each tree
> As if it envied the old Paradice,
> Strives to bring forth immortal fruit; the spices
> Renewing nature, though not deifying,
> And when that fals by time, scorning the earth,
> The sullen earth, should taint or sucke their beauties,
> But as we dreamt, for ever so preserve us:
> Nothing we see, but breeds an admiration;
> The very rivers as we floate along,
> Throw up their pearles, and curle their heads to court us;
> The bowels of the earth swell with the births
> Of thousand unknowne gems, and thousand riches;

> Nothing that beares a life, but brings a treasure;
> The people they show brave too, civill manner'd,
> Proportioned like the Mastres of great minds,
> The women which I wonder at —
> *Pyniero.*                    Ye speak well.
> *Armusia.* Of delicate aspects, faire, clearly beauteous...
> (I.iii, p. 561)[34]

While Armusia is admiring, he admires with an acquisitive eye ('Nothing that beares a life, but brings a treasure'). And as Finkelpearl points out, we are meant to view Armusia's idealising portrait of the islands' inhabitants ironically: they have earlier been revealed to us as treacherous.[35] To this colonial eye, all is objectified, including the 'faire' women, who are exemplified in the figure of the island princess, Quisara. Quisara is desired by a number of men besides Armusia; she is, like her island, a lodestar for colonisers. The plot reaches its culmination when Armusia emerges as most worthy wooer, but is asked by Quisara to renounce his religion for hers. A startling debate then takes place, as the normally courteous Armusia becomes furious:

> *Quisara.* Are not our powers eternal? so their comforts
> As great and full of hopes as yours?
> *Armusia.*                    They are puppits.
> (IV.v, p. 624)

Not only does Armusia curse Quisara's religion, he curses the princess herself:

> Get from me, I despise ye, and know woman,
> That for all this trap you have laid to catch my life in,
> To catch my immortall life, I hate and curse ye,
> Contemne your deities, spurne at their powers,
> And where I meet your maumet Gods, I'le swing 'em
> Thus o're my head, and kick 'em into puddles
> (IV.v, p. 625)

Armusia admits that he was expecting to convert Quisara to Christianity, which is, of course, the usual next step in colonisation. Paradoxically, Armusia's curses evoke Quisara's admiration for him and for his religion. As Finkelpearl notes, we are invited to view this final turn of events in the princess's tempestuous character 'with amusement and suspicion'.[36]

The ironic elements in the play stressed in Finkelpearl's reading do not diminish its complex illustration of early modern colonialism – indeed, in some respects Fletcher's knowing tone underlines the ease with which colonialist paradigms can be assimilated into a spirit of gentlemanly insouciance. In comparison with *The Tempest*, now the subject of so many readings which stress its relationship to colonialism, *The Island Princess* seems, at first glance, quite at ease with its colonial themes.[37] However, the abrupt shifts in tone, particularly in the religious dispute between Quisara and Armusia, point to an interesting tension between Fletcher's debunking of over-idealised heroism and his investment in at least some admiration for Armusia's valour. It is worth noting that *The Island Princess* appeared not long after Ralegh's disastrous final voyage underlined the problems in heroicising colonial endeavours. Where *The Tempest*, as Peter Hulme points out, registers the physical intricacies of colonial encounters, such as exchanges of food and hospitality that degenerate under the solipsism of Europeans into conflict, *The Island Princess* attends to ideological conflict in a very sophisticated fashion.[38]

For example, the religious conflict between Quisara and Armusia discussed above is sparked by the fact that the man who spurs Quisara on to a defence of her religion is not, in fact, the priest he pretends to be, but the treacherous governor of Ternata (the 'rival' island to Quisara's Tidore). On the other hand, the native inhabitants of Ternata and Tidore are seen as both 'false and desperate people' (Pyniero's words at the opening of the play) and as potentially noble and admirable, 'goodly persons', as Armusia describes them (I.iii, p. 562). Quisara embodies this typical colonial paradox: she is most admirable when she is most like a European woman ('most faire', I.iii, p. 568). Her passionate desire for a heroic fate is matched by the figure of Armusia, who wins her over to his religion with his passion. After that has occurred, Quisara represents an easy reconciliation between indigenous and colonising desires, as her brother promises: 'No more guns now, nor hates, but joyes and triumphes' (V.v, p. 642).

These difficult issues are absent from *The Wild Goose Chase*, a play in Fletcher's more straightforward comic mode. The play centres on the 'wild goose', Mirabell, a rather clichéd cavalier figure who despises constancy and, one suspects, for all his Casanova-like speeches, despises and fears women. Pitted against him are three women: Oriana, who loves him, and the sisters Rosalura and Lillia-Bianca. The sisters have been educated by a tutor who schools them, not only in classical learning, but in confidence and an aggressive stance towards men. As the play unfolds, it becomes a fascinating, comic treatment of gender tensions.

At one point, the sisters round upon their tutor for giving them unrealistic expectations. Lillia-Bianca says to Lugier, the tutor, that his principles:

> help to hinder us of all Acquaintance,
> They have frighted off all Friends: what am I better
> For all my Learning, if I love a Dunce,
> A handsome dunce? to what use serves my Reading?
> You should have taught me what belongs to Horses,
> Doggs, dice, Hawkes, Banketts, masks, free and faire
> Meetings, To have studied Gownes and Dressings.

> (III.i, p. 287)[39]

But once again, Fletcher is at pains to produce a genial solution to the issues raised in the play. Mirabell begins as a rake (it is not hard at all to see the appeal of this play to a Restoration audience) with a fine line in rake's rhetoric:

> Thou thinkst I am mad for a Maiden-head, thou art cozn'd;
> Or if I were addicted to that diet
> Can you tell me where I should have one? thou art eighteen now,
> And if thou hast thy Maiden-head yet extant,
> Sure 'tis as big as Cods-head: and those grave dishes
> I never like to deal withall

> (II.i, p. 272)

Mirabell exemplifies the world that provides no space whatsoever for the values that the women in the play attempt to maintain; women are less than objects in his eyes: they are just like melons:

> Musk-Melons are the Emblems of these Mayds;
> Now they are ripe, now cut 'em, they taste pleasantly,
> And are a dainty fruit, digested easily:
> Neglect this present time, and com to morrow,
> They are so ripe they are rotten gon, their sweetness
> Run into humour, and their taste to surfeit.

> (I.iii, p. 263)

However, Oriana eventually catches her wild goose (after a series of tricks and schemes), and the play asks us to believe that he is a worthy catch simply because she loves him so much. Mirabell is an interesting contrast to the noble and ideal (but hot-tempered and didactic) Armusia. Given that both *The Island Princess* and *The Wild Goose Chase* were chosen for performance at court during the Christmas festivities, it is possible to see both as appealing to a court spirit of bravado and witty/rakish comedy, as well as offering a critique of such values. In *The Wild Goose Chase* it is particularly difficult to know or decide just how we are meant to take the conversion of Mirabell into a married man (a problem with so much comedy of this kind). The strength of the female characters is, ultimately, compromised by their desperate desire for marriage, so that the values instilled in them by Lugier, the tutor, are in the end seen to be unrealistic. On the other hand, they demonstrate an ability to outsmart the men within the limits of one particular game: the pursuit of matrimony and the undermining of male resistance to it. The play registers gender tensions in a way that might potentially be quite radical, but it is very hard to pin down.

Fletcher was also co-author, with Beaumont (probably) and Massinger, of one of the few plays which were published in 1621: *The Tragedy of Thierry and Theodoret*. (It is possible that this play was also performed in 1621, but no evidence for this is available.)[40] This play sounds a much less ambiguous note of conventional misogyny. Its dramatic opening involves an oedipally charged confrontation between Theodoret and his mother, Brunhalt. Theodoret accuses Brunhalt of being notorious for her sexual licence:

> Witnesse the daily Libels, almost Ballads,
> In every place, almost in every Province,
> Are made upon your lust
>
> (I.i, p. 379)[41]

Brunhalt flees to the sanctuary provided by her other son, Thierry, who is both naive in his attachment to her and hot-headed in his designs against his brother. The political dimension to this is Thierry's confidence in his position as an absolute prince, whose subjects are meant to be happy that Thierry has the self-control to 'forebeare/Their daughters, and their wives' (II.i, p. 388). When the brothers are reconciled and conflict averted, Brunhalt sets to work to destroy Thierry's new marriage by arranging for him to be fed a drug which induces impotence. The play contrasts the unnatural, devilish Brunhalt with Thierry's virtuous and infinitely long-suffering wife Ordella. In strong contrast to *The Wild Goose Chase*, *Thierry and Theodoret* splits women entirely into whores and saints, and seems to revel in the vicious antics of Brunhalt, whose amoral lust and love of power are meant to be quite appealing:

> Preach not to me of punishments, or feares,
> Or what I ought to be, but what I am,
> A woman in her liberall will defeated,
> In all her greatnesse crost, in pleasure blasted;
> My angers have bin laught at, my ends slighted,
> And all those glories that had crownd my fortunes,
> Suffer'd by blasted vertue to be scatter'd:
> I am the fruitfull mother of these angers,
> And what such have done, reade, and know thy ruine.
>
> (V.ii, p. 453)

Many of the play's themes coalesce in this speech: Brunhalt's unnaturalness as a mother is also linked to her deliberate attempts to render Ordella unfruitful, in order to ensure that Thierry's marriage will not undermine Brunhalt's power. Brunhalt is a fruitful mother of anger – one of her schemes involves convincing Thierry that his brother is only a half-brother, and that Thierry should marry Theodoret's daughter! If *The Wild Goose Chase* reflects gender tensions in 1621, *Thierry and Theodoret* reflects something more like the gender war of the tracts that debated the nature of women.

## Massinger and the state

Massinger produced three plays which are dated around 1621/1622: *The Maid of Honour* and *The Duke of Milan*, both solely by Massinger, and *The Double Marriage*, a collaborative play written with Fletcher. Both *The Maid of Honour* and *The Duke of Milan* benefit from being placed in the context of attitudes towards Buckingham that were growing in intensity in 1621, and continued until his assassination in 1628 (even if neither play can be dated with absolute certainty).

I have already discussed James and Buckingham in relation to John Chamberlain's account of James's visit to Burleigh and his celebration of Buckingham's marriage (see above, pp. 9–11). In 1621, Buckingham had been James's sole favourite for five years. The young George Villiers (he became Earl of Buckingham in 1617, then marquess in 1618, and then Duke in 1623) was seen by Pembroke and others ranged against the Howard faction in court as a tool to block the influence of Robert

Carr, Earl of Somerset, the current favourite who had come to England from Scotland with the King in 1603. Villiers immediately attracted James's interest; he was renowned for his good looks, and James was soon completely under his spell: in 1617, he said to his council 'Christ had his John and I have my George'.[42] By 1621, Buckingham's whole family had benefited from his elevation and he was enormously powerful – and much resented. While Buckingham's biographer, Roger Lockyer, has tried simultaneously to defend Buckingham from charges of excessive power and to argue that he attempted, in 1621, to widen his support in parliament by moving towards the militant Protestant position of support for Frederick and Elizabeth, Buckingham's contemporaries did not see him in this way at all.[43] The 1621 parliament became focused on Buckingham as part of its attack on monopolies and abuses.[44] In particular, the numerous verse libels which circulated about Buckingham testified to the anger and suspicion directed at him. These verse libels were prepared to promulgate attacks on James' relationship with Buckingham, seen at least in some instances in sexual terms, and on Buckingham's supposed corruption, sexual and otherwise.[45]

In *The Maid of Honour*, Massinger seems to me clearly to be evoking James and Buckingham in the relationship he depicts between Roberto, King of Sicily, and his favourite Fulgentio.[46] The play opens with a satirical conversation between two courtiers that centres on Fulgentio's venality and the impossibility of effecting any court business without offering him a bribe. Astutio describes Fulgentio's power: 'In the time of trussing a point, he can undoe / Or make a man' (I.i., p. 122).[47] As the play (a slick tragi-comedy) unfolds, parallels between Roberto and James seem quite clear (though it is important to note that Massinger's criticism of Roberto is veiled, unlike the clear condemnation of Fulgentio). Roberto is faced by a rebellious faction of courtiers who want to aid the Duke of Urbino. Roberto makes a passionate speech in favour of peace that would sit easily with James's views:

> Let other Monarchs
> Contend to be made glorious by proud warre,
> And with the blood of their poore subjects purchase
> Increase of Empire, and augment their cares
> In keeping that which was by wrongs extorted;
> Guilding unjust invasions with the trimme
> Of glorious conquests; wee that would be knowne
> The father of our people in our study,

And vigilance for their safety, must not change
Their plough-shares into swords . . .

(I.i, p. 126)

The debate between Roberto and his half-brother Bertoldo over the
necessity to go to war over a matter of principle again sounds very
much like debates over the Bohemia crisis and the necessity for England
to stand shoulder to shoulder with European Protestants in general and
with Frederick and Elizabeth in particular. It is Bertoldo who gains the
best of the argument; as he states: 'May you live long, Sir, / The King of
peace, so you deny not us / The glory of war' (I.i, p. 128). The war itself
complicates the parallel, because Massinger avoids any real connection
between it and the religious conflict of the 1620s, and indeed the plot
indicates that the war is a futile, not to say foolish, endeavour. It is, one
must admit, this haziness of specific topical reference that has led to
some very disparate dates being ascribed to the play, which in turn led
its editor, Philip Edwards, to diminish suggestions of political purpose
on Massinger's part. Nevertheless, the evocation of Buckingham and
James seems difficult to resist. This is even more the case when Camiola,
the play's maid of honour, turns upon Fulgentio when he proposes to
marry her. She describes him as:

A suit-broker in Court, He has the worst
Report among good men I ever heard of,
For briberie and extortion. In their prayers
Widdowes and Orphans curse him for a canker,
And caterpiller in the state.

(II.ii, p. 142)

At this point one might say that there were many Jacobean and Caroline satirical portraits of favourites, and while many were indeed topical,
some were of types rather than individuals. But attacks on Buckingham
in particular come more clearly to mind when Camiola turns to Fulgentio's
masculinity:

First I am doubtfull whether you are a man,
Since for your shape trimmd up in a Ladies dressing
You might passe for a woman: now I love
To deale on certainties. And for the fairenes
Of your complexion, which you thinke will take me,
The colour I must tell you in a man
Is weake and faint, and never will hold out

> If put to labour, give me the lovely browne,
> A thicke curl's hayre of the same dye, broad shoulders,
> A brawnie arme full of veines, a legge without
> An artificiall calfe, I suspect yours,
> But let that passe.
>
> (II.ii, p. 143)

We have already seen how James responded to Buckingham's wedding (see above, Chapter 1, pp. 9–11), and it might be worth noting that Fulgentio's courtship of Camiola is endorsed by King Roberto. The passionate nature of James's attachment to Buckingham was noted in many slanderous comments. While such slanders intensified later in the 1620s, already in 1621 Buckingham and James's relationship was alluded to through reference to Jove and Ganymede.[48] Fulgentio's suspicious calf is a marvellous image that may well have evoked, for a suspicious audience, James's fondness for a courtier with a good leg. The diarist Simonds D'Ewes wrote of Buckingham, 'his hands and face seemed to me especially effeminate and curious'.[49] Later in the play, Camiola throws out a further insult (concerning Roberto's reluctance to ransom his half-brother) that could easily be read as a reference to James: 'He that can spare more / To his minion for a masque, cannot but ransome / Such a brother at a million' (III.iii, p. 163). In a final irony, Fulgentio is almost assassinated by Adorni, albeit not for political reasons. (Unlike Buckingham, who was assassinated by John Felton in 1628, Fulgentio is spared.)

*The Duke of Milan* is a very different kind of play, both in tone (it is an Italianate revenge tragedy) and in its treatment of the relationship between ruler and favourite. *The Duke of Milan* hinges on the relationship between love and jealousy and Massinger evokes *Othello* at times in the way that Francisco, the favourite, is able to play upon the jealousy of the Duke. In this play, the favourite is far less like Buckingham than Fulgentio, and I would not want to argue for anything like the same political allusiveness. Nevertheless, the play is certainly interested in exploring the problems caused by the Duke's excessive reliance upon Francisco. (There is, in this play, a complicated familial entanglement, as the Duke has earlier seduced and abandoned Francisco's sister – it is this that fuels Francisco's desires for revenge – but bound Francisco to him by marrying him to his sister Mariana.) As a kind of revenge tragedy, *The Duke of Milan* is notable for the close attention Massinger gives to the Duke's relationship with his wife (perhaps under the influence of *Othello*), and this side of the Duke also indicates how unlike King James he is. There is a greater interest in character and relationship than in more baroque Jacobean revenge tragedies, such as *The Revenger's Tragedy*. This is notably the case in Massinger's treatment of the Duke's wife Marcelia, who tries to alert the Duke to his all-consuming jealousy by deliberately feeding it, and thereby undoes herself: 'I haue fool'd my selfe / Into my graue' (IV.iii, p. 284).

## Double writing/double marriage

Massinger collaborated with Fletcher on some nineteen plays from 1616 until Fletcher's death in 1625 (eight of the nineteen probably involved other dramatists as well).[50] *The Double Marriage* was most probably written and performed in 1621, according to its editor, Cyrus Hoy.[51] Set in a Naples tyrannically ruled by the usurping Aragonese King Ferrand, the plot depends upon a series of doubled actions: the noble Virolet, who opposes Ferrand, is tricked into serving him and rescuing Ferrand's beloved friend Ascanio from the Duke of Sesse. Sesse captures Virolet, but he and Ascanio are freed by Sesse's daughter, Martia, who has fallen passionately in love with Virolet. Virolet agrees to divorce his loyal and brave wife Juliana, who has previously suffered the torture of the rack in order to save him and his father from being executed by Ferrand, in order to marry Martia. However, he refuses to sleep with Martia, who accordingly turns upon him and ends up in the arms of Ferrand, while plotting to have Virolet murdered. The play revels in the 'double marriage' of its title, and provides an efficient portrait of two formidable women. But many other doublings occur, including a fine comic scene involving the 'court parasite' Castruchio 'doubled' as the King and being tormented by having a banquet snatched away from him by doctor's orders. There are dizzying changes of loyalty from secondary characters, who set off the central devotion of Virolet and Juliana.

Gordon McMullan notes that *The Double Marriage* 're-presents a series of key moments' from *The Tempest*, notably the relationship between an exiled father and his daughter and the insurrection of Trinculo and Stephano.[52] McMullan also places this collaborative work within a much richer theoretical context by noting how, as a collaborator, Fletcher likes raising, rather than solving, problems (reflected in *The Double Marriage* in the fact that, as was often the case, Massinger wrote the first and last scenes of the play, while Fletcher concentrated on the twists and turns of the middle).[53] As well as this kind of echoing and doubling, the play examines the 'doubleness' induced by Ferrand's corrupt and tyrannical rule over Naples. The play begins with a conspiracy to overthrow Ferrand, which fails because only Virolet is smart enough to realise that it is folly to trust the 'double-agent' Ronvere. Virolet is alert to the fact that there are spies everywhere in this kind of society, just as, by 1621, only a fool would be unaware of the constant surveillance that surrounded the Jacobean court. Virolet pronounces, to his co-conspirators:

> You are cozend
> And all undone; every Intelligencer
> Speakes treason with like license.
>
> (I.i, p. 113)

In this uneasy space of tyranny and conspiracy, Ferrand has tried to protect himself by forbidding all possible means for conspiracy to flourish: all association is forbidden in this state: 'Tis death here, above two, to talk together' (III.ii, p. 151). Ferrand forbids 'all meetings, / All private conferences in the City: / To feast a neighbour shall be death' (III.i, p. 146). Indeed, Ferrand goes one step further and announces later in the play:

> The people have abus'd the liberty
> I late allowed, I now proclaime it straighter,
> No men shall walk together, nor salute;
> For they that doe shall dye.
>
> (III.ii, p. 154)

The play therefore offers an ironic and perhaps only slightly exaggerated image of the London of 1621, at which time, as we have seen in Chapter 2, James issued proclamations in an attempt to stem political dissent and discontent while his foreign policy was increasingly questioned by a wide variety of people. Fletcher and Massinger join together the theme of political duplicity and the doubling of incident and character through the double marriage that gives the play its title. The play begins with a scene in which Virolet explains rather tediously to his beloved wife Juliana that the suffering of his country moves him far more than any action of a woman might do, even, for example, 'Shouldst thou be, / As chastity forbid, false to my bed' (I.i, p. 109). As it turns out, Virolet's relationship with Juliana becomes a matter of state politics, as she is tortured to attempt to force her to reveal Virolet's whereabouts (she resists), while he must cast her off in payment for being rescued by Martia. An even deeper irony is set up by the fact that the ground for Virolet's divorce from Juliana is her barrenness, which has been confirmed, if not created, by her torture.

In his provocative analysis of collaboration by Renaissance dramatists, Jeffrey Masten shifts the norm of composition away from post-Romantic notions of individual authorship towards a general scene in which early modern dramatists 'wrote within a paradigm that insistently figured writing as mutual imitation, collaboration, and homoerotic exchange'.[54] In *The Double Marriage*, an example of what we might now call standard Renaissance homoerotic attachment is Ferrand's obsessive desire to rescue his friend Ascanio: 'What power has my command, when from my bosom / *Ascanio* my most dear, and lov'd *Ascanio*, / Was snatch'd' (III.i, pp. 144–5). (At the end of the play we are told that Ascanio is Ferrand's nephew, which sits oddly with earlier references to him, especially by Ferrand himself.) But the main erotic charge in this play stems from the doubled female desire of Juliana and Martia. As I have mentioned, this desire has significant political consequences, for the state as a whole, not just for Virolet. For example, Martia's desire for Virolet ultimately leads to her father's triumph in Naples over Ferrand; indeed, the restoration of liberty to Naples seems secondary to the Duke of Sesse's need to take revenge on his daughter. So, while Virolet at the beginning of the play mused upon the distance between matters of state and matters of the heart, the play's particular kind of doubling joins those matters together. Juliana channels her desire into a series of self-sacrificing acts, which, in the greatest irony of the plot, culminate in her fatally stabbing Virolet because she is fooled by his disguise into thinking he is the duplicitous villain Ronvere. Martia, on the other hand, is made furious by Virolet's loyalty to Juliana and again her thwarted desire has political consequences, as she plots against Virolet and ultimately becomes Ferrand's mistress.

The most lingering image of power in the play is provided in the comic scenes involving Castruchio, who is made king for a day, supposedly to bear out Ferrand's sense of 'The weighty sorrowes, that sit on a Crown' (III.i, p. 147). Sesse's uprising breaks in upon a Castruchio who accedes to Ferrand's self-indulgent notion, only because he has been teased by having the expected glut of food and women withdrawn from under his very nose, supposedly in order to protect him. A common satirical view of court indulgence becomes, in *The Double Marriage*, a powerful method of setting up the intersection between private desire and public responsibility. The play is quite unsettling in its presentation of cruelty (particularly in the graphic on-stage torture of Juliana) and in its depiction of the impossibility of finding a space free from state control.

## The witch

It is intriguing that *The Double Marriage* was not chosen for a court performance (perhaps because of some of the political implications I have examined here, but that seems unlikely), while *The Witch of Edmonton* was performed for the court on 29 December 1621. *The Witch of Edmonton* also includes a version of a double marriage, but linked to a case of witchcraft that would, no doubt, have appealed to King James, given his abiding fascination with the topic. (Another aspect of the play that may have appealed to James was its significant use of the morris dance, one of the customs encouraged, or at least authorised, by James in *The Book of Sports* of 1618, which was intended to reinforce traditional and presumably socially cohesive rituals.)[55] *The Witch of Edmonton* was written by a particularly skilled team of dramatists: William Rowley, Thomas Dekker and John Ford. Of these three, Dekker was the most experienced, having begun his career in 1598 writing extensively for Henslowe's company, the Lord Admiral's Men. By 1621 he had written a great many plays in a variety of modes, including (with Middleton) *The Roaring Girl*, which was, like part of *The Witch of Edmonton*, loosely based upon a real character. *The Witch of Edmonton* was Ford's first play; he went on to write a series of tragedies in the late 1620s and early 1630s, including *The Broken Heart* and *'Tis Pity She's a Whore*. Rowley was an actor who often played clown parts, but who also wrote some plays with Middleton, including *The Fair Quarrel* and *The Changeling*.

The three dramatists skilfully combine a domestic tragedy plot with a plot based upon the recently executed witch, Elizabeth Sawyer. The tragedy plot revolves around the bigamy of Frank Thorney, who marries the pregnant Winifred without knowing that she has already slept with her master, Sir Arthur Clarington. Having kept his marriage to Winifred secret, Frank decides that he will then marry his father's choice, Susan Carter, in order to ensure access to her wealthy dowry. Frank eventually murders Susan, spurred on by Mother Sawyer's familiar, Dog. Indeed, in this play it is perhaps misleading to speak of two plots, because the links between the account of Mother Sawyer and the tragedy of Frank, Susan and Winifred are numerous and complex. The witch herself provides the main link between the plots, not directly, but through both her familiar and her disruptive effect on the community which surrounds her. This intersection has been pointed to by a number of critics, notably Anthony B. Dawson, who observes that 'in both plots social pressure and a desire for individual autonomy come into conflict and in both infraction of social order and of ritual is the result'.[56]

In April 1621 Elizabeth Sawyer was tried for witchcraft, found guilty and hanged. Almost immediately, an account of her trial was published by Henry Goodcole, a chaplain who attended prisoners at Newgate (and seems to have made a practice of publishing accounts of the most notorious). Diane Purkiss has cautioned against the tendency for critics to be seduced by the realism of *The Witch of Edmonton* into seeing the play as offering some kind of 'truth' about early modern attitudes towards witches. Instead, Purkiss suggests that the play is particularly conscious of the theatricality of the witch, both as a role and as a social event.[57] It is certainly true that the play portrays Mother Sawyer as a figure who exists in the context of what I would prefer to call ritual, rather than theatrical, behaviour, including the extensive treatment of the morris dance which runs through the play's events. However, when Sawyer first appears, she offers a particularly modern-sounding explanation for the 'construction' of the role of witch:

> And why on me? why should the envious world
> Throw all their scandalous malice upon me?
> 'Cause I am poor, deform'd and ignorant,
> And like a Bow buckl'd and bent together
> By some more strong in mischiefs then my self?
> Must I for that be made a common sink,
> For all the filth and rubbish of Men's tongues
> To fall and run into? some call me Witch;
> And being ignorant of my self, they go
> About to teach me how to be one: urging,
> That my bad tongue (by their bad usage made so)
> Forespeaks their Cattle, doth bewitch their Corn,
> Themselves, their Servants, and their Babes at nurse.
>
> (II.i, p. 506)[58]

At first sight this reads like an explanation for the witch as a projection by disgruntled people onto an innocent victim. However, Sawyer, through her curse, does indeed call up the Devil in the form of a familiar called Dog (who is manifested as a dog): the audience is privy to the Devil's actions, which include the delusion of Cuddy Banks in the comic plot but also, indirectly, the murder of Sue in the tragic plot. We are therefore, in the theatre, simultaneously presented with an explanation of the witch as a social phenomenon and an exposure to the power of the Devil and the effectiveness of a witch's curse. In the play, Sawyer clearly does 'cause' the events detailed in the trial of the actual Elizabeth Sawyer, from the comic forcing of Old Banks to kiss his cow's arse, to the madness and suicide of Anne Ratcliffe. This dualist attitude towards witchcraft is also reflected in the way that the play shifts between a comic response, particularly evident in the character of Cuddy Banks, and a serious response, which, as mentioned above, entails a crossover between the plots via the familiar, Dog, who nudges Frank Thorney towards the murder of Sue. Banks's comic story involves the morris dance, which requires, in his view, a mock witch, but he is told 'Witches are so common now adays, that the counterfeit will not be regarded' (III.i, p. 520). The morris dance itself therefore involves a kind of mockery of witchcraft, but it is infiltrated by Dog, and the morris is 'slain' when the news of the murder reaches the town.

The play's most recent editor, Arthur Kinney, has stressed the way in which Edmonton as a community is presented in some detail, and the cohesion of that community is tested by both the outcast figure of Mother Sawyer and by the social disruption of Thorney's bigamy.[59] Both these disruptive figures are carried away to be executed at the end of the play, and there is a clear parallel drawn between them. Mother Sawyer articulates, at several points in the play, a biting social criticism, which might be seen as a response to her ostracism from the community. This is particularly evident in her examination by the justice, when she utters such comments as the following:

> A witch? who is not?
> Hold not that universal Name in scorne then.
> What are your painted things in Princes Courts?
> Upon whose Eye-lids Lust sits blowing fires
> To burn Mens Souls in sensual hot desires:
> Upon whose naked Paps, a leachers thought
> Acts sin in fouler shapes then can be wrought.
>
> (IV.i, p. 538)

This attack continues through to a catalogue of court and city crimes, particularly focusing on the conspicuous consumption that had become virtually a satirical leitmotif directed against James's court:

> These, by Inchantments, can whole Lordships change
> To Trunks of rich Attire: turn Ploughs and Teams
> To *Flanders* Mares and Coaches; and huge trains
> Of servitors, to a *French* Butter-Flie.
>
> (ibid.)

This satire is reinforced by Dog, who proclaims that he won't waste his time on small fry like Cuddy Banks, but is now off in search of some corrupt official to hang upon:

> I am for greatness now, corrupted greatness;
> There I'll shug in, and get a noble countenance:
> Serve some Briarean Footcloth-strider,
> That has an hundred hands to catch at Bribes,
> But not a Fingers-nayl of Charity.
>
> (V.i, p. 556)

This image must have had some resonance in the year of Bacon's impeachment, and the image of the corrupt, bribe-taker with hands constantly out (Briareus had 100 hands) would surely have raised a few eyebrows at the court performance of the play.[60] Here Sawyer and her familiar are joined in contempt for court (and social) corruption and moral hypocrisy, and whatever ambivalent feelings an audience may have had for the figure of the witch herself, the play encourages at least some identification, particularly with this element of social satire. *The Witch of Edmonton* also demonstrates the way a successful play could move between public and court performance at this time, which underlines the fact that socially critical elements in plays did not hamper their chances of a court performance. Indeed, the play would clearly have appealed to King James's longstanding interest in witches. Its very complexity in relation to the nature of a witch intersects with James's active engagement with the legal and religious status of witches.

## Masques

We have seen in Chapter 1 how John Chamberlain reported on performances of Jonson's masques, *The Gypsies Metamorphosed* and *Pan's Anniversary*. The Jacobean masque has been the subject of considerable critical attention since Stephen Orgel reminded us that we need to see the political and social resonances at work under a form that seemed artificial and in many ways antipathetic to modern readers/viewers.[61] As a form, the masque does still offer an extreme case of the gap between a performance and its textual record. As Jerzy Limon has emphasised, masque texts bear a very distant relationship to masque performances, given how important music, dance and stage spectacle were to the form.[62] It was Ben Jonson who gradually turned the masque text into something approaching a literary genre, rather than merely a performance record.

By 1621 the masque had become firmly attached to a court schedule. Although masques were commonly performed on Twelfth Night, they might be attached to any ceremonial occasion (for example, a marriage, such as that of Princess Elizabeth to Frederick, or an investiture, such as the inauguration of Prince Henry as Duke of Wales). Masques were also performed outside the court, in the country houses of those who could afford to put them on (or who were prepared to add the cost to their debts). Because masques were so costly, they were something of a calculated risk for devisers and writers; unlike a stage play, they could not quickly be replaced with a more successful or popular performance.

In 1621, *Pan's Anniversary* was the Twelfth Night masque, while *The Gypsies Metamorphosed*, 'devised' by Buckingham, written by Jonson, was performed for James three times (in three versions): on 3 August at Burley (Buckingham's estate); on 5 August at Belvoir, the estate of Buckingham's father-in-law; and at Windsor in September.[63] Recently, Timothy Raylor has identified and edited a third masque from 1621, which was performed at Essex House.

My interpretation of Jonson's two 1621 masques is heavily reliant upon the pioneering work on their political significance by Martin Butler (who also solved a long-standing problem over the dating of *Pan's Anniversary*, through a wholly convincing argument that it is the supposedly 'missing' twelfth night masque).[64] *Pan's Anniversary* is a comparatively short, pastoral masque. As pastoral, the masque enters into potentially dangerous territory, given that the genre was often favoured by Spenserian poets who opposed James's policies (most particularly his reluctance to engage in the defence of European Protestantism).[65] Butler notes that, in paying homage to James through the figure of Pan, Jonson is able to 'promote a particular view of the priorities of Jacobean kingship' through Pan's power: Pan presides over a peaceful Arcadia, but he is extremely powerful (376–7). However, as Butler goes on to explain at length, Jonson had to walk a difficult line between confirmation of James's attempts to avoid engagement with the Palatine conflict and at the same time convey to Spain the possibility that he might be pushed into war. We have, by now, seen this particular political situation reflected everywhere in the writing of 1621, and Jonson's masque is no exception. However, as a form of entertainment intended both for James's delectation and as a court event which foreign ambassadors attended, the masque had many demands to satisfy. Butler emphasises that *Pan's Anniversary* is a reflection of James's political agenda early in 1621: 'It sets out to counter the current expectations of a more aggressive position on European affairs and to restrain them within limits of deference to

James's kingship, and it does this by propounding an ideology which subordinates plebeian impudence to aristocratic control and in which Protestant enthusiam for a confessional politics is discredited' (385–6).

This is achieved, in part, through Jonson's depiction of a heavily satirised Puritan figure, brought into the anti-masque as a discredited and absurd prophet. This is the figure who, as Butler explains, led to the controversy when the masque was performed that was described by John Chamberlain in his report on the performance. Chamberlain, as has already been noted in Chapter 1, offered an account of the visit of the French ambassador, the Marquis de Cadenet, whose presence meant that the anti-Puritan incident was something of an embarrassment: Chamberlain wrote that the masque 'was handsomly performed, but that there was a puritan brought in to be flowted and abused, which was somewhat unseemly and unseasonable, specially as matters now stand with those of the religion in France'.[66] As Butler explains, the problem with *Pan's Anniversary*'s relationship to James's foreign policy was that it was unable to negotiate the contradictions between a general pacifism and appeasement of Spain and a need to convince the French that James would not tolerate the persecution of Protestants (389–92). Therefore, in the end '*Pan's Anniversary* is an eloquent testimony to the difficulty of writing political panegyric at a time of emerging ideological polarization' (392).

Apart from its interest as testimony to the complex political situation in 1621, *Pan's Anniversary* is a competent but not particularly exciting masque. However, Jonson's second masque for 1621 is a much more complex and challenging work. *The Gypsies Metamorphosed* is particularly difficult to write about because it exists in three distinct versions, each representing a separate performance. In Chapter 1, I discussed John Chamberlain's account of James's visit in August to Burley on the Hill, the estate recently acquired by Buckingham. On 3 August, Buckingham presented James with a performance of a long and elaborate masque in which Buckingham himself took a major part: that of the captain of a band of gypsies. The masque is dominated by what might be seen as its anti-masque elements: that is, the gypsies and their antics. The metamorphosis of the gypsies back into noblemen only takes place at the very end of the masque (especially in the Burley performance). As a whole, the masque is a wonderful showcase for Buckingham, especially when the gypsies tell the fortunes of a group of spectators (at Burley, these are, apart from the King and Prince Charles, female members of Buckingham's family), starting with Buckingham as captain telling the fortune of the King: 'here's a gentleman's hand; / Ile kisse it for lucks sake' (134).[67] The gypsies, in 'traditional' fashion, pick pockets as well as tell fortunes. The Patrico sings the cock-lorel ballad, which includes ribald social satire along with references to the local geographical feature known as the Devil's Arse.

With some variations, the masque was performed again on 5 August at Belvoir, the estate of Buckingham's father-in-law, the Earl of Rutland. It then had a third performance at Windsor in September, and for that performance it was heavily revised. The revisions of Windsor reflect the change from a Burley performance that was largely before an audience of Buckingham's relatives, to a performance before a more general noble audience. This change is easily seen in the revised fortune-telling sequence, where female members of Buckingham's family are replaced by figures such as the Lord Chamberlain, Lord Keeper and Lord Treasurer. The three performances are clear evidence of the success of *The Gypsies Metamorphosed*, and there seems no doubt that Buckingham's prominent part in the masque ensured a favourable reception from James. Modern critics have also seen this masque as perhaps Jonson's finest, Stephen Orgel memorably characterising it as a 'vast triumph of vulgarity and wit, crudity and finesse, tastelessness and grace'.[68] The energy of the masque is immediately evident from the arresting opening moment, when a gypsy enters 'leading a horse laden with five little children' (120). However, the two major critical treatments of the masque differ somewhat in their interpretation of its political significance. In an extremely detailed, book-length study, Dale Randall, while helpfully placing the masque in a variety of contexts, argues that it is shot through with implied criticisms of Buckingham, a figure all too easily seen as a marauding gypsy who, on his rise to favour, dragged along with him a whole band of greedy and self-aggrandising relatives.[69] It is indeed tempting for modern readers to see such a critique embedded in the masque, given its gypsy theme.

But Randall's interpretation has been modified convincingly by Martin Butler, who sees it as much more a process of defusing anxieties about Buckingham, especially given the favourite's successful negotiation of parliamentary attacks on monopolies and general corruption (parliament being in recess when the masque was performed at Burley and Belvoir). Butler, I think rightly, notes the 'playful, teasing tone' of the masque, and the way that Buckingham delighted in playing the rogue (but within limits) before an indulgent James.[70] Indeed, Butler notes that Buckingham plays out a carefully controlled version of his political escape from censure because of his unassailable attachment to James: 'the favourite's integrity is playfully questioned but, under the friendly eye of the king, is found to be above suspicion and intact'.[71] This side of the masque becomes even more interesting in the performance at Windsor before a potentially much more hostile audience, which included William Herbert, the Earl of Pembroke, centre of what was still a powerful counter to Buckingham's power at court and also centre of opposition to any appeasement of Spain, especially through a match between Charles and the Spanish infanta. Again Butler notes the uneasiness at this point in the Windsor version, when the genial fortunes of the Burley version have to turn to stagey flattery when transformed to fit powerful men at court.

As a whole, *The Gypsies Metamorphosed* can also be seen as an indication of how, partly in accommodating both James's taste and Buckingham's ambitions, the masque can incorporate popular forms (such as the ballad) and the energetic vulgarity nurtured on the popular stage within the costly and elaborate court world of the masque. It is a particularly fine example of Jonson's negotiation of what might be seen as competing generic forces.

A third masque from the 1621 winter season has recently been discovered by Timothy Raylor.[72] This is the masque that was performed as part of James Hay, Earl of Carlisle's elaborate reception for the French ambassador, the Marquis de Cadenet, an occasion I have discussed previously in the context of John Chamberlain's account of the elaborate banquet Hay prepared (see above Chapter 1). The masque (given the title *The Essex House Masque* by Raylor), was performed on 8 January, two days after Jonson's *Pan's Anniversary* had been staged at Whitehall. Like *Pan's Anniversary* (and unlike *The Gypsies Metamorphosed*), the Essex House masque is a fairly brief description of a relatively conventional masque. The scenario centres on the subduing of nine giants, who are transformed into stone and then later into men, interlinked with a depiction of Prometheus. Raylor notes that Hay, as someone who favoured a French marriage for Charles over a Spanish match, had to tread a careful line during Cadenet's visit, and that on the surface *The Essex House Masque* is a celebration of the peaceful overcoming of rebellion.[73] It therefore could be seen as a message to the French which would take into account English concern over treatment of the Huguenots and James's attempts to balance his European policies in the midst of the 1621 crisis.

## Audiences

Theatre historians have long debated the exact nature of audiences during this period. The latest position is something of a *via media* between the monolithic popular audience posited by Alfred Harbage in the 1940s (perhaps unconsciously reflected in the sense of total community in the audience depicted in the Olivier film of *Henry V*, made in 1945) and the elite audience posited by Ann Jennalie Cook in the late 1970s.[74] In Andrew Gurr's clear and convincing summing up, these two polarised accounts are taken to task for ignoring the distinctions between theatre locations, as well as changes over time.[75] Accordingly, as my account of individual performances in 1621 certainly indicates, there was still considerable crossover between the King's Men's repertoire at The Globe and Blackfriars, the former a 'popular', accessible, outdoor playhouse, the latter a smaller, more expensive and therefore more exclusive indoor venue. On the other hand, when Christopher Beeston moved much of the Red Bull's repertoire to the indoor Cockpit, the London apprentices rioted in 1617 and attacked the Cockpit, damaging both the theatre and the playscripts it contained, presumably because Beeston's move priced the plays they enjoyed out of their reach.[76] Nevertheless, court performances for 1621 included the popular *Witch of Edmonton* as well as the more obviously 'courtly' *Island Princess*, and I have just noted how a masque like *The Gypsies Metamorphosed* was successful with the king, one can assume, because it contained popular and vulgar material like the cock-lorel ballad.

The early modern 'performance year' had a specific pattern, focused on the rhythm of, in particular, the dramatic calendar, which was concentrated on the period from late Autumn to early Spring. Drama at court became more intense during the Christmas season and the public theatres were also focused on a winter season. Civic entertainment in London was focused on the October Lord Mayor's inauguration – this involved a shift from an earlier, sixteenth-century focus on midsummer.[77] In Summer, performances tended to be focused away from London, both at the aristocratic level (with *The Gypsies Metamorphosed* performed in country estate locations in August and September), and at the popular level, with London theatre companies likely to be touring the provinces. Changing focus in the course of the performance year reflects the generic interaction I have been discussing. This generic interaction indicates that the social divisions between particular kinds of audience, or readers, had not yet hardened in 1621. This is also evident in the way that poetry written, distributed or published during the year crosses genres and, in a similar way to drama, reaches out beyond fixed categories of reader.

# 5
# Poetry

For, I am free; and no Mans power (I know)
Did make Me thus, nor shall vnmake me now.
George Wither, *Wither's Motto*

## 'Pamphilia to Amphilanthus': freely expressing the captive self

I have discussed Rachel Speght's poetry in Chapter 2 and Mary Wroth's prose romance, *Urania*, in Chapter 3. Here I return to Wroth in a consideration of the remarkable sequence of poems appended to the incomplete published text of *Urania*. While I have read *Urania*, in the context of its publication in 1621, as a political act by Wroth, the appended song and sonnet sequence offers a complex engagement with a poetic genre that would have seemed to many readers to be on its last legs, if not *passé*. The characters depicted in *Urania* often produce songs and poems, replicating the way that Jacobean aristocrats, such as Mary Wroth and her cousin and lover William Herbert (who are represented in the romance in the figures of Pamphilia and Amphilanthus), were expected to have some poetic facility. In particular, Wroth's *alter-ego*, Pamphilia, is depicted as a poet, and as well as occasional verse written during the narrative, Pamphilia is the 'author' of the song and sonnet sequence that follows the incomplete book four of the romance. 'Pamphilia to Amphilanthus' is a sequence that, for the reader of *Urania*, fulfils the nature of the relationship between the thwarted Pamphilia and her wayward lover Amphilanthus. Indeed, the sonnet sequence could be seen as a kind of conclusion to the published romance, in so far as it explores the emotional and psychological state of its main female character (though it is worth noting that other women in the romance also write poems, notably Urania and Antissia, who are very different from Pamphilia, and this difference is also evident in the kind of poetry they write).

The poems in 'Pamphilia to Amphilanthus' also exist in earlier versions in a manuscript in Wroth's own hand, which is now in the Folger Shakespeare Library.[1] The manuscript sequence includes some poems which are redistributed through the narrative of *Urania*, a number of them attributed to characters other than Pamphilia.[2] Some poems were discarded and many were revised for publication. 'Pamphilia to Amphilanthus' as a mixed sequence of songs and sonnets has many links to Philip Sidney's 'Astrophil and Stella' and to Wroth's father Robert Sidney's manuscript collection of sonnets and songs.[3] But while Wroth's sequence shares a number of key images with those of her uncle and father, from the very first sonnet the reader is aware of a unique voice created through Wroth's use of a particularly dense syntax, which at times makes the poetry extremely difficult to interpret. This effect can be illustrated by the first stanza of the first sonnet:

> When night's blacke mantle could most darknesse proue,
>   And sleepe (deaths Image) did my senses hyre,
>   From Knowledge of my selfe, then thoughts did moue
>   Swifter then those, most swiftnesse neede require.[4]

Here is Pamphilia characteristically visualising herself in an occluded environment; she is engaged, quite literally, in self-examination, seeking to find an essence that might escape the constraints that surround her. Within the tangled syntax there seems to lurk a paradox: that thought will be most free when, in the death-like state of sleep, the senses are wrenched away from self-knowledge. It is at this moment that, as the sonnet goes on to explain, Pamphilia sees a vision of Venus and Cupid – a vision which will not be dispelled when she wakes, but which rather confirms her as captive to love: 'I waking hop'd as dreames it would depart, / Yet since, O me, a Louer I haue beene'.

On the one hand, Pamphilia is tormented by love, as she remains locked in a relationship with Amphilanthus which, like Wroth's relationship with her first cousin William Herbert, is both passionate, illicit and frustrated, ultimately including – as the narrative of *Urania* continues in the manuscript version that stretches beyond the published version, and therefore beyond the 'concluding' song and sonnet sequence – their marriages to other people. On the other hand, as many critics have pointed out, 'Pamphilia to Amphilanthus' balances the typical male-authored and voiced sonnet sequence with a powerful female voice: powerful as a form of expression, if not as an actual social or romantic position.[5]

As the sonnet sequence unfolds, Pamphilia turns to what might be described as a counter-world, set against the court environment which disallows female subjectivity. This is dramatically expressed in a frequently anthologised sonnet which sets the solitary and inward-gazing Pamphilia against a glittering but hollow court:

> When euery one to pleasing pastime hies,
>> Some hunt, some hauke, some play while some
>> In sweet discourse, and musicke shewes ioyes might:
> Yet I my thoughts doe farre aboue these prize.
>
> The joy which I take is, that free from eyes
>> I sit and wonder at this day-like night,
>> So to dispose themselues as void of right,
> And leaue true pleasure for poore vanities.
>
> When others hunt, my thoughts I haue in chase;
>> If hauke, my minde at wishes end doth flye:
>> Discourse, I with my spirit talke and cry;
> While others musicke choose as greatest grace.
>
> O God say I, can these fond pleasures moue,
> Or musicke bee but in sweet thoughts of Loue?

The speaker separates herself from the activities of a court that indulges in the pleasures central to James's own court (indeed, Wroth herself danced in Ben Jonson's *Masque of Blackness* in 1605), in order to converse with her own spirit, creating and developing a subjectivity which can only flourish away from the surface values of the court. The only freedom achieved by the speaker, who is, after all, in thrall to love, is an internal freedom of self-conversation, reproduced in the idea of the female poet creating a space for her voice within a male poetic tradition.

Through Pamphilia, Wroth explores the self-protection required by any woman who negotiates a position in a court dominated by attitudes ranging from merely predatory to misogynistic. As I noted in Chapter 3, Wroth's venture into print caused Edward Denny to label her a 'monster', and while Pamphilia's writing is viewed benignly in the romance, and she is protected by her position of authority, far above anything achieved by Wroth, Pamphilia still sees her writing as something to be kept secret, just as her feelings have to be guarded. This situation is depicted in a wonderful sonnet that takes up the constant image of eyes (common to many sonnet sequences) in order to show how a woman at court might ward off the male gaze that attempts to deny her any interiority:

Take heed mine eyes, how you your looks doe cast,
    Lest they betray my hearts most secret thought:
    Be true vnto your selues; for nothing's bought
    More deare then Doubt, which brings a Louers fast.

Catch you al watching eyes ere they be past,
    Or take yours fix't, where your best Loue hath sought
    The pride of your desires; let them be taught
    Their faults for shame they could no truer last.

Then looke, and looke with ioy, for conquest won,
    Of those that search'd your hurt in double kinde:
    So you kept safe, let them themselues looke blinde,
    Watch, gaze, and marke till they to madnesse run.

While you mine eyes enioy full sight of Loue,
Contented that such happinesses moue.

The woman's eyes do not simply protect her by refusing to reveal her heart's secret, but they in turn take on the penetration of the male gaze, and drive those who attempt to infiltrate her defences into madness. Characteristically, on close examination the first two stanzas are rather impenetrable themselves: 'lovers fast', for example, may be both the starvation pangs of love which follow from allowing doubt (that is, possibility) to the lover, or it may be the process of holding the lover fast. Once the threat of having her thoughts revealed has been circum-vented, Pamphilia is able, with some sense of autonomy, to contemplate her love, but the autonomy is only relative, because she is caught by the significantly blind Cupid in the bonds of love, and is, in that sense, never free. This lack of freedom is exemplified in the Crown of sonnets placed towards the end of the sequence, a *tour de force* consisting of fourteen sonnets where the last line of one sonnet is repeated as the first line of the next, forming a linked chain. The image that entangles these sonnets is the labyrinth, an image present throughout *Urania* in various ways as a representation of the entrapment that desire produces, especially for women. The Crown begins and ends with a line that stresses Pamphilia's bewilderment: 'In this strange Labyrinth how shall I turne'. Pamphilia is, at one level, trapped by her love, but as a poet, she has an inner freedom, which might be said to replicate Wroth's own paradoxical position: removed from the court and castigated for writing about it, yet free enough to continue *Urania* in manuscript.

## George Wither: the poet in prison

In the middle of 1621, George Wither was imprisoned for writing *Wither's Motto*. He had spent time in the Marshalsea Prison in 1614 because the Earl of Northampton was incensed by libellous reflections in Wither's satirical collection of 1613, *Abuses Stripped, and Whipped*. By 1621, Wither was a poet with a reputation for controversy and at the beginning of the year, he seems to have entered into an agreement with his printers to intervene in the debates over foreign policy and freedom of speech by arranging for the publication of *Wither's Motto* without a licence. The unlicensed poem was entered in the Stationers' Register on 14 May 1621, where it was prohibited from publication 'untill he bring further aucthority'.[6] A version of the poem appeared without the engraved frontispiece (depicting Wither lying gazing at the Heavens); this was followed, after being re-entered on 16 June 'to be printed as it is corrected by Master Tauernor', by another edition with the frontispiece and a postscript detailing the fame of the first edition.[7] On 27 June, Wither was called before the House of Lords and immediately committed to the Marshalsea Prison, following some questioning as to whether he knew of the Proclamation 'against lavish and licentious speech of Matters of State' of December 1620. Wither replied that he 'thinks there is nothing in it contrary to the proclamation restraining writing on matters of government'.[8] The House was clearly unimpressed by Wither's protestations and he remained in jail for the rest of the year, and was not released until March 1622.

The poem that caused all this trouble runs to about 2,000 lines of loose, heroic couplets, organised in three sections reflecting the motto of the title: 'Nec habeo, nec careo, nec curo' [I neither have, nor want, nor care]. As a whole, the poem is an autobiographical reflection on the state of the times, filled with oblique comments on topical issues, especially the relationship between the individual citizen and the nexus of religion and politics. In a detailed account of Wither as a 'citizen prophet', Michelle O'Callaghan suggests that, in the course of *Wither's Motto*, the poet 'becomes the faithful servant of Truth who challenges the powers of corrupt authorities in a way that draws attention to the

*Figure 3* Title-page of *Wither's Motto* (1621), by permission of The British Library, 1076.c.19, p. 163.

limitations of the state to control the individual conscience'.[9] Wither dedicates the poem 'To any body', and begins with a prickly address to readers which sets the tone for the poem as a whole: 'Proud Arrogance (I know) and enough too; will be layd to my charge' (A3).[10]

In the first section, Wither lays claim to a position as truth-teller and potential martyr:

> For now, these guilty Times so captious be
> That such, as loue in speaking to be free:
> May for their freedome to their cost be shent,
> How harmlesse e'er they be, in their intent. (A6)

O'Callaghan notes that Wither slyly disclaims direct comment on political issues, thereby drawing the reader's attention to those very issues, most particularly to the crisis over the Palatine and the actions of the Spanish ambassador, Gondomar, who had, in the previous year, been instrumental in the imprisonment of Thomas Gainsford for Gainsford's inflammatory anti-Spanish pamphlet *Vox Spiritus*:

> You are deceiu'd, if the *Bohemian* state
> You think I touch; or the *Palatinate*:
> Or that, this ought of *Eighty-eight* containes;
> The *Powder-plot*, or any thing of *Spaines*:
> That their *Ambassador* need question me,
> Or bring me iustly for it on my knee.
> The state of those Occurrences I know
> Too well; my Raptures that way to bestow. (A6v)[11]

The clever use of the negative construction is part of the overall structure of the poem, which has as its theme the motto 'I neither have, nor want, nor care'. In fact, just as Wither reveals by indirection a list of what he indeed has, desires and cares for, so the list of key anti-Spanish and anti-Catholic icons (Bohemia, Spanish Armada, Gunpowder Plot; Gondomar) is intended to alert the reader to a political agenda beneath the disingenuous disclaimer.[12] One particularly sensitive theme which Wither returns to throughout the poem concerns position and status, especially in relation to people who might move above their proper station. In the first section Wither proudly identifies himself as a writer who fears no one and flatters no one: 'I cannot giue a *Plaudit* (I protest) / When as his Lordship thinkes, he breakes a Iest: / Vnles it mooue me'

(B2v). In particular, Wither claims to be free from any materialistic desire which would leave him dependent upon any person or institution:

> The value of a penny *haue I not*,
> That was by bribry, or extortion got.
> *I haue no* lands that from the Church were pild,
> To bring (hereafter) ruine to my child. (B6v)

By the third section, Wither is prepared to belittle 'our relying on weake *Polecy*' (D2v) and he then moves on to a detailed account of public scandals, including what would seem to be a clear reference to Buckingham as favourite, followed by an indictment of the abuse of monopolies that formed such a key theme in parliament:

> Yes, Princes (by experience) we haue seene,
> By those they loue, haue greatly wronged beene.
> Their too much trust, doth often danger breed,
> And Serpents in their Royall bosomes feed.
> For, all the fauours, guifts, and places, which
> Should honour them; doe but these men enrich.
> With those, they further their owne priuate ends,
> Their faction strengthen, gratifies their Friends:
> Gayne new Associates, daily to their parts,
> And from their Soueraigne, steale away the harts,
> Of such as are about them; For those be
> Their Creatures; and but rarely thankes hath Hee,
> Because the Grants of *Pension*, and of *Place*;
> Are taken as Their fauors, not His grace. (D5)

The notion here that favourites are a problem because they create their own dependants, who are alienated from the king, is an acute criticism that was to be repeated often by those alarmed at Buckingham's influence. Wither actually goes on to accuse those who 'grinde the faces of the poore' in the King's name of treason. By the time *Wither's Motto* was published, Bacon had fallen and the attack on monopolies had become a key element in the criticism aimed at Buckingham. Accordingly, Wither's comments on the Parliament would have stung:

> *I care not* when there comes a *Parliament*:
> For I am no Proiector who inuent
> New *Monopolies*, or such *Suites*, as Those,

> Who, wickedly pretending, goodly showes,
> *Abuses* to reforme; engender more. (E8)

Wither also lashes out at those who are 'clad with Title of a Lord';
they are 'gaudy Vpstarts', who are hardly worth his attention. Once
again, in the context of a parliament that was heatedly pursuing both
those engaged in monopolies and those who had been elevated principally
because of their links to Buckingham, Wither's satirical reflections would
have been extremely provocative. They were, of course, intended to be
provocative and, as O'Callaghan notes, the whole production of *Wither's
Motto* relied upon the deliberate creation of controversy – a strategy that
was successful, given the enormous success of the poem, which ran into
eight editions in 1621 alone.[13]

In the second edition, Wither added a postscript (written, he claims,
twenty days after the first edition appeared), which boasts of the poem's
success: 'Qvite through this *Iland* has my *Motto* rung' (D3). Full of defiance, the postscript claims that, as well as setting the whole of Britain
stirring ('the good approve it'), *Wither's Motto* has aroused the ire of
opponents who will attempt to answer it in verse. Imprisoned, Wither
was able to advertise himself as a martyr for the Protestant cause, and
indeed one might say that imprisonment was necessary in order to testify
to the success of *Wither's Motto*.

At first glance, the other volume of poetry which Wither published in
1621 seems far less controversial than *Wither's Motto*. Entitled *The Songs
of the Old Testament*, this was a volume containing fourteen translations
of songs from a variety of Old Testament sources. But this apparently
pious work, complete with a dedication to the Archbishop of Canterbury,
is part of another of the combative poet's struggles with authority. The
Stationers' Company had bought the Royal Patent allowing for the
publication of psalters and psalms in 1603.[14] This gave them a monopoly
for the publication of the standard Sternhold and Hopkins psalter, and
a veto over the publication of any new translations (the famous translations of Philip and Mary Sidney were, of course, not affected as they
circulated in manuscript). The interest of the Sidneys in the psalms
points to the role that the psalms played in engaged Protestantism.
Given Wither's self-representation as Protestant 'agitator' and martyr, it
is no wonder that he was drawn to the psalms as a literary project.
Wither apparently began to translate the psalms in 1619, but the Stationers' Company repeatedly blocked his attempts to publish them, despite
the fact that Wither obtained a patent from King James in 1623 which
required Wither's *Songs and Hymns of the Church* to be bound with copies

of the English Psalter.[15] Accordingly, the 1621 publication of *The Songs of the Old Testament* forms part of Wither's challenge to the Stationers' Company monopoly, and is therefore interconnected with the attack on monopolies that is part of the theme of *Wither's Motto*, as well as the exemplification of Wither's position as Protestant champion/martyr.

*The Songs of the Old Testament* therefore appears to be a case of testing the waters: while it contains only fourteen translated songs, it has, as well as the dedication to the Archbishop of Canterbury, an opening 'Epistle to the Clergy', which specifically asks the bishops to authorise the use of the songs in churches. Wither stresses his pious purpose – although, of course, if he broke the Stationers' Company monopoly, he stood to make a great deal of money, given that the Company had paid £9,000 for the monopoly in 1603. In particular, Wither emphasises, in addressing the bishops, his disdain for any merely fashionable or purely literary criticism of his volume:

> And if your Reverences be herewith satisfied, I value not how the wits of our age shall censure the Stile I haue vsed; for though many of them are well acquainted with the raptures in *Hero* and *Leander*, the expressions in *Venus* and *Adonis*, and with the elegancies becoming a wanton Sonnet; yet in these *Lyricks*, in the naturall straine of these Poems, in the power of these voyces, and in the proprieties befitting these sprituall things, their sensuall capacities, are as ignorant as meere Ideots: and had it the Poeticall phrases they fancy, I should hate it; or were it such as they might praise, I would burne it. (A5)

This is calculated to appeal to the bishops' sense of what might be appropriate literary activity, while at the same time defending the nature of the translation itself (in other circumstances, Wither himself was quite capable of writing amorous verse).

Each of the fourteen songs is preceded by a brief essay on its 'argument and use' and each includes a musical setting. While Wither's general project of translation clearly had a pious (and perhaps also economic) purpose, a number of the translations in *The Songs of the Old Testament* intersect with the political themes of *Wither's Motto* in a more direct way. Song Number 3, which is from Judges 5, is described as one which might be sung:

> as a thanks-giuing for euery particular deliuerance, which is vouchsafed to the visible Church in these times. As in memoriall of our miraculous

preseruation, in the year 1588. when our Princely Deborah (the Queene
of this kingdome) gaue an ouerthrow to the Spanish Sisera. (16–17)[16]

Here Wither evokes the favourite icon of those who favoured intervention in Bohemia for the Protestant cause; in particular, the evocation
of Elizabeth as a militant Deborah is calculated to annoy those who
supported James's policy of Spanish appeasement (although one needs
to bear in mind that Wither sought and gained James's support for his
project of translating the psalms). A similar ideological purpose is
apparent in the next song (1 Samuel 2), which is described as a hymn
that 'may be sung in our reformed Churches, to comfort vs against the
pride and arrogancie of the Romish Strumpet' (26). Several other songs
have, as their central theme, the need to rally the Church against its
enemies, and accordingly they would, in 1621, have seemed particularly
relevant to the Bohemia crisis. In the decades that followed, Wither
continued to be a poet who revelled in controversy, and he took an
active part in the civil war.[17]

### John Taylor: waterman/satirist

Two days after the authorised edition of *Wither's Motto* was entered in
the Stationers' Register, John Taylor entered a work entitled *Taylor's
Motto: Et Habeo, et Careo, et Curo*.[18] Taylor was a self-educated writer,
who worked as a waterman – someone who rowed passengers up and
down the Thames.[19] Taylor published his first work in 1612: a highly
miscellaneous collection of poetry entitled *The Sculler*. By 1621 he had
published a wide variety of work, including eccentric travel narratives,
satirical verse and comic elegies. While they ended up on opposite sides
in the civil war (Taylor became involved in writing Royalist propaganda),
Taylor was an admirer of Wither and in 1621 shared many of Wither's
political views. In 1620 Taylor wrote a pamphlet to encourage volunteers
to aid Frederick and Elizabeth; he himself visited Prague in the same
year and his account is clearly in favour of intervention.[20] In *The
Subjects Joy, for the Parliament*, published early in 1621, Taylor enthusias-
tically greeted the prospect of a parliament that would attack monopolies
and protect Frederick and Elizabeth:

> The Prince and Princesse Palatines high Grace
> With all the Royall and the hopefull Race:
> Defend them Against all that them oppose,
> And fight their Battels still against their Foes.[21]

*Figure 4* Title-page of *Taylor's Motto* (1621), The Huntington Library, San Marino, 69646.

*Taylor's Motto* does, therefore, echo some of Wither's themes, but it is also a comic parody of Wither's solemn (some might say self-regarding) style and technique. Such a satirical parody was not new to Taylor, who had earlier engaged in a series of comic attacks on and parodies of Thomas Coryate, whom he clearly saw as a rival in the production of travel narratives. Taylor had an eye for the main chance, and knew how to cash in on someone else's fame, and such a motive is also obviously behind his response to the notoriety of Wither and the immense success of *Wither's Motto*.

The parody begins with the engraved frontispiece: instead of Wither's reclining figure, Taylor has a portrait of himself holding an oar, standing straddled over a globe of the world, which itself lies upon a small rocky island in the midst of a turbulent sea. Taylor overturns Wither's actual motto by changing 'nec habeo, nec careo, nec curo' to 'et habeo, et careo, et curo' ['I have, and want, and care']. In contrast to Wither's ironic preface 'To Anybody', Taylor's preface is addressed 'To Euerybody' (A3).[22] This preface sets the tone for Taylor's work, which is, as Bernard Capp notes, quite different from Wither's: 'a relatively contented detachment from the world, far removed from Wither's bitter alienation'.[23] Nevertheless, Taylor does see himself as a satirist, it is just that he is a circumspect one: 'I haue not heere reuil'd against my betters, / Which makes me feare no dungeon, bolts, or fetters' (A5v). This seems a specific dig at Wither, who was already notorious for the time he spent in prison and who was to be imprisoned again for *Wither's Motto*. Taylor echoes Wither in proclaiming that he has no specific political target in mind, but unlike Wither, he does not mention Bohemia and the Palatine.[24]

After the preface and introduction, *Taylor's Motto* again mimics *Wither's Motto* in being structured in three sections, which echo the tripartite motto itself. Given that Taylor begins with 'I have', as opposed to Wither's 'I have not', it is significant that he begins with his spiritual assets (starting with his soul), while Wither began by proclaiming his poverty: 'I Have a Soule which though it be not good, / 'twas bought at a deere rate, my Sauiours Blood' (A6v). Taylor's self-reflection does tend to decline into cliché in this first section of the poem; perhaps that is the price of his geniality, as opposed to Wither's bitter originality. But he does echo Wither in proclaiming his independence as a poet who cannot be bought or sold: 'Rewards or bribes my Muse shall ne're entice, / To wrong faire Vertue, or to honor Vice' (B4).[25] Towards the end of the first section Taylor offers the reader a more intimate piece of autobiographical reflection than Wither is prepared to reveal, noting in particular his attitude towards his wife, starting with some misogynistic commonplaces, but concluding '*I haue* my bonds of marriage long enioy'd, / And do not wish my obligation voyd' (C2).

In the 'I want' section, Taylor again echoes Wither quite closely, turning Wither's rather egotistical list of traits he does not want into a considerably more modest self-appraisal:

> For ought I know, *I want* a courage stout,
> Afflictions and temptations to keepe out:
> And I do feare should time of triall come,
> My constancy would abide no Martyrdome. (C3)

Wither's third section gathers together many of the attacks on Buckingham and on monopolies. Taylor again offers an explicit, humorous contrast with Wither:

> Vpon *I care not*, my swift Muse could iog,
> Like to an Irish Lackey o're a bog;
> But my poore wit must worke vpon *I care*,
> Which is a subject (like my wit) most bare. (D2)

Taylor simply glances at a general and fairly unoriginal list of abuses in society and moves on to an account of his trade as a waterman. He finishes with a lengthy self-justification for his writing and an advertisement for his other works; the poem ends in jovial self-puffery. In many ways *Wither's Motto* becomes, by the end of *Taylor's Motto*, simply a convenient peg upon which Taylor can hang the conceit of a piece of moderately witty and entertaining autobiography. This is not to say that Taylor didn't take himself seriously as a writer – quite the contrary, as evidenced by the publication of his collected works in a handsome folio edition in 1630 (the only precedents at that stage being the Shakespeare, Daniel and Jonson folios).

Taylor's serious vein is evident in a second major work which he published in 1621: *Superbiae Flagellum, or The Whip of Pride*. The commonplace image of the whip may have been intended as another evocation of Wither's *Abuses Stripped, and Whipped*, and Taylor clearly intends to lay claim to the title of satirist. He writes an earnest epistle to the reader stressing his serious intentions and follows this up with a poetic preface decrying the current taste for 'paltry Riming, Libells, jigges and Iests' (A3v). The poem itself begins in a lofty style, recounting the creation of man and the entry of pride into the world. While Taylor again tends to deal in clichés, he always has an adept turn of phrase:

> Pride of our Riches is most Transitory,
> Pride of our Beauty is a fading Glory:
> Pride of our wisedom is most foolish folly,
> Pride of our holines is most vnholy,
> Pride of our strength is weaknes in our thought,
> And Pride in any thing will come to nought. (B4v)

At the level of social satire, Taylor is able to hit home, with an effective image of rack-renting landlords exploiting tenants in order to parade their status: 'Let him and his be hunger-staru'd and pin'de, / His Land-lord hath decreed his bones to grinde' (Cv). He also spends some time on the absurd vanity associated with clothing – again a common Jacobean theme, but one handled adroitly: 'A good man to his suite is a repute, / A knaues repute lyes onely in his sute' (C4v). Taylor offers a quick recapitulation of the debate over the position of women in Jacobean society, evoking *Hic Mulier* and *Haec Vir* and re-emphasising the foolishness of women acting and dressing like men.[26] Taylor does balance the portrait of vain women with a witty, satirical account of men's fashionable beards, though as someone who sported a rather natty beard himself, he allows for fashion so long as it does not involve pride ('Yet though with beards thus merrily I play, / 'Tis onely against *Pride* which I inueigh').

Given Taylor's own propensity for satire, however mild, it is worth noting that he includes a section 'Against Libellers', which is particularly scathing about those who resort to anonymity:

> They are the vilest cowards on the earth:
> For there's not one that doth a libell frame,
> Dares for his eares subscribe to it his name. (D2v)

Wither's satire appeared under his own name, but anonymous libels were on the increase throughout this period (and will be discussed below). Taylor's attack on them is consistent with his persona as genial social commentator, rather than fierce political satirist. This is evident in another 1621 poem: *The Praise, Antiquity and Commodity of Beggery, Beggers and Begging*, an example of the mock encomium, a form which Taylor embraced with great enthusiasm.[27] The poem begins with a clever conceit whereby the lot of a beggar is far better than that of anyone above him in the social hierarchy (mostly because a beggar is free from care): 'A Duke, is a degree magnificent, / But yet a beggar may haue more content' (95).[28] Taylor offers a close association between the poet and the beggar, as well as a humorous personal association, typical of the vivid snippets of autobiography that characterise his writing:

> When I would Cry, as Children vse to doe:
> My Nurse to still me, or to make me cease
> From crying, would say, Hush lambe, pray thee peace.
> But I (like many other froward boyes)
> Would yawle, & bawle, and make a wawling noyse,
> Then she (in anger) in her armes would snatch me,
> And bid the beggar, or Bull-begger catch me;
> With take him Beggar, take him, would she say,
> Then did the Beggar such hard holdfast lay
> Vpon my backe, that yet I neuer could,
> Nor euer shall inforce him leaue his hold. (97)

Taylor produced a similar mock encomium in *Taylor's Goose*, but this is a particularly clever piece of work which plays with the various meanings attributed to the word 'goose'. The full title indicates Taylor's playful variations: 'describing the wilde goose, the tame goose, the Taylors goose, the Winchester goose, the clack goose, the Soleand goose, the Huniburne goose, goose vpon goose, the true nature and profit of all geese, the honourable victories of the gray-goose-wing, the worthinesse of the pen, the description of goosetost, and goose fayre, with the valour of the gander'. This vein of Taylor's is reminiscent of the great Elizabethan prose writers, notably Thomas Nashe in works like *Lenten Stuff* (1599), Nashe's mock encomium on the red herring. Unlike Nashe, Taylor favours verse over prose, and writes *Taylor's Goose* in his usual, serviceable couplets. The account glides from the properties of real geese to the Winchester goose – slang term for a prostitute – to the uses of goose feathers, amounting to the kind of light-hearted and witty entertainment at which Taylor excelled. Taylor is particularly delighted by the sport created by the fact that writers use a goose quill:

> The Gooses Quill, the Ganders praise hath writ.
> Thus for the Goose I hauing done my best,
> My toyled Muse retires vnto her rest:
> Ile shut my Inckhorne, and put vp my Pen,
> So take my Goose amongst you, Gentlemen.[29]

A similar *tour de force* is evident in *A Shilling, Or, The Travels of Twelue-Pence*, which hangs upon the conceit of a coin that passes from hand to hand. The coin tells its own story in the first-person, beginning with an arresting account of its 'birth': 'A hundred strong men-midwiues, digg'd their way / Into her bowels, to finde where I lay' (66).[30] The very origins of coinage are examined and Taylor ranges through places and times in order to establish the nature of monetary transactions. The coin then describes its passage from one person to another: from knave, to whore, to surgeon, physician, apothecary and so on – part of the poem's pleasure comes from the ingeniously varied list of those who possess the coin:

> To Players, Bearewards, Fencers, to good fellowes,
> To those that make no breath, yet can make bellows,
> To Pewt'rers, Shoomakers, and Buttonmakers,
> To Marshals men, and dirty kenell-rakers,
> To Leather-sellers, Armourers, and Curriers,
> To Iuglers, Iesters, Masons, Barbers, Spurriers,
> To Woodmongers, to Tapsters, and to Salters,
> To Rope makers, for Cables, Ropes, and Halters . . . [31]

Taylor is also able to include some general social satire: 'That where I had one Master lou'd the poore, / I had ten Drunkards, that did loue a Whore' (71). The poem ends with Taylor promising the reader that he can proffer more information if more money is forthcoming.

The range of poetry published by Taylor in 1621 demonstrates not just his own proficiency but also the market for verse that was both entertaining and satiric. Taylor's purpose could be seen as far less serious than Wither's, but both point to the general interest in satire and social commentary in the Jacobean period as a whole.[32] This is also evident in the range of verse that circulated in manuscript at this time.

## Manuscript poetry: libels, lyrics and anthologies

In recent years, scholars such as Arthur Marotti and Harold Love have changed our understanding of how writing circulated in manuscript in the early modern period.[33] Despite the increasing number of works in print, manuscript 'publication' was still extremely important in the early seventeenth century, especially for certain genres, such as poetry. Works in manuscript might be confined to a few readers or they might have a wide circulation. In the case of poetry, the most common form of manuscript publication occurred in verse anthologies and miscellanies, which were kept by a very large range of people. Individual poems might be copied in a large number of such anthologies, some of which grew as collections over a long period of time, some of which were more topical and confined to the collection of pieces within a few years. Indeed, Peter Beal has noted that the 1620s and 1630s were 'the golden age of MS verse compilation', although the practice continued through to the end of the seventeenth century (and beyond).[34]

Most of the poems that appeared in these collections cannot be dated to within a single year, so my discussion here will be curtailed. Nevertheless, there are a few examples of specific 1621 poems in manuscript which are of particular interest because they are further examples of the interest in satire and libel. Marotti describes Bodleian MS Malone 23, 'which looks like a presentation volume to a social superior', as a 'manuscript taken up almost entirely with political poetry dealing with events from the beginning of the reign of King James I through the assassination of the Duke of Buckingham in 1628'.[35] Clearly the majority of the poems in this manuscript do not relate directly to 1621, although many might be called stock political satires which would have appealed to a 1621 reader. The best example of this phenomenon is a poem often entitled 'The Commons' Petition', the full title being 'To the Blessed St Eliza of Most Famous Memory: The Humble Petition of Her Now Most Wretched and Most Contemptible the Commons of Poore Distressed England'. This poem appears in a significant number of manuscripts and eventually found its way into print in 1642.[36] In Bodleian Manuscript Malone 23, the poem is prefaced by a more elaborate, explanatory title: 'The Coppie of a Libell put into the hand of Queene Elizabeths statue in Westminster by an vnknowne person Anno domini 1619 [this date is crossed out] / 1621 vltimo Martii 1623'.[37] Its date of composition is unclear: the title in Malone 23 seems to be claiming 1623 as the date at which the 1621 (or originally 1619) poem was made public – or this might simply be part of the ludic element implied in the very existence of a 'petition' to Queen Elizabeth in the person of her memorialising Westminster statue.[38]

As a political satire, the poem is particularly relevant to the 1621 parliament, given that it claims to be a petition from 'the Commons of poore, distressed England'.[39] In harking back to Elizabeth, indeed supposedly petitioning her for aid, the poem aligns itself to Protestant expressions of discontent and to general disgruntled feelings about James's reign which produced a retrospective use of Elizabeth as an icon of English freedom, martial spirit and just rule. In particular, the poem takes up the issue, so much in the public eye in 1621, of the role of parliament in the correction of social abuses. The 'petition' asks Elizabeth to tender the Commons' complaints to the bar of Heaven, where 'Nor fauorites nor parasites nor Minion' can change the 'opinion / Of that great Chancellor' – with the clearly intended contrast to James's practices. The petition itself, which begins 'If bleeding harts dijected soules find grace', mourns the loss of Prince Henry, the embryonic Protestant champion, and compares contemporary England to Sodom. Monopolists and 'parasites' are everywhere and 'base informers / Lyke toades and frogges lye croaking in all corners' (157).[40] There is fierce condemnation of corruption throughout the state: 'Justice is bought and sold, become a trade; / Honours conferred on base unworthy groomes' (159). Buckingham and his followers are clear targets:

> Where is our Ancient nobility become?
> Alas, they are supprest, and in their roome,
> (Lyke proud insultinge Lucifers) ther sitts
> A sort of vpstart fawninge Parasites. (159)

There is a third poem in this series, which also appears in a variety of manuscripts (including the two cited here): a purported reply from Elizabeth to the petition, which underlines the supposed decline from the proud and wealthy nation that existed under her rule. A barbed attack on Scotland (and accordingly an attack on James) forms an important part of the satire, and the country's 'lust' for a king is roundly condemned, given the unfortunate consequences that followed from gaining one.[41]

These fierce satires clearly had wide manuscript circulation and they testify to the way that certain forms of poetry carried an intense political charge in 1621 (as they did throughout the early modern period). Numerous verse libels circulated during the same period, which addressed at a more personal level the failings of significant court figures, notably Buckingham, but many others, such as Northampton and Bacon.[42] Libels were topical, but like the Commons Petition, they remained in manuscript circulation after the figures they were first directed at were out of the limelight; thus libels aimed at Northampton remained in circulation well after his death. In 1621, the libels and satires generated by the Overbury scandal continued to circulate in many forms (including in disguised form in Mary Wroth's *Urania*), because the events formed part of the ongoing unease generated by King James, especially in relation to the treatment of favourites.[43]

As well as these libels directed at prominent individuals, people of lesser status could be the butt of satirical poetry if they were in the right place at the right time. In August 1621, James paid a visit to Oxford. He was preached to by Richard Corbett, Dean of Christ Church and a strong supporter of Buckingham. Corbett wrote a good deal of poetry which circulated in manuscript. One 1621 example was a poem dedicated to Buckingham which appears in a number of manuscripts.[44] The poem begins 'When I can pay my parents or my Kinge, / For life or peace or any dearer thing', and it goes on to compare Corbett's address to Buckingham with more venal (and critical) applications: 'But that a prayer from the Convocation / Is better than your Commons Protestation' (107).[45] The manuscript anthologies that contain a lot of satirical material, such as Malone 23 and the Herrick manuscript, are able to juxtapose a poem like Corbett's and a satirical poem on Corbett that mocked a famous incident during James's visit, involving Corbett's inability to deliver a sermon to the king because he was so distracted by James's gift of a ring suspended from a ribbon. Corbett retired to laughter from the congregation and was commemorated in this squib:

> A reverend deane
> With his band starcht cleane
> Late preached before the king;
> A ring was espied
> At his band string tyed,
> Was not that a prettie thing?
> The ring out of doubt
> Was that put him out,
> He knew not well what was next:
> For most that were there
> Did think, I dare sweare,
> He handled that more than his text.[46]

During the same visit to Oxford by James, a play was performed at Woodstock: Barten Holyday's *Technogamia* (which was first performed in 1618). The performance was a much commented-upon fiasco. Anthony a Wood noted that the performance was 'too grave for the king, and too scholastic for the auditory, (or as some have said, that the actors had taken too much wine before they began) his majesty (Jam. I.) after two acts, off'rd several times to withdraw'.[47] Holyday was a member of Christ Church College, and the embarrassing performance of *Technogamia* produced a number of satirical poems from within the university, which were copied in a number of manuscripts. For example, British Library Sloane Manuscript 542 has a series of poems on the *Technogamia* incident, beginning with 'Certain verses made upon Christ Church men in Oxford, concerning the play which they made before the King and Prince at Woodstock, 1621'.[48] The poems unmercifully mock the whole affair which, they claim, made 'poore Oxford a pure laughing stock' (fol. 39).

Reading individual poems (or small groups of poems) like this is very different from the experience of readers and compilers who worked with manuscript collections, many of which grew over a large number of years. The poems that 'belong' to 1621 are simply a small sample of manuscript poetry in general; like other topical satirical poems, even those devoted to the follies attendant upon James's visit to Oxford had a long life after their first appearance, in part because the satirical impulse behind them uses such incidents to characterise the failing of whole groups of people or areas of society.

## John Ashmore and Joseph Martyn: translations, epigrams and satire

Horace's Odes were published in English translation for the first time in 1621.[49] The translator was John Ashmore, about whom little is known, although a number of his poems point to connections with Ripon in Yorkshire. The Odes were later to inspire a number of politically charged poems, most famously Andrew Marvell's 'An Horatian Ode upon Cromwel's Return from Ireland'.[50] Ashmore offers a series of serviceable translations, which occasionally reach impressive levels of lyric grace:

> Why doe we, short-liv'd things, on tentars set
> Our greedy thoughts with vaine desire of pelf?
> In climats farthest off, What would we get?
> Who, from his Countrey exil'd, flees from himselfe?

Ashmore appended, with a separate title-page, a series of original poems: 'Epigrammes, Epitaphs, Anagrammes, and other Poems of divers subiects'. These are a combination of English and Latin poems, and begin with a verse speech made in 1617 at Ripon to King James when he was on a progress, followed by a series of epigrams on members of the royal family. Ashmore has a particularly obsequious poem to Buckingham congratulating him on becoming Lord Admiral, and an unfortunately timed epigram on Bacon, proudly expanding the idea that his name is an anagram for Beacon.[51] The strongest poems are in fact adaptations of Virgil and Martial, especially a dexterous version of *Georgics* Book 2, part of a concluding section of the volume entitled 'The Praise of a Country Life'.

Joseph Martyn's *New Epigrams and a Satire* is a much more adept collection than Ashmore's. The form of the epigram, exemplified in the Latin poetry of Martial, became extremely popular in the sixteenth century, when Martial was translated and imitated by poets such as Henry Howard, Earl of Surrey. Ben Jonson's publication of his *Epigrams* in his 1616 *Collected Works* is one example of many Jacobean homages to Martial and the genre. Martyn's collection of epigrams is varied and he is able to achieve some of the concision and wit characteristic of true inheritors of Martial; a good example is 'To Iocosa a Nightwalker':

> I wonder much, why she in all things Light,
> Should loue to do her Busines in the night,
> The reason; Foule within, without shews faire,
> Though she be light her workes of darkenes are. (XX)[52]

Martyn's epigrams are addressed to general types, rather than the specific individuals so often addressed or described in epigrams by writers like Jonson or John Harington. After sixty varied epigrams, Martyn appends a satire, dedicated to his kinsman William and written, he states, 'in times dispite'. The satire, in fairly general terms, describes how city, court and country are corrupt; great men 'Delight in great offences; and support / Injurious rapines, with a friend in Court' (X). The law in particular is seen as open to bribery: 'he that could procure a Great Ones Letter / To colour wrong, was sure to fare the better'. The fact that the country is just as subject to corruption as the city lends gravity to Martyn's charges, and he includes an interesting passage lamenting the decline of tradition in the country towns: echoing James's views on traditional sports and pastimes by noting 'Where (once their Ioy) the Maypole, was pul'd downe, / And asking why; Twas told her by a Swaine; / The better sort, did hold it was prophane'. Martyn ends with his Muse retiring from the fray, unable to engage further with such an unsympathetic age.

## Elegy: Donne and the reprinting of mourning

The elegy was a more popular seventeenth-century genre of poetry than the epigram or satire; amateur and professional writers turned out elegies for people they knew and for prominent figures for either fame or gain.

Collections of elegies appeared following the death of individuals such as Philip Sidney, or Prince Henry. Donne contributed an elegy on Prince Henry's death to the commemorative collection *Lachrymae Lachrymarum* (1613). In 1611, in response to the death of a rather less famous figure, Elizabeth Drury, who died in December 1610 at the age of fourteen, Donne published *An Anatomy of the World*, a small volume which contained a prefatory poem, probably written by Joseph Hall, and Donne's two elegies: 'An Anatomy of the World', which was later renamed 'The First Anniversary' and 'A Funeral Elegy'.[53] In 1612 these poems were reprinted together with a further elegy, 'Of the Progress of the Soul' or 'The Second Anniversary'. This volume was reprinted in 1621 with the same title-pages (though the volume had a new publisher).

While Donne's name does not appear on any of these editions, his authorship was clearly known to a large number of people, and the 1621 edition presumably reflects Donne's increasing prominence in the year in which he was made Dean of St Paul's.[54] The nature of the 1621 text (which does not correct errata listed in at least one copy of 1612 and which introduces further errors) indicates that Donne had no hand in the edition, but rather, that the publisher saw an opportunity to reprint poems by someone in the public eye.[55] The 1621 edition was published by Thomas Dew (the first two editions of 1611 and 1612 were published by Samuel Macham), and R.C. Bald has pointed out that Dew, like a number of other stationers, had his shop in the churchyard of St Dunstan's, where Donne was vicar from 1624.[56] Continuing interest in Donne is attested to by the edition of 1625, which was set from 1621. Unlike Donne's love poetry, which had extensive manuscript circulation, interest in *The Anniversaries* was satisfied by the published editions.[57]

These ambitious poems generated some controversy from their first appearance; the most famous response to them was Ben Jonson's, reported in his conversation with Drummond: 'that Dones Anniversarie was profane and full of Blasphemies / that he told Mr Donne, if it had been written of ye Virgin Marie it had been something to which he answered that he described the Idea of a Woman and not as she was'.[58] Jonson's criticism was not unique, and Donne made a number of defensive remarks that were triggered by what seems to have been a number of critical comments on the volume. In 1612 Donne wrote to his friend Goodyer while he was in France with Elizabeth Drury's father, who had become an important patron for Donne after the poem was produced:

I hear from England of many censures of my book, of Mris. Drury; if any of those censures do but pardon me my descent in Printing any thing in verse, (which if they do, they are more charitable then my self; for I do not pardon my self, but confesse that I did it against my conscience, that is, against my own opinion, that I should not have done so) I doubt not but that they will soon give over that other part of that indictment, which is that I have said so much; for no body can imagine, that I who never saw her, could have any other purpose in that, than that when I had received so very good testimony of her worthinesse, and was gone down to print verses, it became me to say, not what I was sure was just truth, but the best that I could conceive; for that had been a new weaknesse in me, to have praised any body in printed verses, that had not been capable of the best praise that I could give.[59]

By 1621, the nature of Donne's sermons would have provided, for the perceptive reader, a paradigm for the way the *Anniversaries* treat the 'fit' between Elizabeth Drury and the conceit that her death symbolizes the world's diminution:

> Sicke world, yea dead, yea putrified, since shee
> Thy 'ntrinsique Balme, and thy preseruatiue,
> Can neuer be renew'd, thou never liue (8)[60]

The elegies are opportunistic in so far as they take the death of Elizabeth Drury as a ground upon which the conceit of the poems might be developed; like all such public elegies, their 'sincerity' should not really be an issue. The fact that Jonson and others criticised Donne for an inappropriate response is more a reflection of the status of Elizabeth Drury (compared, say, to Prince Henry) than of Donne's relationship to her and her family.[61] Given that both poems see the world as corrupt and constricting, it is worth reiterating R.C. Bald's observation that in 1611 Robert Drury was, like Donne, frustrated in his ambitions.[62] After he wrote the *Anniversaries*, Donne was taken up by Drury and accompanied him on his trip to France and Germany.[63] Neither Drury nor Donne gained any real political advancement from the trip. *The Second Anniversary* in particular expresses considerable frustration at the state of a world which, at the time of its first publication, was not granting Donne his due advancement:

> With whom wilt thou Conuerse? What station
> Canst thou choose out, free from infection,
> That wil nor giue thee theirs, nor drinke in thine?

> Shalt thou not finde a spungy slack Diuine
> Drinke and sucke in th'Instructions of Great men,
> And for the word of God, vent them agen?
> Are there not some Courts, (And then, no thinge bee
> So like as Courts) which, in this let vs see,
> That wits and tongues of Libellars are weake,
> Because they doe more ill, then these can speake? (32)

Arthur Marotti interprets the *Anniversaries* as poems which enabled 'Donne to engage in intense meditation and speculation, but also the means to express feelings associated with his personal disappointments arising from his experiences in the decade preceding their publication'.[64] It is impossible to say how much more evident this aspect of the poems would have seemed on their 1621 publication; perhaps lines that touch on the corruption of favourites would have stood out: 'Thinke thee a Prince, who of themselues create / Wormes which insensibly deuoure their state' (27). On the other hand, Donne as preacher might have been even more evident in the meditative passages:

> Thinke then, My soule, that death is but a Groome,
> Which brings a Taper to the outward romme,
> Whence thou spiest first a little glimmering light,
> And after brings it nearer to thy sight:
> For such approches doth Heauen make in death. (27)

Eleven years after Elizabeth Drury's death, the poems' more abstract and meditative features would have stood out, although the 1621 edition kept the original title for each poem and therefore the name of Elizabeth Drury as, at some level, each poem's subject: 'The First Anniversary. An Anatomie of the World. Wherein, by occasion of the vntimely death of Mistris Elizabeth Drvry, the frailtie and decay of this whole World is represented'; 'The Second Anniversary. Of the Progres of the Soule. Wherein: By occasion of the religious death of Mistris Elizabeth Drvry, the incommodities of the Soule in this life and her exaltation in the next, are contemplated'. Donne's association with the Drurys had not proved particularly profitable, as Robert Drury's quest for advancement in 1611/12 was no more successful than Donne's, Drury being hampered by a temperament quite unsuited to diplomacy.[65] Drury died in April 1615, soon after Donne was ordained. Donne composed Drury's epitaph, which was carved on Drury's monument around 1618. Drury's wife Anne was leading a fairly retired life by 1621, though Donne retained some links with her, including some involvement in the transfer of the lease of two Drury properties in London to Donne's friend Christopher Brooke.[66] Donne wrote *The Second Anniversary* while in France with the Drurys, and he evokes this setting at the end of the poem, in lines which may well have had interesting resonances in 1621, the speaker now being a prominent Churchman and preacher, and relations with European Catholicism at a particularly delicate stage:

> Here in a place, where mis-deuotion frames
> A thousand praiers to saints, whose very names
> The ancient Church knew not, Heauen knows not yet,
> And where, what lawes of poetry admit,
> Lawes of religion, haue at least the same,
> Immortal Maid, I might inuoque thy name.
> Could any Saint prouoke that appetite,
> Thou here shouldst make me a french conuertite.
> But thou wouldst not; nor wouldst thou be content,
> To take this for my second yeeres true rent,
> Did this Coine beare any other stampe, then his,
> That gaue thee power to do, me to say this.
> Since his will is, that to posteritee,
> Thou shouldest for life, and death, a patterne bee,
> And that the world should notice haue of this,
> The purpose, and th'Autority is his;
> Thou art the Proclamation; and I ame
> The Trumpet, at whose voice the people came. (36–7)

In 1621, Donne's evocation of Elizabeth Drury as 'proclamation' may have been distanced from its immediate cause, but Donne himself was certainly fulfilling the role of 'trumpet'.

## *Envoi*: elegy for Hugh Atwell

I end this chapter with a much more modest example of the elegy: William Rowley's elegy for the death of the actor Hugh Atwell. Rowley and Atwell were both members of the same acting company: Prince Charles's Men (formerly Elizabeth's, the Prince's and the Queen's Revels), associated with the Hope Theatre.[67] Rowley was both a playwright and an actor, and his admiration for Atwell seems that of one professional for another.[68] Rowley's elegy has a particularly strong opening, setting up an image of Atwell as a player who struggled with death, as an acting company struggled with its rivals:

> So, now Hee's downe, the other side may shout:
> But did he not play faire? Held he not out
> With courage beyond his bone? Full sixe yeares
> To wrastle and tugge with Death? The strong'st feares
> To meet at such a Match.[69]

In this wrestling match, Atwell is a 'little' man who will not give up the match with death, until 'At last, death gets within, and with a hugge / The faint Soule crushes'. Atwell is praised by Rowley for his sweet tongue, which has sung to princes. The elegy directs our attention to Atwell's courage, which comes to seem intermixed with his skill as an actor: just as his tongue was a 'siluer-bell', so he struggled for six years of illness against death, and continued to perform during that time (he is, for example, listed in the part of New Year for the Inner Temple Masque of 1619).[70] Rowley shifts the public element of the elegy just slightly so that we sense a real relationship between writer and subject, before closing with a painful final line which cannot resist the too obvious pun: 'He chang'd his Hugh, yet he remaines At-well'.

Like so much of the printed poetry I have discussed in this chapter, Rowley's elegy is a poem that crosses between a court context, at least peripherally (Atwell was a servant of Prince Charles; his theatre company performed for the court) and what we might call a popular audience – something that characterises Rowley's plays as well. At first glance, little else might seem to bind together such diverse poets as Wroth, Wither, Donne, Taylor, anonymous satirists and diverse elegists. But it is clear that all these poets, writing in such different forms, shared an interest in the social in its broadest sense, and moved across a range of readers (and, one assumes, readings). I have often had cause to address the way that writing shifts between social groups in this way, and this issue is particularly important in relation to 'news', which is part of the focus of the next chapter.

# 6
# News

'I'll give anything for a good copy now, be't true or false, so't be news.'

Ben Jonson, *News From the New World* (1620)

I have already discussed the growing hunger for news in the early seventeenth century in relation to a number of genres and issues, from sermons to plays, and in Chapter 1 analysed John Chamberlain as a reader and processor of news. In this chapter, I move on to some forms of writing which 'carry' news more directly, although even here I range widely, from the obvious modes such as the coranto or ballad through to almanacs and more miscellaneous instructive works.[1] Richard Cust, in an influential article on the whole issue of news in the early seventeenth century, noted how historians had underestimated the importance of a variety of methods of news transmission in the period.[2] Cust suggests that 'news contributed to a process of political polarisation in the early seventeenth century', but warns that there were many news sources and they were processed in a variety of ways.[3] More recently, F.J. Levy has also emphasised the variety of ways in which 'news' was transmitted through diverse genres.[4] In his important study of the newsbooks of the 1640s, Joad Raymond points out that a key achievement linking the corantos of the 1620s with the later newsbooks is the notion of widespread distribution, rather than any textual characteristic.[5] Raymond also notes how anxious the distribution of news made those in authority.[6] But it is important to realise, as this chapter demonstrates, that 'news' was conveyed through a wide variety of genres and texts, and the hunger for news was satisfied through very diverse methods. In contrast to the politically self-conscious corantos of the 1640s, news in 1621, while eagerly sought out and political in effect, was conveyed both through news-books and through a very heterogeneous series of modes and genres which may not, at first glance, seem relevant to the category of 'news', but which, as this chapter is intended to show, participate in the growing fervour for news of all kinds. As I have noted in previous chapters, 1621 readers and audiences, in all their diversity, were catered for by a concomitantly diverse array of texts, and this is particularly evident in relation to news and (as the next chapter indicates) to its allied category of informative and didactic writing, which also often involved political commentary.

## News-paper: the coranto

Historians of the English newspaper rush past the examples of 1621 in their eagerness to examine the infinitely more sophisticated products of the civil war period.[7] However, we need to recapture the excitement that must have greeted the often crude corantos of 1621, which provided news of the Bohemia crisis to their readers. This process began in December 1620, when George Veseler and Pieter van den Keere produced an English language coranto in Amsterdam, which had become a centre for the publication of news.[8] Entitled *Corrant out of Italy, Germany etc.*, this single sheet of news (in folio) appeared at regular intervals in 1621, and was joined by a second Amsterdam coranto in April.[9] As early as January 1621, King James requested the States General of The Netherlands to ban the export of corantos to England, but the ban was never enforced.[10] The first coranto published in England appeared in August, and Thomas Archer, the bookseller who produced it, was promptly imprisoned.[11] Despite Archer's treatment, in September another printer, coyly named N.B., claimed a licence to publish corantos translated from the Dutch and produced seven in 1621, before changing the single sheet to a larger quarto format by early 1622.[12] However skimpy they may look to the modern reader, these corantos were seen as serious conveyors of news. Interesting testimony to this is contained in a letter of Dudley Carleton to John Chamberlain written on 20 March 1621. Just as Chamberlain conveyed domestic news to Carleton, so Carleton conveyed European news to Chamberlain, including news about the progress of the conflict in Bohemia. In his letter, Carleton suggests: 'For the rest of our news I refer you to your gazettas and mr. Salmon's report'.[13] While Mr Salmon was available to convey personal news, Carleton clearly believed that a gazetto, or coranto, would also serve to bring Chamberlain up to date on state affairs.

In the issue of *Corrant out of Italy, Germany etc.* for 21 January 1621, much of the news dates from late December 1620. This typical coranto consists of a series of items, generally of around 150–200 words, each one headed with the place and date of the news; for example, the item from Prague, dated 29 December, notes that there is rioting in the city in the aftermath of Frederick's defeat.[14] The emphasis is certainly on the unfolding Bohemia crisis, although there are also snippets of what might be described as diplomatic despatches, such as: 'Letters from Paris declare that the Mareschal Cadinet with a great suite is departed to his Maiestie of great Brittayne'.[15]

The next issue, dated 31 March, has news from Venice, Vienna, Prague, Berlin, Breslau, Augsburg, Worms and Frankfurt; it contains important news from Prague of the persecution of the Protestant rebels in one of the notorious acts at the early stages of the Thirty Years' War. Like all the information provided in the corantos, the news is offered without comment as a series of factual statements, but any reader sympathetic to the Protestant cause would interpret the news as a comment upon the lack of active engagement by England on behalf of Frederick and Elizabeth. No specifically English news was published in these corantos, so that the reader who relied on them for news from Europe needed to find other sources for domestic news. Details of the Bohemia crisis and the onset of the Thirty Years' War are often connected to the threat of Turkey, ruled by Osman II, who was laying siege to Poland in 1621 (though he was defeated at Khoczim).[16] In Veseler's coranto of 9 April, the Turkish Emperor's threatening letter to the King of Poland is reproduced.[17]

In his discussion of the development of periodical news publication in the seventeenth century, C. John Sommerville notes a certain tension between the continuing flow of information suggested by the name coranto (which implies both senses of the word 'current'), and the separation of each 'instalment' of a recounted event which 'tended to fragment experience'.[18] The constant accounts of European conflict in the corantos from the Netherlands reinforce the first aspect noted by Sommerville, because the growing sense of crisis is, it seems to me, conveyed quite clearly to the reader, despite the dry style and minimal descriptive detail. As the religious conflict heightened, one would expect that most readers would eagerly await the next piece of news, and the individual items from various European locations fit together to provide strong sense of how wide-ranging that conflict was. For the English reader, this European news could be set against the domestic situation, as parliament boldly debated foreign policy and, throughout society, tension over possible English intervention was manifested in a variety of ways, as we have seen in earlier chapters.

One can only assume that readers would have appreciated some domestic news in these corantos, but it was not forthcoming until some years later, when the turmoil of the civil war allowed enterprising people on both sides to publish details of the conflict.[19] Not only were the later newsbooks able to convey the kind of detailed domestic news previously confined to the much more expensive and narrowly distributed manuscript newsletters, they characteristically produced 'thicker' news items, written in more detail and from a clear point of view.[20]

When corantos were produced in England they were almost indistinguishable from the corantos produced in the Netherlands. While the corantos that landed Thomas Archer in jail have not survived, those published by N.B., beginning on 24 September, are available. N.B. has been identified as Nathaniel Butter, a bookseller who was closely involved in various forms of news publication since 1604.[21] Butter's first coranto was entitled *Corante, or news from Italy, Germany, Hungarie, Spaine and France* and it was described as a translation 'out of the hie Dutch coppy printed at Franckford'. Indeed, all of Butter's 1621 corantos proclaim themselves to be translation from the Dutch.[22] Butter's corantos cite European news only and their style is similar to the corantos published in the Netherlands (which is scarcely surprising if they were translations of Dutch originals). Butter's first coranto, of 24 September, offered news from Rome, Genoa, Vienna, Presburg, Prague, The Hague, Wesell, Brussels and Cologne.[23] Butter's five other 1621 corantos are all very similar to the first one. By September, the European situation was steadily worsening, and Butter's corantos would have emphasised the increasing desperation of the Protestant cause, as James continued to hold back from any intervention, while castigating any subject who dared to comment on foreign policy.

## Foreign correspondence

As well as the corantos, there were many other ways that information about European affairs, and indeed matters from further afield, were conveyed to those who were interested. A great deal of foreign news was filtered through the conduit of correspondence such as that between Carleton and Chamberlain. The idea of the foreign correspondent conveying reliable news is reflected in a publication like *Certain Letters declaring in part the passage of affaires in the Palatinate, from September to this present Moneth of April*.[24] This purports to be a collection of seven letters detailing events from September 1620 to April 1621 written by an English soldier under the command of Sir Horace Vere.[25] While quite short, the letters are vivid and would certainly serve to rally support for the Protestant cause.

A variety of pamphlets could be seen as providing 'news' that would confirm English sympathy for Frederick. These pamphlets, like the sermons discussed in Chapter 2, participated in the public debate over English involvement in the conflict. Some of these pamphlets closely resembled the corantos on which they may well have been modelled. A good example is *The Certaine and True Newes, from all the parts of Germany and Poland, to this Present of October 1621*, which differs from the corantos only in being more detailed and focused on fewer events.[26] Other pamphlets offer an argument, even an analysis, of events, while reinforcing the Protestant cause; for example, *A Brief Description of the reasons that make the Declaration of the Ban made against the King of Bohemia, as being Elector palatine, Dated the 22 of Ianuarie last past, of no value nor worth, and therefore not to be respected.*[27] Not all the pamphlets support the cause of Frederick and the Protestant Netherlands. A clever debunking of English support for the Dutch, which criticises Elizabeth's policy and argues that Dutch Protestantism is completely removed from England's religion, is set out as a series of observations from an informant in Paris to a friend in England: *Observations Concerning the Present Affaires of Holland and the Vnited Provinces*. This pamphlet, published as, essentially, a piece of Catholic propaganda by the English College at St Omer, was evidently written by Richard Rowlands (also known as Richard Verstegan), a Catholic antiquarian who was educated at Christ Church, Oxford, before moving to Antwerp and then Paris, where he produced a number of works of Catholic polemic and also acted as a publisher and printer for similar works.[28]

Another group of pamphlets reported on the situation in France. The Huguenot situation had declined steadily after the assassination of Henry IV in 1610. When Louis XIII decided to assert his power, he led a series of campaigns against the Huguenots from mid-1620.[29] The Huguenot cause rallied at the fortified port city of La Rochelle, beginning with a defiant assembly held in November 1620. In 1621 a campaign against this Huguenot defiance led to the Royalist defeat of the city of St Jean d'Angély, leaving La Rochelle exposed. The struggle is reflected in pamphlets from both sides. From La Rochelle itself came *The declaration of the Reformed Church of France and the Soveraigntie of Bearn of their unjust persecution by the enemies of the State and their Religion. And of their lawful and necessarie defence.*[30] The exchange between Louis and the assembly at La Rochelle is reproduced in *Letters Patent made by the French King, Declaring his intent touching those of the Reformed Religion. Published in*

*Roane in the Court of Parliament the seventh day of Iune An 1621 With two letters of the Assembly at Rochell unto the Duke de Lesdiguieres.*[31] Readers also had access to attempts to persuade La Rochelle to surrender, such as *The Last Summons, or an Oration Sent to the Inhabitants of the Towne of Rochell, To mooue them to yield the Towne vnto his Maiestie, and to obay his Commandments*, a translation of the Marquis de Berguille's speech to the town.[32]

Not all the news from France was quite so political; indeed, the pamphlet entitled *Newes from France* is perhaps indirectly intended as praise for the good governance of Paris, but it is in essence a report of a 'notable' occurrence (a fire which burned the merchants' quarter of the city), like the reports of 'notable' events in England.[33] A similar pamphlet in the style of a newsbook was published conveying news from Spain, specifically following on from the accession of Philip IV in March. *The Copy of Two Letters Sent from Spain* is a curious amalgam, in that it begins with Philip's court reforms, but ends with an account of a house in Grenada collapsing under the weight of spectators at the proclamation of the new king.[34]

Pamphlets also provided news from much further afield; there are three good examples that were published in 1621. The first is *A Letter Written by Captaine Edward Winne, to the Right Honourable, Sir George Calvert, Knight, His Maiesties Principall Secretary: From Feryland in Newfoundland.*[35] This is Wynne's account of the newly formed colony in Newfoundland, which Calvert, who was secretary of state, sent Wynne to establish in June 1621. After a brief description of an uneventful voyage, Wynne briefly outlines the advantages of the area for a colony: 'Both Sea and Land heere swarme (as it were) with benefits and blessings of God for mans vse and reliefe' (6).

Rather more craft is involved in *Algiers Voyage*, an account of a naval expedition under Sir Robert Mansel, Vice-Admiral of England, that set out in October 1620 to combat Algerian piracy. The expedition was not particularly successful and returned to England in July 1621. The author of this pamphlet, 'one that went along in the Voyage' (tp), offers the reader a monthly journal that promises a vivid account: 'Imagine (as thou readest) that thou hearest the Canon playing' (A3v). The account is quite substantial, and full of minute (and rather dull) detail, offering an almost day-by-day account of the voyage, enlivened, on occasion, by descriptions of combat.

The third example of this form of news is focused upon a single naval encounter. The title-page offers a good summary of the contents: *A True Relation of a Wonderfull Sea Fight between two great and well appointed*

*Spanish ships or Men of Warre and A small and not very well provided English ship, who was constrained to enter into this conflict at the Iland of Dominico in her passage to Virginia, as shee was determined to take in fresh water there.*[36] In this work the style is the standard plain and factual English found in so many of the voyage narratives of the period, but the description of the sea battle is quite passionate: 'O the ambition and turbulency of mens natures, and the ill condition of reuenge, that cannot be contented with faire satisfaction, vnlesse it be answered with death and blood' (C2v).

## News from parliament

The very existence of a parliament in 1621 meant that the constant appetite for information had a source that participated in both the generation and dissemination of news. Parliamentary news was a significant part of the manuscript newsletters that circulated at the time. Harold Love notes that reports of parliamentary proceedings were a key element in the publication of manuscript 'separates', which were sold as newsletters to clients around the country.[37] Those who had the money to spend could read quite detailed accounts of parliamentary speeches and motions, some of which also appeared as printed pamphlets. A great deal of information about parliament stems from the diaries kept by individual members. The editors of *Commons Debates 1621* found ten surviving private journals, as well as official notes of parliamentary proceedings. Clearly a number of these journals were not just private compilations by an MP for his own use, but rather they circulated in manuscript: two good examples are the anonymous diary labelled 'X' by the editors, which exists in at least five versions, and the diary of John Pym, which also exists in a number of copies.[38] The diary of John Pym has particular significance for parliamentary historians, given his later political career: 1621 was his first parliament, and his diary is detailed and highly organised, though the editors note that he had an eye only for argument and was not interested in the 'racy idiom and interesting expressions of the speakers'.[39] The diaries vary greatly, from the detail of Pym's or the diary of Sir Thomas Barrington, which each take up an entire volume of the *Commons Debates 1621* series, to brief and partial notes and memoranda that were much more restricted and probably for private use (such as that of the antiquarian John Smyth).[40]

The parliament of 1621 initially focused public interest on a number of issues unconnected with the religious conflict in Europe.[41] In a period of considerable economic hardship, the issue of patents and monopolies loomed large in the first session.[42] These served to focus a large amount of general discontent with the perceived inequities brought about by the favouritism and exploitation generated by the parcelling up of economic opportunities as a reward. The Commons' attention was, in February, focused most strongly on Sir Giles Mompesson, who held the patent for inns. The associated patent for ale-houses was also considered – a potentially dangerous move given that it involved Buckingham's younger brother Kit Villiers. Led on by Edward Coke, the House of Commons decided to revive the judicial function of the House of Lords and send Mompesson (who was a member of the Commons) to the Lords for trial, a process that was then used in the impeachment of Francis Bacon.[43] The proceedings against the monopolists generated enormous public interest which is reflected in a variety of news sources that connect to the parliamentary proceedings. These even include a ballad: *The Description of Giles Mompesson late knight censured by Parliament*, in which Mompesson is made to lament his activities: 'Woe worthe the time when first on Innes I thought / Those Monopolies cursed bee with shame, / Which have my reputation thus made lame'.[44]

John Chamberlain followed parliament's pursuit of these issues closely, and wrote detailed accounts to Dudley Carleton. Initially, Chamberlain thought that Mompesson might escape censure: 'he makes such humble submission, and promises such service in discoverie of secrets in case he may find favor, that yt is likely he may scape better cheape then Justice Michell, who on Friday had his patent of alehouses taken from him and was sent to the Towre on foot'.[45] By 10 March, Chamberlain realised which way the wind was blowing: 'Touching the parliament they are very busie about Sir Giles Mompesson and the rest of that crue, in which number they are willing to spare none no not Sir Edward Villers, nor the refferrees be they never so great'.[46] The referees were those who approved the patents, and they included Bacon as Attorney General (despite the fact that Bacon was advising on what became a Bill against monopolies and had certainly suggested that many patents were contrary to accepted practice).[47] Chamberlain describes the pursuit of Mompesson, who fled and ended up in exile in France. People could also follow this process in the published proclamations issued by the King; this began on 3 March with *A Proclamation for the finding out and apprehending of Sir Giles Mompesson Knight*, and was followed on 30 March by *A Proclamation for the Banishing of Giles Mompesson*.[48] A proclamation repealing the patents for inns, ale-houses and the manufacture of gold and silver thread was also printed on 30 March (the gold and silver thread monopoly was controlled by Buckingham's older brother Edward Villiers); in repealing the patents, this proclamation offers a particularly apologetic account of how James was unaware of the abuses that had occurred:

> By the fraud and abuse of some persons, who with much confidence and assurance undertooke to his Majesty, to manage and execute the said Patents, Proclamations, and Commissions, for his majesties honour, and the good of the Publike; the same have beene perverted, to the disturbance of the Justice of the realme, affront to Justices of Assise, and Justices of the Peace, and to the great damage, hurt, and oppression of many of his Majesties Subjects; which abuses were altogether unknowne to his most Excellent Majestie, untill they were discovered by the complaint of the Commons in this present Parliament which (had they sooner come to his majesties knowledge) he would have punished with all severitie. (504)

This proclamation is an interesting example of how far James was prepared to justify his actions, and it would certainly have provided extra information for those who followed the proceedings in parliament through the various sources of knowledge that were available. I have noted in Chapter 1 how Chamberlain interpreted the renewal of the 1620 proclamation against 'excesse of lavish and licentious speech of matters of State', which was a clear response to the way that issues over the Palatine were being discussed throughout the country.[49] Again, in this proclamation James was responding to the way that news, its dissemination and analysis, was rife and was potentially undermining his authority.

As the case against the patent holders was followed by the case against Bacon, so Chamberlain wrote in detail about Bacon's isolation and precarious situation: 'Many indignities are said and don against him, and divers libells cast abroad to his disgrace not worth the repeating as savoring of too much malice and scurrilitie: God send him patience and that he may make the best use of his affliction' (356). Chamberlain also offered Carleton a detailed account of the way that Buckingham rode out the threat against him, which centred on the trial by the Lords of Sir Henry Yelverton, the former Attorney who had been ordered by Buckingham to enforce the patents for gold and silver thread and for inns. Yelverton was prepared to point the finger directly at Buckingham, at one point comparing him to Edward II's favourite Hugh Spencer. James made his support for Buckingham clear and Yelverton was disgraced; Chamberlain again astutely noted how the course of the proceedings actually made Buckingham's position even stronger: 'Thus we see that great men weakly opposed, thereby become the stronger, and yt is no small comfort to him and his (as he professes) that he is found parlement proofe' (374).

When parliament resumed on 20 November, relations with James (who was in Newmarket) broke down over the whole issue of foreign policy. In the belief that the King was asking for a direct statement (and money) supporting war against Spain (as opposed to the complex conciliation efforts James was actually pursuing), the House of Commons infuriated him by sending him a petition which not only supported war, but opposed any further negotiations for a Spanish match for Prince Charles. James was so angry that he sent a furious letter of remonstrance to the speaker before the petition even reached him. The confrontation continued as King and Commons moved into a bitter argument over privileges and freedom of speech.[50] The Commons attempted to be placatory, but stuck at the defence of their 'ancient Liberty of Parliament for freedom of Speech'.[51] This stand-off culminated in the Commons' Protestation, affirming their rights and privileges. While the dissolution of parliament would mean that James was unable to secure supply, and therefore would not be able to threaten Spain with possible war, he was unable to countenance such opposition; accordingly, Coke was imprisoned, James summoned the clerk of Commons, tore the Protestation out of the Commons Journal, and dissolved parliament.[52]

While the King's proclamations were published and therefore offered some limited sense of how the Crown was responding to events in parliament, parliamentary petitions were also published, and they offered some sense of how parliament was being approached on a variety of issues. There were a number of petitions generated by the abuses of patents, and their publication would certainly have fuelled the general controversy over patents and monopolies; for example, there were petitions against the patent for lighthouses in Dungeness and Winterton; petitions from bookbinders over the import of gold leaf.[53] In some instances the petitions were responses to parliamentary bills: for example, a petition from dyers against the bill which was intended to stamp out abuses in their trade.[54] Some bills were also published, and in some instances commentaries on the bills appeared; for example, *The Contents of the Water-mans Bill* is an argument against a bill which attempted to regulate and control the activities of the watermen, who plied the Thames as a taxi service.[55] A complex quarrel between Sir Francis Englefield and Sir Henry Montagu, the Lord High Treasurer, over Montagu's management of his estates being held in trust in order to provide dowers for his daughters, led to parliamentary bills and answers to them being published, presumably because Montagu was a figure of intense interest, given that he was in danger of being impeached alongside Francis Bacon because of his role as referee for monopolies, and the case in question was a chancery case that involved bribery.[56]

Ironically, the only published speech from the 1621 parliament is a fake. Two editions appeared of *A Speech Made in the Lower House of Parliament, Anno. 1621 By Sir Edward Cicill, Colonell*.[57] Sir Edward Cecil was certainly a member of the parliament and was a strong supporter of intervention on behalf of Frederick and Elizabeth. He had originally been appointed to lead the troops which Sir Horace Vere commanded. The speech published as his is a rousing call to battle: 'The defence of Religion, and the safetie of the Land, are the things in danger' (A2). The speaker condemns the ambitions of the Pope, of Spain, and the House of Austria, quickly sums up the danger to the Protestants in Europe (including the Huguenots), and warns against the dangers of English Catholics, who undermine the security of the state. The speech concludes by calling for a subsidy and for an immediate army to reclaim the Palatine. Cecil would certainly concur with all the arguments in the speech attributed to him; he is recorded as seconding Sir James Perrot's call to parliament to be ready to go to war for the Palatine with the statement that 'this Declaration is come from Heaven'.[58] However, there is no record of Cecil ever making such a speech, and S.R. Gardiner was forced to conclude that the published speech was most probably by the notorious Thomas Scott, whose anti-Catholic/anti-Spanish pamphlet *Vox Populi* of 1620 cleverly indicted Gondomar by purporting to reveal the Spanish ambassador's secret plans to undermine England.[59] But while this sole published example of a 1621 parliamentary speech was not made in parliament, Cecil would certainly have agreed with its sentiments (and may well have been in correspondence with Scott on the subject of the 'speech'), and many readers would have been enthusiastic about its call to arms.

## Ballads and broadsheets

The pioneering work of Margaret Spufford alerted historians to the importance of the chapbook trade in the seventeenth century.[60] Spufford traced the impressive network of chapbook distribution – a network that ensured that virtually no area in England was without access to chapbooks and ballads. This material offers some insight into the cultural milieu of those far down the social scale from the consumers of news discussed thus far. Spufford notes that she set out to 'establish the nature of the world of imagination, fiction and fantasy opened to the unlettered reader of the seventeenth century, who had 2*d* or 3*d* to spend'.[61] In the case of ballads, and other genres as well, the audience stretched well beyond those who could read or purchase chapbooks: there was an audience of hearers that would have been much larger than the readers and singers who entertained them. And while 'fiction and fantasy' are important elements in this material, news was also conveyed to the most humble of listeners through the chapbook and ballad.

In her detailed study of religious chapbook material, Tessa Watt notes the enormous number of ballads in circulation in early modern England; she estimates that there may have been three or four million in the late sixteenth century, and probably more by the seventeenth century.[62] Contemporary comments indicate that the use of the ballad to convey news was well recognised; for example, Henry Peacham notes in 1641 that 'For a peny you may have all the Newes in England, of Murders, Flouds, Witches, Fires, Tempests, and what not, in one of Martin Parkers Ballads'.[63]

There are two 1621 ballads extant which clearly have 'news' as a significant component. The first signals the fashionable reference to news in its title: *The Post of Ware: With a packet full of Strange Newes out of Diverse Countries.* Hyder Rollins explains that a post boy (who would be engaged in spreading news) would arrive at Ware as the first significant stage in a journey North from London.[64] This ballad is broadly satirical, and indeed could be seen as making fun of the passion for news; it works through a series of paradoxical, 'world upside-down' images, including 'All Cittizens Wiues / Are grown constant and sound', and the idea that Spain is grown so rich that Spinola will recall his troops from Bohemia and march home. All the news relayed by the post boy is of this comic kind:

> By Merchants rich is giuen much,
> To Bankrupts newly decay'd,
> The Merchants store, shall help the poore,
> That want, to set vp their Trade;
> From *Lud-gate* stones none shal heare mones
> Which haue so long beene made;
> The Usurers, fiue

> In the hundred will take,
> Promoters all shall Soldiers make,
> And Whores are turnd honest,
> For conscience sake. (143)

This ballad seems to smile at the passion for 'strange news', while at the same time offering a satirical perspective on the theme of the country going to the bad. The concluding verse promises that those who come to London especially to 'peruse' the topsy-turvy state of affairs outlined in the body of the ballad will find all to be true 'betwixt this and Doomes-day'.

A more serious response to political news is exemplified by a ballad responding to the downfall of Sir Francis Mitchell, who was condemned by parliament along with Mompesson for the gold and silver thread monopoly. Entitled 'The Deserved Downfall of a Corrupted Conscience', this ballad details the humiliating punishment meted out to Mitchell, and notes how Mitchell's crime (like all the monopolists') struck against ordinary citizens:

> By wrongs instead of right,
> Great benefits gain'd he:
> By wrested Lawes
> Much wealth he drawes
> From many a poore mans state,
> For which it seem'd
> He thus was deem'd
> A bribed Magistrate. (146)[65]

While the ballad details the stripping of Mitchell's honours, it indicates that Mitchell has brought knighthood itself into question (a common criticism at the time, especially given the general condemnation of knighthood as a degraded honour that could be bought cheaply under James's reign): 'see / in what degree / Degraded Knighthood lies'. The final stanza offers a general criticism of 'this plague of pence, / That stood with open hand', indicating that the tone taken by Wither in his satirical account of the ills of society reached downwards to the audience for popular ballads.[66]

Ballads also expressed popular support for the Protestant cause; a good example is *Gallants to Bohemia, or, Let Us to the warres again*, which is dated *circa* 1620 by the STC, but would certainly still be in circulation in 1621 and would have appealed to patriotic sentiments.[67]

But a great many ballads, rather than purveyors of news, were either pure entertainment, or didactic. A sample of ballads dated by the STC around 1620 (and therefore almost certainly available in 1621) illustrates the typical series of ballad subjects: *Good Sir You Wrong Your Britches* (a mildly bawdy courting song); *A Merry ballad of a rich maid that had 18 severall suitors* (each suitor is of a different nationality, allowing for a series of stock satirical comments); *Anything for a Quiet Life or the Married mans Bondage* (stock satire on a shrewish wife); *The two Leicestershire Lovers* (another wooing ballad); *A Pleasant ditty, of a maidens vow, that fain would marry, and yet knew not how* (a warning against the wiles of young men); *Master Basse his careere or the New Hunting of the Hare* (a fairly literary hunting ballad); *A Caveat or Warning for all sorts of men both young and olde, to avoid the company of lewd and wicked Woemen* (didactic, with the chorus line 'take heed trust not a whore'); and *The second part of Barrow-Faustus Dreame* (no extant first part, this is a dream of the judgement meted out to an uncaring, rich Lord).

The other popular form that conveyed news and was carried by the chapmen who hawked ballads was the small book retailing sensational news of one kind or another: murders, unnatural wonders, witch trials, natural phenomena, and so on. A third edition of an account of a notorious witch trial, which took place in 1618, was published in 1621: *The Wonderful discouerie of the witchcrafts of Margaret and Phillip Flower, daughters of Ioane Flower, by Beuer-Castle, and executed at Lincolne, the 11. Of March, 1618.*[68] This case involved Buckingham's future father-in-law, the Earl of Rutland. Joan Flower and her daughters Margaret and Philip worked as charwomen in the Rutland castle of Belvoir, but were dismissed, initially because of Margaret's 'undecencies both in her life and neglect of her business' (B4v). Suspicion fell upon the three women some years later, after the death of the Earl's younger son Francis, which followed some years after the death of his elder son Henry – the Earl's daughter Katherine, Buckingham's future wife, was also ill at this time. The women were examined at Lincoln, where Joan died before trial under circumstances that, according to the account, seemed to prove her to be a witch: she 'called for bread and butter and wished it might never go through her if she were guilty of that whereupon she was examined; so mumbling it in her mouth, never spake more words after, but fell down and died' (C1v). During the examinations, various women testified that they saw the Flowers practising witchcraft, giving suck to familiars and casting spells against the Earl's children. Margaret and Philip then confessed – the witchcraft in part involved Margaret's delivery of Henry's glove to her mother who 'buried it in the yard, wishing the Lord Roos might never thrive; and so her sister Margaret continued with her other, where she often saw the cat Rutterkin leap on her shoulder and suck her neck' (D1). Margaret and Philip were hanged.

The case of the Flower witches attracted considerable attention, mainly owing to the involvement of what was probably the wealthiest family in England. While this alone accounts for the popularity of the pamphlet retailing the events and examinations, a reprint in 1621 may well have been stimulated by the family connection with Buckingham, especially given that the witches succeeded in making Katherine Manners (who was the Earl's daughter by his first wife, Frances Knevet) the Earl's sole heir.

The account of a murder, especially in the form of autobiographical confession, was also a popular form, and it is a mode allied quite directly with the conveyance of news. Nathaniel Butter, the printer associated with corantos discussed above, published *The Life, Confession and Heartie Repentance of Francis Cartwright, Gentleman, For his bloodie sinne in killing of one Master Storr, Master of Arts, and Minister of Market Rason in Lincolnshire.* This narrative is rather like a spiritual autobiography, in so far as Cartwright sees the hand of God in his story (which includes not one but two murders), and concludes his narrative with a profession of his religious faith and adherence to the Church of England. Cartwright's succinct life story is full of vivid details, and it resembles the kind of repentance narrative produced by condemned criminals before their execution, except that Cartwright escaped punishment for his two acts (the first, the murder of Storr, was in anger, the second was provoked by the victim).

## Almanacs

The range of information conveyed in the ballads and pamphlets is matched by their ability to pitch to a market hungry for news, but equally hungry for entertainment. The final form I want to consider here was extremely popular, but it has to be placed somewhere between popular news and the category considered in detail in the next chapter: didactic writing. Keith Thomas has described the almanac as 'the most widespread form of fugitive literature in early modern England'.[69] By 1621 the almanac had reached a set form: it generally contained the year's astronomical events, a calendar which set out church festivals, and a 'prognostication' predicting the year's major events. A great variety of miscellaneous information also appeared in many different forms; usually medical, including a figure of an anatomical man, showing the influence of the zodiac over the zones of the human body; sometimes legal, such as tables showing the correct language to use in drawing a will; timetables for fairs and markets; road distances, and so on, and often a series of blank pages designed for use as a factual diary.[70] The almanac, as Bernard Capp points out, 'was successful because it filled a wide variety of roles, cheaply and concisely'.[71] Almanacs had an extraordinarily large circulation; by 1621, most almanacs would have cost around 2d or 3d and the print-run for an almanac could be as high as 12,000.[72] While exact circulation figures are difficult to determine for the early seventeenth century, it has been estimated that in the Restoration, one family in three was buying an almanac annually, and in the early seventeenth century the distribution, while perhaps not quite as great, may well have approached one family in four.[73]

Thirteen almanacs have survived from 1621 and they represent the range of authors and works in circulation at the time. Richard Allstree, for example, published almanacs from 1617 to 1643 – his 1621 almanac was (like many others he produced) prepared for Derby, but, as the title-page noted, 'may serue generally, for the most part of Great-Brittaine'. Other well-known authors who delivered almanacs for 1621 were John Johnson, Jeffrey Neve and Daniel Browne.

Browne's almanac may serve as a detailed example here. It begins with a tide table, then has a table and explanation of the four law terms (Hilary, Easter, Trinity and Michaelmas), a table showing the dates of moveable feasts integrated with a table showing eclipses and planetary movements. Then Browne has the illustration of the anatomical man – this illustration, which ascribes planetary influences to the various parts of the body (e.g. Taurus to the neck and throat), has a very long history stretching back to classical times.[74] Then Browne begins the almanac proper, each month set out on a double page, headed by a summary of advice and *bons mots* (so January's summary begins 'Now warme meats, warme clothes, with warme exercise embrace. Drowsinesse and venery, bathes and phlebotomy abandon'). On the left-hand page the month is divided into days, with the astrological details set out. The right-hand page has space to allow the owner to make brief diary entries (a number of examples are extant which show typical entries, which might range from comments on the weather to political observations).[75] Browne's prognostication begins with a separate title-page. The preface to the reader attacks the influence of Jesuits and Catholics, 'traitors, that would haue wrought the ouerthrow of King and Countrey' (B2v). This anti-Catholic preface could be seen as a forerunner of the increasingly political nature of the almanac during the civil war, when prognostications

*Figure 5*  Anatomical man from Daniel Browne, *Almanac* (1621), British Library, P.P. 2465.

in particular became extremely partisan.[76] (Browne's almanac is unique, in that this veiled piece of political comment is the only example of anything that could even faintly be construed as political to be contained in a 1621 almanac.) The actual quarterly prognostications which follow are very general in nature, largely confined to meteorological and medical predictions ('Sicknesses of the Summer season, are continuall feuers, burning feuers, vomits, watering eyes, paines of the eares, blisters, and sores of the mouth', B4), as was typical during this earlier period, when the publication of almanacs was under the strict control of the Stationers' Company and the almanacs themselves were subject to censorship.

The buyer of a 1621 almanac did have a certain amount of choice. For example, Jeffrey Neve offers very detailed husbandry notes on a month by month basis: advice for January includes 'Take away the Mosse and superfluous branches from your trees, & this month it is good to set Beanes, pease, parsneps, Radish, Leekes, Garlike, Turneps, and Onions, if the weather be mild, and the moone past her ful'.[77] Similarly detailed advice on husbandry is offered by John Johnson, but with the added attraction of the advice being delivered in verse:

> Cold *Ianuary* wils prepare
> Yee things that fit the season,
> Then cloth and fuell is a iewell
> Esteemed by men of reason:
> Cut downe your timber now, or December
> Last quarter of the Moone.
> Rouncifall pease sowe if you please,
> And Beanes, tis not too soone.[78]

The 'packaging' of the information contained in almanacs was clearly important, given that they all worked from similar premises and supplied similar kinds of advice. While the calendar sections are a significant feature of all the 1621 almanacs, some present each month as scientifically and factually as possible (such as Browne, who heads each month with factual information about what is best for one's health in that month), some offer poetic aphorisms of a moral/instructive nature; to take a random example, John White for March: 'Grosse meates doe hurt, vse foode that's fine, / Let blood, and take some Medicine'.[79] Some writers frame their practical information with reasonably detailed accounts of astrology as a scientific system.[80] While some almanacs were directed towards readers from a particular town (such as Gilden's for Shipston upon Stour), most purchasers would have been able to choose an almanac tailored at least to some degree to their particular interests and needs. The almanac was a handbook and a book of advice; part of its appeal would surely have been a sense that the owner was to some extent less subject to the vagaries of natural events because the almanac both predicted the 'natural' course of the coming year and offered remedies and information to combat ills and uncertainties. The almanac satisfied a need for information that permeated all levels of early modern society; this need is evident when one considers all the forms of news dissemination available in 1621 and outlined in this chapter. The line between information and instruction was a very fine one, and didactic writing of various kinds served some of the same purposes as the modes outlined here. There is, however, a clear distinction between the desire for news that is immediate and related to present-day concerns, and the at least purportedly timeless moral weight that lies behind much didactic writing during this period, the details of which are considered in the next chapter.

# 7
# Instruction

'it hath given life to our understanding'

Walter Ralegh

## Religion

If we use the word 'didactic' in its broadest context, then a very substantial amount of early modern writing falls into that category. This is particularly the case with religious writing, which makes up the bulk of all published and unpublished writing in 1621, as it does for the early modern period as a whole. While sermons have already been considered at length in Chapter 2 as political (and personal) documents, sermons, along with catechisms, meditations, prayerbooks and theological commentaries, were principally marketed as forms of religious instruction, with particular versions of these genres aimed at a wide variety of social groups. Historians remain divided over the whole issue of religion in Jacobean society. This is particularly the case in relation to what was once called Puritanism, but is now seen as a variety of religious positions, both within and outside of the established Church. At present, there is some agreement that, at least in the period under consideration here, there was room within the Church for a variety of doctrinal and ceremonial positions.[1] However, tensions existed between various positions that might be taken on anything from the doctrine of predestination to the significance of baptism. Anthony Milton cites the Venetian ambassador's view in 1616 that there were twelve different religious parties in England, including 'four of the religion of his Majesty'![2] All the religious writing of 1621 positioned itself, implicitly or explicitly, in relation to a series of ongoing controversies, and didactic material that might seem bland to the modern reader could be quite inflammatory when it was first written. This is especially the case if we take into account the large amount of Catholic and anti-Catholic writing published and/or circulated in Britain.[3]

Sermons circulated for many reasons: because they allowed an eager audience access to a popular preacher; because they satisfied the vanity of a preacher, popular or unpopular; because even in 1621 many more remote areas of Britain did not have access to a clergyman who could deliver a sermon.[4] I have already discussed at some length in Chapter 2 the variety of forms taken by sermons, which ranged from the highly abstruse and literary to the declamatory and polemical. The other forms of religious writing addressed an equally diverse audience, and ranged from massive and complex works of theology to catechisms and explanatory works about doctrine, right down to the most popular kinds of religious writing, described in Tessa Watt's careful study of 'the dissemination of Protestant ideas' through chapbooks, ballads and woodcuts.[5] Every area of life was addressed by religious writers, and most particularly the rites of passage recently studied in great detail by David Cressy, who stresses the significance of ritual (often by no means only religious), and points out that 'Despite the adoption of protestantism, with its denial of sacramental efficacy, the spiritual and social drama of the life cycle remained freighted with religious meaning and graced with elaborate ceremony', and that 'these ceremonies were politicised'.[6]

## The sermon as instruction

No sermon can be seen as entirely free from the kinds of political and religious controversies outlined in my earlier discussion of sermons in Chapter 2, even those that were clearly directed towards a general didactic purpose and tried to remain unchallengingly constrained by the boundaries of particular doctrines within the established Church. A good representative example is Robert Lovell's *Two Soveraigne Salves for the Souls Sicknesse*. This is the text of a sermon preached by Lovell when he was a minister at Hurstchurch in Berkshire, but at the time of publication he was at St Michael's, Crooked Lane, London.[7] The text for the sermon is John 5.14: 'Behold, thou art made whole, Sinne no more: lest a worse thing come unto thee'. In essence, Lovell argues the case for Christ as healer, 'that good Physitian of the soule' (1).[8] The sermon as a whole takes the comforting position that the fight against sin is able to be won, given the right armour and weapons.

While Lovell keeps to generalities, his position on sin would offend few readers. But then he comes to the specific charge of 'Sabbath-breaking' (20), and enters a contentious area. Lovell exclaims that this practice 'is but the *Citties day of Dalliance and delight, Pride and Gluttonie*; and the *Country-mans Leisure day*, wherein if they should not *Recreate* themselues in *Dauncing, Dicing, Drinking*, and such like *Deuillish pastimes*, they would think themselues much wrong'd' (20). This brings Lovell's sermon into alignment with attacks on the abuse of the Sabbath that were a challenge to King James's defence of traditional Sabbath games and leisure activities, recently affirmed (in 1618) in the 'Book of Sports'. In this declaration, which was entitled *The Kings Maiesties Declaration to his Subjects, concerning lawfull sports to be vsed*, James reaffirmed his long-standing belief in traditional sports and pastimes practised on certain holidays, but also on Sundays:

> Our pleasure likewise is, That after the end of Diuine Seruice, Our good people be not disturbed, letted, or discouraged from any lawfull Rec-reation; Such as dauncing, either men or women, Archery for men, leaping, vaulting, or any other such harmelesse Recreation, nor from hauing of May-Games, Whitson Ales, and Morrisdances, and the setting vp of Maypoles and other sports therewith vsed, so as the same be had in due and conuenient time, without impediment or neglect of diuine Seruice.[9]

The declaration gave rise to considerable controversy, given the intense opposition that had been expressed by various 'Puritan' writers to such forms of entertainment – opposition that extended into such areas as the attack on the theatre that lasted from Elizabeth's reign through to James's and Charles's. Christopher Hill's important account of Sabba-tarianism in the early modern period examines the Puritan stress on Sunday as 'the day for edification', a concept that gathered momentum in the 1590s, though it had its roots in earlier Reformation arguments.[10] James's Declaration became a key political test upon its reissue by Charles in 1633, when ministers were asked to read it in church, and a number of those who refused to do so were suspended.[11]

In 1621, James's Declaration was potentially divisive, part of that divisiveness being exacerbated by debates over the parliamentary bill for the Sabbath (a bill described by Robert Zaller as 'perennial', given that one was first introduced in the 1584 parliament).[12] The bill was denounced by Thomas Shepherd for its defiance of the Book of Sports and Shepherd was expelled for his pains.[13] The bill was one of many that Edward Coke steered through the House of Commons; it was then criticised in the House of Lords for the use of the word 'Sabbath', because that word potentially appealed to those who favoured adopting the Jewish sabbath day. The apocalyptic implications of this move were emphasised in the prosecution in 1618 of John Traske, who maintained that the Jewish sabbath should be observed.[14] In 1621 the lawyer John Finch was imprisoned for publishing *The Worlds Great Restauration or the calling of the Jews*, an apocalyptic text which offered some inflammatory comments on the actions of God's justice in 'tumbling down the enemies of God's people, notwithstanding all their might'. Finch's book and the controversy over the Sabbath bill undoubtedly provoked William Laud into a sermon preached in June before the King on Psalm 122, in which Laud argued strongly for the necessity to recognise the intertwining of Church and State and, in a move which would have especially appealed to James, he stresses the need for peace and the King's authority over peace and war, and then moves on to attack those who see millennarian possibilities which involve the rebuilding of Jerusalem and the reassembling of the Jews: 'doe you not thinke the Papists will triumph, that such monstrous opinions are hatched among vs?'[15]

In this context, Robert Lovell's sermon becomes increasingly controversial, despite its apparently bland and simple didactic tone. Towards the end of the sermon, Lovell becomes much more explicit in his attack on Sabbath-breakers, 'who would out face all goodnesse and commit all euill (and that *By Booke*:)'(35). One can only assume that 'By Booke' glances at the Book of Sports, as Lovell goes on to condemn some of James's allowed pastimes: 'God is certainly yet much dishonoured among vs in this place, by our *Cardings and Kittleings, by our Dancings and Daliances, by our seruants Idlenes, and Childrens Vanities*, which they vse on Gods holy day, and therefore I pray you in Christs stead, let your hands be against such in a heauier manner then formerly they haue beene' (35). Lovell may not have been a polemical preacher like Samuel Ward, whom I used as an example in Chapter 2 and who was also a Sabbatarian (see above, pp. 54–8), but his sermon indicates that no didactic writing could rely on being seen as 'neutral' moral instruction.

### Religious guides

The issue of Sabbatarianism can be traced through to a leading example of a second popular form of religious writing: the guide to conduct. Guides to achieving a proper Christian life were extremely popular and came in a variety of forms. In 1621 Lewis Bayly, Bishop of Bangor, published the thirteenth edition of his spiritual guide, *The Practise of Piety*. Bayly's volume is subtitled 'Directing a Christian how to walke that he may please God'. The first edition is not extant, but it was dedicated to Prince Henry (Bayly was Henry's chaplain) and its popularity grew rapidly:

it reached something approaching fifty-nine editions by the early eighteenth century and was, during the seventeenth, translated into numerous languages, including French, German and Polish and even, in 1665, into that of the Indians in the Cambridge, Massachusetts area. As the dedication to Prince Henry indicates, Bayly had Puritan leanings and this is reflected in various ways in *The Practice of Piety*. In contrast to his book's advocacy of restraint and moral uprightness, the Bishop's own conduct was often extremely provocative. In 1621 Bayly was called before the Privy Council and censured over a conflict with his Dean, and he was also in trouble over the way he favoured the Wynn family in the parliamentary elections.[16] In the area of Sabbatarianism, chapter 17 of *The Practise of Piety* offers a strong argument 'that the fourth commandment is perpetual and morall vnder the new Testament'. Bayly overstepped the mark in defending his position in 1621, as reported by John Chamberlain: 'Dr. Baylie bishop of Bangor was committed to the Fleet for disputing (they say) somwhat malapertly with the King about the Sabbath'.[17]

As a whole, *The Practise of Piety* offers a spiritual guide which speaks directly to its reader:

> *Who-euer* thou art that lookest into this *Booke*, neuer vndertake to read it; vnlesse thou first resoluest to become from thy heart, an vnfained *Practitioner* of *Piety*. Yet reade it, and that *speedily*, lest before thou shalt read it ouer, *God* (by some vnexpected death) cut thee off, for thine inueterate *Impiety*. (1)

Bayly's style was clearly an important part of the appeal of his book, an appeal testified to by John Bunyan's account in *Grace Abounding* of his encounter with it:

> Presently after this, I changed my condition into a married state; and my mercy was, to light upon a Wife whose Father was counted godly: this Woman and I, though we came together as poor as poor might be, (not having so much as a Dish or Spoon betwixt us both) yet this she had for her part, *The Plain Mans Path-way to Heaven*, and *The Practice of Piety*, which her Father had left her when he died. In these two Books I should sometimes read with her, wherein I also found some things that were somewhat pleasing to me: (but all this while I met with no conviction.)[18]

*The Practise of Piety* takes the reader through a description of God's qualities, a series of meditations and instructions for daily prayers, prayers for the Sabbath, advice about holy communion and general advice about absolution, death and the nature of the soul. This structure was common to such books, which offered the comfort of firm advice and the consolation of set prayers, meditations and summations of theology. That *The Practise of Piety* was so much more popular than many of its rivals clearly owes something to the appeal of Bayly's Puritan precepts for a particular (and growing) seventeenth-century audience, but even more to the clarity of his style.

The theological stance of Bayly's book can be compared to an interesting example of a guide specifically designed to offer a moderate account of reformed English church doctrine, which might help to bring recusants over from the Church of Rome: *A Booke of Christian Exercise*. This is an adaptation by Edmund Bunny of a Roman Catholic religious guide written by the Jesuit Robert Parsons. First published in 1584, Bunny's adaptation was in its tenth edition by 1621.[19] *A Booke of Christian Exercise* is written more as a point-by-point account of doctrine than as a manual for religious practice, but its purpose is similar: 'to perswade a Christian by name to become a true Christian indeed, at the least, in resolution of minde' (B4).[20] The rhetoric is much stronger than Bayly's, in so far as the book is partly designed to lead waverers into a Christian life:

> walke on thy carelesse life as quietly as before: what hope (I beseech thee) may there be conceiued of thy saluation? Wilt thou goe to heauen, liuing as thy doest? It is impossible. As soone thou maist driue God out of heauen, as get thither thy selfe in this kind of life: What then? Wilt thou forgoe heauen, and yet escape hell too? This is lesse possible, whatsoeuer the Atheists of this world doe perswade thee. (491)

A third substantial example in this genre is Thomas Tymme's *A Silver Watchbell*, which was first published in 1609 and had its fourteenth edition in 1621. This is a firm account of the superiority of the English Church, which includes an exposition of Calvinist views on predestination.[21] The premiss of Tymme's book is that the sound of the silver watchbell should remind the reader of the inevitability of death and the necessity therefore to allow oneself to 'become a true Christian indeed' – 'if there be but the least sparke of Grace remayning in him'.[22] Tymme dedicated the 1621 edition to Edward Coke, noting in the dedication that '*Religion*, is the foundation of all well-gouerned Commonweales; of the execution of *Lawes*' (A3v). Given Coke's role in the 1621 parliament, notably his early speech denouncing Catholics, Tymme's book was well calculated to appeal to him.[23] In chapter 12, Tymme attacks papists vigorously and, in another move that would have appealed to many opposing James's policy of appeasement in 1621, he harks back to the age of Elizabeth:

> in the beginning of Queene Elizabeths most happy raigne, wee all, as men almost hunger-starued for lack of the spirituall food of GODS Word, the Manna of our Soule, were right glad on what occasion, or from what manner, of person soeuer we might hear that Angelical tidings (as it were from heauen) of our saluation in Christ, & of our iustification throw faith in him: Yea, how ioyfull were we then to hear GOD serued in our vulgar tongue: but now either through negligence or lazinesse, we sit at home: or if we come to Church, it is either to heare newes, or eloquent phrases from the Preacher, or to undermine and intrap him, or peraduenture fetch a nap or two, or to meet a friend, etc. (220)

*A Silver Watchbell* begins, like *A Booke of Christian Exercise*, by reminding the reader of 'the shortnesse, frailty, and miseries of mans life' and calling for repentance. But Tymme, in chapter 5, offers a firm argument for the limited number of the elect and against any meliorist attempts to ease the possibility of personal salvation. He also appends a treatise titled 'The Court of Conscience', which instructs the reader how to approach the sacrament of communion, and ends the book with a short series of prayers.

It is perhaps worth considering, given the large number of religious guides available, how readers chose which one to purchase. It is quite clear that the specific audiences for works like the three I have considered here as representative examples would have grown, following on from the response of readers addressed by the books themselves. These books sought out readers who would agree with their basic premisses, so that, by the time Bunyan's wife brought him *The Practise of Piety* as her dowry, it would have been most unlikely that Bayly's guide would have been read by a disinterested seeker after Christian truth, as opposed to those who knew that it provided an account of religious practice acceptable to those with broadly Puritan sympathies.

These books are all substantial works (Bayly's runs to just over 800 pages), but forms of religious guidance were available in less substantial and even more easily accessible genres. A good example is James Warre's *The Touchstone of Truth*. This book is a set of tables setting out principal points of doctrine and texts supporting them that can be found in the

Old and New Testaments. Warre's essential purpose is anti-Catholic, and the book is designed as a guide for those 'of meane capacity' who needed to be able to refute the arguments of Papists. Anthony Milton notes Warre's book as part of the move 'to protect the vulnerable laiety from Romanist proselytizers'.[24] It accordingly covers such topics as purgatory, prayers for the dead, and so on, in a very easily digested form (although one which still depends upon an ability to read the Bible).

For those who were not literate, the final form to be considered in this category was, at least potentially, a powerful conduit for religious doctrine: the catechism. The 'authorised' catechism that was part of the Book of Common Prayer was extremely brief in comparison to the catechisms of the European reformed churches, lacking as it did, for example, any reference to preparation for communion. A large number of catechisms were published to fill the gap, many for private household use, as well as ones intended to be used by clergymen.[25] Patrick Collinson notes how 'catechisms were well adjusted to an oral, at best semi-literate, culture', and catechising was a powerful way to reach those who might not have fully accepted the shift to a Protestant religion that stressed words, not images.[26] There were numerous sixteenth-century catechisms which remained popular in the seventeenth century, but there was also an increase in number after the Bishops confirmed the importance of catechising as a pre-requisite for confirmation.[27] Catechisms reflected the same conflicts over doctrine as the more substantial religious guides. Margarita Hutchison notes that there was an increase in the number of broadly Puritan catechisms after the 1604 Hampton Court Conference, but that the 1620s were dominated by catechisms that were less challenging.[28] 1621 saw the thirty-first edition of Stephen Egerton's *Brief Method of Catechizing*, which first appeared in 1593 and remained popular well into the seventeenth century.

The two new catechisms published in 1621 are an interesting contrast, which can once again be represented by their stances in relation to the issue of the Sabbath and the Book of Sports. John Mayer's *The English Catechism* has the following exchange:

> QUESTION: Are we bound to the holy duties of God's worship all this time, without ceasing?
> ANSWER: No, for we may refresh ourselves with eating and drinking, singing and music, and with any honest delight whatsoever, whereby the mind is cheered up, and joy and gladness befitting the Lord's holy day is expressed. (C2v–C3)

John Frewen's *Certain Choise Grounds and Principles of Our Christian Religion* is dedicated to Sir Thomas Coventry, who was the King's Attorney-General, and was admired for his moderation. Frewen also addresses his catechism to the members of his flock, for whom he expresses a pastoral care. But he chastises those who do not take the sabbath and church-going seriously:

> So, are there many ... whose mindes and affections are so wholly set vpon the profits & pleasures of this world, as that they seem almost vtterly vncapable of the heauenly things. If they come to the Church (as sometimes they do) when the holy exercises of Religion are in hand, either they are asleepe, or so giue place to idle, and carnall cogitations, that they nothing profit by any thing spoken: but returne to their houses as carelesse and secure, as ignorant and senceless in the mysteries of saluation, as they came from thence. Nay, some of them as vaine and common swearers; as wilful prophaners of the Lords day; as malicious, as proud and couetous, as filthy talkers, as very lyers, slanderers, tale-carryers, Alehouse-haunters, and the like, as euer before. (A4v–A5)

The subjects of catechising, as opposed to the readers of catechisms, were presumed to be wholly dependent upon the catechiser, and were characteristically pictured as ignorant and in need of instruction – Frewen specifically addresses women in his preface, and catechisms were also aimed directly at children and servants. But the multiplicity of catechisms with different ideological points of view meant that the public act of catechising also had a private side, and at least at the level of the individual household, considerable choice was available for a form of religious guidance that could reflect the views of very specific groups. This more private side of an apparently public institution is even more apparent in the form of the prayer and/or meditation.

### Meditation

While, as noted above, many of the religious guides contained some prayers and occasionally a meditation, the meditation was a separate and influential genre in the seventeenth century. Meditation was recommended even to the audience for Stephen Egerton's *Brief Method of Catechizing* as a devotional practice which will 'Not only ... keep the mind free from wicked and idle thoughts, but also to fill it with some holy and profitable matter' (18). In its Protestant form, the meditation in the early seventeenth century was dominated by the theory and practice of Bishop Joseph Hall. In 1605 Hall, already known for his satirical poetry, published *Meditations and Vows, Divine and Moral*. As well as gaining Hall preferment as Prince Henry's chaplain, the *Meditations* became extremely influential, especially when they were joined in 1606 by Hall's theoretical exposition of the genre, *The Art of Divine Meditation*. As Richard McCabe points out, in his study of Hall, 'Among the more devout the practice of private contemplation became under his guidance one of the distinguishing features of the godly'.[29] By the time that Hall wrote in the genre, the meditation had become associated, by Protestants, with Roman Catholic forms of devotion.[30] Hall was able to counter this by offering a convincing example of the Protestant possibilities of the genre, stressing in particular its utility as a form that crossed between private religious contemplation and public spiritual guidance.

In *The Art of Divine Meditation*, Hall describes the form as 'nothing else but a bending of the mind upon some spirituall object, through divers formes of discourse, untill our thoughts come to an issue: and this must needs bee either Extemporall, and occasioned by outward occurrences offered to the mind; or deliberate, and wrought out of our owne heart'.[31] Accordingly, the meditation was able to take its place within the range of devotional material I have been discussing, because published meditations offered a template for private devotion. By 1621, Hall had successfully captured the genre for the English Church. Both the *Meditations* and the theoretical *Art of Divine Meditation* went through a number of editions in the early seventeenth century, but in 1621 a compendium volume was produced, which combined these two works with Hall's *Characters of Virtues and Vices*, which was first published in 1608 – the volume also included two other meditative works: *Holy Observations* (1608) and *Heaven Upon Earth* (1606).

The combination in one volume of Hall's meditative works and his *Characters* might at first seem no more than an example of the random yoking together of works by popular authors which was engaged in by many printers at the time. But Richard McCabe has offered a convincing argument that the meditative tradition also lies behind Hall's use of the Character form, a genre which Hall pioneered in English in the seventeenth century, modelling his work on Theophrastus, and which was immediately popular and much imitated. McCabe argues that Hall is able, in the Character form, to combine the two central impulses in his work: meditation and satire.[32] The 1621 combined volume neatly illustrates McCabe's thesis and testifies to the popularity of Hall's efforts in both forms.

Hall's opening meditation is a good example of his approach to the genre and it also exemplifies his profound sense of how the form of meditation enables the individual to achieve a guided spiritual connection with God:

> In meditation, those which begin Heauenly thoughts, and prosecute them not, are like those which kindle a fire vnder greene Wood, and leaue it so soone as it but begins to flame; leesing the hope of a good beginning, for want of seconding it with a sutable proceeding: When I set my selfe to meditate, I will not giue ouer, till I come to an Issue. It hath beene said by some, that the beginning is as much as the midst; yea, more then all: but I say, the ending is more then the beginning. (1–2)[33]

Hall's clipped, Senecan prose style emphasises the movement of this meditation to a firm conclusion: the reader, or imitator, is not invited to extemporise, but rather to allow him/herself to be guided to an appropriate attitude. Hall's meditations are, like the general spiritual guides, forms of religious instruction, not suggestions for the reader to invent either a theological position or a form of reflection. The arrangement of the 1621 volume means that the reader moves from the meditations themselves to the theory behind them, outlined in *The Art of Divine Meditation*. Somewhat disingenuously, Hall explains, in the original dedication to Richard Lea, that he envisages the form as uncontroversial – indeed, as a counter to controversy: 'I perceiued the number of Polemicall books rather to breede, than end strifes: and those which are doctrinall, by reason of their multitude, rather to oppresse then satisfie the Reader' (T5–T5v). I have already argued that no religious writing in 1621 could be uncontroversial, but Hall's approach to the meditation was certainly an attempt to offer the sympathetic reader a model for a moderate position, as exemplified in the third meditation of book one:

> As there is a foolish Wisedome, so there is a wise Ignorance; in not prying into Gods Arke; not inquiring into things not reuealed. I would faine know all that I need, and all that I may: I leaue Gods secrets to himselfe. It is happie for me, that God makes me of his Court, though not of his Counsell. (3)

A second 1621 compendium volume included Hall's *Contemplations*, a massive, ongoing project, begun in 1612 and not completed until 1634.

The *Contemplations* were written very much under the influence of Calvin, in that they eschewed Catholic allegorical interpretation in favour of a 'literal' reading of the text.[34] However, rather than biblical commentary, the *Contemplations* were another form of meditation, taking biblical texts as their starting point. Hall accordingly appeals to the reader's imagination and in his use of the vivid, dramatic detail inherent in the genre of meditation, he paradoxically evokes, not Calvin, but rather the Catholic meditative tradition.[35] This may be a generic effect, but Hall's didactic purpose is determinedly anti-Catholic. As a prominent objector to King James's rapprochement with Spain, Hall was quite prepared to make oblique comment, via the *Contemplations*, on the dangers of foreign wives and alien religious practices.[36]

The *Contemplations* are placed at the end of this large collection, which pretty much sums up Hall's writings as they stood in 1621. Hall retains the original dedication of the first volume of the *Contemplations* to Prince Henry, which in 1621 would clearly underline Hall's political allegiances. Hall's account of some of the work's themes would also have had added resonance in 1621: 'Both your Peace and Warre shall finde here holy and great examples' (733).[37] Hall then dedicated the second volume to Prince Charles, offering a hope that Charles, 'the heire of his Honor, and vertues' (Zzz3), might take up Henry's mantle. In his dedication of the fourteenth book to Philip Herbert, Hall offers a rather ambivalent account of his desire to leave polemical writing in favour of meditative work, such as the *Contemplations*: 'How earnestly doth my heart rather wish an universal cessation of these Armes; that all the Professors of the deare Name of Christ might bee taken vp with nothing, but holy and peaceable thoughts of Deuotion' (Fv). Hall's forthright account of the marriage of Samson to a daughter of the Philistines, with reflections on the great dangers of marrying into a foreign and antipathetic religion, would have struck readers in 1621 as being even more relevant to the Catholic marriage negotiations than readers of book ten in 1615, when it was first published.[38] In one powerful passage, Hall has Samson's parents anguish over 'the inconueniences of an vnequall yoke; corruption in religion, alienation of afections, distraction of thoughts, conniuence at Idolatry, death of zeale, dangerous underminings, and lastly, an vnholy seed' (928).

### Maternal advice

Coming somewhere in between the impersonal religious guide and the introspective meditation we find a fascinating example of the book of spiritual advice: Dorothy Leigh's *The Mother's Blessing*. This book was first published in 1616 and was in its seventh edition by 1621. The sub-title makes it plain that Leigh's book is a kind of conduct manual which moves between the private reflections of a mother left as a legacy for her children, and a public, published document presented as a template for godly parental advice: 'The godly Counsaile of a Gentlewoman, not long since deceased, left behind her for her children: Contayning many good exhortations, and godly admonitions profitable for all parents, to leaue as a legacy to their children'.[39] Throughout the book, Leigh directly addresses her three sons, telling them that her purpose is 'to see you grow in godlinesse' (A5v). But Leigh's consciousness of a public voice is emphasised by her dedication of the volume to James's daughter Elizabeth: a dedication which would have taken on added significance in 1621 following the crisis in Bohemia, especially given that Leigh's religious precepts could be described as, not exactly militant, but firmly Protestant; Lloyd Davis notes that, even in 1616, 'The princess acts as a socially elevated version of the author, whose personal advice to her sons is thus associated with a wider patriotic, protestant significance'.[40]

Leigh uses her role as a mother to overcome prescriptions against women's authorship:

> But lest you should maruaile, my children, why I doe not according to the vsuall custome of women, exhort you by words and admonitions, rather then by writing: a thing so vnusually among vs, and especially in such a time, when there bee so many Godly bookes in the World, that they mould in some mens Studies, while their Masters are mard... know therefore that it was the Motherly affection that I bare vnto you all, which made mee now (as it often hath done heretofore) forget my selfe. (3–4)

Having justified herself as a writer, Leigh goes on to, in Davis's words, make 'use of the family's institutional and figural centrality to social order to reconceive the maternal role as one that includes public utterance and work'.[41]From a religious point of view, this is reinforced by Leigh's 'reformist agenda', which includes many of the exhortations characteristic of books like *The Practise of Piety*. But Leigh sees the maternal role as intimately bound up in religious teaching; she stresses that a mother's close relationship with her children makes her desire their salvation, and one can draw this out into an explanation for her public voice: that she can exemplify the necessary link between the care she evinces and her spiritual message, which is universal. Leigh emphasises a series of commonplaces centred on reading the Bible and meditating on the word of God. The universal messages are intermingled with extremely personal addresses to her sons, such as her explanation of how she has chosen names for all the children they might have: Philip, Elizabeth, James, Anna, John and Susanna (29). She also offers advice on how her sons might choose their wives, noting especially that they should 'Loue not the vngodly' (52). Leigh's message about the importance of women both within the family and as spiritual exemplars leads quite naturally to her determination that her sons should choose only wives they will love 'to the end', and that they should be seen as a husband's 'fellow', not a drudge or servant (55). Indeed, the fundamental importance of the effect of the word of God on daily life extends to the treatment of servants, who should be taught to read the Bible if they are not already literate.

Leigh also counteracts Christian examples of women as sinners who are tainted by the example of Eve; for the godly, Eve should be seen as she who caused Christ to come to save us (35–6). This is part of her argument that a woman might lead men (who are all sons), as well as women, towards a godly life. Leigh specifies the details of this life, again in a manner reminiscent of the religious guides discussed above, noting the need for regular, private morning prayers and bible reading (she offers a short prayer as an example). Reading in particular is, for Leigh, a key to godliness:

> Reading good bookes, worketh a mans heart to godlinesse ... I will tell you what good writing of bookes doth: It makes the way to Christ easie to those that desire to goe in it. And I will tell you who are they that are angry with writing of Books: they are such as are ignorant; and the more ignorant they are, the more angry: they are those that loue the world so well, that they cannot finde leasure to read bookes. (92–3)

By implication, *The Mothers Blessing* is just such a good book.

Leigh has a forthright section on the importance of the Sabbath, stating that church should be attended both morning and afternoon and stressing the importance of a preaching minister (she expresses a desire that her sons might become just such ministers). The final sections stress the way that a godly life will manifest itself both inwardly (especially through private prayer) and outwardly, through adherence to an upright manner of living as well as due observance of religious precepts. The reader, placed in the position of Leigh's sons, is exhorted to uphold the religious precepts of Protestant faith, with *The Mothers Blessing* as something more than just an impersonal guide to conduct, but rather a maternal testament.

## Religious controversy

While guides to spiritual conduct were always potentially controversial, overt religious controversy accounts for a large number of books published in 1621, as it did in previous years. In particular, the battle between Catholic and Protestant apologists is well represented, both through new works and the reprinting of popular, earlier works. In his detailed study of English Protestant attitudes towards Catholicism in the period, Anthony Milton points out that 'anti-Papal writings...were the most distinctive feature of English Protestant theology and occupied the energies of all the principal members of the Jacobean episcopate'.[42] However, by 1621, especially under James's rapprochement with Spain, there was some tension between the aggressive anti-Catholic writing we have already seen manifested in, for example, sermons, and those who were following the King's lead and pulling back a bit, especially from 'Puritan' anti-Catholicism. We still find, in 1621, a large sample of the estimated 500 works of controversy published by Protestant and Catholic writers between 1605 and 1625.[43] The sheer variety of these works leads to some similar questions to those I have raised in relation to religious guides: were these works addressing uncommitted or wavering audiences and, in theory, winning conversions, or, rather, were they polemic aimed at an assenting reader? The fierce nature of many of these works seems to me to signal the latter explanation; despite the fact that conversions took place in both directions, most of the works of controversy would be unlikely to convince someone who wasn't already inclined to the writer's point of view.

Two representative examples of popular polemic can illustrate this and also serve to show how such polemic often works as a kind of see-saw in which one text feeds off another. In *The Reformed Protestant*, James Anderton, writing under the pseudonym of John Brerely, offers a clear, simple Catholic attack on the reformation, and in particular on Calvinist views of salvation and predestination. Given that these views were the subject of intense debate within the Church of England, the pamphlet's strong defence of free will would have been particularly provocative:

> Now how directly this [Calvin's doctrine] fighteth with the Sacred Scriptures, with the doctrine of the Primitiue Church, yea, with the goodnesse and wisedome of God, and indeed with all true and vertuous Reformation of mans life, let the sequele make good. In proofe then

of our Catholike doctrine concerning Free will, the sacred Scriptures do teach that God doth to the enabling thereof offer vs his sufficient grace, to that end. (39)[44]

Turning Anderton's title around is *The Reformed Spaniard*, a narrative of the conversion of a Spanish doctor, John de Nicholas y Sacharles, who claims that he moved to England in order to live 'under the Gouernment of the most gracious King Iames, the most powerful defender of the sincere & unpolluted faith' (D4v).[45] *The Reformed Spaniard* has the distinct advantage of being a clear and well-told narrative, beginning with Sacharles's childhood, when 'with my nurses milk I haue sucked in the corruptions of popery' (A3), and moving through his time as a novice monk. Sacharles claims that, from the time he came to 'yeares of discretion' he questioned the absurdities of Catholic doctrine and practice, but did not finally convert to the reformed church until he visited Rome and was scandalised by church corruption there. The reformed doctrine expressed in this book is moderate; the attack on Catholic doctrine is very predictable, moving through issues such as the worship of images, communion in only one kind and a subject's right to depose a ruler.

As a conversion narrative, Sacharles's book is part of a popular genre, which in 1621 included Christopher Musgrave's *Musgrave's Motives*, the full title of which conveys the book's contents: 'Musgraues Motiues and reasons for his secession and disseuering from the Church of Rome and her doctrine after that hee had for 20 yeeres liued a Carthusian monke returning at easter last into England'.[46] Dedicated to Archbishop Abbot, the book is again a simple and quite compelling narrative, outlining corrupt practices amongst the Carthusians and going over the usual criticisms of Catholic doctrine, such as the nature of the mass or the belief in purgatory.

These short, popular works of polemic can be contrasted with fiercer and more detailed arguments, of which there are numerous 1621 representatives. A good example is Alexander Cooke's *More Work for a Masse Priest*, an expanded version of *Work For a Masse Priest*, which was published in 1617. Cooke's swingeing excoriation of the priest, addressed directly and taken to task for his absurd beliefs, was clearly very popular: not only was the 1621 *More Work* an expansion of the earlier book, but it went through two impressions in 1621, another in 1622, as well as undergoing a further 1622 expansion into *Yet More Work* and a 1628 expansion into *Work, More Work, & A Little More Work*. Cooke's technique is quite simple: he itemises a series of standard criticisms of Catholic doctrine and Catholic practices: 'I reade in your bookes, that

you had one *boy Pope* of twelue yeares old, viz. *Benedict* the nineth: and
a *May-pole-morrice-dancer* Pope of 18 yeares old viz., John 12 alias 13 who
made the *Lateran* a plaine *Stewes'* (22).[47] Cooke offers careful footnoting
of his sources, and while his arguments are fairly simple, he does use
a certain amount of Latin and obviously intended to reach a moderately
educated audience.

Another good example of this kind of book is Robert Jenison's *Height
of Israel's Heathenish Idolatry.* Jenison begins by praising the godly city
fathers of Newcastle, where he was a preacher, and moves on to a detailed
attack on Catholicism's worship of idols. But as a whole, the book ranges
much more widely in its critique of Catholic doctrine. Jenison focuses
at one point on the dangers of Catholicism both for ordinary Protestants
and for Protestant rulers, claiming that Catholics advocate 'shedding
the innocent blood of harmlesse Protestants, and especially of religious
Kings . . . Hereupon they most deuilishly practise and most shamelessly,
by writing, excuse, yea warrant and giue allowance to the murthering of
Christian Kings and Princes' (60). Jenison integrates this political critique
with stories of Papal iniquity and Jesuit conspiracy.

Anthony Milton notes that criticism of Catholic idolatry is a key
component in Protestant polemic. The idea of Catholic political conspiracy, highlighted by Jenison and most other authors cited here, was
particularly provocative in 1621 when King James was trying to avoid
disputes over Catholic loyalty. As we have seen in relation to many of
the sermons discussed in Chapter 2, Protestant writers rallying support
for the Bohemian cause constantly reminded hearers and readers of the
Gunpowder Plot and the slippery Catholic response to James's Oath of
Allegiance. The controversial works discussed here were equally wedded
to a notion of the pernicious nature of Catholic doctrine and the political,
as well as religious, threat that reached from the Pope, to the Jesuits,
down to James's Catholic subjects.

As well as these relatively popular controversial works, more ambitious and scholarly (albeit still polemical) works defending English Protestantism were published and republished in large numbers. The works
of the Elizabethan Puritan divine William Perkins are a good example.
Perkins's elaborate defence of the doctrine of double predestination,
*The Golden Chain,* first published in 1591 and often reprinted, was
adapted by Robert Hill in 1612 into a question and answer format, to,
in Hill's words, 'cause it to be read with more delight' (π2v). This
version was reprinted in 1621 and it exemplified what might be called
the hard Protestant line on predestination, always a difficult topic for
the reformed churches and made even more fraught by disagreements

following the 1618/19 Synod of Dort. A work like *The Golden Chain* as read in 1621 was both a rebuttal of Catholic doctrine and a statement of a particular attitude within the Church of England.[48]

This leads on to the important fact that controversy and battles over doctrine raged within the Church of England, as well as against the Catholic Church. Most of the controversial works discussed above could be said to have an eye on disputes within the Church of England even as they attacked Papists. More overt interventions in Church disputes ranged from highly specific quarrels about ceremony through to elaborate theological disquisitions. For example, James Wats devoted an entire pamphlet to the issue of whether members of the congregation should kneel when receiving communion, arguing in favour of that ceremony against those who thought that it savoured of papist idolatry.[49] Wats's discussion is a reminder that the disputes over ceremony that reached a head under Archbishop Laud in the late 1620s and 1630s have a prehistory. Disputes over kneeling were also held with an eye on the practices of European Protestant churches, as English divines argued over uniquely English ceremonies (especially those which might seem allied to Catholic ceremonies).[50] Richard Bernard's popular manual for the instruction of clergymen, *The Faithful Shepherd*, first published in 1607, offers a moderate view of church practice but makes plain Bernard's adherence to the idea of a preaching ministry through an elaborate set of instructions about how to construct and deliver a good sermon.

More scholarly works still had to be self-conscious about their intersection with controversy within and outside of the Church. For example, Thomas Granger's *A Familiar Exposition or Commentarie on Ecclesiastes* is a careful, verse by verse exposition, which nevertheless reaches an apocalyptic note towards the end: 'Neither haue there bene so many tongue-tied Christians in times of Popery, as there shall be phantasticall babblers and deceitfull Satanists in these last times, whose words and deeds are all falsehoods and lies: yet it is but a multitude of malignants, who wil either be idolaters, or Atheists, of a false religion, or of no religion' (343).[51] Any theological work was, inevitably, a work of controversy; as Anthony Milton has cautioned:

> The more that the polemical nature of theological discourse is grasped, the more its relationship with more popular and political perceptions of religion becomes clear. Even if degrees of theological sophistication undoubtedly varied, university disputations, religious pamphlets, parliamentary debates and popular lay religion all shared a common manipulation of the symbols of orthodoxy and heterodoxy.[52]

## Providence and punishment: *The Triumphs of God's Revenge*

Religious instruction and entertainment intermingle in an astonishing way in one of the seventeenth century's most popular works of prose fiction, John Reynolds's *The Triumphs of God's Revenge Against the Crying and Execrable Sin of Murder*. In 1621 Reynolds published the first book of what was to become, by 1635, a six-book collection of thirty stories, with numerous succeeding editions through to the late eighteenth century.[53] In his own day, Reynolds was categorised (at times stigmatised) as an Exeter merchant, but he was educated at Oxford and began writing poetry and romances at an early age.[54] Reynolds combined his business activities with connections to artistic and aristocratic circles; he was a friend of Drayton, and seems to have been in the service of Edward Sackville, spending some time with him in France. In 1624, during the French marriage negotiations for Prince Charles, Reynolds published two pamphlets: *Vox Coeli*, a fierce attack on Spain and the then defunct Spanish marriage negotiations, and *Votivae Angliae*, an appeal to King James to take up arms for the Palatine cause.

The preface to *Votivae Angliae*, addressed to the 1624 parliament, makes it plain that Reynolds wrote the main text in 1621 but was (understandably) reluctant to submit it to the press, having noted the fates of Thomas Scott and Samuel Ward. Reynolds was clearly less smart in gauging James's reaction in 1624; he seems particularly naïve in this, given that *Votivae Angliae* suggests that Charles should persuade his father to draw his sword in favour of the Palatine cause, and that *Vox Coeli* conjures up a dialogue in Heaven between Henry VIII, Edward VI, Prince Henry, Queen Mary, Queen Elizabeth and Queen Anne, all except Mary suitably incensed at England's reluctance to attack Spain! *Vox Coeli* would certainly have been a particularly inflammatory pamphlet in 1621, but it fits in to the context of the mass of anti-Spanish/anti-Catholic material produced around it. The 1624 publication of these pamphlets led to Reynolds's imprisonment and he seems to have been released only after James's death.

Reynolds claims that his purpose, in *God's Revenges*, is a kind of moral crusade against the 'bewitching World, the alluring Flesh' (A2v).[55] Reynolds's vivid sense of what the world offers points to his narrative powers, even as he professes his dismay at such temptations:

> The World, that it may bewitch vs to its will, assayles vs with Wealth, Riches, Dignities, Honours, Preferments, Sumptuous houses, Perfumed Beds, vessels of Gold and Siluer, Pompous Apparell, Delicious fare, variety of sweet Musike, Dancing, Maskes and Stage-playes, delicate

Horses, rich Coaches, and infinite Attendants, with a thousand other inticements and allurements. (A2v)

When Reynolds gets into stride, the preface becomes something like a sermon, complete with marginal biblical glosses. He claims a simple didactic purpose: reading about the 'bloody and mournefull Tragedies' (B2) that strike down those who transgress will help the reader to avoid temptation:

My intent, desire, and prayer is, that if thou art strong in Christ, the perusing and reading of these Histories may confirme thy faith, and thy defiance of all sinnes in generall, and of Murther in particular: or if thou art but weake in the rules of Christian fortitude and piety, that hereby it may incourage and arm thee against the allurements of the World and the Flesh: but especially against the snares and inticements of the diuell, which may stirre thee vp, either to Wrath, Despaire, Reuenge, or Murther: that by the contemplation thereof, thou mayest resemble the Bee, and not the Spider: and so draw honey from all flowers, but poyson from none. (B3)

Reynolds's stories are set in Italy or France and the plots resemble those of many Jacobean tragedies – indeed History 4 of Book 1 is a source for *The Changeling*. It is, of course, a Renaissance cliché to claim that sensationalist fiction may supply a moral lesson and that readers or viewers can be relied upon to balance the allure of sin with the certainty of punishment. Reynolds is constantly anxious to guard his reader against being seduced by the events he recounts, while at the same time demonstrating a clear relish for the lurid detail. We can take the first story as a typical example; the plot is conveniently summarised by Reynolds himself:

Hautesilia causeth La Fresnay an Apothecary, to poyson her brother Grand Pre and his wife Mermanda, and is likewise the cause that her said brother kils de Malleray her owne husband in a Duell: la Fresnay condemned to be hanged for a rape, on the ladder confesseth his two former murthers, and saies that Hautesilia seduced and hired him to perform them: Hautesilia is likewise apprehended: and so for these cruell murthers, they are both put to seuere and cruell deaths. (1)

While all of Reynolds's characters are vividly drawn, he is especially interested in powerful (and sinful) women, and sees them as particular harbingers of evil events: 'I wish the euent of this History would giue the lie to this ensuing position, that there is no pride nor malice, to that of a woman; but I haue more reason to feare, then hope to beleeue the contrary' (10). Such women may serve to exemplify Reynolds's didactic stance, in so far as providence punishes them, but he is also drawn to them as, generally, the most satisfying examples of his narrative technique. This reminds us, once again, of the paradox at the heart of such didactic, religious fiction: the allure of the evil character may outweigh their role in the narrator's moral lesson. In this first story, Hautesilia is just such a character. She is driven by jealousy of her sister-in-law:

> shee likes not to giue the hand to her whom she knowes, is by descent her inferiour; and to speake truth, preferres a scarlet cloake before a blacke, and a Sword-man before a Pen-man: these ambitious conceits of hers, proceeding from hell, will breed bad blood, and produce mournefull effects; yea peraduenture strangle her, who embraceth and practiseth them. (11)

Reynolds constantly strives to ensure that the reader will be alert to the correct manner in which the story is to be interpreted: 'Iudge, Christian Reader, what simple reasons and triuiall motiues, this inconsiderate Gentlewoman hath for her malice' (12). When Hautesilia has her sister-in-law murdered, Reynolds, despite having already informed us of her ultimate fate in the précis at the beginning of the story, constantly reminds us that she will not get away with her evil actions: 'Which inhumane murther, we shall see, God in his due time will miraculously detect, and seuerely reuenge and punish' (26); 'Hautesilia exceedingly triumphes and reioyces hereat, but this bloudy victory shall cost her deare' (27). Reynolds depicts for us a God who is always alive to sin and who actively punishes the sinner: 'although murther be for a time concealed, yet the finger of God will in due time detect and discouer it; for hee will make inquisition for blood, and will seuerely and sharpely reuenge the death of his children' (34). Reynolds goes on to offer an account of the workings of providence which underlies all the stories:

> But Gods prouidence, and iuistice in the discouery thereof, is as different as miraculous: for sometimes hee protracts and deferres it of purpose, either to mollifie or to harden our hearts, as seemes best to his inscrutable will, and diuine pleasure: or as may chiefly serue and tend to his glorie, yea sometimes he makes the murtherer himselfe as well an instrument to discouer, as he hath beene an actor to commit

murther: yea and many times hee punisheth one sinne by and in another, and when the murtherer sits most secure, and thinkes least of it, then hee heapes coales of fire on his head, and sodainely cuts him off with the reuenging sword of his fierce wrath and indignation. (35)

Indeed, one might see Reynolds as standing in for God, given that his narration brings about just such a demonstration of the workings of providence. Reynolds typically ends this first story in his collection by hammering home his didactic purpose:

Now to gather some profit by reading this History: or indeed rather by the memory of the History it selfe, let us obserue, nay let us imprint in our hearts and soules, how busie the diuell was by ambition, couetousnesse, malice and reuenge, to seduce and perswade Hautesilia and la Fresnay to commit these murthers; and also how iust God was in the detection and punishment thereof, that the feare of the one may terrifie vs from imbracing and attempting the other, to the end, that as they liued in sinne, and died in shame; so we may liue in righteousnes, and dye in peace; thereby to liue in eternall felicity and glorie. (37–8)

The constant repetition of these moral saws would certainly have appealed to readers who agreed with Reynolds's view of providence, but such repetition also reveals some nervousness about the lack of control that an author has over interpretation. As far as the whole issue of 'authorship' is concerned, Reynolds sees his murderous protagonists as authors (for example, Christeneta in the second story is 'the Author of so execrable and lamentable a murther', 65), by which he means creators, but then over all human action stands God, who 'authors' the providence which metes out the sinners' fates. In her wide-ranging account of providence in early modern England, Alexandra Walsham notes that 'Providentialism was not a marginal feature of the religious culture of early modern England, but part of the mainstream, a cluster of presuppositions which enjoyed near universal acceptance'.[56] Walsham believes that Reynolds offers 'no more than parenthetical deference to the workings of providence in these absorbing novellas', but it seems to me that these numerous parentheses are a vital part of the texture of Reynolds's narration.[57] Indeed, the reader's pleasure is twofold: fuelled by the combination of lurid murder and forceful, even alluring murderers, with a satisfying sense of divine retribution and didactic justification.

The great success of Reynolds's multiplying collections of stories reinforces Walsham's key argument that stories of providential, divine retribution crossed the boundaries of genre and also the boundaries of the status of readers and listeners: 'They were aspects of an idiom capable of uniting godly and ungodly, literate and illiterate, privileged and poor'.[58] This balance can be seen in the way that Reynolds narrates History 4, the major source for *The Changeling*. For Reynolds's purposes, the relationship between Beatrice-Joanna and de Flores is perfectly straightforward, free from any of the complex tussle depicted by Middleton and Rowley in *The Changeling*. Because, in the story, Beatrice-Joanna is typical of Reynolds's sinful female protagonists, she readily accedes to de Flores's desires: 'shee, considering what he hath done for her seruice, and ioyning therewith her husbands iealousie, not onely ingageth her selfe to him for the time present, but for the future, and bids him visit her often' (134). Beatrice-Joanna confesses straight away to Alsemero, and the maid, Diaphanta, so pivotal in the play, is merely Alsemero's spy. This is not to criticise Reynolds for being less subtle than Middleton and Rowley, but simply to stress how Reynolds's didactic framework affects his view of human nature. The lurid details of Reynolds's bloody stories are explained by an overriding notion of inherent sin, and their denouements are all due to God's providential care. Reynolds provides the dual satisfaction of sensational narrative events and moral righteousness, as he suggests when he offers the hope, at the end of this first volume, that his histories 'may proue to be as great a consolation to the godly, as a terror to the vnrighteous' (178).

## History

### Ralegh: history and power

Providence is a key idea behind the most notable work of history published in 1621: Ralegh's *The History of the World*. Ralegh's work stands head and shoulders above other Jacobean histories, in part because of its ambitious scale, in part because Ralegh was intent upon testing the limits of early modern historiography. D.R. Woolf, in his comprehensive account of historical thought in the period, acutely notes that Ralegh demonstrates a fundamental paradox at the heart of the didactic approach to history: 'How was one supposed to learn valuable lessons from the past when the future was already mapped out is a tension in the didactic view of historiography that did not resolve itself in Ralegh's day, nor in the rest of this period; indeed, its resolution required an abandoning of strict predestinarianism that could only come slowly, in the course of the century.'[59] Woolf goes on to point out that Ralegh has (we might say in contrast to Reynolds) a particularly pessimistic view of providence:

> There is no discernible telos to the chaos of historical events which the *History* depicts, not even the providential goal of man's salvation. Providence itself figures not as a benevolent guide of the collective human destiny, only as an unseen, incomprehensible and generally hostile force.[60]

Given Ralegh's circumstances when he wrote the *History* (in the Tower since his death sentence for treason in 1603 had been commuted to indefinite confinement), it is scarcely surprising that he produced such a challenging work. There is an interesting attempt to fit the effects of providence into a more conventional (one might even say Reynolds-like) frame by Ben Jonson, in the poem entitled 'The Mind of the Front', which he composed to face the elaborately engraved title-page for the first edition of *The History of the World* in 1614. In it Jonson claims that Ralegh offers the reader a view of 'High Providence' meting out fit rewards for the great and good. This reassuring view is contradicted everywhere in the *History* itself, where Ralegh constantly shows us the gap between greatness and goodness. It is certainly true that the frontispiece depicts the eye of Providence above the globe (which is flanked by figures representing good and evil reputation), but it is placed at the top of the page staring out at the reader, judging us as coldly as it judges and pre-ordains the events of the past.

Ralegh wrote *The History of the World* under the patronage of Prince Henry and it was entered into the Stationers' Register in 1611. By the time it was actually published, in 1614, Prince Henry was dead. Ralegh's book was published without the author's name on the title-page, and it quickly raised the ire of the king and copies were seized by order of the Archbishop of Canterbury. James had reportedly noted that Ralegh was 'too saucy in censuring princes'.[61] This underlines the gamble that Ralegh took; if indeed, as Christopher Hill notes in his acute study of Ralegh, the *History* was written in part 'to rehabilitate himself with James I', he was bold not just in his censure of princes, but in his covert and overt criticisms of Spain, which are scattered throughout the *History*.[62] By the time the second edition was published in 1617, Ralegh had passed from his moment of freedom and his doomed expedition to Guiana, back to being a condemned man whose punishment was held out by James as a gesture of conciliation with Spain. The 1617 edition was again

*Figure 6* Title-page of Walter Ralegh, *History of the World* (1614), British Library, C.38.i.10.

published without Ralegh's name on the title-page, but his role of author was acknowledged, with considerable irony, by the Lord Chief Justice, who, in passing sentence at Ralegh's trial in 1618, stated 'I am resolved you are a good Christian, for your book which is an admirable work, doth testify as much'.[63]

In 1621 *The History of the World* was reprinted and all copies signal Ralegh's authorship on the title-page.[64] The solemn portrait of the author, which takes up half the title-page, is inscribed 'The true and lively portraiture of the honourable and learned Knight Sr Walter Ralegh', and its appearance for the first time serves to underline Ralegh's importance – stronger than ever in 1621 – as a symbol of opposition to Spain, and to mark the *History* as, at least in part, a treatise on power, full of lessons directing England to resist its old enemy. By 1621 the idea of Ralegh as a martyr, whose downfall was brought about by Spain and (some would venture) the collusion of Spain and King James, was firmly established, and the *History* was his monument.

Ralegh's history of the world begins with creation, but extends only as far as the Roman empire. However, Ralegh is always drawing parallels and lessons from ancient history for contemporary England. For example, in the preface, he notes that 'those that are wise, or whose wisedome, if it bee not great, yet is true and well grounded; will be able to discerne the bitter fruites of irreligious policie, as well among those examples that are found in ages remoued farre from the present, as in those of latter times' (A2v).[65] Ralegh goes on to note how 'the secret and vnsearchable iudgement of God' acted upon English monarchs, beginning with the 'remarkable example of Gods Iustice' upon the children of Henry I, and moving through the fates of Edward II, Edward III, Richard II, passing stern judgement along the way, especially on Henry VIII (judgement calculated to please King James). One need not be as sensitive as James was to see a certain irony in the panegyric to the king which follows the negative account of his predecessors; indeed, much of the praise directed at James is negative (for example, he didn't force his claim on the crown while Elizabeth was on the throne).

Ralegh moves from the rulers of England to the rulers of Spain, and offers a fierce account of their tyranny which would, once again, have appealed greatly to anti-Spanish feeling in 1621. Ralegh is, at the end of the preface, prepared to admit how dangerous it is to comment on contemporary events: 'whosoeuer in writing a moderne History, shall follow truth too neare the heeles, it may haply strike out his teeth', but he then disingenuously indicates how his history of the past has a moral relevance: 'in speaking of the past, I point at the present' (C4v).

*Figure 7*   Frontispiece/title-page of Walter Ralegh, *History of the World* (1621), The Bodleian Library, Oxford University, Antiq.C.E.1621.1.

Indeed, Ralegh has a constant string of digressions that comment on contemporary or near-contemporary issues, such as his discussion, in Book 5, of the English fleet and the necessity for its maintenance. This issue again hits directly at relations with Spain.

For those who persevere with the massive volume, which ends with Rome at its height, just before its empire topples, Ralegh concludes with an ominous and wholly explicit attack on Spain:

> Since the fall of the Roman Empire (omitting that of the Germanes which had neither greatnesse nor continuance) there hath beene no State fearefull in the East, but that of the Turk; nor in the West any Prince that hath spread his wings farre ouer his nest, but the Spaniard; who since the time that Ferdinand expel'd the Moores out of Granado, haue made many attempts to make themselues Masters of all Europe. And it is true, that by the treasures of both Indies, and by the many kingdoms which they possesse in Europe, they are at this day the most powerfull. But as the Turke is now counterpoysed by the Persian, so in stead of so many Millions as haue beene spent by the English, French and Netherlands in a defensiue Warre, and in diuersions against them, it is easie to demonstrate that with the charge of two hundred thousand pound continued but for two yeeres, or three at the most, they may not onely be perswaded to liue in peace, but all their swelling and ouer-flowing streames may be brought back into their naturall channels and old bankes. These two Nations, I say, are at this day the most eminent, and to be regarded; the one seeking to roote out the Christian Religion altogether, the other the truth and sincere profession thereof, the one to ioyne all Europe to Asia, the other the rest of all Europe to Spain. (V.669)

This call to arms would have rung all the more loudly in 1621 than in 1614, and Ralegh joins the religious opposition to Spain to his long-standing colonial ambitions, pointing to the very Spanish wealth that he proposed to counter, in 1616, with gold from Guiana (and from Spain itself). This is part of the political thread running through the *History* which stresses English superiority, even at a time when that superiority is held in check by James's foreign policy. One can assume that, like many others, Ralegh believed that Prince Henry would fulfil the English martial and colonial promise outlined in so many passages in the *History*.[66]

This political side of Ralegh's work needs to be seen alongside the more personal nature of the *History*, which has been strikingly outlined in Stephen Greenblatt's influential account of Ralegh as a paradigm for the Renaissance man as role-player. The *History* fits into Greenblatt's account of Ralegh's life as an exemplar of his 'inner anxieties', tugged paradoxically between 'grandeur and futility'.[67] Of course, Ralegh's personal 'crisis of the self' is also a political crisis, and the *History* addresses the dilemma he faced by stressing a dark view of providence and the futility of human action, while at the same time offering a muted call to arms and a catalogue of princely errors.[68] Greenblatt notes that the *History* ends with an address to death and a sense that all faith in human achievement must be abandoned:

> O eloquent, iust and mighty Death! whom none could aduise, thou hast perswaded; what none hath dared, thou hast done; and whom all the world hath flattered, thou only hast cast out of the world and despised: thou has drawne together all the farre stretched greatnesse, all the pride, crueltie, and ambition of man, and couered it all ouer with these two narrow words, *Hic iacet.* (V.669)[69]

For Greenblatt, the conclusion implies that 'History itself is no longer possible', but the last book in the volume, as well as examining the ironies of Roman history, takes the closest possible look at contemporary England, complete with a justification of Ralegh's past actions and a programme for the future. Ralegh may well have foreseen the futility of such political dreams, and his own fate bears out such a pessimistic view, but later readers of the *History* were able to see it as a challenge for England, as well as an ironic statement about human endeavour. To take one example of this, in Book 5 Ralegh analyses the political institution of tyranny, noting in particular that this is an unstable form of government (V. 325). Ralegh argues against slavery (including villeinage) and praises the kind of state which would exist under a king who is not a tyrant and who subscribes to Ralegh's own colonial and religious agenda: 'Vnder such a King, it is likely by Gods blessing, that a Land shall flourish, with increase of Trade, in countries before vnknowne; that Ciuilitie and Religion shall be propagated, into barbarous and heathen countries; and that the happinesse of his subiects, shall cause the Nations farre off remoued, to wish him their Souereigne' (V.327). As J.P. Sommerville has stressed, arguments against villeinage were linked to the anti-absolutist argument that the king does not have extra-legal powers over property, and, as a consequence, the subject's rights to property are linked to the powers of parliament.[70] James hardly fits Ralegh's description of the ideal ruler; the question for a 1621 reader might well be whether Ralegh pessimistically describes an unachievable ideal, or whether he prescribes a model for a future ruler to follow.

Another irony for readers of the *History* is Ralegh's treatment of the great battles of ancient history. While Ralegh offers detailed treatment of such events and is able to praise the brave actions of commanders and rulers, military prowess is ultimately seen to be futile, as all victorious generals, armies and civilisations are subject to death and decay. The very scope of the *History* militates against a triumphalist interpretation of local success. Many of Ralegh's asides adducing contemporary examples are meditations upon a human inability to learn by example. Following his account of the Roman response to Hannibal, Ralegh raises the highly contentious example of Ireland to illustrate his point about the need for continuity of command, but also to underline his moral: that we do not gain wisdom incrementally (by implication, this is a pessimistic summing up of the likelihood that the *History* itself will not teach readers anything):

> Our Princes haue commonly left their Deputies in *Ireland* three yeeres; whence, by reason of the shortnesse of that their time, many of them haue returned as wise as they went out; others haue profited more, and yet when they began but to know the first rudiments of Warre, and Gouernment, fitting the Countrie, they haue beene called home, and new Apprentices sent in their places, to the great preiudice both of this and that Estate. But it hath euer beene the course of the World, rather to follow old errours, than to examine them: and of Princes and Gouernours, to vp-hold their slothfull ignorance, by the olde examples and policie of other ages and people; though neither likenesse of time, of occasion, or of any other circumstance, haue perswaded the imitation. (V.373)

Ambition is worthless but it is ubiquitous: 'the Kings and princes of the world haue alwaies laid before them, the actions, but not the ends of those great Ones which preceded them. They are always transported with the glory of the one, but they neuer minde the miserie of the other, till they finde the experience in themselues' (V.669). Prince Henry's death allows him to be held up in the preface as the impossible ideal, who, now absent, will only serve to underline the sense of desertion felt by Ralegh, the Prince's followers, and the *History* itself:

> it was for the seruice of that inestimable Prince Henry, the successive hope, and one of the greatest of the Christian World, that I vndertook this Worke. It pleased him to peruse some part thereof, and to pardon what was amisse. It is now left to the world without a Maister: (C4v)

While the *History* entered the world without a patron, by 1621 it stood for its deceased patron's cause and its deceased author's memorial.

## Bacon: power and history

In May 1621, the process of removing Francis Bacon, Lord Chancellor, from office was complete.[71] Bacon had been accused of taking bribes and was impeached in the House of Lords; his response was, ultimately, to confess to the charges. As well as being stripped of his office and fined, Bacon was sent into a limited exile, forbidden to come within twelve miles of the court. While Bacon made efforts towards his recuperation, he seems from an early stage of the proceedings to have anticipated (as long as he was spared from the most severe of punishments) an exile in which he would fulfil some of his intellectual ambitions, writing to King James: 'if your Majesty give me peace and leisure, and God give me life, I will present your Majesty with a good history of England, and a better digest of your laws'.[72] Bacon's most recent biographers note that his disgrace did indeed allow him to produce the bulk of his scientific and philosophical work.[73] Bacon's first project was a segment of his long-promised history of the Tudors: *The History of the Reign of King Henry VII*. He finished the manuscript by October and sent it to James for his approval on 8 October, explaining in an accompanying letter that Henry was James's 'forerunner', 'whose spirit, as well as his blood, is doubled upon your Majesty'.[74]

James evidently read Bacon's manuscript carefully and approved of it, only asking for the deletion of a passage examining whether parliamentary representatives who were attainted should be allowed to serve without new writs being issued after their sentences were reversed.[75] The *History* was published early in 1622 with a dedication to Prince Charles. Bacon, like Ralegh, may have seen history as a genre with potential appeal for King James, but he had a more astute sense of how James could be flattered through the way history might be presented. Nevertheless, Bacon's account of Henry VII raises some very touchy issues of political doctrine which may well have troubled James, had he been alert to their presence in the work. Bacon narrates the events of Henry's reign and saves an assessment of the king's character until the end. There, he puzzles over the contradictions of Henry's somewhat enigmatic character: 'He was a Prince, sad, and serious, and full of thoughts and secret observations' (202). Henry's reign was a catalogue of true and false conspiracies, and Bacon would certainly have been aware of James's own anxiety about conspiracy and his distrust of his subjects. Perhaps James read Bacon's life of Henry as an exemplary account of a king who, seemingly without much effort, withstood all the conspiracies raised against him. How James read Bacon's account of Henry's greed and distrust of his nobility is another matter – many readers would surely have seen parallels that apparently escaped James's notice. Bacon noted that while Henry was peaceable (like James), his greed was oppressive: 'But the less blood he drew the more he took of treasure; and as some construed it, he was the more sparing in the one that he might be the more pressing in the other, for both would have been intolerable' (198).

Bacon offers a detailed account of Henry's distrust of his nobility, partly fuelled by his sense that they might always be involved in fomenting rebellion. This aspect of Bacon's work has led to some discussion of how far Bacon can be seen to be sowing the seeds of later Republican thought (especially in James Harrington) through an account of the separation of Henry's realm into 'a dichotomy of king and independent people'.[76] But Bacon is drawn to Henry's enigmatic nature, rather than to any freedom his subjects may have derived from his mistrust of his nobility; for Bacon, Henry was 'a Prince, sad, serious, and full of thoughts and secret observations' (202). Indeed, as Judith Anderson notes in her sensitive account of the complex narrative strategies employed by Bacon in the *History*, Bacon sees in Henry a parallel which points to the self-conscious way in which Bacon approached history writing.[77] Bacon is particularly drawn to Henry's legislative programme: 'here I do desire those into whose hands this work shall fall, that they do take in good part my long insisting upon the laws that were made in this King's reign; whereof I have these reasons, both because it was the pre-eminent virtue and merit of this King, to whose memory I do honour, and because it hath some correspondence to my person' (68). Bacon would have been conscious, when he was writing the *History*, that his legal career was now a matter for retrospective reflection, and that undoubtedly reinforced his interest in the long-lasting effects of Henry VII's legislative programme.

The other main theme of the *History* that offers some ironic reflection on Bacon's own times is the extensive treatment of the two duplicitous figures who challenged Henry's right to the throne: Lambert Simnell and Perkin Warbeck. Simnell's imposture as Edward Plantagenet and Warbeck's as Richard Duke of York cast a shadow over Henry's reign, and their activities fascinated many more Jacobeans than just Bacon, especially Perkin Warbeck, subject of the popular play by John Ford. No one writing a history of Henry VII's reign could ignore Simnell and Warbeck, but Bacon makes Warbeck in particular a centrepiece of his account. He actually links the mysterious nature of Warbeck's impersonation with Henry's enigmatic character: 'Wherefore this being one of the strangest examples of a personation that ever was in elder or later times, it deserveth to be discovered and related at the full; although the King's manner of shewing things by pieces and dark-lights, hath so muffled it that it hath left it almost as a mystery to this day' (96).

In his fanciful opening remarks about Warbeck, Bacon describes the impostor as appearing like a ghost raised by Margaret Duchess of Burgundy (sister of Edward IV): 'At this time the King began again to be haunted with sprites by the magic and curious arts of the Lady Margaret, who raised up the ghost of Richard Duke of York' (95). This piece of wit points to Bacon's largely secular approach to the writing of history. In complete contrast to Ralegh's pessimistic articulation of providence, Bacon offers an account of Henry's reign that seeks meaning in the human interpretation of human action, even if Henry's character remains somewhat enigmatic. D.R. Woolf aptly describes Bacon's methodology in the *History* as 'pragmatic'; Bacon seeks to instruct through a largely negative example.[78] Perhaps for that reason, the colourful impostors, Simnell and Warbeck, exert a spell over writer and reader far in excess of any attraction held by the colourless and even unknowable Henry VII.

### Samuel Daniel: history and the English state

In comparison to Ralegh and Bacon, Samuel Daniel has struggled to emerge from the negative characterisation that dates back as far as Ben Jonson's rather spiteful remark that he was 'a good honest man . . . but no Poet'.[79] Daniel may or may not have taken Jonson's hint, but he moved from poetry (including the historical poetry of *The Civil Wars*) to prose history late in his career. His ambitious plan for a complete history of England was unrealised, but he began by publishing a first part (for a limited audience) in 1613, expanding that to a larger version, which still ends with Edward III, published in 1618 as *The Collection of the Historie of England*. As D.R. Woolf explains, Daniel was particularly interested in the development of what he called the English state, by which he meant a national community.[80] The second edition of *The Collection* was published in 1621, two years after Daniel's death. In the preface, Daniel explains that, rather than attempt to penetrate the misty beginnings of England, he decided to begin his history when the nation was already formed: 'For States (as men) are ever best seene, when they are vp, and as they are, not as they were' (1).[81]

Daniel formed part of the group of Elizabethans characterised acutely by Richard Helgerson as poets who 'sought to articulate a national community'.[82] While in 1621 Michael Drayton was still working on his historical and topographical (or in Helgerson's terms chorographic) poem *Poly-Olbion*, the Elizabethan ambition to write the story and map the geographical and ideological boundaries of the nation had to deal with the fact that James's reign was so antipathetic to such endeavours. Indeed, as Helgerson points out, 'By the second decade of James's reign, chorography had become a dangerously political activity', in part because such a view of the country often involved an implicit undermining of royal authority in favour of local power and local identity.[83] Nevertheless, as D.R. Woolf points out, Daniel used *The Collection* to trace out a clear narrative of historical development, paying particular attention to the law (Daniel saw the common law as essentially forged after the Norman Conquest) and the unification of Britain into a nation. The latter progress clearly culminates in James's ideal of united kingdoms, even though the direct history in *The Collection* ends generations before James's accession.[84]

From the very beginning of *The Collection*, Daniel stresses his concern for the exact nature of a national, political identity: 'But now, what was the state, and forme of gouernment among the Britaines before this subiection [i.e. the Roman conquest]' (2). Daniel's careful consideration of the mixed origins of English common law, which he sees as essentially arising from the Norman Conquest, though with a few Saxon antecedents, placed him directly at odds with Edward Coke's insistence on the immemorial pre-Conquest origins of the common law which he defended so vigorously. Given the fact that Coke, as defender of common law, had such a clear symbolic victory in the 1621 parliament over the impeached Bacon, defender of legal codification and royal prerogative, Daniel's careful assessment of the history of common law is worth noting.[85] Daniel characterises the Norman Conquest as a historical barrier beyond which it is hard to penetrate: 'by these passages, we see what way wee came, where wee are, and the furthest end wee can discouer of the originall of our Common-law; and to looke beyond this, is to looke into an vncertaine vastnesse, beyond our discerning' (37). Daniel states that English law before the Conquest was 'plaine, briefe, and simple' (37) and that 'the maine streame of our Common-law, with the practice thereof, flowed out of Normandy, notwithstanding all obiections can be made to the contrary' (36). Part of his interest in the Conquest is to do with the way it unified a divided country and thus helped to forge the state. Similarly, Daniel ends *The Collection* when the state is ordered (although in typically balanced mode he notes some of the disorders that were to follow):

Thus farre haue I brought this Collection, of our History, and am now come to the highest exaltation of this Kingdome, to a State full built, to a Gouernment reared vp with all those maine Couplements of Forme and Order, as haue held it together euer since: notwithstanding those dilapidations made by our ciuill discord, by the Nonage or negligence of Princes, by the alterations of Religion, by all those corruptions which Time hath brought forth to fret and canker-eate the same. (222)

As well as the Norman Conquest, Daniel concentrates on what he sees as some key moments of historical change which affect the composition of the state, so that, while he offers an account of each ruler from William I onwards, some have a more significant impact than others (Henry II is a good example). Wales's unity with England under Edward I is of particular significance because it forms part of Daniel's argument for British unity: 'The Deusion and Plurality of States in this Isle, hauing euer made it the Stage of blood, and confusion: as if nature that had ordained it but one Peece, would haue it to bee gouerned but by one Prince, and one Law, as the most absolute glory and strength thereof, which otherwise it could neuer enioy' (159). Daniel is also at pains to stress the necessity for co-operation between prince and people (including through the process of parliament), noting, in his account of Edward I, 'it is not well with a State, where the Prince, and people seeke but to obtaine their seuerall ends, and worke vpon the aduantages of each others necessities: for as it is vn-sincere, so it is often vnsuccessful, and the good so done hurts more, then it pleasures' (165).

Daniel abandoned historical poetry in favour of history, but the example of Daniel's poetry, and even more so of Drayton's historical poetry, was carried forward in 1621 by Drayton's friend William Slatyer. As noted above, Drayton was still writing parts of his topographical/historical epic *Poly-Olbion*, which was first published in 1613 but only completed in 1622, when Slatyer published *The History of Great Britanie*, a ten-book poem which extends from (in Slatyer's opinion) the earliest kings down to the reign of James.[86] Slatyer's poem is heavily annotated with his historical sources, and the historical observations attracted the admiration of Camden, who commended Slatyer's 'historical learning'.[87]

In his rather ponderous preface, Slatyer takes readers to task for preferring foreign heroes and tales to native ones, and sets out to remedy this defect. The poem itself consists of a series of ten 'odes' in Latin with a facing parallel English version (the English poems carry the heavy historical annotations). Slatyer literally begins with the Creation and outlines Britain's peopling by Samothes, son of Japhet, 131 years after the flood (7).[88] Slatyer's description of Britain is very much in Drayton's mode, noting its topographical features and celebrating 'our pleasant seate' (13). Slatyer extends his boasts from the countryside itself to the nature of the people and their society: 'scarce any Nation more ingenious: since Christianitie, more zealously giuen and religious' (15).

Slatyer's historical speculation is more interesting than his limping couplets; he is particularly concerned to interrogate the legendary beginnings of Britain, and here he differs from Daniel's discreet avoidance of the earliest legends about the nation. He is especially interested to prove the existence of Brute and argues strongly in favour of English legends and chroniclers against 'foreigners', such as Polydore Virgil (83, 105). He also continues his combination of historical and geographical information, listing the origins of notable towns and cities. Slatyer offers a clear account of the tangled genealogy of British rulers and his narrative becomes particularly brisk and effective when he reaches the time of Egbert. Here, he reveals his allegiances to both Drayton and (as signalled by Camden's admiring remark) to the antiquarian interest in the past which itself was seen by James as a potential threat because such an interest, like that of the chorographers in local and national identity, could potentially bypass the direct identification of nationality with the sovereign.[89] But unlike Drayton, Slatyer counterbalances this by his concentration on rulers, who (as is the case in Daniel's *Collection*) mark out the phases of national history.

Slatyer compresses the period from William the Conqueror to Henry VII into a single book. In the last book, he is able to celebrate James as a unifier of the kingdom, but he awards Elizabeth due praise, taking special and personal note of the defeat of the Armada: 'So triumphs cheere, / Our natiue soil; and my first yeere' (281). The celebration of James's accession requires a lightning history of Scottish rulers, and the poem as a whole ends with James as symbol of British greatness. Slatyer's celebratory style is a long way from Daniel's more subtle account of the English state, but it would still have appealed to nationalist instincts.

## Heylyn's *Microcosmus*: historical/geographical/ political/theological

In 1621, at the age of 22, a precocious Peter Heylyn published a highly ambitious account of the geography and (potted) history of the entire known world. The table at the front of the book runs from Aragon to Zagataie (in Tartaria). Heylyn dedicated *Microcosmus* to Prince Charles and he was eventually to become a chaplain to Charles in 1630 and an associate of Archbishop Laud. Heylyn went on to write a series of historical works that offered support for Charles's personal rule and for absolutist views of sovereignty.[90] In *Microcosmus* he begins with an exposition of geographical knowledge and its importance, but then moves on to link that knowledge to historical knowledge: 'As Geographie without Historie hath life and motion but at randome, and vnstable: so Historie without Geographie like a dead carkasse hath neither life nor motion at all' (11).[91] Heylyn offers a schematic view of history, which has its origins in four genres: commentaries, annals, diaries and chronologies (12). For Heylyn, true history melds these genres into a coherent account of either 'universal' history or the 'lesser' history of man and his works, the latter exemplified by Heylyn's own book. Heylyn offers a traditional but rather perfunctory series of didactic justifications for history, before he embarks on his world tour.

The encyclopaedic methodology of *Microcosmus* is endearing, as Heylyn offers lively introductions to countries, starting with Europe, moving briskly through geographical description and historical summarising. Heylyn's concept of geography includes thumb-nail sketches of the nature and temperament of the inhabitants of each country, most of them breathtakingly sweeping; Spaniards, for example, 'are much giuen to women, impudent braggers, and extremely proud in the lowest ebbe of fortune' (23). Heylyn walks nervously through the political minefield as he describes European countries; for example, noting of the Bohemian crisis during his description of the Palatine 'I say nothing of the deplored state of this countrey, holding it more fit for my prayers, than safe for my penne' (154), and hoping for the martial success of Frederick's troops 'that hee may tread vpon the necke of the *Romish Adder*' (166).

When he reaches Britain, Heylyn leans heavily on Camden for his information. His praise of his own country is lavish, as one might expect. In particular, he notes the favourable position of women, the fair, local administration of justice, the great learning of the clergy, the might of army and navy, the universities, and the sensible approach to Reformation of the English Church. From Britain, Heylyn moves through Asia, Africa and America – at which point he stops abruptly, not wanting to venture anything about the 'unknowne parts of the world' (319).

## History as exemplary knowledge

The popularity of history as a genre is attested to by the publication or republication in 1621 of a miscellaneous selection of works that ranged from the ambitious and magisterial to the fairly slight and easily consumed. A work that in some ways rivalled the scope of *The History of the World* was Richard Knollys's *The Generall History of the Turkes*, first published in 1603. Already a massive folio volume on its first publication, Knollys's history, which begins with the origins of the Turkish nation, was expanded for the third edition of 1621 by Edward Grimeston, who took the history up to 1620.[92] Grimeston was the author of *The Generall History of the Netherlands* (1608), and these substantial folios were intended to supply those wealthy enough to buy them with a comprehensive historical survey. (Indeed, one might speculate about the response of those who bought these large, 'general' histories to the truncated nature of Ralegh's history, which promised to encompass the world but stopped considerably short.)

Grimeston, like Knollys, writes in a simple, straightforward style using an annals approach to the year-by-year ordering of events. In particular, Grimeston outlines the Turkish response to the situation in Bohemia, which essentially involved their allegiance with Transylvania (1382–4). At the conclusion of his continuation, Grimeston notes how the Turks attribute their martial success to the constant divisions between Christian princes and throws out a rather casual, apocalyptic prediction that these divisions will cease and the Turks will be driven out of the east into Sythia (1387).

Roman history was a popular and politically suggestive subject for Jacobean writers; it is represented in 1621 by the translation of a minor Roman historian, Lucius Florus, best known for his 'epitome' of Livy.[93] Florus's epitome was used by Philemon Holland in his translation of Livy in 1600.[94] Edmond Bolton's translation of Florus was first published in 1619 and dedicated to Buckingham. D.R. Woolf notes that Florus 'became the most readily available synopsis of republican history', and was read widely as a more accessible source than Sallust or Livy.[95] Woolf also notes that Florus's depiction of Augustus appealed to James's sense of himself as an Augustan ruler.[96] Bolton himself was particularly interested in historical methodology, and wrote a treatise, entitled *The Hypercritica, or a Rule of Judgement for Writing or Reading Our Histories*, which outlines a scheme for writing British history in part along the compact and elegant lines of Florus.[97] Bolton's translation is in keeping with the qualities he admires in Florus's Latin.

As a final example, the ubiquitous John Taylor, recognising the interest in history as a genre at the popular end of the market, published *A Brief Remembrance of All the English Monarchs* in 1618. This had a second edition in 1621. It is an ingenious volume, which offers the reader a portrait, a very brief biography beneath the portrait, and a sonnet, for each ruler from William the Conqueror to King James. Each sonnet is written in the first person, as if spoken by the appropriate monarch, except for the last two, where Taylor tactfully switches to third person paeans to James and Prince Charles.

History was, in nearly all cases, presented to the reader as a didactic genre, but as the examples published in 1621 indicate, the lessons it supposedly taught were often highly sensitive, from a political point of view. In the cases of Ralegh, Bacon and Daniel, the ideological conflicts of the period can be seen manifested in the authors' approaches to the genre of history and in the stories they chose to relate.

## Secular instruction

Early modern equivalents of modern self-help manuals, advice books and practical guides were available in large quantities. Examples published in 1621 indicate the enormous range of these books, which, like so many genres considered in this study, were published in a wide variety of formats with prices that catered for rich and poor buyers. The topics covered include grammars, language books, books on how to run a household, how to spell phonetically, gardening, how to remember things, fowling, cooking, letter writing, mathematics, marriage and accounting. Some were already best-sellers and some were published for the first time. In their very different ways, they all address a need for information which the printing-press was able to supply with increasing efficiency.

### Education

A large number of these works could be grouped under the general heading of education, although they address a very wide range of issues for diverse audiences. At the more formal level, some classic works that addressed educational issues were reprinted in 1621. The most famous of Renaissance treatises that revised approaches to rhetoric, Ramus's *Rhetorica*, was reprinted in Edinburgh in 1621.[98] As well as this Latin edition, commentaries and digests of Ramus were available, as were English translations.[99] Ramus's analytical approach is, to take just one example, demonstrated in Heylyn's table outlining the nature of history in *Microcosmus*.

Grammars were also extremely popular, headed by the most famous of Latin grammar books, William Lily's *A Short Introduction of Grammar*, which had its twenty-third edition in 1621. John Davies's Welsh grammar,

*Antiquae linguae Britannicae* was published for the first time in 1621. At the more popular level, Pierre Erondelle's French grammar was marketed for a female readership with a clever title: *A French Garden for English ladyes and gentlewomen to walke in: or, a sommer dayes labovr. Being an instruction for the attayning vnto the knowledge of the French tongue.* Other textbooks of this kind include *A New Booke of Spelling With Syllables,* which is a guide for children to learn handwriting and spelling. A more radical approach to the issue of spelling is taken in Alexander Gil's *Logonomia Angliae,* which uses illustrations from *The Faerie Queene.* John Evans's *The Palace of Profitable Pleasure* combines instructions for spelling, grammar, and arithmetical tables.

The letter-writing manual was another popular form of textbook in the period, and 1621 saw the re-issue of the standard book on the subject, Angel Day's *The English Secretarie,* first published in 1586. As an Elizabethan letter-writing manual, Day's book was a fashionable exposition of the principles of the elegant and practical epistle, with examples of a variety of letters analysed to show what style was appropriate for each particular circumstance. The 1621 edition, still printed in black-letter, would surely have seemed slightly old-fashioned, especially if set beside the more modern example of William Fulwood's translation of a French original, *The Enemy of Idleness,* though it follows the same format of a series of sample letters for a variety of occasions.

## Practical arts

At a more practical level, books were available to teach readers a variety of useful skills; two representative examples worth mentioning here cover fowling and cooking.[100] Gervase Markham, a prolific author who specialised in books on husbandry, gardening, horsemanship and housewife-skills, offers an extremely detailed account of the art of fowling in the delightfully-titled *Hungers Preuention: or, The whole art of fowling by water and land.* Markham dedicates the book to the Virginia Company, and offers it to the reader as both a practical guide to the various methods of fowling and a salutary example of self-sufficiency. Markham's detailed, practical guide not only details ways to catch birds of all kinds, but he so empathises with his prey that he is able to offer a vivid picture of the birds he discusses and their societies, noting, for example, how water fowl are 'the subtillest and wisest of Birds' (3), with a social system rather like a human camp complete with soldiers and scouts.[101] Similar imaginative identification lies behind his instructions on how to train a dog to fetch game birds. Markham also possesses a charming didactic style, which always has in mind 'the industrious and diligent Reader' (285), who is made to feel wholly competent by the time the book ends. Unlike many of Markham's other guides, which went through numerous editions, *Hungers Preuention* was not reprinted after 1621.

The cookbook is John Murrell's *A Delightful Daily Exercise for Ladies and Gentlewomen*. This is in fact a compendium volume, joining together two of Murrell's previously published cookbooks: *A Daily Exercise* (1617), which is devoted to cakes, sweetmeats and preserves, and *A New Book of Cookery* (1615), a plain and sensible collection of savoury recipes. Murrell begins the book with an interesting piece of marketing, informing the reader that 'If any of you are desirous of any of the Moulds mentioned in the Booke, you may enquire at the shoppe of Thomas Dewe in St Dunstons Church-yarde in Fleetstreete, where you may haue them' ($\pi$4).[102] Murrell, like Markham (albeit in a very different genre) has a clear sense of how to address his readers, and his recipes are extremely well set-out and easy to follow, with an admirable anticipation of possible problems and explanations for anything in a recipe that might seem unusual. For example, in his recipe for green, as opposed to white, 'mackroones', he explains: 'the reason why you have the white of an egge lesse then in the other, is because you haue more water to moysten your Almonds' (B5).

### Economics

One of the major economic controversies addressed in parliament and elsewhere in 1621 was the crisis over the supply of silver coin, and this became interconnected with debates over the relationship between national wealth and foreign trade. The activities of the East India Company were defended by the merchant Thomas Mun in *A Discourse of Trade, From England Vnto the east Indies*, which went through two editions in the course of the year. Mun painstakingly answers a series of criticisms which were directed against the company and its activities. His main argument is that trade is always of benefit to the national economy; he describes it as the 'Touchstone of a kingdoms prosperity' (1), and makes particular capital out of the fact that the East India Company has ensured that England can cut out the former trade with the Turks for commodities such as spices and drugs.[103] Mun argues that the East Indies trade actually brings coin (and wealth) in to the kingdom, and that it provides essential employment. Mun's argument is largely an economic one; while he acknowledges the political importance of an English presence in the East Indies, he defends trade essentially in terms of wealth-creation. Mun's defence is particularly important, given the pressure on the East India Company at this stage of its existence, and the second edition of his book points to the fact that he struck a chord with 1621 readers.

## Psychology

The early modern interest in the workings of the mind is attested to most impressively in *The Anatomy of Melancholy*, which I have discussed in detail in Chapter 2. Three other 1621 books are, in different ways, examinations of what we might loosely call psychology. The first two are devoted to human emotions. F.N. Coeffeteau's *A Table of Humane Passions*, translated by Edward Grimeston, offers a catalogue of emotions based upon the premise that the soul and the body are involved in constant interaction. In this theory, humans are constantly driven by the 'sensitive appetite' (10), as the impressions made by the external world are processed: 'The obiects of the senses strike first vpon the imagination' (15).[104] The passions are therefore examined from this perspective, as the book outlines the causes and effects of love, desire, pleasure, envy, grief, shame, and so on. Thomas Dewe's *Passions of the Mind in General*, first published in 1601 but published in 1620 and 1621 in a revised edition augmented by Thomas Wright, similarly outlines the effects of the passions on human behaviour, but emphasises the need to control them and harness them to the individual's advantage. Both these works take the tone of instruction manuals, their purpose being to allow the reader to understand the workings of the passions and to put that knowledge to use, in so far as the regulation of the passions allows for both self-control and a knowledge of the people one encounters in everyday life. In this sense, they are both very different in tone to Burton's self-reflexive and pessimistic sense, in *The Anatomy of Melancholy*, of the way one's mind works.

The third book, John Willis's *The Art of Memory*, the author's own translation of an earlier Latin treatise, is a straightforward account of classical mnemonic theory, which uses visualisation in order to commit ideas and speeches to memory. Willis's book is typical of many such volumes published in the period, and it specifically addresses what he calls the 'common sort' (A3v) of reader, allowing such a reader access to techniques more often restricted to scholarly, Latin volumes. The concept of memory behind these treatises is mechanistic, and while the techniques were certainly effective, little insight into the process of remembering is generated.

## Living

There is a fine line between the books of religious instruction discussed above and the more secular guides which I will discuss here. A good example is the popular guide published by Robert Cleaver in 1598 and expanded with the assistance of John Dod in the early seventeenth century: *A Godly Form of Household Gouernment: for the ordering of priuate families, according to the direction of Gods word*, which reached its fourth edition in 1621. As the subtitle implies, the maxims provided relate to proper religious conduct within the household, but they also cover day to day living. Dod and Cleaver see the household as a mirror of society – 'An Household is as it were a little Commonwealth' (Av) – and they stress the need for companionable marriage, though the husband remains the clear head of the family: 'the dutie common both to the husband and wife, importeth, that the one should aide and helpe the other' (M2v). Dod and Cleaver are careful to defend women against accusations that they are inferior to men, just because they are ultimately subservient: 'women are as men are, reasonable creatures' (K6v). The essence of a Christian marriage is a mutual trust and an avoidance of tyranny, though the husband must be the head of the household: 'in a well ordered household, there must be a communication and consent of counsell and will between the husband and the wife: yet such as the counsell and commandment may rest in the husband' (O7).

Dod and Cleaver offer an extremely detailed account of the religious and moral duties entailed upon the three elements of the household: husband to wife, wife to husband, parents to children, children to parents, masters and mistresses to servants, and servants to masters and mistresses. Christian conduct is the essential subject of this guide, and although it does cover some practical elements of household management, they are seen as part of the fundamental Christian message; so, for example, Dod and Cleaver urge mothers to breast feed their own children, but offer no real details about nurture or nutrition. But on their main theme of true Christian life within the home, Dod and Cleaver offer extremely precise and elaborate advice.[105]

The scope of *A Godly Form of Household Government* can be contrasted to a little book of moral instruction by Robert Crowley: *The Schoole of Vertue and Book of Good Nurture, teaching children and youth their dutie*. This small black-letter quarto is mostly in verse and it offers a simple guide to good conduct for children, covering such things as how they should rise in the morning: 'Thy hands see thou wash, / thy head likewise keame, [i.e. comb] / And of thine apparell / See torne be no seame'

(A4v). Crowley includes some poems about general social degree and good conduct.

One can also admire Dod and Cleaver's view of companionable marriage if one turns to *A Discourse of the Married and Single Life*, an anonymous adaptation of a French text by Roland du Jardin which offers a 'witty' argument against marriage by trotting out a stream of early modern clichés about women's failings. In contrast to Dod and Cleaver's interest in a balanced form of household government, we are offered such aphorisms as: 'If thou giuest her the gouernment of thy whole house, thou must then serue her at command. If thou reseruest any part thereof to thy selfe, shee then complaineth of the little trust thou reposest in her' (35).[106] Women are, in this dichotomising style, damned if they do and damned if they don't: 'If shee can read printed Bookes, in reading, shee mingleth that of the Serpent, with that of the Scorpion. If she cannot read, then being idle, she hath many euill thoughts, which produce and grow to euill actions' (37–8). One might characterise this as advice turned to misogynistic polemic, and it can be related to the pamphlet debates over the nature of women discussed in Chapter 2.

### Knowledge on the market

The length of this chapter points to the large readership for didactic material of all kinds, religious and secular. With this disparate range of books, we come closest to an understanding of just how diverse the market for information was in 1621, and how effectively the market was supplied with material. Given the controversial nature of so many forms of writing considered here, especially in the categories of religion and history, it is tempting to ask exactly how readers were able to determine which books to buy and even more tempting to ask how they were read. In many cases, readers were addressed directly by books (such as the religious guides) which shared their religious beliefs. But readers must also have been prepared to be addressed by books arguing a case with which they might not agree.

Many of the examples discussed in this chapter also demonstrate the significance of reprinted works which change their signification in a changed context. While this is demonstrated most dramatically in the case of Ralegh's *History*, which becomes a memorial to Ralegh as Protestant martyr in 1621, especially given his sudden elevation to prominence on the title-page, it is also evident in the reprint of a religious work like Perkins's *Golden Chain*, which by 1621 has a long and complex history within religious controversy.

It is also worth remembering that didactic material was inherently entertaining – a point that can be lost in solemn theorising and a modern perspective that might wonder at the early modern appetite for religious tracts, sermons, or historical chronicles.

# Conclusion

In a project that in many ways complements mine, Kevin Sharpe has studied an early modern reader in order to shed light on the way that early modern individuals processed information and 'read' the world, particularly in relation to the construction of authority, power and counter-authority.[1] Sharpe exploits the rich archive left behind by Sir William Drake, a gentleman whose notebooks, diaries and annotated books chart the responses of a deeply committed 'reader' from the late 1620s to the Restoration. Unlike John Chamberlain, my analogous early modern reader and paradigm for my own reading practices, Drake had a sharp focus on serious, humanist texts and had no discernible interest in popular culture. In a most illuminating fashion, Sharpe is able to explore the way that Drake represents early modern reading as, at least potentially, an escape from certain social constraints: 'whatever the directives of the magistracy or the codes of the village, each subject read authority and constructed his or her own worldview differently'.[2] Sharpe's book involves a detailed incorporation of literary theory, especially reader response theory, into an assessment of how historians might recover early modern attitudes and practices.

In this book, I have moved between a parallel endeavour to Sharpe's, and a rather more self-conscious presentation of *my* reading of 1621's texts, taking John Chamberlain as an example of a certain kind of early modern reader (much more catholic in taste than Drake), but also as an example of a certain kind of *modern* reader, who might address the past by as full as possible an immersion into the texts of a manageable period of time; say a single year. Not even the omnivorous John Chamberlain came close to reading all that was written in 1621. I have tried to do so, but to make this book a readable analysis, rather than an encyclopaedia, I have tried to digest the writing of 1621 and order it into a series of categories, mostly thematic and generic, but also ideological and political. I am left with writing that, for various reasons, does not fit into such a scheme, however ingeniously I might try to tweak it. The most obvious example is music. For example, John Adson published *Courtly Masquing Ayres*, a collection of music 'for violins, consorts and cornets'. Adson's music won't fit into my categories, and while I could easily have created a category for music, my narrative of 1621 would have been made more unwieldy by its creation.

I have, as I noted in my introduction, always been conscious that my attempt to enter into a dialogue with the writing of my chosen year has involved, not just reading the year, but also re-writing it. The categories, like the idea of studying the year itself, act as a heuristic device, allowing me not just to find out as much as possible about 1621, but also to see what kind of history might be written if one can gain detailed knowledge of the minutiae of early modern writing.[3] I hope that the reader of this book will benefit from my immersion in 1621 in a variety of ways. At the most obvious level, I have tried to convey my experience of the many and varied kinds of writing that were available in 1621. As my work progressed, it became clear that much of this writing has what we would now call a political or ideological dimension, and I have been conscious of the arguments between political historians, such as Conrad Russell, Glenn Burgess and Johann Sommerville, to name three prominent examples, over just how self-conscious and sophisticated ideological debates were at this time.[4] Much of my reading of sermons and other religious writing in particular tends to support Sommerville's account of ideological conflict in the period. But I have also resisted the pull towards political history, because while this book acknowledges its importance, I have been conscious that many 1621 works were prized for what we might bravely call literary qualities, as well as for the information they conveyed or the ideological points that they scored.

Allied to the political implications of many works discussed here is a heightened sense of local contexts for various kinds of writing – contexts that change as writing first published earlier is republished and re-read in 1621. My examples of this have ranged from Ralegh's *History of the World* to Donne's *Anniversaries*. Once again, my intention is that this way of reading might be applied in a more wide-ranging fashion: that early modern writing in general might be seen, not as frozen at the moment it is first published, but as constantly changing within the period. I have tried to avoid freezing early modern writing into the patterns imposed by modern interpretations.

When I began this study, it was suggested to me that it might be rewarding to compare 1621 to one or two other years. Given that this book has taken close to a decade to write, I am relieved that I shied away from the suggestion, but some comparison can at least be hinted at here. The political story of 1621 is continued in impressive detail by Thomas Cogswell in *The Blessed Revolution: English Politics and the Coming of War, 1621–1624.*[5] Cogswell is particularly conscious of the importance of literary and cultural sources as he traces the shift away from James's rapprochement with Spain, culminating in the 1624 parliament, when Charles and Buckingham, still smarting from their Spanish visit of 1623, pushed for war. Many of the writers prominent for their political comment in 1621 were equally prominent in 1624, which saw the most significant example of political commentary through cultural performance for the whole period when Middleton staged *A Game at Chess*, a fiercely anti-Spanish political allegory that was a scandalous and outstanding success. Cogswell sees a rise in political commentary in 1622/3, but it seems to me, looking at his examples, that such writing, until the moment of *A Game at Chess*, is not very different from that of 1621 in either quantity or intensity.

It might be useful to compare 1621 specifically to other years when parliament sat, given that the existence of parliament clearly provoked both politically-oriented writing and, even more importantly, a real hunger for the news purveyed by such writing. The comparison I have just made with 1624, courtesy of Cogswell's study, might also profitably be made with the parliament year that preceded 1621: 1614. And then one might want to look at a year without a parliament. But I don't want to end with a prescription for future research projects, because I am not really concerned to determine whether 1621 was a 'typical' year (although I think it was to the degree that any year can be typical). Rather, I want this book to allow readers of early modern writing some insight into just how different the period looks when we read well beyond the constrictions of the canon (even if it is an expanded one) that lingers on in many approaches to the period. I have found that the enriched knowledge generated by the detailed account allowed for by 'knowing' 1621 spills over into how I now read other early modern works from other years; the narrative provided by this book is intended to offer the reader a fresh vision of the year, but also of the period as a whole.

Some more general conclusions might be drawn about other issues that have been traced through the preceding chapters. As I noted in Chapter 2, much recent work on the early modern period has been interested in unravelling the modern distinction between public and private. A number of apparently disparate genres discussed in this book are concerned with this intersection between private and public spheres. In Chapter 2, I specifically related this to the way that clear self-reflection, such as *The Anatomy of Melancholy*, had a political/social dimension, and correspondingly, sermons crossed boundaries between the private examination of the individual conscience and the public, rhetorical presentation of a series of moral and political issues. In the case of sermons, this issue also crosses what we might call barriers of status, as politically-oriented sermons had a very wide audience (including those who were not literate). The issue was also raised in Chapter 3 in relation to the romance, given that the two major 1621 examples of romance, *Urania* and *Argenis*, look once again at political issues in relation to the depiction of inwardness – notably in *Urania*, where Wroth offers portraits of subjectivity that explore the position of women in relation to political power and the politics of gender. Much of the poetry discussed in Chapter 5, including Wroth's, integrates some notion of the personal with a public realm.

Another general issue in early modern studies which is illuminated by an analysis of a year is the relationship of genre to political expression. The choice of a genre – history is a notable example – has political implications. King James's hasty attempt to prohibit the importation of corantos (see Chapter 6) signals the alarm raised by any form of writing that announced itself as news. On the other hand, a play in 1621 could get away with more overt political criticism, and even find itself performed at court.

I raise the issue of gender myself as a modern question we ask the past, and by choosing 1621, the year of Wroth's *Urania*, I give the issue great prominence. But *Urania* was noticed as a significant publishing event by a number of 1621 readers, and when Wroth's work is examined alongside that of Speght and Leigh (discussed in Chapter 2 and Chapter 7 respectively), one can see that women writers were a significant presence in a variety of genres: fiction, poetry, autobiography, meditation and religious advice, to name those represented here.

Evidence of the flourishing early modern book trade is present throughout this study, but the continuing vitality of manuscript publication is also apparent. While I have inevitably had to centre my account on texts of various kinds, it is important to note that 'literary culture' in the broadest possible sense had a vital life beyond writing and print, as evidenced by forms of performance, from plays to civic pageants to sermons. The final issue raised by my reading of 1621 is how this very diversity of material might reflect early modern reading practices. While I have been careful to guard against taking John Chamberlain, compulsive reader, as a representative early modern reader, at the same time I believe that individuals in 1621 were addressed by an enormous network of entertainment, information, commentary, political critique, reflection and self-examination. Doubtless many people read only within a small number of works that suited them, many people did not read writing at all, although they 'read' events, ideas, performances, speeches, and so on. At the same time, Chamberlain's omnivorous crossing of genre boundaries is evidenced even in a reader like King James, who enjoyed scholarly works *and* the cock-lorel ballad. The texts of 1621 also testify to the large number of *writers* in this society: they range from those we might see as professionals (Middleton, Massinger); to scholars (Burton); to clergymen of all political hues (Donne, Andrewes, Ward); to journalists (Butter); to more ordinary members of society wanting to testify to their own experience and influence others (Leigh, Speght); to serious creative writers (Wroth, Wither). Even the most private of these writers enters, in 1621, something like an early modern public sphere, including those whose work was reprinted/recopied/recirculated and accordingly placed in a new political context. My own readings of 1621 are intended to reflect this heterogeneity; my readers are of course free to draw their own conclusions.

# Notes

## Preface

1. The bibliography for the debate over new historicism is now substantial. The best introduction is perhaps the collection of essays in H. Aram Veeser, ed., *The New Historicism* (London: Routledge, 1989); and for the feminist critique see also Carol Thomas Neely, 'Constructing the Subject: Feminist Practice and the New Renaissance Discourses', *ELR* 18 (1988), 5–18. I have found Lee Patterson's analysis of the relationship between historicism, new historicism and humanism particularly helpful, although his emphasis is on medieval studies: see *Negotiating the Past* (Madison: University of Wisconsin Press, 1987), chs 1 and 2.
2. Leah Marcus, *Puzzling Shakespeare* (Berkeley: University of California Press, 1988); Annabel Patterson, *Reading Holinshed's Chronicles* (Chicago: University of Chicago Press, 1994).
3. See especially Arthur Marotti, *Manuscript, Print and the English Renaissance* (Ithaca: Cornell University Press, 1995); Wendy Wall, *The Imprint of Gender* (Ithaca: Cornell University Press, 1993); and especially on the spread of manuscript publication through scriptoria, Harold Love, *Scribal Publication in Seventeenth-Century England* (Oxford: Clarendon Press, 1995).
4. Nigel Smith, *Literature and Revolution in England 1640–1660* (New Haven: Yale University Press, 1994), p. 12.
5. Ibid., p. 19.
6. Having been found guilty in 1616 of the murder of Carr's friend Thomas Overbury (who had opposed their marriage while Devereux was married to the Earl of Essex), in 1621 Carr and his wife were in the tower, thanks to James, who commuted their death sentences. Of the many accounts of the Overbury scandal, the most comprehensive are David Lindley, *The Trials of Frances Howard: Fact and Fiction at the Court of King James* (London: Routledge, 1993); and Anne Somerset, *Unnatural Murder: Passion at the Court of James I* (London: Weidenfeld and Nicolson, 1997); recently much more attention has been paid to attitudes towards James's relationship with his favourites: see especially David M. Bergeron, *Royal Family, Royal Lovers* (Columbia: University of Missouri Press, 1991); and Michael B. Young, *James I and the History of Homosexuality* (London: Macmillan – now Palgrave Macmillan, 2000).
7. The most relevant example is perhaps Thomas Cogswell, *The Blessed Revolution: English Politics and the Coming of War 1621–1624* (Cambridge: Cambridge University Press, 1989).
8. I want to thank Tom Healy for reminding me of the importance of this issue.
9. James Chandler, *England in 1819* (Chicago: University of Chicago Press, 1998); Chandler's extremely sophisticated account of his methodology stresses the crucial interconnection between romanticism and issues of historicism.

10. See the detailed account of Ralegh in Chapter 7.
11. Though he focuses on a slightly later period, the importance of processing printed material in particular as news has been pointed out in Richard Cust's influential article, 'News and Politics in Early Seventeenth Century England', *Past and Present* 112 (1986), 60–90; the issue of news is then taken up in greater detail below in Chapter 6.
12. Some of the more general theoretical conclusions one might draw from this process are outlined below in the Conclusion.
13. H.S. Bennett, *English Books and Readers 1603–1640* (Cambridge: Cambridge University Press, 1970); I do not mean to imply that Bennett's overall view of the publications of the period is wrong, simply that his general statistics cannot be applied to a single year without some refinement.
14. See the detailed account below in Chapters 2 and 7.
15. See Mary Hobbs, *Early Seventeenth-Century Verse Miscellany Manuscripts* (Aldershot: Scolar Press, 1992).

## Chapter 1: John Chamberlain Reads the Year

1. *The Letters of John Chamberlain*, ed. Norman Egbert McClure (Philadelphia: American Philosophical Society, 1939), 2 vols., further references in parentheses to this edition.
2. A selection of Carleton's letters replying to Chamberlain may be found in *Dudley Carleton to John Chamberlain 1603–1624: Jacobean Letters*, ed. Maurice Lee Jr. (New Brunswick: Rutgers University Press, 1972).
3. For an account of them, see Wilfred R. Prest, *The Inns of Court Under Elizabeth I and the Early Stuarts, 1590–1640* (London: Longman, 1972).
4. Wallace Notestein, *Four Worthies* (London: Jonathan Cape, 1956), p. 33.
5. For a full account, see Roy E. Schrieber, *The First Carlisle, Sir James Hay, First Earl of Carlisle as Courtier, Diplomat and Entrepreneur* (Philadelphia: American Philosophical Society, 1984), pp. 22–36.
6. See in particular Stephen Orgel, *The Jonsonian Masque* (Cambridge, Mass.: Harvard University Press, 1965) and *The Illusion of Power* (Berkeley: University of California Press, 1975); and among more recent studies Jerzy Limon, *The Masque of Stuart Culture* (Newark: University of Delaware Press, 1990).
7. Schrieber, p. 11.
8. See Martin Butler, 'Ben Jonson's *Pan's Anniversary* and the Politics of Early Stuart Pastoral', *ELR*, 22 (1992), 369–404.
9. Ibid., p. 391.
10. See Katherine Duncan-Jones, 'Philip Sidney's Toys', in Dennis Kay, ed., *Sir Philip Sidney: An Anthology of Modern Criticism* (Oxford: Clarendon Press, 1987), 61–80.
11. Unfortunately, a search of the Public Record Office indicates that all the enclosures with Chamberlain's letters were either never deposited with them or have disappeared.
12. It seems most likely that the song in question was the Cock Lorel ballad, a popular satirical piece, reproduced in a number of commonplace books etc. It begins:

Cock Lorel would needs have the devil his guest,
And bade him once into the Peak to dinner,
Where never the fiend had such a feast
Provided him yet at the charge of a sinner.

His stomach was queasy for coming there coached;
The jogging had caused some crudities rise;
To help it he called for a Puritan poached,
That used to turn up the eggs of his eyes.

*Ben Jonson: Complete Masques*, ed. Stephen Orgel (New Haven: Yale University Press, 1969), pp. 356–7.

13. James F. Larkin and Paul L. Hughes, eds., *Stuart Royal Proclamations* (Oxford: Clarendon Press, 1973), Vol. 1, pp. 495–6.

14. *The Poems of James VI of Scotland*, ed. James Craigie (Edinburgh: William Blackwood, 1958), Vol. 2, p. 177.

15. The most comprehensive and sophisticated account of James's relationship with Buckingham is contained in David M. Bergeron, *Royal Family, Royal Lovers: King James of England and Scotland* (Columbia: University of Missouri Press, 1991), pp. 160–85. See also the glancing reference to the smiling boy in Jonathan Goldberg, *James I and the Politics of Literature* (1983, rpt. Stanford: Stanford University Press, 1989), p. 142, although Goldberg, removing the couplet from its context, also removes any ambiguity of reference.

16. Craigie's text's 'fatt' is from the Bodleian Library Rawlinson MS Poet. 26, which I have checked; he notes the Conway Griffith's manuscript reading of 'full' (p. 261).

17. I will be returning in Chapter 3 to Chamberlain's literary judgement when I discuss two works published in 1621 which he comments on in 1622: John Barclay's *Argenis* and Mary Wroth's *Urania*.

18. Stephen Greenblatt, *Shakespearean Negotiations* (Oxford: Clarendon Press, 1988): 'I began with the desire to speak with the dead' (p. 1).

# Chapter 2: Selves

1. Stephen Greenblatt, *Renaissance Self-Fashioning* (Chicago: University of Chicago Press, 1980), p. 256.

2. Francis Barker, *The Tremulous Private Body: Essays on Subjection* (London: Methuen, 1984), p. 31.

3. Katherine Eisaman Maus, 'Proof and Consequences: Inwardness and its Exposure in the English Renaissance', *Representations* 34 (1991), 37; see the elaboration of her argument in *Inwardness and Theater in the English Renaissance* (Chicago: University of Chicago Press, 1995).

4. Barbara K. Lewalski, *Writing Women in Jacobean England* (Cambridge, Mass.: Harvard University Press, 1993), p. 3.

5. But see the next chapter for an account of one of the most important of all early modern women writers. One example that has attracted considerable attention recently is Anne Clifford's diary and autobiographical writing. The diary covers 1603, 1616–1617 and then stops tantalisingly at the end of

1619: see the important edition of the diary edited by Katherine O. Acheson, *The Diary of Anne Clifford 1616–1619* (New York: Garland, 1995); also critical studies such as Mary Ellen Lamb, 'The Agency of the Split Subject: Lady Anne Clifford and the Uses of Reading, *ELR* 22 (1992), 347–68; Lewalski, ch. 5. Other important examples that precede 1621 include Arbella Stuart's letters, now edited by Sara Jayne Steen (New York: Oxford University Press, 1994); and an increasing number of examples after 1621, some of them well known for some time, such as the autobiographies of Ann Fanshawe, Margaret Cavendish and Anne Halkett, some only more recently examined in any detail, such as the prophetic writings of Anna Trapnel. An excellent introduction and selection of these autobiographical texts is *Her Own Life*, edited by Elaine Hobby, Elspeth Graham, Hilary Hinds and Helen Wilcox (London: Routledge, 1989). Of the older, general accounts of autobiographical writing in the seventeenth century, the most useful general introduction remains Paul Delany, *British Autobiography in the Seventeenth Century* (London: Routledge, 1969).

6. For an account of this, see Lewalski, pp. 153–8.
7. Ibid., p. 157.
8. All references are to *Mortalities Memorandum* (1621); the text is available in an excellent edition prepared by Barbara Lewalski, *The Polemics and Poems of Rachel Speght* (New York: Oxford University Press, 1996).
9. Elaine Beilin, *Redeeming Eve: Women Writers of the English Renaissance* (Princeton: Princeton University Press, 1987), p. 115.
10. Elaine Beilin, 'Writing Public Poetry: Humanism and the Woman Writer', *MLQ* 51 (1990), p. 269.
11. Thomas Faulkner, Nicolas Kiessling, Rhonda Blair, J.B. Bamborough, Martin Dodsworth, eds, *Robert Burton's The Anatomy of Melancholy* (Oxford: Clarendon Press, 5 vols. 1989–2000).
12. I have used the information from the bibliographical introduction to volume 1 of the Oxford edition (1989).
13. The three editions usually used are: Arthur Shilleto's (London: George Bell and Sons, 1893, reissued in one volume 1923), based on the seventh edition of 1660; Floyd Dell and Paul Jordan Smith's (New York: Tudor Press, 1927), based on the sixth edition of 1651 with translations of much Latin but the omission of many marginal notes; Holbrook Jackson's Everyman edition (London: Dent, 1932), based on the sixth edition of 1651 with some limited collation, described by the Oxford editors as the 'most accurate' (xliv).
14. See the description of the editions in the Oxford textual introduction, vol. 1, pp. xliv–xlviii.
15. Reproduced in the Oxford edition and in many discussions; the most detailed account of the title-page is in Margery Corbett and Ronald Lightbown, *The Comely Frontispiece* (London: Routledge, 1979), pp. 191–200.
16. References are to the facsimile of the Bodleian copy of the 1621 *Anatomy of Melancholy*, published by Theatrum Orbis Terrarum (Amsterdam, 1971). I will also provide part, section, member and subsection references before each page number – except for the preface, which only has page numbers, and the conclusion, which only has signatures. I have often omitted Burton's marginal notes, but when including them, I have placed them within square brackets.

17. Devon L. Hodges, *Renaissance Fictions of Anatomy* (Amherst: University of Massachusetts Press, 1985), p. 118.
18. Joan Webber, *The Eloquent 'I': Style and Self in Seventeenth-Century Prose* (Madison: University of Wisconsin Press, 1968), p. 110.
19. The best account of the paradoxical nature of the *Anatomy* remains Rosalie Colie, *Paradoxia Epidemica: The Renaissance Tradition of Paradox* (Princeton: Princeton University Press, 1966), ch. 14.
20. See William R. Mueller, *The Anatomy of Robert Burton's England* (Berkeley: University of California Press, 1952), passim.
21. See the discussion in Mueller, passim.
22. For a detailed discussion of this aspect of the preface, see J. Max Patrick, 'Robert Burton's Utopianism', *PQ* 27 (1948), 345–58; Patrick describes the expansion of the Utopia section in later editions, especially the second, but notes that the 1621 version 'was an attempt to remove anomalies and abuses, to increase efficiency and productivity, and to ensure the maximum use of available resources' (356).
23. See the discussion below in this chapter and in Chapters 5 and 7.
24. For this aspect of Burton see Jonathan Sawday, 'Shapeless Elegance: Robert Burton's Anatomy of Knowledge', in Neil Rhodes, ed., *English Renaissance Prose: History. Language and Politics* (Tempe: MRTS, 1997), pp. 173–202.
25. Lawrence Babb, *Sanity in Bedlam: A Study of Robert Burton's Anatomy of Melancholy* (Michigan: Michigan State University Press, 1959), p. 9.
26. Colie, passim; Mueller; passim; Ruth A. Fox, *The Tangled Chain: The Structure of Disorder in the Anatomy of Melancholy* (Berkeley: University of California Press, 1976); Stanley Fish, *Self-Consuming Artifacts* (Berkeley: University of California Press, 1972), ch. 6; E. Patricia Vicari, *The View From Minerva's Tower: Learning and Imagination in The Anatomy of Melancholy* (Toronto: University of Toronto Press, 1989); John Stachniewski, *The Persecutory Imagination: English Puritanism and the Literature of Religious Despair* (Oxford: Clarendon Press, 1991); Bridget Gellert Lyons, *Voices of Melancholy* (London: Routledge, 1971); Hodges, passim.
27. Mark Breitenberg, *Anxious Masculinity in Early Modern England* (Cambridge: Cambridge University Press, 1996); see also Juliana Schiesari, *The Gendering of Melancholia* (Ithaca: Cornell University Press, 1992), ch. 5.
28. Webber, p. 112.
29. On this, see especially Colie, p. 431.
30. Breitenberg, p. 40.
31. Ibid., p. 49.
32. It is unfortunate that Breitenberg doesn't discuss the conclusion, presumably because he follows the Dell/Jordan-Smith text.
33. For the passage see the Oxford edition, vol. 1, p. 18.
34. It is worth noting that the Burton revealed in biographical details is not all that different to the 'Burton' within the *Anatomy*, see in particular information in Jean Robert Simon, *Robert Burton (1577–1640) L'Anatomie de la Mélancolie* (Paris: Didier, 1964); Richard L. Nochimson, 'Studies in the Life of Robert Burton', *YES* 4 (1974), 85–111; Oxford edition, vol. 1, xiii–xxii.
35. For an interesting account of Burton's geographical knowledge see Anne S. Chapple, 'Robert Burton's Geography of Melancholy', *SEL* 33 (1993), 99–130.

36. See Nochimson, pp. 93–7.
37. See Nicolas K. Kiessling, *The Library of Robert Burton* (Oxford: Oxford Bibliographical Society, 1988).
38. Ibid., p. xxxi.
39. Patrick Collinson, *The Religion of Protestants* (Oxford: Clarendon Press, 1982), pp. 133–4.
40. Peter McCullough, *Sermons at Court: Politics and Religion in Elizabethan and Jacobean Preaching* (Cambridge: Cambridge University Press, 1998), esp. chs. 3 and 4; see p. 5. I discuss a sermon by Laud below in Chapter 7, p. 162.
41. The key figures in this debate are Glenn Burgess, who, especially in *The Politics of the Ancient Constitution* (London: Macmillan, 1992) and *Absolute Monarchy and the Stuart Constitution* (New Haven: Yale University Press, 1996), argues for the consensual model, and J.P. Sommerville, who sums up his case for true ideological difference and debate in the revised edition of *Royalists and Patriots: Politics and Ideology in England 1603–1640* (London: Longman, 1999). Kevin Sharpe offers a complex engagement with these issues in *Remapping Early Modern England* (Cambridge: Cambridge University Press, 2000), especially in chapter 1, where he underlines his own belief in the necessity to cut through dichotomising views of early modern society and, in particular, to trace political ideas in cultural, as well as overtly political, texts. I also discuss some of these issues below in Chapter 7, especially in relation to the genre of history.
42. McCullough notes that James's support of preaching complicates any simple alignment of positions along preaching/anti-preaching lines, p. 156. The debates over the exact nature of anti-Calvinism before Laud can be traced especially through Patrick Collinson, *The Birthpangs of Protestant England* (London: Macmillan, 1988); Nicholas Tyacke, *Anti-Calvinists: The Rise of English Arminianism c. 1590–1640* (Oxford: Clarendon Press, 1987); Peter White, *Predestination, Policy and Polemic: Conflict and Consensus in the English Church from the Reformation to the Civil War* (Cambridge: Cambridge University Press, 1992); the issues are judiciously summed up in Anthony Milton's *Catholic and Reformed: The Roman and Protestant Churches in English Protestant Thought 1600–1640* (Cambridge: Cambridge University Press, 1995); Milton himself sees strong divisions in the Jacobean Church.
43. See *The Sermons of John Donne*, ed. George Potter and Evelyn Simpson, Vol. 3 (Berkeley: University of California Press, 1957), introduction; all page references in parentheses are to this volume.
44. Izaak Walton, *Lives*, ed. S.B. Carter (London: Falcon, 1951), p. 31.
45. Joan Webber, *Contrary Music: The Prose Style of John Donne* (Madison: University of Wisconsin Press, 1963), p. 28. The other standard studies of Donne's sermons concur; see William Mueller, *John Donne: Preacher* (Princeton: Princeton University Press, 1962); Winifried Schleiner, *The Imagery of John Donne's Sermons* (Providence: Brown University Press, 1970); Janel Mueller, ed., *Donne's Prebend Sermons* (Cambridge, Mass.: Harvard University Press, 1971), introduction; Gale H. Carrithers Jr., *Donne At Sermons: A Christian Existential World* (Albany: State University of New York Press, 1972).
46. See particularly the special issue of the *John Donne Journal*, edited by Jeanne Shami, focusing on the sermons, 11 (1992), Nos. 1 and 2, especially articles by Gale Carrithers Jr. and James D. Hardy Jr. and M.L. Donnelly; Jeanne

Shami's earlier article 'Kings and Desperate Men: John Donne Preaches at Court, *John Donne Journal* 6 (1987), 9–23); see also, for the period immediately leading up to 1621 when Donne was part of Doncaster's embassy, Paul R. Sellin, *So Doth, So Is Religion: John Donne and Diplomatic Contexts in the Reformed Netherlands, 1619–1620* (Columbia: University of Missouri Press, 1988).

47. I take my cue from the observations of Debora Kuller Shuger, *Habits of Thought in the English Renaissance: Religion, Politics and the Dominant Culture* (Berkeley: University of California Press, 1990), who points to Donne's sense of sin as rooted in the self, but also that 'the inner and outer man are both constructed politically', p. 209.

48. R.C. Bald, *John Donne: A Life* (Oxford: Clarendon Press, 1970), p. 174.

49. Ibid.

50. This is the same Burley noted in the previous chapter as the location for the performance of Jonson's *Gipsies Metamorphosed*, see above p. 9.

51. Shuger, p. 209.

52. See the discussion of Doncaster's banquet in the previous chapter, pp. 2–4.

53. Jonathan Sawday, *The Body Emblazoned: Dissection and the Human Body in Renaissance Culture* (London: Routledge, 1995), p. 21.

54. T.S. Eliot, *For Lancelot Andrewes* (1928: rpt. London: Faber, 1970), p. 11.

55. Ibid., p. 20.

56. References are to Lancelot Andrewes, *CXVI Sermons* (1629): this is the posthumous collection edited by Laud and Buckeridge. For an account of the texts and a good general introduction see G.M. Story, ed., Lancelot Andrewes, *Sermons* (Oxford: Clarendon Press, 1967).

57. This is emphasised by Joan Webber: 'The liveliness of Andrewes' sermons always comes from his colloquial ability to make a scene or attitude familiar by bringing it close', 'Celebration of Word and World in Lancelot Andrewes' Style', *JEGP* 64 (1965), 263.

58. Horton Davies describes Andrewes as having a 'spirit less contentious than that of many other preachers, especially when dealing with dissent from Roman Catholicism', *Like Angels from a Cloud: The English Metaphysical Preachers 1588–1645* (San Marino: Huntington Library, 1986), p. 196; one might also note that Andrewes's views fit perfectly into James's policy of toleration in 1621 – McCullough stresses that Andrewes's moderated anti-Catholicism mirrors 'James's own political distinction between moderate and radical Catholics', p. 123.

59. Story, p. xxiv.

60. Shuger, p. 63.

61. Ibid., p. 150.

62. Paul A. Welsby, *Lancelot Andrewes 1555–1626* (London: SPCK, 1958), p. 224.

63. The main studies of this aspect of the 1621 parliament that I have benefited from consulting are Robert Zaller, *The Parliament of 1621* (Berkeley: University of California Press, 1971); Conrad Russell, *Parliaments and English Politics* (Oxford: Clarendon Press, 1979), Chap. 2; S.L. Adams, 'Foreign Policy and the Parliaments of 1621 and 1624', in Kevin Sharpe, ed., *Faction and Parliament* (Oxford: Clarendon Press, 1978).

64. See Zaller, pp. 27–8.

65. Ibid., p. 30.

66. Shuger, p. 145.
67. The sermon was entered in the Stationers' register on 13 June.
68. Bald, p. 368.
69. Ibid., p. 370.
70. References are to Edward May, *A Sermon of the Communion of the Saints* (1621).
71. Bald, p. 370.
72. Wilfred R. Prest, *The Inns of Court under Elizabeth I and the Early Stuarts, 1590–1640* (London: Longman, 1972), p. 197.
73. May's sermon was delivered before Ussher's was preached, but the published sermon, with its newly written preface, seems (though I cannot prove this) to have something like Ussher's sermon in mind as its target.
74. Zaller, p. 33.
75. Ibid., p. 36.
76. Ibid., pp. 42–3.
77. *Commons Debates 1621*, ed. Notestein, Relf and Simpson (New Haven: Yale University Press, 1935), Vol. 4, p. 11.
78. References are to *The Substance of That Which Was Delivered in a Sermon Before the Commons House of Parliament, the 18. of February 1620 [ie 1621]* (1621).
79. Chamberlain, II (347).
80. *Commons Debates*, IV, p. 75.
81. Anthony Milton has pointed out that May's sermon attracted the attention of the licensing authorities Daniel Featley and Richard Sheldon: 'As Archbishop Abbot's licenser, Featley attempted in vain to ensure that Maie inserted a passage condemning the doctrine of transubstantiation in order to balance the incautious references to ministers as the "makers of Christ his body" in Maie's sermon', Milton, p. 199.
82. Burgess, *Politics*, p. 171.
83. Sommerville, passim, see esp. his postscript.
84. These issues will be discussed in more detail below in Chapters 5 and 6, which return to the subject of parliamentary debates.
85. J.R. Tanner, *Constitutional Documents of the Reign of James I* (Cambridge: Cambridge University Press, 1952), p. 80.
86. Ibid., p. 82. Nicholas Tyacke notes that the Directions were, in fact, 'largely inoperative', p. 103.
87. References to Thomas Gataker, *A Sparke Toward the Kindling of Sorrow for Sion* (1621).
88. Milton, p. 504.
89. For a good general account, see Marvin Arthur Breslow, *A Mirror of England: English Puritan Views of Foreign Nations, 1618–1640* (Cambridge, Mass.: Harvard University Press, 1970), ch. 2.
90. Zaller, p. 137.
91. Some further examples which I have reluctantly set aside are: Robert Jenison, *The Height of Israel's Heathenish Idolatry*, a pair of sermons, as the title-page goes on to explain, 'With a large application to our times, against Popery'; Henry King's Paul's Cross sermon of November 25, which set out to vindicate his recently deceased father, John King, Bishop of London, from (false) charges that he had died a Roman Catholic – this even

included a transcript of the examination by the Archbishop of Canterbury of the priest implicated in the charge; the sharply argued sermons of John Prideaux, Regius Professor at Oxford, collected as *Eight Sermons*, including one commemorating the discovery of the Gunpowder Plot (a popular theme for sermons, but still pointed in the midst of the 1621 controversies over Prince Charles's potential Catholic marriage); one should also note more popular anti-Catholic works, some of which I discuss in chapter 7, such as Alexander Cooke's *More Work for a Masse Priest*, or Thomas Clarke's *The Pope's Deadly Wound*, written as a kind of collection of easily understood objections to Catholicism for use by the ordinary person. Timothy Rogers offers a wonderful redefinition of the word 'Puritan' and defence against its pejorative use in *The Roman Catharist: Or, The Papist is a Puritan*, arguing that 'Puritan' should be reserved for heresy (the prime example being the Church of Rome), and offering such stout accounts of true godliness as: 'if a man will not swagger, and sweare and forsweare, drinke and be drunken, and play the Ruffian, and conforme himself to euerie apish, or rather monstrous attire, and cut himselfe out into euerie fashionless fashion and newfangled shape, that will not lie for aduantage, cousen, game, cheate, dissemble, followe unlawfull gaine, and pleasures and run to the same excesse of riot with others, straightway he shall bee sure of this benevolence (which is no better then malevolence) to bee bestowed on him, O you are so pure, and holy, too pure for our companie, you are one of those Puritanes, one of the holy brethren &c.' (39–40).

92. References to Samuel Ward, *The Happiness of Practice* (1621).
93. Arthur Hind, in *Engraving in England in the Sixteenth and Seventeenth Centuries* (Cambridge: Cambridge University Press, 1955), Vol. 2, reproduces the engraving as plate 247, and sees Ward as the originator of the engraving's concept, rather than its executioner: 'There is in fact a MS. in the British Museum (Marl. MS. 389.f.15) which appears to be Samuel Ward's directions to the engraver rather than notes after the engraving' (p. 394).
94. *Pace* Hind, to my eyes this figure resembles portraits of Gondomar far more than the figure seated beside the General of the Jesuits.
95. *The Life of Faith. The second Edition* (1621), p. 24.
96. See Milton, pp. 94–5; also Kenneth Fincham and Peter Lake, 'The Ecclesiastical Policy of King James I', *Journal of British Studies* 24 (1985), 169–207; and W.B. Patterson, 'King James and the Protestant Cause in the Crisis of 1618–22', *Studies in Church History* 18 (1982), 319–34. On the importance of the Book of Sports, discussed further in Chapter 7, see Leah S. Marcus, *The Politics of Mirth* (Chicago: University of Chicago Press, 1986).
97. For a detailed account of Bacon in 1621 see Jonathan Marwil, *The Trial of Counsel: Francis Bacon in 1621* (Detroit: Wayne State University Press, 1976), and my discussion in Chapter 6.
98. References to Samuel Ward, *Jethro's Justice of the Peace* (1621).
99. Zaller, pp. 44–5.
100. McCullough points out that Charles's chaplains, like his deceased brother Henry's, were generally evangelical Calvinists who espoused strong anti-Catholic views, pp. 200–2.
101. References to the revised edition, *The Vanity of the Eye* (1633).

102. *Boswell's Life of Johnson*, ed., G.B. Hill, rev. L.F. Powell (Oxford: Clarendon Press, 1971), Vol. 1, p. 219.
103. References to George Hakewill, *King David's Vow for Reformation of Himself his Family his Kingdom* (1621).
104. A most interesting parallel is found in the examination of Samuel Philips later in the year (in November) over a sermon he delivered at St Paul's, 'concerning the Mariadg of Protestants wth Papists'; Philips included a discussion of the unlawfulness of Protestant Princes marrying Catholic Princesses: 'Being asked further what reasons he vsed to prove this doctrine of his, he aunswereth that first it was against the commandment of God who forbids vs to marry with Idolaters . . . Being asked whether he thought ye Papists idolaters, or no; he aunswereth that he thinkes most of them are, but he will not say so of all.' Philips tried a bit of disingenuous reasoning at the very end to exonerate himself: 'Lastly he desired this to be added that he did not mean any Prince in particular but spoke yt he did of Princes in generall & further that he never knew of any treaty betwixt his majesty & the King of Spain concerning any marriadg for the Prince wth a daughter of Spain.' See PRO *State Papers Domestic, James I*, 14/123, fol. 105.
105. See Pauline Gregg, *King Charles I* (London: Dent, 1981), pp. 73–4; see also Fincham and Lake, p. 200; Milton, p. 193.
106. PRO *State Papers Domestic, James I*, 14/122, fol. 88–88v.
107. Two manuscripts of *The Wedding Robe* are in the Bodleian Library: the presentation copy in Hakewill's own hand, in Bodleian MS Rawlinson D 853, and a scribal copy, in Bodleian MS Jones 14, which is identical except that it omits the prefatory letter and a final sentence.
108. Rawlinson D 853, preface.
109. References in parentheses are to Bodleian MS Jones 14.

## Chapter 3: Transformations of Romance

1. I have outlined some of these developments in *English Prose Fiction 1558–1700: A Critical History* (Oxford: Clarendon Press, 1985), chs 10 and 11.
2. Josephine A. Roberts, ed., *The Poems of Lady Mary Wroth* (Baton Rouge: Louisiana State University Press: 1983); Josephine A. Roberts, ed., Mary Wroth, *The First Part of the Countess of Montgomery's Urania* (Binghampton: Medieval and Renaissance Texts and Studies, 1995); this volume is the printed 1621 *Urania*, the manuscript continuation is published as *The Second Part of the Countess of Montgomery's Urania*, ed. Roberts, completed by Suzanne Gossett and Janel Mueller (Tempe: Renaissance English Text Society, 1999); Naomi J. Miller and Gary Waller, eds., *Reading Mary Wroth: Representing Alternatives in Early Modern England* (Knoxville: University of Tennessee Press, 1992). This recent attention to Wroth could be seen as answering Carol Neely's feminist challenge to new historicism, both through her suggestion that there is a need to 'overread men's canonical texts with women's uncanonical ones' and the need to example the implications of gender in Renaissance literature and its criticism. See Carol Thomas Neely, 'Constructing the Subject: Feminist Practice and the New Renaissance Discourses', *English Literary Renaissance* 18 (1988), 5–18.

3. See especially Mary Ellen Lamb, *Gender and Authorship in the Sidney Circle* (Madison: University of Wisconsin Press, 1990); Gary Waller, 'Mother/Son, Father/Daughter, Brother/Sister, Cousins: the Sidney Family Romance', *Modern Philology* 88 (1991), 401–14, 'The Sidney Family Romance: Mary Wroth and Gender Construction in Early Modern England', in Miller and Waller, and *The Sidney Family Romance: Mary Wroth, William Herbert and the Early Modern Construction of Gender* (Detroit: Wayne State University Press, 1993); P.J. Croft, ed., *The Poems of Robert Sidney* (Oxford: Clarendon Press, 1988). Gary Waller contends that 'The Sidney family ... was not merely a collection of individual men and women linked by kinship, but also a major site of contradictory cultural forces, a discursive formation in miniature in which the broader conflicts of the age were being enacted', in 'The Countess of Pembroke and Gendered Reading', in Anne M. Haselkorn and Betty S. Travitsky, eds., *The Renaissance Englishwoman In Print* (Amherst: University of Massachusetts Press, 1990), p. 334.

4. For this approach see, for example, Lamb, *Gender and Authorship*; and, in a context wider than simply Sidney, see Naomi Miller, '"Not much to be marked": Narrative of the Woman's Part in Lady Mary Wroth's *Urania*', *SEL* 29 (1989), 120–37; Maureen Quilligan, in an extremely suggestive article, points to the empowerment for Wroth of her alliance with her cousin, and of 'brother–sister' ties in general: 'Lady Mary Wroth: Female Authority and the Family Romance', in *Unfolded Tales: Essays on Renaissance Romance*, ed. George Logan and Gordon Teskey (Ithaca: Cornell University Press, 1989), 257–80; Josephine A. Roberts, 'Labyrinths of Desire: Lady Mary Wroth's Reconstruction of Romance', *Women's Studies* 19 (1991), 183–92; and a judicious summing up in Helen Hackett, *Women and Romance Fiction in the English Renaissance* (Cambridge: Cambridge University Press, 2000), ch. 10.

5. See John J. O'Connor, 'James Hay and the Countess of Montgomery's *Urania*', *Notes and Queries* 200 (1955), 150–2; Josephine A. Roberts, 'An Unpublished Literary Quarrel Concerning the Suppression of Mary Wroth's *Urania*', *Notes and Queries* 222 (1977), 532–5; Paul Salzman, 'Contemporary References in Mary Wroth's *Urania*', *Review of English Studies* 29 (1978), 178–81; there is a full account in Roberts's edition of Wroth's poetry, which includes complete transcripts of the poems exchanged by Wroth and Denny, pp. 31–5. Denny's daughter Honora married James Hay in 1607 (she died in 1614); see the discussion of Hay's 1621 banquet in chapter 1, above.

6. Roberts, *Poems of Mary Wroth*, p. 32.

7. This aspect of Denny's response is discussed cogently by Mary Ellen Lamb, who stresses the sexual ambivalence present in Denny's imagery, in *Gender and Authorship*, 156–9.

8. Roberts, *Poems of Mary Wroth*, p. 239.

9. Ibid., p. 33.

10. *Letters of John Chamberlain*, ed. N. E. McClure (Philadelphia: American Philosophical Society, 1939), 2, p. 427.

11. Throughout this chapter, references are to Josephine Roberts's edition of the printed text of *Urania* (1621), cited as 1, and to the manuscript continuation held in the Newberry Library (Case MS fY 1565.W95),

described as the 'second part', cited as 2. The continuation is in two parts.

12. Philippa Berry, *Of Chastity and Power: Elizabethan Literature and the Unmarried Queen* (London: Routledge, 1989), p. 69.

13. On this aspect of Sidney, see Katherine Duncan-Jones, 'Philip Sidney's Toys', *Proceedings of the British Academy* 46 (1986): 161–78, repr. in Dennis Kay, ed., *Sir Philip Sidney: An Anthology of Modern Criticism* (Oxford: Clarendon Press, 1987), pp. 61–80.

14. Roberts, *Poems of Mary Wroth*, p. 236.

15. Ibid.

16. Annabel Patterson, *Censorship and Interpretation: The Conditions of Writing and Reading in Early Modern England* (Madison: University of Wisconsin Press, 1984), p. 18. For Sidney's influence in the seventeenth century, see, among other studies, John Buxton, *Sir Philip Sidney and the English Renaissance* (London, 1964); W. H. Bond, 'The Reputation and Influence of Sir Philip Sidney', (unpublished PhD Dissertation, Harvard University, 1941); Dennis Kay, 'Sidney – A Critical Heritage', in Kay, *Sir Philip Sidney*, pp. 3–41; and Jackson Boswell and H. R. Woudhuysen, 'Some Unfamiliar Sidney Allusions', in Jan Van Dorsten et al., *Sir Philip Sidney: 1586 and the Creation of a Legend* (Leiden: E.J. Brill, 1986), pp. 221–37.

17. For a general account of these, see Paul Salzman, *English Prose Fiction 1558–1700: A Critical History* (Oxford: Clarendon Press, 1985), ch. 10.

18. David Norbrook, *Poetry and Politics in the English Renaissance* (London: Routledge, 1984), p. 207; see also Michelle O'Callaghan, *The 'Shepheard's Nation': Jacobean Spenserians and Early Stuart Political Culture 1612–1625* (Oxford: Clarendon Press, 2000); and Michael Brennan, *Literary Patronage in the English Renaissance: The Pembroke Family* (London: Routledge, 1988), p. 134.

19. See Margot Heinemann, *Puritanism and Theatre: Thomas Middleton and Opposition Drama Under the Stuarts* (Cambridge: Cambridge University Press, 1980), pp. 264–83, for the strongest statement of this view of Herbert, a view which may be countered somewhat by David Norbrook, who sees the Herbert group as less coherently oppositional, in *Poetry and Politics*, p. 185. The complex and ongoing debate between historians over the nature of political factions at this time is obviously relevant to my account of Wroth's position at court. The most convincing adjustment of the views of revisionist historians (e.g. Kevin Sharpe, ed., *Faction and Parliament: Essays on Early Stuart History* [Oxford: Clarendon Press, 1978]; and Kevin Sharpe, 'Faction at the Early Stuart Court', *History Today* 33 [1983], 39–46) is Linda Levy Peck, *Court Patronage and Corruption in Early Stuart England* (Boston: Unwin Hyman, 1990), esp. ch. 3. Peck stresses 'the fluidity and fragility of patronage networks', p. 54.

20. See Wallace Notestein, *The House of Commons 1604–10* (New Haven: Yale University Press, 1971) p. 63.

21. Roberts, *Poems of Mary Wroth*, p. 12.

22. Ethel Carleton Williams, *Anne of Denmark* (London: Longman, 1970), p. 76; for an interesting account of Anne's court as a realm of female resistance see Barbara Lewalski, *Writing Women in Jacobean England* (Cambridge, Mass.: Harvard University Press, 1993), ch. 1.

23. In this respect, James's court may be contrasted with Elizabeth's; see the interesting discussion in Philippa Berry, who stresses the challenge of Elizabeth to 'conventional ideas both of masculine and feminine identity', and notes the roles allowed for noble women, in contrast to their marginalisation under James, *Of Chastity and Power*, pp. 68 and 79; see also Peck, *Court Patronage*, pp. 68–74.

24. Roy Strong, *Henry, Prince of Wales and England's Lost Renaissance* (London: Thames and Hudson, 1986), p. 145; and see also Graham Parry, *The Golden Age Restor'd: The Culture of the Stuart Court 1603–1640* (Manchester: Manchester University Press, 1981), ch. 3.

25. Strong, pp. 141 and 158.

26. For some examples of significant masques in *Urania*, see 1.144, 2.i.14v–15v, 2.i.41–41v, 2.ii.26; for tilts see 1.77, 92, 120, 196, 415.

27. There are many studies on this; see in particular Richard C. McCoy, *Sir Philip Sidney: Rebellion in Arcadia* (Brighton: Harvester Press, 1979); Alan Sinfield, 'Power and Ideology: An Outline Theory and Sidney's *Arcadia*', *ELH* 52 (1985), 259–77; Christopher Martin, 'Misdoubting His Estate: Dynastic Anxiety In Sidney's *Arcadia*', *English Literary Renaissance* 18 (1988), 369–88; Blair Worden, *The Sound of Virtue: Philip Sidney's Arcadia and Elizabethan Politics* (New Haven: Yale University Press, 1996).

28. Sir Fulke Greville, *Life of Sir Philip Sidney*, ed. Nowell Smith (Oxford, 1907), pp. 13 and 11.

29. See Margaret P. Hannay, *Philip's Phoenix: Mary Sidney Countess of Pembroke* (New York: Oxford University Press, 1990), passim.

30. See Bent Juel-Jensen, 'Sir Philip Sidney, 1554–1586: A Check-List of Early Editions of his Works', in Kay, pp. 289–314.

31. Roberts, *First Part of Urania*, pp. xxxix–xl.

32. Leah S. Marcus, *Puzzling Shakespeare: Local Reading and its Discontents* (Berkeley: University of California Press, 1988), p. 104. Among the many important accounts of how Elizabeth's reign unsettled assumptions about gender and ideology, see especially Louis Adrian Montrose, '"Shaping Fantasies": Figurations of Gender and Power in Elizabethan Culture', *Representations* 1 (1983), 61–94; Berry offers a counter view to Montrose, suggesting that Elizabeth's reign was a much more 'radical event' (see *Of Chastity and Power*, ch. 3).

33. Josephine A. Roberts, 'Radigund Revisited: Perspectives on Women Rulers in Lady Mary Wroth's *Urania*', in Haselkorn and Travitsky, p. 202; the concept of the Queen's two bodies is analysed in Marie Axton, *The Queen's Two Bodies* (London: Royal Historical Society, 1977), which in turn draws on Ernst H. Kantorowicz, *The King's Two Bodies* (Princeton: Princeton University Press, 1957).

34. Jeff Masten, '"Shall I turne blabb?": Circulation, Gender and Subjectivity in Mary Wroth's Sonnets', in Miller and Waller, pp. 70 and 76.

35. Ann Rosalind Jones, 'Designing Women: The Self as Spectacle in Mary Wroth and Veronica Franco', in Miller and Waller, pp. 135–53.

36. For an excellent example of this, see Marion Wynne Davies, '"Et in Arcadia Ego": Lady Mary Wroth's Excursion into Renaissance Pastoral', in Kate Chedgzoy et al., *Voicing Women: Gender and Sexuality in Early Modern Writing* (Keele: Keele University Press, 1996).

37. Jonathan Goldberg, *James I and the Politics of Literature* (Baltimore and London: Johns Hopkins University Press, 1983), p. 150; Susan Dwyer Amussen, *An Ordered Society: Gender and Class in Early Modern England* (Oxford: Basil Blackwell, 1988), p. 2.
38. Roberts, *Poems of Mary Wroth*, p. 34.
39. Mary Ellen Lamb stresses the sense of sexual anxiety behind Denny's response; see *Gender and Authorship*, pp. 154–9.
40. The two most dramatically opposed views on this debate are contained in Caroline Ruth Swift, 'Female Identity in Lady Mary Wroth's Romance *Urania*', *English Literary Renaissance* 14 (1984), which sees the female characters as victims, and Naomi Miller, '"Not much to be marked"', and 'Women's Voices in Wroth's *Urania* and Shakespeare's Plays', in Miller and Waller, who sees female solidarity and resistance. Accounts more sympathetic to the argument I am putting forward here include Hackett, '"Yet Tell Me Some Such Fiction"', and Roberts, 'Labyrinths of Desire'. For a fascinating account of Wroth's 'manipulation of cultural constructions of the woman reader to provide some degree of dignity to women's reading', thereby enabling a precarious negotiation of the pressures of the masculine world of letters, see Mary Ellen Lamb, 'Women Readers in Mary Wroth's *Urania*', in Miller and Waller, p. 225, and see also Lamb's analysis of *Urania* in *Gender and Authorship*. Patricia Parker has offered an excellent account of the way in which attitudes towards rhetoric replicate the gendered dimension of the public/private dichotomy, noting that 'the clear link that would keep women from learning rhetoric as specifically public speech is the long association in which a "public woman," and especially one who spoke in public, could only be called a whore', *Literary Fat Ladies* (London: Methuen, 1987), p. 104; once again, this particular set of prejudices is reflected in Denny's response to Wroth.
41. Roberts, 'Radigund Revisited', p. 200.
42. See especially the discussion in Lamb, *Gender and Authorship*.
43. The whole issue of the gaze in *Urania* has been discussed cogently by Helen Hackett, '"Yet Tell Me Some Such Fiction"', in Clare Brant and Diane Purkiss, *Women, Texts and Histories 1575–1760* (London: Routledge, 1992), p. 56 and also in her essay 'The Torture of Limena', in Kate Chedgzoy, Melanie Hansen and Suzanne Trill, eds., *Voicing Women* (Edinburgh: Edinburgh University Press, 1998), pp. 93–110.
44. Wroth here offers an important counterbalance to the rigid gender divisions reinforced by the blazon as a rhetorical device which have been examined by Patricia Parker in *Literary Fat Ladies*, drawing also on the work of Nancy Vickers in 'Diana Described: Scattered Woman and Scattered Rhyme', *Critical Inquiry* 8 (1981), 265–79; and '"The blazon of sweet beauty's best": Shakespeare's Lucrece', in Patricia Parker and Geoffrey Hartman, eds., *Shakespeare and the Question of Theory* (New York: Methuen, 1985).
45. There have been many attempts to pin down the exact genre of both *Arcadias*; of particular relevance to my argument about the nature of generic interaction in *Urania* is Peter Lindenbaum's thesis about Sidney as an 'anti-pastoral' writer in *Changing Landscapes: Anti-Pastoral Sentiment in The English Renaissance* (Athens: University of Georgia Press, 1986), chs. 2 and 3, and

also his essay 'Sidney and the Active Life', in M.J.B. Allen et al., eds., *Sir Philip Sidney's Achievements* (New York: AMS Press, 1990).

46. *A Defence of Poetry*, ed. J.A. Van Dorsten (Oxford: Oxford University Press, 1966), pp. 40–1; for a general account of the influence of *Amadis* on Elizabethan literature, see John J. O'Connor, *Amadis de Gaule and its Influence on Elizabethan Literature* (New Brunswick: Rutgers University Press, 1970); O'Connor makes no mention of *Urania*; the influence of *Amadis* on Wroth is noted in Josephine Roberts, 'The Marriage Controversy in Wroth's *Urania*', in Miller and Waller, p. 126.

47. For an important analysis of Tyler, see Tina Krontiris, 'Breaking the Barriers of Genre and Gender: Margaret Tyler's Translation of The Mirrour of Knighthood', *English Literary Renaissance* 18 (1988): 19–39; see also Hackett, '"Yet Tell Me Some Such Fiction"', 44–5.

48. Of the many studies of pastoral, see in particular Helen Cooper, *Pastoral: Medieval into Renaissance* (Ipswich: D.S. Brewer/Rowman and Littlefield, 1977), chs. 4–6; Andrew V. Ettin, *Literature and the Pastoral* (New Haven: Yale University Press, 1984).

49. *Urania*'s unfinished state can be viewed as part of Wroth's homage to Sidney, echoing the unfinished *New Arcadia*; but it can also be seen as part of the resistance to closure of the romance form itself; see Patricia Parker, *Inescapable Romance: The Poetics of a Mode* (Princeton: Princeton University Press, 1979).

50. Roberts, *Poems of Mary Wroth*, p. 236.

51. See DNB.

52. See Ben Jonson, *Works*, ed., C.H. Herford and P. Simpson (Oxford: Oxford University Press, 1925), vol. 1, pp. 74–5, Vol. 11, p. 78.

53. An abridged translation published by John Jacob in 1734, and Clara Reeve's translation, *The Phoenix*, published in 1772.

54. Annabel Patterson, *Censorship and Interpretation* (Madison: University of Wisconsin Press, 1984), p. 180; see Patterson's general account, pp. 180–5, and see also Salzman, *English Prose Fiction*, pp. 149–55.

55. Unless otherwise noted, references are to *Barclay His Argenis*, trans. Kingesmill Long, 2nd edition (1636); references for Latin quotations are to John Barclay, *Argenis*, ed. secunda (Paris, 1627).

56. For example, see the defence of a monastic life on pp. 652ff; for the critical account of Calvin, see pp. 134ff.

57. Patterson offers a fascinating reading of this aspect of *Argenis* in relation to Charles' situation in 1628/9, when the Le Grys translation was published (see pp. 183–4). It seems to me to be even more relevant to James's situation in 1621/2.

58. 'Scilicet neruos imperii, id est aerarium, in potestate populi esse; Hunc arbitrum rerum, & suorum Regum Regem vno hoc iure publicis omnibus coeptis, consiliis, viribus, moderare? Certe non regnandi veras leges hoc pati; non cum sumni imerii convenire' (790).

59. 'Indulgere plus iusto venatui, in cuius varia genera annum distinxerat. Non consilio amicitias fortiri, impetuque eas colere: largiri immodice, horrere a negociorum summa, quam plerumque insidis credebat' (14).

60. Patterson, p. 160.

61. See especially Roberts's introduction pp. xxxix–lxix.

## Chapter 4: Performances

1. Amongst many studies, those particularly related to this book include A.A. Bromham and Zara Bruzzi, *The Changeling and the Years of Crisis* (London: Pinter, 1990); Margot Heinemann, *Puritanism and Theatre: Thomas Middleton and Opposition Drama Under the Early Stuarts* (Cambridge: Cambridge University Press, 1980); Jerzy Limon, *Dangerous Matter: English Drama and Politics in 1623/4* (Cambridge: Cambridge University Press, 1986); and although it concentrates on a later period, Martin Butler, *Theatre and Crisis 1632-1642* (Cambridge: Cambridge University Press, 1984) has become particularly influential.

2. The information that follows is taken from a number of sources, principally E.K. Chambers, *The Elizabethan Stage* (Oxford: Clarendon Press, 1951), 4 vols; G.E. Bentley, *The Jacobean and Caroline Stage* (Oxford: Clarendon Press, 1941-68), 7 vols; Andrew Gurr, *The Shakespearean Stage 1574-1642*, 3rd edition (Cambridge: Cambridge University Press, 1992); Alexander Leggatt, *Jacobean Public Theatre* (London: Routledge, 1992); Keith Sturgess, *Jacobean Private Theatre* (London: Routledge, 1987); Andrew Gurr, *Playgoing in Shakespeare's London* (Cambridge: Cambridge University Press, 1987).

3. For plays and performances, as well as Chambers and Bentley, I have consulted Alfred Harbage rev. S. Schoenbaum, *Annals of English Drama 975-1700* (London: Routledge, 1989) and Yoshiko Kawachi, *Calendar of English Renaissance Drama 1558-1642* (New York: Garland, 1986).

4. REED, *Norwich 1540-1642*, ed. David Galloway (Toronto: University of Toronto Press, 1984), p. 165. There are numerous other examples in the various volumes of REED published thus (2001) far.

5. REED, *Cambridge*, ed. Alan H. Nelson (Toronto: University of Toronto Press, 1989), vol. 2, pp. 713-14.

6. Ibid., p. 975; for James's visit to Oxford in 1621 see Chapter 5, p. 132.

7. Plays definitely performed in 1621: Dekker, Ford and Rowley's *Witch of Edmonton*; Fletcher's *Island Princess*; Jasper Garnett's *Tenants' Complaint Against the Landlords* (lost); Massinger's *The Woman's Plot* (lost); Middleton's *Anything For A Quiet Life*; *The Woman is Too Hard For Him* (lost); *Grammercy Wit* (lost) and *The Man in the Moon Drinks Claret* (lost). Plays almost certainly performed in 1621: Fletcher's *Pilgrim* and *Wild Goose Chase*; Massinger's *Duke of Milan* and *Maid of Honour*; plays probably performed in 1621: Middleton's *Women Beware Women*.

8. See in particular Margot Heinemann, *Puritanism and Theatre: Thomas Middleton and Opposition Drama Under the Stuarts* (Cambridge: Cambridge University Press, 1980); Heinemann also offers a useful general approach to early modern drama as a whole in 'Political Drama', in A.R. Braunmuller and Michael Hattaway, eds., *The Cambridge Companion to English Renaissance Drama* (Cambridge: Cambridge University Press, 1990).

9. Middleton and Rowley's *The Changeling* (1622) has also been the subject of an elaborate political reading in A.A. Bromham and Zara Bruzzi, *The Changeling and the Years of Crisis* (London: Pinter, 1990).

10. *Puritanism and Theatre*, p. 180.

11. Ibid., p. 198.

12. See *Women Beware Women* I.3.91. There is a lengthy discussion of the play's date in the Revels edition, ed. J.R. Mulryne (London: Methuen, 1975), pp. xxxii–xxxviii.
13. Page references are to ibid.
14. A.A. Bromham, 'The Tragedy of Peace: Political Meaning in *Women Beware Women*', *SEL*, 26 (1986), 309–29.
15. Albert H. Tricomi, *Anticourt Drama in England 1603–1642* (Charlotteville: University Press of Virginia, 1989).
16. I have mentioned this debate briefly in relation to Rachel Speght (see above, Chapter 2). An important reassessment of the debate, which stresses intersections of class as well as gender issues, and which examines the whole issue of the desire for an uncontested female authorship for the tracts which defended women in the debate, may be found in Diane Purkiss, 'Material Girls: The Seventeenth-Century Woman Debate', in Clare Brant and Diane Purkiss, *Women, Texts & Histories* (London: Routledge, 1993), 69–101.
17. One of these types of pamphlet published in 1621, *A Discourse of the Married and Single Life*, is discussed below in Chapter 7.
18. See F.L. Lucas, *The Complete Works of John Webster* (1927, rpt. London: Chatto and Windus, 1966), vol. 4 – references are to this edition; Heinemann, *Puritanism and Theatre*, pp. 116–20; Bromham and Bruzzi, pp. 166–9.
19. *Puritanism and Theatre*, p. 117.
20. Ibid., p. 119.
21. Bromham and Bruzzi, p. 168.
22. See the description of this and other shows in David M. Bergeron, *English Civic Pageantry 1558–1642* (London: Edward Arnold, 1971), pp. 179–200.
23. Ibid., p. 200.
24. Lawrence Manley, *Literature and Culture in Early Modern London* (Cambridge: Cambridge University Press, 1995), p. 262.
25. Ibid., p. 282.
26. See Thomas Middleton, *Honourable Entertainments* ed. R.C. Bald (Oxford: Malone Society, 1953), facsimile, B6–B7. Further references are to this edition.
27. See Robert Ashton, *The City and the Court 1603–1643* (Cambridge: Cambridge University Press, 1979), p. 108.
28. For a description, see Chamberlain, p. 361 (letter 377).
29. James F. Larkin and Paul L. Hughes, *Stuart Royal Proclamations* (Oxford: Clarendon Press, 1973), vol. 1.
30. Ibid., p. 509.
31. For dates, see G.E. Bentley, *The Jacobean and Caroline Stage*, vol. 3 (Oxford: Clarendon Press, 1956), pp. 347–50 and 425–30.
32. See the work of Philip Finkelpearl; in particular, *Court and Country Politics in the Plays of Beaumont and Fletcher* (Princeton: Princeton University Press, 1990); '"The Comedians' Liberty": Censorship of the Jacobean Stage Reconsidered', *ELR*, 16 (1986), 123–38; and 'John Fletcher as Spenserian Playwright: The Faithful Shepherdess and The Island Princess', *SEL*, 27 (1987), 285–302; and Gordon McMullan, *The Politics of Unease in the Plays of John Fletcher* (Amherst: University of Massachusetts Press, 1994).
33. McMullan offers a detailed interpretation of this aspect of *The Island Princess*, pp. 224–36 and see the suggestive reading by Andrew Hadfield, which

brings out some of the complexities of the play's treatment of the colonial experience, in *Literature, Travel and Colonial Writing in the English Renaissance 1545–1625* (Oxford: Clarendon Press, 1998), pp. 254–64.

34.  References are to *The Dramatic Works in the Beaumont and Fletcher Canon*, ed. Fredson Bowers, vol. 5 (Cambridge: Cambridge University Press, 1982).
35.  'John Fletcher as Spenserian Poet', p. 290.
36.  Ibid., p. 295.
37.  The most sophisticated and wide ranging of these readings remains Peter Hulme's in *Colonial Encounters* (London: Methuen, 1986), ch. 3.
38.  Ibid., pp. 130–1.
39.  References are to *The Dramatic Works in tne Beaumont and Fletcher Canon*, ed. Fredson Bowers, vol. 6 (Cambridge: Cambridge University Press, 1985).
40.  For information on *Thierry and Theodoret* see E.K. Chambers, *The Elizabethan Stage*, vol. 3 (Oxford: Clarendon Press, 1951), p. 230.
41.  References are to *The Dramatic Works in the Beaumont and Fletcher Canon*, ed., Fredson Bowers, vol. 3 (Cambridge: Cambridge University Press, 1976).
42.  David Harris Wilson, *King James VI and I* (London: Jonathan Cape, 1956), p. 384.
43.  See Roger Lockyer, 'An English *Valido*? Buckingham and James I', Richard Ollard and Pamela Tudor-Craig, *For Veronica Wedgwood These* (London: Collins, 1986), p. 55 and passim; and his biography *Buckingham* (London: Longman, 1981).
44.  See Robert Zaller, *The Parliament of 1621* (Berkeley: University of California Press, 1971), pp. 116–25; and my discussion of parliament in Chapter 2 and Chapter 6.
45.  For an important account of these verse libels, see Alastair Bellany, '"Rayling Rymes and Vaunting Verse": Libellous Politics in Early Stuart England, 1603–1628', in Kevin Sharpe and Peter Lake, eds., *Culture and Politics in Early Stuart England* (London: Macmillan, 1994), pp. 285–310; and Andrew McRae, 'The Literary Culture of Early Stuart Libeling', *MP*, 97 (2000), 364–92; some of the libels (but not the most obscene ones) were collected by Frederick Fairholt, *Poems and Songs Relating to George Villiers, Duke of Buckingham* (London: Percy Society, 1850).
46.  I am encouraged in my political reading of Massinger by Annabel Patterson, who makes a strong case for such a reading in *Censorship and Interpretation* (Madison: University of Wisconsin Press, 1984), pp. 79–84; she offers a suggestive account of the political reverberations of the idea of honour in *The Maid of Honour*, but then concentrates on later plays: *The Bondman* and *The Roman Actor*.
47.  References are to *The Plays and Poems of Philip Massinger*, ed. P. Edwards and C. Gibson (Oxford: Clarendon Press, 1976), vol. 1.
48.  See Bellany, pp. 297–8.
49.  Quoted in Wilson, pp. 384–5.
50.  See Cyrus Hoy, 'Massinger as Collaborator: The Plays with Fletcher and Others', in Douglas Howard, ed., *Philip Massinger: A Critical Reassessment* (Cambridge: Cambridge University Press, 1985), 51–82.
51.  *The Dramatic Works in the Beaumont and Fletcher Canon*, ed. Fredson Bowers, vol. 9 (Cambridge: Cambridge University Press, 1994); references are to this edition

52. McMullan, p. 183.
53. Ibid., pp. 152–3; Hoy outlines the division between the two playwrights in his introduction, p. 98.
54. Jeffrey Masten, *Textual Intercourse: Collaboration, Authorship, and Sexualities in Renaissance Drama* (Cambridge: Cambridge University Press, 1997), p. 9.
55. See my discussions of 'The Book of Sports' in Chapters 2 and 7.
56. Anthony B. Dawson, 'Witchcraft/Bigamy: Cultural Conflict in The Witch of Edmonton', *Renaissance Drama* n.s. 20 (1989), p. 78; while Lena Orlin has many fascinating things to say about the domestic tragedy aspect of the play, her decision to set aside the witch skews her argument, see *Private Matters and Public Culture in Post-Reformation England* (Ithaca: Cornell University Press, 1994), p. 251.
57. See Diane Purkiss, *The Witch in History* (London: Routledge, 1996), p. 232.
58. References are to Fredson Bowers, ed., *The Dramatic Works of Thomas Dekker*, vol. 3 (Cambridge: Cambridge University Press, 1958).
59. *The Witch of Edmonton*, ed. Arthur Kinney (New York: Norton, 1998), pp. xxiii–xxviii.
60. For a more detailed account of Bacon's impeachment in 1621, see Chapter 7.
61. See especially Stephen Orgel, *The Illusion of Power: Political Theatre in the English Renaissance* (Berkeley: University of California Press, 1975). The shift from Orgel's sense of the masque as replicating James's ideal of the monarchy towards a notion of the form as much more contested politically is evident in Lawrence Venuti's Marxist account, *Our Halcyon Days* (Madison: University of Wisconsin Press, 1989), ch. 4, and in the diverse essays in David Bevington and Peter Holbrook, eds., *The Politics of The Stuart Court Masque* (Cambridge: Cambridge University Press, 1998). The shift is concisely summed up in Leah Marcus's conclusion to the Bevington/Holbrook volume.
62. Jerzy Limon, *The Masque of Stuart Culture* (Newark: University of Delaware Press, 1990), pp. 19–24.
63. The Burley performance has been discussed above in Chapter 1.
64. Martin Butler, 'Ben Jonson's *Pan's Anniversary* and the Politics of Early Stuart Pastoral', *ELR*, 22 (1992), 369–404; and '"We are one mans all": Jonson's The Gipsies Metamorphosed', in Cedric Brown, ed., *Patronage, Politics and Literary Traditions in England 1558–1658* (Detroit: Wayne State University Press, 1991), pp. 247–67.
65. See, for example, Michelle O'Callaghan, *The 'Shepheard's Nation': Jacobean Spenserians and Early Stuart Political Culture 1612–1625* (Oxford: Clarendon Press, 2000).
66. Chamberlain, Letters, II, 333.
67. References are to W.W. Greg, ed., *Jonson's Masque of Gipsies* (London: British Academy, 1952).
68. Stephen Orgel, 'To Make Boards Speak: Inigo Jones's Stage and the Jonsonian Masque', in Samuel Schoenbaum, ed., *Renaissance Drama*, 1 (1968), p. 44.
69. Dale B.J. Randall, *Jonson Gypsies Unmasked: Background and Theme of The Gypsies Metamorphosed* (Durham NC: Duke University Press, 1975), passim.
70. Butler, '"We are one mans all"', p. 253.

71. Ibid., p. 251.
72. Timothy Raylor, 'The "Lost" *Essex House Masque* (1621): A Manuscript Text Discovered', *English Manuscript Studies 1100–1700*, 7 (1998), 86–130; and see also his 'The Design and Authorship of The Essex House Masque (1621)', *Medieval and Renaissance Drama in England*, 10 (1998), 218–37.
73. 'The "Lost": *Essex House Masque*', p. 112.
74. Alfred Harbage, *Shakespeare's Audience* (New York: Columbia University Press, 1941); Ann Jennalie Cook, *The Privileged Playgoers of Shakespeare's London* (Princeton: Princeton University Press, 1981).
75. Andrew Gurr, *Playgoing in Shakespeare's London*, 2nd edition (Cambridge: Cambridge University Press, 1996), p. 4 and passim; see also his important account of the theatre companies in *The Shakespearian Playing Companies* (Oxford: Clarendon Press, 1996).
76. See Gurr, *Playgoing*, p. 177.
77. See Manley, chapter 5 for a detailed account of the changing rhythm of the London ritual year. For an elaborate account of the ritual/festive year focused on the 'winter' half (with the summer reserved for work), see Francois Laroque, *Shakespeare's Festive World* (Cambridge: Cambridge University Press, 1991).

## Chapter 5: Poetry

1. For detailed information on the relationship between the manuscript and published poems, see Josephine Roberts's invaluable edition, *The Poems of Lady Mary Wroth* (Baton Rouge: Louisiana State University Press, 1992), pp. 62–5.
2. Poems are ascribed to Philarcos, Antissia, Meriana, the Queen of Naples, and the Duke of Wertenberg; see ibid., p. 62.
3. See *The Poems of Robert Sidney*, ed. P.J. Croft (Oxford: Clarendon Press, 1983).
4. All quotations are from Mary Wroth, *The Countess of Montgomeries Urania* (1621), STC 26051; the sonnet sequence is separately paginated.
5. This interpretation of the significance of 'Pamphilia to Amphilanthus' is argued most convincingly in the context of European women poets in Ann Rosalind Jones, *The Currency of Eros: Women's Love Lyric in Europe, 1540–1620* (Bloomington: Indiana University Press, 1990), pp. 141–54; see also Elaine Beilin, *Redeeming Eve* (Princeton: Princeton University Press, 1987), pp. 232–43; Barbara K. Lewalski, *Writing Women in Jacobean England* (Cambridge, Mass.: Harvard University Press, 1993), pp. 251–63.
6. E. Arber, ed., *A Transcript of the Registers of the Company of Stationers of London* (Gloucester, Mass.: Peter Smith, 1967), vol. 4, p. 15.
7. Ibid., p. 18.
8. On the imprisonment, see J. Milton French, 'George Wither in Prison', *PMLA*, 45 (1930), 960; *Calendar of State Papers Domestic, 1619–1623*, p. 268.
9. Michelle O'Callaghan, *The 'Shepheard's Nation': Jacobean Spenserians and Early Stuart Political Culture* (Oxford: Clarendon Press, 2000), p. 157.
10. Except where otherwise noted, references are to the first edition of *Wither's Motto* published by Marriot and Grismond (1621); the complicated textual history is discussed at length in O'Callaghan.

11. O'Callaghan, p. 180; and for more on this context, see Chapter 2 above.
12. Again O'Callaghan is enlightening on this aspect of the poem and its political context, see pp. 180–7.
13. Ibid., p. 181.
14. For my account, I rely upon the authoritative article by James Doelman, 'George Wither, the Stationers Company and the English Psalter, *SP*, 90 (1993), 74–82.
15. Ibid., p. 77; see also Jocelyn C. Creigh, 'George Wither and the Stationers', *PBSA*, 74 (1980), 49–57.
16. References are to *The Songs of the Old Testament* (1621); italic type has been changed to roman.
17. Wither's literary activities in the civil war have finally received their due attention from David Norbrook, especially in *Writing the English Republic: Poetry, Rhetoric and Politics 1627–1660* (Cambridge: Cambridge University Press, 1999), pp. 140–58.
18. Stationers' Register, 18 June 1621.
19. For biographical information, see Bernard Capp, *The World of John Taylor the Water Poet* (Oxford: Clarendon Press, 1994).
20. See ibid., pp. 126–7.
21. *The Subjects Joy, for the Parliament* (1621), 1.
22. References are to *Taylor's Motto* (1621).
23. Capp, p. 83; see the comparison between Wither and Taylor in Michelle O'Callaghan, 'Three Jacobean Spenserians: William Browne, George Wither and Christopher Brooke', unpublished Oxford DPhil. Dissertation (1993), pp. 290–3.
24. See the passage on A6 which echoes *Wither's Motto*, A6v.
25. This echoes *Wither's Motto*, B2.
26. For a fuller account of the controversy see the discussion in Chapter 2.
27. See the excellent discussion of the genre by Capp, pp. 85–6.
28. References are to the text in *All the Works of John Taylor* (1630); the text is identical to that of 1621, except for the omission of the engraved frontispiece.
29. Ibid., p. 111.
30. References to the text in ibid.
31. Ibid., a spurrier is a maker of spurs; a salter a dealer in salt.
32. An edition of the Latin satires of Juvenal and Persius, edited by Thomas Farnaby, was published in 1621 (STC 14891). An example of a rather more bland approach to social commentary in 1621 is Richard Brathwait's *Time's Curtain's Drawn, or, The Anatomie of Vanity*, a miscellaneous collection of poems including some very mild and general social criticism and a prayer addressed to the 1621 parliament. Brathwait's criticism of those who soar with 'ambitious wings' (E3) is unlikely to have offended anyone; this is also true of a second volume of poetry published by Brathwait in 1621: *Natures Embassie, or the Wilde Mans Measures*, which contains a similar collection of general satires as well as elegies and eclogues.
33. Arthur Marotti, *Manuscript, Print, and The English Renaissance Lyric* (Ithaca: Cornell University Press, 1995); Harold Love, *Scribal Publication in Seventeenth Century England* (Oxford: Clarendon Press, 1993); see also Wendy Wall, *The Imprint of Gender* (Ithaca: Cornell University Press, 1993); Henry

Woudhuysen, *Sir Philip Sidney and the Circulation of Manuscripts* (Oxford: Oxford University Press, 1996); Peter Beal, *In Praise of Scribes* (Oxford: Oxford University Press, 1998).

34. Peter Beal, *Index of English Literary Manuscripts*, quoted in Marotti, p. 68.
35. Marotti, p. 85.
36. Gerald MacLean discusses the printed version without reference to earlier manuscript versions, but his discussion underlines how relevant the sentiments were even a generation after the poem's first appearance; see Gerald MacLean, *Time's Witness: Historical Representation in English Poetry, 1603–1660* (Madison: University of Wisconsin Press, 1990), pp. 163–7. See also Ann Coiro's important discussion of the poems in relation to the 'Herrick' MS as a whole: Coiro believes that the poems mock the Commons' nostalgia for Elizabeth, but it seems to me that the real satiric force is reserved for James: Ann Coiro, 'Milton and Class Identity', *Journal of Medieval and Renaissance Studies*, 22 (1992), 274–5.
37. Bodleian MS Malone 23, fol. 32.
38. The title varies from manuscript to manuscript; in Malone 23 the description of the libel being placed in the hand of Elizabeth's statue, and the date(s), introduce and contextualise a poem that elsewhere appears simply introduced as 'To the Blessed St Eliza . . . '; see for example the copy in the so-called 'Herrick' manuscript at the University of Texas, edited in facsimile by Norman K. Farmer, *Texas Quarterly*, 16 (1973), 122–85.
39. Quotations are from Bodleian MS Malone 23.
40. Quotations from the petition are from the Herrick MS in the Farmer facsimile (see note 38), as the version in Malone 23 is incomplete.
41. See Malone 23, fols. 14–16; Herrick MS pp. 163–9.
42. See the discussion of libels in relation to Buckingham in the previous chapter, pp. 97–100; Andrew McRae offers an important account of the libel as a genre in 'The Literary Culture of Early Stuart Libeling', MP, 97 (2000), 364–92.
43. See Chapter 3 above; McRae also makes this point about the way that libels transcend immediate topical reference, p. 385.
44. See Marotti, p. 12.
45. References to the version of the poem in the Herrick MS, ed. Farmer.
46. Ibid., p. 123; see the account on p. 16.
47. Quoted in G.E. Bentley, *The Jacobean and Caroline Stage*, vol. 4 (Oxford: Clarendon Press, 1956), p. 590.
48. British Library MS Sloane 542, fol. 38.
49. Ashmore translated a substantial selection; there were previous translations and imitations of individual odes by notable writers, such as Surrey, Sidney and Jonson.
50. David Norbrook has an important reading of Marvell's Ode in relation to the royalist-leaning Horatian translations of Richard Fanshawe and Mildmay Fane in *Writing the English Republic*, pp. 249–71.
51. John Ashmore, *Epigrams, Epitaphs, Anagrams* (1621), pp. 41–3.
52. References to Joseph Martyn, *New Epigrams and a Satire* (1621).
53. The most detailed bibliographical information is provided in *The Variorum Edition of the Poetry of John Donne*, ed. Gary Stringer et al., vol. 6 (Bloomington: Indiana University Press, 1995), pp. 38–9.

54. See R.C. Bald, *John Donne: A Life* (Oxford: Clarendon Press, 1970), p. 249.
55. On the state of the 1621 text, see *Variorum Donne*, p. 38.
56. Bald, p. 459.
57. There is a manuscript derived from the 1621 text which, according to the *Variorum* editors, was probably intended as a printer's copy for a new edition, see p. 39.
58. Jonson, 'Conversations with William Drummond' (1619), *Complete Works*, ed. Herford and Simpson, vol. 1 (Oxford: Clarendon Press, 1925), p. 133.
59. Quoted in *Variorum*, pp. 239–40.
60. All references are to the *Variorum* edition of the poems.
61. The most illuminating discussion of the generic context for the *Anniversaries* and the way in which they might be interpreted in relation to disquiet over their subject remains Barbara Lewalski's *Donne's Anniversaries and the Poetry of Praise* (Princeton: Princeton University Press, 1973).
62. Bald, pp. 240–1.
63. Arthur Marotti goes so far as to describe the *Anniversaries* as 'patronage verse' in *John Donne, Coterie Poet* (Madison: University of Wisconsin Press, 1986), p. 235.
64. Ibid., p. 236.
65. See R.C. Bald, *Donne and the Drurys* (Cambridge: Cambridge University Press, 1959), p. 103.
66. Ibid., pp. 153–5.
67. See Bentley, vol. 1, p. 199.
68. See the previous chapter for an account of Rowley's co-authored *The Witch of Edmonton*, pp. 104–7.
69. William Rowley, 'For a Funerall Elegie on the death of Hvgh Atwell', single page.
70. Bentley, vol. 1, p. 211.

## Chapter 6: News

1. M.A. Shaaber includes proclamations, ballads, chapbooks, broadsides and speeches as 'news' in his study *Some Forerunners of the Newspaper in England 1476–1622* (1929, rpt. London: Frank Cass, 1966).
2. Richard Cust, 'News and Politics in Early Seventeenth-Century England', *Past and Present*, 112 (1986), 60–90.
3. Ibid., p. 87.
4. F.J. Levy, 'Staging the News', in Arthur Marotti and Michael Bristol, eds., *Print, Manuscript, Performance* (Columbus: Ohio State University Press, 2000), 252–78; while Levy is particularly interested in the relationship between news and drama, he offers a useful summary of the various sources for news, especially in the early 1620s.
5. Joad Raymond, *The Invention of the Newspaper: English Newsbooks 1641–1649* (Oxford: Clarendon Press, 1996), p. 9.
6. Ibid., p. 10.
7. The standard study is still Joseph Frank, *The Beginnings of the English News-paper 1620–1660* (Cambridge, Mass.: Harvard University Press, 1961), which only devotes six pages to the corantos of 1620–22; Raymond largely

supersedes Frank and offers much more detail and a sophisticated methodology, but his study centres on the newsbooks of the 1640s.

8. See ibid., p. 3.
9. Van den Keere/Veseler produced thirteen English-language corantos in
   1621; Broer Jansz produced eight, beginning on 9 April; see Folke Dahl,
   *A Bibliography of English Corantos and Periodical Newsbooks 1620–1642*
   (Stockholm: Almqvist and Wiksell, 1953).
10. See Frank, p. 6.
11. Dahl, p. 49: Archer's corantos, none of which has survived, are mentioned
    in a letter from Joseph Mead to Sir Martin Stuteville on 22 September 1621.
12. Frank, p. 7.
13. *Dudley Carleton to John Chamberlain 1603–1624: Jacobean Letters*, ed. Maurice
    Lee Jr. (New Brunswick: Rutgers University Press, 1972), p. 282.
14. This coranto is STC 18507.4.
15. For Cadenet's visit, see Chapter 1, pp. 2–4.
16. See David Ogg, *Europe in the Seventeenth Century* (London: A. and C. Black,
    1976), p. 475.
17. STC 18507.6; this letter was reproduced in a different translation as part of
    a more detailed account of the encounter between Turkey and Poland: *Trve
    Copies of the Insolent, Cruell, Barbarous, and Blasphemous Letter lately written
    by the Great Turke* (1621), which also contains a reply from the king of
    Poland and a commentary. A summary account of the Turkish threat to
    Poland was also printed in 1621: *Newes from Poland* (STC 18507.35A).
    Presumably in response to the interest in Polish affairs at this time, the Pol-
    ish ambassador's speech, made to King James in March 1620, was published
    together with an English translation in 1621 as *A true copy of the Latine
    oration of the excellent Lord George Ossolinski* (STC 18890).
18. C. John Sommerville, *The News Revolution in England* (New York: Oxford
    University Press, 1996), p. 23.
19. See the detailed account of this in Raymond; Raymond emphasises how
    the existence of parliament generated news – this is significant in 1621, as
    I discuss below.
20. Raymond is again illuminating on this aspect of the newsbooks; see esp. ch. 3.
21. See Frank, p. 6; and Dahl, p. 51.
22. Dahl is unable to trace the original sources for N.B.'s corantos.
23. This coranto is STC 18507.29.
24. 'At Ampsterdam Printed this present Moneth of April'; STC 1037.
25. Simon Adams notes that Vere's Palatine regiment was in service in the
    Netherlands under the States General, 'Spain or the Netherlands? The
    Dilemmas of Early Stuart Foreign Policy', *Before the English Civil War*, ed.
    Howard Tomlinson (London: Macmillan, 1983), p. 85.
26. STC 18507.35c.
27. STC 11353.
28. See STC 13576; DNB Rowlands alias Verstegan, Richard. This seems likely to
    be the pamphlet that infuriated Sir Edward Coke to such a degree that he
    declared his intention to refute it in a speech to parliament on 27 November,
    when, as discussed below, the Commons became entangled in the whole
    issue of foreign policy, notably war with Spain and the Spanish match for
    Prince Charles. The Commons Journal reports Coke as saying he 'Hath

a Book in his Hand, made, as he saith, by an *Englishman* turned *Romish*, and *Hispanilized*, so as hath a *Spanish* Heart, written from *Parys* to a Friend in *England*... That this Book extolleth the King of *Spayne*, and dishonoureth Queen *Eliz*. And religion. – Will answer this Book.' *Journals of the House of Commons* (1803), p. 648.

29.  See Mack P. Holt, *The French Wars of Religion, 1562–1629* (Cambridge: Cambridge University Press, 1995), p. 177.
30.  STC 11300.3; Béarn was a Huguenot, Bourbon principality.
31.  STC 16840; Lesdiguieres had been the leader of the Protestant party in Dauphiné, but he changed his faith and went over to the Royalist side in 1621.
32.  STC 1901.
33.  STC 11279.5.
34.  This pamphlet is printed in London 'by F.K. for William Lee', STC 19843.5.
35.  STC 25854.
36.  This was printed for Nathaniel Butter, STC22130
37.  Harold Love, *Scribal Publication in Seventeenth Century England* (Oxford: Clarendon Press, 1993), pp. 9, 17.
38.  *Commons Debates 1621*, ed. W. Notestein, F. Relf and H. Simpson (New Haven: Yale University Press, 1935), vol. 1, pp. 5–6, 26.
39.  Ibid., p. 62.
40.  Ibid., the Pym diary is vol. 4, Barrington vol. 3 and Smyth is in vol. 5.
41.  The most detailed account of the parliament is Robert Zaller, *The Parliament of 1621* (Berkeley: University of California Press, 1971); Conrad Russell's controversial interpretation of this parliament, which stresses its conciliatory nature and suggests that there was little genuine interest in a campaign for the Palatine, is outlined in *Parliaments and English Politics 1621–1629* (Oxford: Clarendon Press, 1979), ch. 2.
42.  For an important account of the general issue of corruption and court favouritism in the period, see Linda Levy Peck, *Court Patronage and Corruption in Early Stuart England* (London: Routledge, 1990); her specific account of the way that the 1621 parliament dealt with these issues is on pp. 185–90.
43.  See Zaller, pp. 56–63.
44.  STC 18003.9; published 1621, not 1620 as listed in STC.
45.  *The Letters of John Chamberlain*, ed. N.E. McClure (Philadelphia: American Philosophical Society, 1939), vol. 2, p. 347; further references in parentheses.
46.  Ibid., p. 350.
47.  See Russell, p. 99.
48.  References to *Stuart Royal Proclamations*, ed. James Larkin and Paul Hughes (Oxford: Clarendon Press, 1973).
49.  See above, pp. 7–8.
50.  This whole aspect of the parliament has intrigued historians, who are not in agreement as to the causes of the dispute, especially the enigmatic first stage when members tried to puzzle out the purpose of Sir George Goring's initial motion to offer the King advice (Goring being closely connected to Buckingham); see especially Conrad Russel, who has offered two different interpretations, in 'The Foreign Policy Debate in the House of Commons in 1621', first published in 1977 and reprinted in *Unrevolutionary England, 1603–1642* (London: Hambledon Press, 1990), pp. 59–79, and in *Parliaments*

*and English Politics*, pp. 133–40; see also S.L. Adams, 'Foreign Policy and the Parliaments of 1621 and 1624', in Kevin Sharpe, ed., *Faction and Parliament* (Oxford: Clarendon Press, 1978), pp. 159–64; see also Zaller's clear account of three alternative explanations of Buckingham's motivation, pp. 152–3.

51. Zaller, p. 159.
52. Ibid., pp. 180–6.
53. STC 7353.8; STC 16768.8.
54. STC 16777.4.
55. STC 16787.
56. See *The effect of a Bill exhibited in Parliament by Sir Francis Englefield* and *The effect of the Viscount Montagues Bill exhibited in Parliament*.
57. STC 22086.5 and STC 22087.
58. Zaller, p. 137.
59. S.R. Gardiner, *History of England*, vol. 4 (London: Longman, 1883), pp. 28–9; the Cecil pamphlet is listed as one of Scott's works on the title-page of a collection apparently published in Utrecht in 1624.
60. Margaret Spufford, *Small Books and Pleasant Histories: Popular fiction and its readership in seventeenth-century England* (London: Methuen, 1981).
61. Ibid., p. 258.
62. Tessa Watt, *Cheap Print and Popular Piety, 1550–1640* (Cambridge: Cambridge University Press, 1994), p. 11.
63. Quoted in ibid., p. 11.
64. See Hyder E. Rollins, *A Pepysian Garland* (1922: rpt. Cambridge, Mass.: Harvard University Press, 1971), p. 139; quotations are from Rollins.
65. References to ibid.
66. See the discussion of Wither in chapter 5, pp. 117–23.
67. STC 3207.
68. STC 11107; references to this edition. Accounts of the Flower witch trial are in Wallace Notestein, *A History of Witchcraft in England from 1558 to 1718* (1911: rpt. New York: Russell and Russell, 1967), pp. 133–5; George Kittredge, *Witchcraft in Old and New England* (1929 rpt New York: Russell and Russell, 1956), p. 324; an abridged version of the pamphlet may be found in Barbara Rosen, ed., *Witchcraft* (London: Edward Arnold, 1969), pp. 369–84.
69. Keith Thomas, *Religion and the Decline of Magic* (New York: Scribners, 1971), p. 292.
70. For general descriptions see Thomas, p. 293 and the comprehensive account in Bernard Capp, *English Almanacs 1500–1800* (Ithaca: Cornell University Press, 1979).
71. Capp, p. 23.
72. Ibid., p. 41.
73. See ibid., p. 23.
74. Ibid., p. 30; eleven of the 1621 almanacs have a version of the anatomical man illustration.
75. Ibid., p. 256; most of the 1621 almanacs simply have a calendar page without a blank facing page for diary entries.
76. See the detailed account in ibid., ch. 3, and also in Patrick Curry, *Prophecy and Power: Astrology in Early Modern England* (Oxford: Polity Press, 1989), ch. 2.
77. STC 489.23.
78. STC 465.9.

79. STC 527.10, A3.
80. See, for example, Gilden, STC 448.6 and Philip Ranger, STC 502.7.

## Chapter 7: Instruction

1. Positions amongst historians vary on this issue: see Patrick Collinson, *The Religion of Protestants* (Oxford: Clarendon Press, 1982); Nicholas Tyacke, *Anti-Calvinists* (Oxford: Clarendon Press, 1987); Peter Lake, *Moderate Puritans and the Elizabethan Church* (Cambridge: Cambridge University Press, 1982); Kenneth Fincham, *Prelate as Pastor* (Oxford: Clarendon Press, 1990); Anthony Milton, *Catholic and Reformed* (Cambridge: Cambridge University Press, 1995); and a judicious summary in Darren Oldridge, *Religion and Society in Early Stuart England* (Aldershot: Ashgate Press, 1998).
2. Milton, p. 7.
3. Milton's focus is on attitudes towards Catholicism within English Protestantism.
4. See Keith Wrightson, *English Society 1580–1680* (London: Hutchinson, 1982), pp. 206–7.
5. Tessa Watt, *Cheap Print and Popular Piety 1550–1640* (Cambridge: Cambridge University Press, 1991), p. 8.
6. David Cressy, *Birth, Marriage, and Death* (Oxford: Oxford University Press, 1997), p. 477.
7. Lovell then became curate at All Hallows, Barking.
8. References to Robert Lovell, *Two Soveraigne Salves for the Soules Sicknesse*, STC 16859.
9. James I, *Kings Maiesties Declaration* (1618), STC 9238.9, pp. 6–7; see the important discussion of the declaration and its relationship to Jacobean culture in Leah Marcus, *The Politics of Mirth* (Chicago: University of Chicago Press, 1986), esp. ch. 4.
10. See Christopher Hill, *Society and Puritanism in Pre-Revolutionary England* (London: Secker and Warburg, 1964), p. 172, see ch. 5 passim; see also Patrick Collinson, 'The Beginnings of English Sabbatarianism', in *Godly People* (London: Hambledon Press, 1983), 429–43.
11. Ibid., p. 200.
12. Robert Zaller, *The Parliament of 1621* (Berkeley: University of California Press, 1971), p. 42; Zaller notes that the 1614 parliament passed a Sabbath bill.
13. Ibid., pp. 42–3.
14. Ibid., pp. 202–3.
15. Laud, *A Sermon Preached Before his Maiestie on Tvesday the nineteenth of June* (1621), STC 15301, p. 27.
16. See Fincham, pp. 81–2.
17. *Letters of John Chamberlain*, ed. N.E. McClure (Philadelphia: American Philosophical Society, 1939), vol. 2, p. 387.
18. John Bunyan, *Grace Abounding to the Chief of Sinners* (1666), p. 4; Arthur Dent's *Plain Man's Pathway to Heaven*, first published in 1601, was nearly as popular as *The Practise of Piety*; Dent's popular *A Sermon of Repentance*, preached in 1581 and often reprinted, had an edition in 1621.

19. See Milton, pp. 234–5; Parsons wrote the treatise to appeal to Protestant readers and Bunny's subtle adaptation echoes Parsons's moderate tone; see the detailed examination in Robert McNulty, 'The Protestant Version of Robert Parsons' *The Firste Booke of the Christian Exercise'*, *HLQ*, 22 (1959), 271–300.

20. References to A *Booke of Christian Exercise* (1621), STC 19375.

21. The extremely complex issue of Calvinist and anti-Calvinist positions in the church, especially in relation to predestination, has been much debated: Nicholas Tyacke's thesis that a general consensus in the Church on Calvinist doctrine was shattered by Charles and Laud in the 1630s has been rebutted in detail by Peter White, who claims in *Predestination, policy and polemic* (Cambridge: Cambridge University Press, 1992) that Calvinist views were contested within the Church from a very early stage. Milton's expansive argument that the Church had many positions, rather than just the easily dichotomised Calvinist/Arminian, is especially useful in the context of my account here of religious guides, given that they clearly reflect a wide range of opinion within the Church in 1621.

22. References to Thomas Tymme, *A Silver Watch-Bell* (1621), STC 24429.

23. See Zaller, p. 42; for a more detailed account of Coke's role in the 1621 parliament see Stephen D. White, *Sir Edward Coke and 'The Grievances of the Commonwealth'* (Chapel Hill: University of North Carolina Press, 1979), esp. chs. 2–5.

24. Milton, p. 38; he cites the expanded 1634 edition.

25. For an extremely detailed account see Margarita Patricia Hutchison, 'Social and Religious Change: The Case of the English Catechism 1560–1640' (unpublished PhD Dissertation, Stanford University, 1984); see also Ian Green, *The Christian's ABC* (Oxford: Clarendon Press, 1996).

26. Collinson, pp. 232–3.

27. See Ian Green, '"For Children in Yeers and Children in Understanding": The Emergence of the English Catechism Under Elizabeth and the Early Stuarts', *Journal of Ecclesiastical History*, 37 (1986), p. 405.

28. Hutchison, p. 212; in this instance, the use of the general term 'Puritan' may be a bit broad but is a fair way to categorise the general nature of these catechisms.

29. Richard A. McCabe, *Joseph Hall: A Study in Satire and Meditation* (Oxford: Clarendon Press, 1982), p. 144.

30. See ibid., pp. 145–7.

31. Ibid., p. 145.

32. Ibid., p. 131.

33. References to *Meditations and Vows*, STC 12684.

34. See McCabe, pp. 219–24.

35. See ibid., pp. 228–31.

36. Ibid., pp. 247–8.

37. References to *A Recollection of Such Treatises as Haue Heretofore Been Severally Published*, STC 12708.

38. See McCabe, pp. 246–7.

39. References to Dorothy Leigh, *The Mothers Blessing* (1621), STC 15404; Kristen Poole points out that Leigh 'is at once the individual mother of three and a role model', in '"The fittest closet for all goodness": Authorial Strategies in Jacobean mothers' Manuals', *SEL* 35 (1995), 83.

40. Lloyd Davis, 'Redemptive Advice: Dorothy Leigh's *The Mother's Blessing*', in Jo Wallwork and Paul Salzman, eds., *Women Writing 1550–1750* (Bundoora: Meridian, 2000), p. 64.
41. Ibid., p. 66.
42. Milton, p. 31.
43. See ibid., pp. 32–3.
44. References to *The Reformed Protestant*, STC 3607.5.
45. References to *The Reformed Spaniard* (1621) STC 18530.5; this is an English translation of a Latin text published the same year.
46. References to *Musgraues Motives*, STC 18316
47. References to *More Work for a Mass Priest*, STC 5663.
48. For a good general account of this vexed issue, see Peter White, *Predestination, Policy and Polemic* (Cambridge: Cambridge University Press, 1992).
49. James Wats, *The Controversie Debated About the Reuerend gesture of Kneeling, in the Act of Receiuing the Holy Communion*, STC 25109.
50. See Milton, pp. 498–9.
51. STC 12178.
52. Milton, p. 542.
53. The bulk of the editions appeared between 1621 and 1640; detailed bibliographical information may be found in Joan M. Walmsley, *John Reynolds, Merchant of Exeter* (Lewiston: Edwin Mellen Press, 1991).
54. All the following biographical information is taken from Walmsley.
55. All References to John Reynolds, *The Triumphs of Gods Revenge* (1621), STC 20942.
56. Alexandra Walsham, *Providence in Early Modern England* (Oxford: Oxford University Press, 1999), p. 2.
57. Ibid., p. 112.
58. Ibid., p. 113.
59. D.R. Woolf, *The Idea of History in Early Stuart England* (Toronto: Toronto University Press, 1990), p. 50.
60. Ibid.
61. Quoted by John Chamberlain, *Letters*, ed. N.E. McClure (Philadelphia: American Philosophical Society, 1939), vol. 1, p. 568.
62. Christopher Hill, *Intellectual Origins of the English Revolution* (Oxford: Clarendon Press, 1965), p. 191; Hill precedes Woolf in his subtle account of Ralegh's complex attitude towards providence and his use of history as social criticism.
63. Stephen Coote, *A Play of Passion: The Life of Sir Walter Ralegh* (London: Macmillan, 1993), p. 372; the extremely complicated publication history of the editions of 1614, 1617 and 1621 is detailed in John Racin Jr, 'The Early Editions of Sir Walter Ralegh's *The History of the World*', *SB*, 17 (1964), 199–209; however it seems clear that all 1617 copies with title-page (printed by Jaggard) were actually printed in 1621.
64. There are different versions of 1621, some misdated 1617, classified by STC as 20638a and 20639; one copy (Bodleian Antiq.C.E.1621.1) drops the engraved frontispiece in favour of a title-page with a large, engraved portrait of Ralegh and an elaborate table of contents; the other (STC 20638a) has the original frontispiece as well as the new title-page with portrait.

65. References are to Walter Ralegh, *The History of the World* (1621), STC 20638a.
66. See, for example, Ralegh's praise of English yeomen, 'freest of all the world' and therefore the best soldiers (V.266).
67. Stephen J. Greenblatt, *Sir Walter Ralegh: The Renaissance Man and his Roles* (New Haven: Yale University Press, 1973), pp. 131 and 128.
68. This case is also made by Anna R. Beer, in *Sir Walter Ralegh and his Readers in the Seventeenth Century* (London: Macmillan, 1997), ch. 2; Beer outlines the increasing significance of Ralegh as a political figure in the seventeenth century, focusing in particular on the late 1620s through to the 1650s.
69. Greenblatt, p. 154.
70. See J.P. Sommerville, *Royalists and Patriots: Politics and Ideology in England 1603–1640* (London: Longman, 1999), pp. 137–8; Sommerville does not refer specifically to Ralegh, but Ralegh's position on villeinage is clearly part of the anti-absolutist case.
71. The most up to date account, which I follow, is Lisa Jardine and Alan Stewart, *Hostage to Fortune: The Troubled Life of Francis Bacon* (London: Victor Gollancz, 1998), ch. 16.
72. Ibid., p. 457.
73. Ibid., p. 473.
74. Ibid., p. 478.
75. Ibid., the excised passage was removed for publication but remains in the manuscript; see Francis Bacon, *The History of the Reign of King Henry VII*, ed. Brian Vickers (Cambridge: Cambridge University Press, 1998), p. 16; further references are to this edition,
76. Jerry Weinberger, 'The Politics of Bacon's History of Henry the Seventh', *The Review of Politics*, 52 (1990), 563; Weinberger is offering an adaptation of J.G.A. Pocock's thesis in *The Machiavellian Moment* (Princeton: Princeton University Press, 1975).
77. Judith H. Anderson, *Biographical Truth: The Representation of Historical Persons in Tudor-Stuart Writing* (New Haven: Yale University Press, 1984), p. 201, and see her illuminating account in ch. 10 passim.
78. Woolf, p. 153.
79. Ben Jonson, 'Conversations With Drummond', *Complete Poems*, ed. George Parfitt (Harmondsworth: Penguin, 1975), p. 461.
80. Woolf, p. 83.
81. References are to Samuel Daniel, *The Collection of the Historie of England* (1621), STC 6249.
82. Richard Helgerson, *Forms of Nationhood: The Elizabethan Writing of England* (Chicago: University of Chicago Press, 1992), p. 2.
83. Helgerson, p. 130; on the implications of the Spenserians as a political grouping, see especially Michelle O'Callaghan, *The 'Shepheard's Nation': Jacobean Spenserians and Early Stuart Political Culture* (Oxford: Clarendon Press, 2000).
84. See Woolf, pp. 97–101.
85. Helgerson offers a particularly perceptive account of Coke, see ch. 2 passim; this issue has been the subject of intense historical debate, much of it centring on interpretations of political conflict versus political consensus

in the period: two representative examples which look in detail at Coke and the symbolic significance of the debate over the origins of common law are Glenn Burgess, *The Politics of the Ancient Constitution* (London: Macmillan, 1992), passim, who would certainly argue for a form of consensus in 1621, and the counterview put most cogently in J.P. Sommerville, *Royalists and Patriots: Politics and Ideology in England 1603–1640* (London: Longman, 1999), ch. 3 and pp. 254–61; unfortunately neither historian discusses Daniel, who in *The Collection* argues a case rather like Burgess's.

86. Slatyer acknowledges his debt to Drayton in a poem at the end of the volume.
87. In his commonplace book; quoted in Woolf, p. 77.
88. References are to William Slatyer, *The History of Great Britanie*, STC 22634.
89. See Helgerson, pp. 127–8.
90. See Woolf, pp. 181–6 for a discussion of Heylyn's *Augustus* (1632); Heylyn's political views are the subject of disagreement between Glenn Burgess in *Absolute Monarchy and the Stuart Constitution* (New Haven: Yale University Press, 1996), and Sommerville, who offers a convincing counter-argument on pp. 240–4.
91. References to Peter Heylyn, *Microcosmus* (1621), STC 13276.
92. STC 15053; Grimeston's continuation begins on fol. 1297.
93. For the Roman influence on the Jacobean court, see Jonathan Goldberg, *James I and the Politics of Literature* (Baltimore: Johns Hopkins University Press, 1983), chs. 3 and 4, and the argument in David Norbrook, *Writing the English Republic: Poetry, Rhetoric and Politics 1627–1660* (Cambridge: Cambridge University Press, 1999), that a more radical use of Roman history was significant, especially from the later 1620s, see esp. ch. 1.
94. See Woolf, p. 172.
95. Ibid., p. 173.
96. Ibid., p. 174; in this case, Florus can be contrasted to the anti-monarchical implications of Tacitus.
97. *Hypercritica* was written mostly in 1621 and remained in manuscript until the eighteenth century; see the account in Woolf, pp. 192–4.
98. STC 23660.
99. No translations were published in 1621 but the fifth edition of Charles Butler's *Ramae rhetoricae libri duo* was published, STC 4199.5.
100. One might place, in this category, Tobias Venner's measured assessment of tobacco, *A Briefe and Accurate Treatise, concerning the taking of the fume of tobacco*, STC 24642. Venner, a doctor, offers a cautious endorsement of the medicinal properties of smoking tobacco, as long as it is done in moderation, and he outlines the correct method whereby a smoker (of the right humour) will gain maximum benefit.
101. References to Gervase Markham, *Hungers Preuention* (1621), STC 17362.
102. References to STC 18302.
103. References to the second edition, STC 18256.
104. References to STC 5473.
105. Dod and Cleaver's notion of the Christian household could be seen as an influence on Dorothy Leigh, whose views on companionate marriage are similar.
106. References to STC 6908.

## Conclusion

1. Kevin Sharpe, *Reading Revolutions: The Politics of Reading in Early Modern England* (New Haven and London: Yale University Press, 2000).
2. Ibid., p. 328.
3. Indeed, as one of my own readers has pointed out, I underline the conceptual gap by 'making' the year begin, as it does for modern readers, on 1 January, whereas for early modern readers 1621 began on 25 March.
4. See especially Conrad Russell, *Parliaments and English Politics 1621–1629* (Oxford: Clarendon Press, 1979); Glenn Burgess, *The Politics of the Ancient Constitution* (London: Macmillan, 1992); J.P. Sommerville, *Royalists and Patriots: Politics and Ideology in England 1603–1640* (London: Longman, 1999).
5. (Cambridge: Cambridge University Press, 1989).

# Bibliography

## Primary

### Manuscripts

Bacon, Francis, *The History of the Reign of King Henry VII*, ed. Brian Vickers (Cambridge: Cambridge University Press, 1998).

Bodleian MS Jones 14.

Bodleian MS Malone 23.

Bodleian MS Rawlinson Poet. 26.

Bodleian MS Rawlinson D 853.

British Library MS Sloane 542.

*Commons Debates 1621*, ed. Notestein, Relf and Simpson (New Haven: Yale University Press, 1935).

PRO State Papers Domestic, James I, 14/122/123.

University of Texas Herrick MS, facsimile ed. Norman Farmer, *Texas Quarterly*, 16 (1974), 122–85.

Wroth, Mary, *Urania* Continuation, Newberry Library, Case MS fY 1565.W95.

### Printed Texts

(I use a short title format; place of publication is London and year of publication is 1621 unless otherwise noted; STC number follows title).

Adams, Thomas, *The White Deuill*, 134.

Adson, John, *Courtly Masquing Ayres*, 153.

Aesop, *Aesopi phrygis fabulae*, 172.6.

Aesop, *The Moral fabl[es] of Esope* (Edinburgh), 186.

Airay, Henry, *The Iust and Necessary Apologie of Henrie Airay*, 244.

Alexander, Daniel ben, trans. Thomas Drewe, *The Converted Jew of Prague in Bohemia*, 6266.

*Algiers Voyage in a Iournall or Briefe Reportary*, 4208.

Almanacs: Allestree, Richard, *New Almanack*, 407.4; Einer, N., *An Almanack*, 438.2; Frende, Gabriel, *A New Almanacke and Prognostication*; Gumdante, Edward, *A New Almanack*, 453.

Anderton, Lawrence, *The Reformed Protestant*, 3607.5.

Andrewes, John, *A Celestiall Looking-Glasse*, 592.

——, *Andrewes Resolution*, 590.

——, *The Brazen Serpent*, 591.

Andrewes, Lancelot, *CXVI Sermons* (1629), 606.

——, G.M. Story, ed., *Lancelot Andrewes, Sermons* (Oxford: Clarendon Press, 1967).

Archibold, John, *The Beauty of Holines*, 731.

Arias, Francisco, *The Iudge* (St Omer), 741.

Ashmore, John, *Epigrams, Epitaphs, Anagrams*, 13799.

*Assize of Bread, The*, 879.

Augustine, St., trans. A. Batt, *A Heavenly Treasure of Comfortable Meditations*, 933.5.

Aylett, Robert, *The Song of Songs*, 2774.

Bacon, Francis, *Certaine Considerations*, 1121.

Barclay, John, *Argenis* (Paris); trans. Long (1625), 1392; trans. Le Grys (1628), 1393.

Baron, Robert, *Philosophia theologi*, 1496.

Bathe, William, trans. William Welde, *Ianua Linguarum*, 14468.

Bayly, Lewis, *The Practice of Piety*, 1604.5.

Bedford, Thomas, *The Sinne Vnto Death*, 1788.

Bergeville, Marquis de, *The Last Summons*, 1901.

Bernard, Richard, *The Faithfull Shepherd*, 1941.

——, *The Seaven Golden Candlestickes*, 1963.

Bradshaw, William, *A Meditation of Mans Mortalitie*, 3521.

Brathwait, Richard, *Natures Embassie*, 3571.

——, *The Shepheards Tales*, 3584.

——, *Times Curtaine Drawn*, 3589.

Breton, Nicholas, *The Mothers Blessing*, 3760.

*Briefe Collection of some part of the exactions . . . done by Alexander Harris*, 12802.

*Briefe contents of the bill exhibited against logwood, and abuses in dying, The*, 16777.2.

*Briefe Description of the Reasons That Make the Declaration of the Ban Made Against the King of Bohemia . . . Of No Value*, A, 11353.

Broughton, Richard, *English Protestants Plea and Petition* (St Omer), 3895.5.

Buchanan, George, *Paraphrasis Psalmorum Dauidis poetica* (Edinburgh), 3987.

Bullokar, John, *An English Expositor*, 4084.

Bunyan, John, *Grace Abounding to the Chief of Sinners* (1666).

Burton, Robert, *The Anatomy of Melancholy*, 4159; Thomas Faulkner, Nicolas Kiessling, Rhonda Blair, J.B. Bamborough, Martin Dodsworth, eds, *Robert Burton's The Anatomy of Melancholy* (Oxford: Clarendon Press, 5 vols. 1989–2000).

Butler, Charles, *Rhetoricae libri duo*, 4199.5.

Cade, Anthony, *A Sermon of the Nature of Conscience*, 4329.

Calderwood, David, *The Altar of Damascus* (Amsterdam), 4352.

Camerarius, Philip, trans. John Molle, *The Walking Librarie*, 4528.

Carleton, Dudley, *Dudley Carleton to John Chamberlain 1603–1624: Jacobean Letters*, ed. Maurice Lee Jr. (New Brunswick: Rutgers University Press, 1972).

Carter, Bezaleel, *Christ his last Will and Iohn his legacy*, 4692.

Cartwright, Francis, *The Life, Confession, and Heartie Repentance of Francis Cartwright, Gentleman*, 4704.

Casaubon, Meric, *Merici Casauboni Is. F. Pietas contra maledicos patrii nominis*, 4749.

*Certain Letters Declaring in Part the Passage of Affaires in the Palatinate*, 1037.

*Certaine and Trewe Newes From all the Parts of Germany and Poland*, 18507.35c.

Chamberlain, John, *The Letters of John Chamberlain*, ed. Norman Egbert McClure (Philadelphia: American Philosophical Society, 1939), 2 vols.

Clarke, Anthony, *The Defence of the Honour of God*, 5352.

Clarke, Thomas, *The Popes deadly Wound*, 5364.

Coeffeteau, Nicolas, trans. Edward Grimeston, *A Table of Humane Passions*, 5473.

Coke, Edward, *La size part des reports*, 5510.

*Collection in English, of the Statutes Now In Force, A*, 9327.
*Contents of the Watermans Bill into the Parliament*, 16787.
Cooke, Alexander, *More Worke for a Masse-Priest*, 5663.
Cooper, Thomas, *Wilie Beguile Ye*, 5710.3.
*Copie of the Submission Which Those of the Reformed Religion in France Requested the Viscount of Doncaster, A*, 11264.
*Copy of Two Letters Sent From Spain, A*, 19843.5
*Corantos*: Veseler [Amsterdam]: *Corrant Out of Italy, Germany etc.*, 4 Jan, 18507.3; 21 Jan., 18507.4; 31 March, 18507.5; 9 April, 18507.6; 5 July, 18507.9; 9 July, 18507.11; 15 July, 18507.12; 9 Aug., 18507.13; 6 Sept., 18507.14; 12 Sept., 18507.16; 18 Sept., 18507.17; Broer Jonson: 9 July, 18507.23; 20 July, 18507.24; 2 Aug., 18507.25; *Newes from the Low Countries*, 18507.26; Clarke: 10 Aug., 18507.28; N. Butter: 30 Sept., 18507.30; 24 Sept., 18507.29; 2 Oct., 18507.31; 6 Oct., 18507.32; 11 Oct., 18507.34; 22 Oct., 18507.35.
Crakanthorp, Richard, *The Defence of Constantine*, 5974.
Crane, Ralph, *The Workes of Mercy*, 5986.
Crashaw, William, *The Iesuites Gospell*, 6017.
Culpeper, Thomas, *A Tract Against Vsurie*, 6108.
Daniel, Samuel, *Collection of the History of England*, 6249.
Davies, John, *Antiquae linguae Britannicae*, 6346.
Davison, Francis, *Dauisons Poems*, 6376.
Day, Angel, *The English Secretorie*, 6406.5.
Day, Martin, *A Monument of Mortalitie*, 6427.5.
De Moulin, Pierre, *A Letter Vnto Them of the Romish Church*, 7331.
*Declaration Made by the Reformed Churches of France, A*, 11300.
*Declaration of the Reformed Churches of France, The*, 11300.3.
*Declaration Set Forth by the Protestants in France, A*, 11303.5.
Denison, John, *De confessionis auricularis vanitate* (Oxford), 6586.
——, *The Christians Care for the Soules Safety*, 6584.
Denison, Stephen, *The Doctrine of Both the Sacraments*, 6601.
Dent, Arthur, *A Sermon of Repentance*, 6663.
*Discourse of the Married and Single Life, A*, 6908.
Dod, John and Cleaver, Robert, *A Godly Forme of Houshold Gouernment*, 5387.5.
Dod, John, *Ten Sermons*, 6946.
Donne, John, *The First Anniuersarie. An Anatomy of the World*, 7024.
——, *The Sermons of John Donne*, ed. George Potter and Evelyn Simpson, Vol. 3 (Berkeley, University of California Press, 1957).
——, Mueller, Janel, ed., *Donne's Prebend Sermons* (Cambridge, Mass.: Harvard University Press, 1971).
Doughty, Thomas, *A Briefe Discouerie of the Craft and Pollicie* (Mechelin), 7072.2.
Downes, Andrew, *Praelectiones in Philippican de pace Demosthenis*, 7154.
Du Bartas, Guillaume de Salluste, trans. Joshua Sylvester, *Du Bartas his Diuine Weekes and Workes*, 21653.
*Effect of a Bill Exhibited in Parliament by Sir Francis Englefield, The*, 10406.5.
*Effect of the Viscount Montagues Bill Exhibited in Parliament, The*, 10406.6.
Egerton, Stephen, *A Briefe Method of Catechizing*, 7533.
*Enemy of Idlenesse, The*, 11483.
Erasmus, Desiderius, *Adagia*, 10441.5.
Erondelle, Pierre, *The French Garden*, 10514.

Evans, John, *The Palace of Profitable Pleasure*, 10585.

Fancan, Francois, *The Favorites Chronicle*, 15203.

Farley, Henry, *St Paules Church her Bill for the Parliament*, 10690.

Finch, Henry, *The Worlds Great Restauration or the Calling of the Jewes*, 10874.5.

Fitzherbert, Thomas, *The Obmutesce of F.T. to the Epphata of D.Collins* (St Omer), 11020.

Fletcher, John, *The Island Princess, The Dramatic Works in the Beaumont and Fletcher Canon*, ed. Fredson Bowers, vol. 5 (Cambridge: Cambridge University Press, 1982).

——, *The Tragedy of Thierry . . . and his Brother Theodoret*, 11074.

——, *The Wild Goose Chase, The Dramatic Works in the Beaumont and Fletcher Canon*, ed. Fredson Bowers, vol. 6 (Cambridge: Cambridge University Press, 1985).

Florus, Lucius, trans Edmund Bolton, *The Roman Histories of Lucius Iulius Florus*, 11104.

Frewen, John, *Certain Choise Grounds and Principles of Our Christian Religion*, 11379.

Gamage, William, *Linsi-Woolsie*, 11545.

Gataker, Thomas, *A Sparke Towards the Kindling of Sorrow for Sion*, 11675.

Gerhard, Johann, trans. Richard Bruch, *The Soules Watch*, 11766.

Gill, Alexander, *Logonomia Anglica*, 11874.

Godwin, Francis, *De Prusulibus Angliae Commentarius*, 11942.

Gohaeus, Gulielmus, *Carmen Panegyrikon*, 11982.5.

Goldwell, Charles, *Reasons Metamorphosis and Restoration*, 11988.

Goodcole, Henry, *The Wonderfull Discouerie of Elizabeth Sawyer a Witch Late of Edmonton*, 12014.

Gouge, William, *A Short Catechisme*, 12127.

Goulart, Simon, *A Learned Summary Upon the Famous Poeme of William of Saluste Lord of Bartas*, 21666.

——, *The Wise Vieillard*, 12136.

Granger, Thomas, *A Familiar Exposition or Commentarie on Ecclesiastes*, 12178.

Greville, Fulke, *Life of Sir Philip Sidney*, ed. Nowell Smith (Oxford, 1907).

Gullemard, Jean, trans. Edward Grimeston, *A Combat Betwixt Man and Death*, 12495.

Hakewill, George, *King Dauids Vow*, 12616.

—— *The Vanity of the Eye* (1633), 12623.

Hall, Joseph, *A Recollection of Such Treatises as Haue Been Heretofore Seuerally Published*, 12708.

——, *Meditations and Vowes, Diuine and Morall*, 12684.

*Helpe to Memorie and Discourse, A*, 13051.

Heron, Edward, *Physicke for Body and Soule*, 13227.

Hewat, Peter, *Three Excellent Points of Christian Doctrine* (Edinburgh), 13258.

Heylyn, Peter, *Microcosmus*, 13276.

Heywood, Thomas, *A Pleasant Conceited Comedy Wherein is Shewed How a Man May Choose a Good Wife from a Bad*, 5598.

Hughes, Lewis, *A Plain and True relation of the Goodnes of God Towards the Sommer Ilands*, 13920.

*Holy Bible, The*, 2263.

Horace, trans. John Ashmore, *Certain Selected Odes*, 13799.

Hume, Patrick, *The Flyting Betwixt Montgomerie and Polwart* (Edinburgh), 13955.

Jackson, Timothy, *A Briefe and Plain . . . Exposition Vpon S. Pauls Second Epistle*, 14320.

James I, King, *His Maiesties Speech in the Vpper House of Parliament*, 14399.

——, Proclamations: . . . *dissoluing . . . Parliament*, 8678; *His Maiesties Declaration*, 9241; *Abraham Lambert of Woodside*, 8651; *Robert Lawe*, 8653; *Thomas Peeke of the towne of Lodden*, 8658; *Concerning the Adiournement of the Parliament*, 8675; *Declaring . . . Grace to his Subiects*, 8667; *Restraint of the Transportation of Corne*, 8669; *William Chapman*, 8654; *Philotheos*, 8673.5; *Anne Callons*, 8652; *Against Abuses*, 8672; *For the Adjournement of the Parliament*, 8671; *Against Excesse of Lavish and Licentious speech of Matters of State*, 8668; *For Suppressing Insolent Abuses Committed by Base people Against Persons of Qualitie*, 8666; *For Abolishing of Abuses*, 8665; *For Repeal of Certain Letters patent . . . concerning Innes, Ale-houses, and the Manufacture of Gold and Silver Threed*, 8664; *For the Finding Out and Apprehending of Sir Giles Mompesson*, 8659; *For restraint of Killing, Dressing and Eating of Flesh in Lent*, 8654.7; James F. Larkin and Paul L. Hughes, eds., *Stuart Royal Proclamations* (Oxford, Clarendon Press, 1973).

——, *The Poems of James VI of Scotland*, ed., James Craigie (Edinburgh: William Blackwood, 1958).

Jenison, Robert, *The Height of Israels Heathenish Idolatrie*, 14491.

John Murrell, *A Delighfful Daily Exercise for Ladies and Gentlewomen*, 18302.

Johnson, Robert, *The Way to Glory*, 14693.5.

Jonson, Ben, *The Masque of Augures*, 14777.

——, *Ben Jonson: Complete Masques*, ed. Stephen Orgel (New Haven: Yale University Press, 1969).

——, W.W. Greg, ed., *Jonson's Masque of Gipsies* (London: British Academy, 1952).

Juvenal, *Iunii Iuuenalis et Auli Persii Flacci Satyrae*, 14891.

Kellison, Matthew, *The Right and Iurisdiction of the Prelate, and the Prince* (Douai), 14911.

King, Henry, *A Sermon Preached at Pauls Crosse the 25 of November 1621*, 14969.

Knolles, Richard, *The Generall Historie of the Turkes*, 15053.

*Lamentable Death of the Earle of Bucquoy, The*, 16798.

Laud, William, *A Sermon Preached Before his Maiesty*, 15301.

*Lawes or Standing Orders of the East India Company, The*, 7447.

Leech, John, *Poematum pars prior*, 15366.

Leigh, Dorothy, *The Mothers Blessing*, 15404.

Leius, Matthias, *Mathiae Leii, Aruillarii vbii Germani*, 15438.

Lessius, Leonardius, trans. John Wilson, *A Treasure of Vowed Chastity in Secular Persons* (St Omer), 15524.

——, trans. William Wright, *A Consultation* (St Omer), 15518.

*Letter Written by Gregory the XV. Pope of Rome to the French King, A*, 12356.

*Letter Written by Those of the Assembly in Rochell, A*, 11304.

Lily, William, *A Short Introduction of Grammar*, 15627.3.

Lindsay, David, *A True Narration of All the Passages of the Proceedings in the Generall Assembly of the Church of Scotland*, 15657.

Littleton, Thomas, *Les Tenures de Monsieur Littleton*, 15758.

——, *Littletons Tenures in English*, 15782.

Loe, William, *Vox Clamantis*, 16691.

*Londons Looking Glass* (St Omer), 18327.

Longford, George, *Manassehs Miraculous Metamorphosis*, 15193a.

*Looking Glasse for Papists, A*, [by R.W.], 24912.

Louis XIII, King, *Letters Patents*, 16840.

Lovell, Robert, *Two Soveraigne Salves for the Soules Sicknesse*, 16859.

Lydiat, Thomas, *Epistola astronomica*, 17039.

Markham, Gervase, *Hungers Preuention*, 17362.

Martyn, Joseph, *New Epigrams and a Satyre*, 17525.

Mason, Francis, *Two Sermons Preached at the Kings Court*, 17600.

Mason, William, *A Handful of Essaies*, 17624.

Massinger, Philip, *The Maid of Honour, The Plays and Poems of Philip Massinger*, ed. P. Edwards and C. Gibson (Oxford: Clarendon Press, 1976), vol. 1.

——, *The Duke of Milan*, in ibid.

——, and John Fletcher, *The Double Marriage, The Dramatic Works in the Beaumont and Fletcher Canon*, ed., Fredson Bowers, vol. 9 (Cambridge: Cambridge University Press, 1994).

May, Edward, *A Sermon of the Communion of Saints*, 17195.

Mayer, John, *The English Catechisme*, 17732.

Middleton, Thomas, and Webster, John, *Anything for a Quiet Life*, F.L. Lucas, *The Complete Works of John Webster* (1927, rpt. London: Chatto and Windus, 1966), vol. 4.

——, *Honourable Entertainments*, 17886.

——, *The Sunne in Aries*, 17895.

——, *Women Beware Women*, ed. J.R. Mulryne (London: Methuen, 1975).

Miller, William, *A Sermon Preached at the Funerall of the Worshipfull Gilbert Davies Esquire*, 17923.5.

Montagu, Richard, *Diatribe Vpon the First Part of the History of Tithes*, 18037.

Mun, Thomas, *A Discourse of Trade*, 18255.

Musgrave, Christopher, *Musgraues Motiues*, 18316.

*New Booke of Spelling with Syllables, A*, 3365.

*Newes from France*, 11279.5.

*Newes from Poland*, 18507.35A.

*Note of the Shipping, Men and Provisions Sent and Prouided for Virginia, A*, 24842a.

*Order of My Lord Maior, the Aldermen, and the Sheriffs for Their Meetings*, 16728.

*Orders and Articles Granted by the High and Mightie Lords of the States General of the Vnited Prouinces*, 18460.

Parsons, Robert, adapted by Edmund Bunny, *A Booke of Christian Exercise*, 19375.

Pasor, George, *Lexico Graeco-Latinum*, 19444.

*Passion of a Discontented Mind, The*, 3681.

Peck, Pierre, *Proposition of the Ambassadour Peckius*, 18460.7.

Perkins, John, *A Profitable Booke . . . Treating of the Lawes of England*, 15758.

Perkins, William, *A Declaration of the True Manner of Knowing Christ Crucified*, 19687.5.

——, *A Direction for the Government of the Tongue*, 19693.

——, *A Golden Chain*, 19664.5.

——, *A Graine of Mustard Seede*, 19726.5.

——, *Two Treatises*, 19761.9.

*Petitions to Parliament*: Carpenters and Bricklayers, 16768.22; Masters of Shipping against the Dungenesse Light, 7353.8; Binders of Books, 16768.8; Felt-Makers,

16777.6; Caleb Morley and Alan Bishop, 18114.5; Dyers Company, 16777.4; Masters of Trinitie House on the Keeping of the Winterton Light, 24283; Prisoners for Debt in the Kings Bench, 14961.5.

Phayer, Thomas, *A Book of Presidents*, 3348.

Playfere, Thomas, *Nine Sermons*, 20006.

Preston, Richard, *Short Questions and Answers*, 20286.

——, *Duties of Communicants*, 20284.

——, *The Doctrine of the Sacrament of the Lords Supper*, 20283.

Prideaux, John, *Eight Sermons*, 20351.

Proctor, Thomas, *The Righteous Mans Way*, 20411.

Quarles, Francis, *Hadassa*, 20546.

Ralegh, Walter, *The History of the World*, 20638a.

Ramus, Petrus, *Audomari Talae Retorica* (Edinburgh), 23660.

Reading, John, *A Faire Warning*, 20789.

——, *The Old Mans Staffe*, 20792.

*Reformed Catholicque, The* (n.p. Netherlands?), 4830.5.

*Relation of Some Special Points Concerning the State of Holland, A* (The Hague), 22083.

*Relation of the Passages of Our English Companies from Time to Time, A*, 17125.

Reynolds, John, *The Triumphs of Gods Reuenge*, 20942.

Robertson, Bartholomew, *Spirituall Encrease*, 21098.7.

Rogers, Nehemiah, *Christian Curtesie*, 21194.

Rogers, Thomas, *A Pretious Booke of Heauenlie Meditations*, 947.5.

——, *The Faith, Doctrine and Religion Professed and Protected in the Realme of England*, 21229.

——, *The Roman-Catharist*, 21250.

Rowley, Samuel, *When You See Me You Know Me*, 21419.

——, Thomas Dekker and John Ford, *The Witch of Edmonton*, ed. Arthur Kinney (New York: Norton, 1998).

Rowley, William, *For a Funerall Elegie on the Death of Hugh Atwell*, 21420.5.

S[egar], F[rancis], *The Schoole of Vertue*, 22137.7.

Sacharles, Juan de Nicholas, *The Reformed Spaniard*, 18530.

Sandys, George, *A Relation of a Iourney Begun An. Dom. 1610*, 21727.

Savile, Henry, *Praelectiones tresdecim in principium Elementorum Euclidis* (Oxford), 21782.

Scot, Patrick, *A Table-Booke for Princes*, 21860.

Scott, Thomas, *A Speech made in the Lower House of Parliament anno. 1621 by Sir Edward Cicill*, 22087.

Shaw, John, *Bibli summula*, 22389.

Sidney, Philip, *The Countesse of Pembrokes Arcadia*, 22545.

——, *A Defence of Poetry*, ed. J.A. Van Dorsten (Oxford: Oxford University Press, 1966).

Sidney, Robert, P.J. Croft, ed., *The Poems of Robert Sidney* (Oxford: Clarendon Press, 1988).

Simson, Archibald, *Heptameron* (St Andrews), 22566.

——, *Samsons Seaven Locks of Haire* (St Andrews), 22570.

Slatyer, William, *The History of Great Britanie*, 22634.

Smith, Henry, *Sixe Sermons*, 22774.

Smith, Richard, *Of the Author and Substance of the Protestant Church and Religion* (St Omer), 22812.

Smith, Samuel, *Aditus ad logicam*, 22830.

Smith, Thomas, *The Common-Wealth of England*, 22864.

Speght, Rachel, *Mortalities Memorandum*, 23057; Barbara Lewalski, ed., *The Polemics and Poems of Rachel Speght* (New York: Oxford University Press, 1996).

Squire, John, *A Sermon*, 23117.

*State of the Suite in Chancerie between Francis Versyln, The*, 24690.

Sternhold, Thomas, Hopkins, Whittingham et al., *The Whole Booke of Dauids Psalmes*, 2573.5.

Stint, Thomas, *An exposition on the CXXIIII, CXXV, CXXVI Psalmes*, 23270.

——, *An Exposition vpon the CXII Psalme*, 23269.

Susenbrotus, Johann, *Syn de theoi makares*, 23441.

Swale, Christopher, *Jacobs Vow*, 23512.

Tapp, John, *The Path-Way to Knowledge; Contayning the Whole Art of Arithmeticke*, 23678.

Taylor, John, *A Briefe Remembrance of all the English Monarchs*, 23737.5.

——, *A Shilling or The Trauailes of Twelue-Pence*, 23793.

——, *Superbiae Flagellum, or, The Whip of Pride*, 23796.

——, *Taylor his Trauels*, 23802.5.

——, *Taylor's Motto*, 23800.

——, *The Cold Tearme*, 23910.

——, *The Praise, Antiquity and Commodity of Beggary, Beggers and Begging*, 23786.

——, *The Subjects Joy for the Parliament*, 23795.7.

——, *The Vnnatural Father*, 23808a.

Taylor, Thomas, *The Parable of the Sower and the Seed*, 23840.

Teelinck, Willem, *Pauls Complaint Against his Naturall Corruption*, 23861.

——, *The Balance of the Sanctuary*, 23860.

Thorius, Raphael, *In obitum Io. Barclaii elegia*, 24034.

Tillesley, Richard, *Animaduersions Vpon M. Seldens History of Tithes*, 24074.

*To the Most Honourably Assembly . . . Petition of the Adventurers in the Ship called the Pearle*, 19519.

*Treves Endt*, 24268.3.

*True Copies of the Insolent, Cruell, barbarous and Blasphemous Letter lately Written by the Great Turke*, 208.

*True Copy of the Latine Oration of the Excellent Lord George Ossolinski, A*, 18890.

*True Medium of the Monies Payable . . . for the Lights at Winterton, A*, 25857.

*True Relation of a Wonderfull Sea Fight, A*, 22130.

*True Relation of the Bloody Execution, A*, 20181.

Tymme, Thomas, *A Silver Watch-Bell*, 24429.

Ussher, James, *The Substance of That Which Was Deliuered in a Sermon before the Commons House of Parliament*, 24553.5.

Vega, Lope de, trans. William Dutton, *The Pilgrime of Casteele*, 24629.

Venner, Thomas, *A Briefe and Accurate Treatise Concerning the Taking of the Fume of Tobacco*, 24642.

Verstegan, Richard, *Obseruations Concerning the Present Affaires of Holland and the Vnited Prouinces* (St Omer), 13576.

Vesey, Henry, *The Scope of the Scripture*, 24694.

Villegas, Alonso de, trans. John Heigham, *The Liues of Saints* (St Omer), 24731b.

Voilleret, Francois, *Le preau des fleurs*, 24871.

Vrillac, Monsieur de, *An Epistle*, 24893.

Ward, Samuel, *Iethro's Iustice of Peace*, 25047.
——, *The Happinesse of Practice*, 25044.
——, *The Happinesse of Practice*, 25044.5.
——, *The Life of Faith*, 25049.
Warre, James, *The Touchstone of Truth*, 25090.
Wats, James, *The Controversie Debated About the Reuerend Gesture of Kneeling*, 25109.
Webbe, George, *Agurs Prayer*, 25155.
*Whole Book of Psalms, The*, 2575.3.
Willis, John, *The Art of Memory*, 25749.
Wing, John, *Abels Offering*, 25842.
——, *Iacobs Staffe*, 25846.
Winne, Edward, *A Letter*, 25854.
Wither, George, *The Songs of the Old Testament*, 25923.
——, *Wither's Motto*, 25925.
*Wonderful Discouerie of the Witch-Crafts of Margaret and Philip Flower, The*, 11107.5.
Woodwall, William, *Englands Vnthankfulnes for Gods Mercie*, 24923.
Wright, Leonard, *A Display of Dutie*, 26029.
Wright, Thomas, *The Passions of the Minde in Generall*, 26042.
Wroth, Mary, *The Counesse of Montgomeries Urania*, 26051.
——, Josephine A. Roberts, ed., *The Poems of Lady Mary Wroth* (Baton Rouge: Louisiana State University Press: 1983).
——, Josephine A. Roberts, ed., Mary Wroth, *The First Part of the Countess of Montgomery's Urania* (Binghampton: Medieval and Renaissance Texts and Studies, 1995).
——, *The Second Part of the Countess of Montgomery's Urania*, ed. Roberts, completed by Suzanne Gossett and Janel Mueller (Tempe: Renaissance English Text Society, 1999).
Yates, John, *A Short and Briefe Summe of Saving Knowledge*, 26088.
Younger, William, *The Vnrighteous Iudge*, 26098.3.

## Secondary

Adams, S.L., 'Foreign Policy and the Parliaments of 1621 and 1624', in Kevin Sharpe, ed., *Faction and Parliament* (Oxford: Clarendon Press, 1978).
Adams, Simon, 'Spain or the Netherlands? The Dilemmas of Early Stuart Foreign Policy', *Before the English Civil War*, ed. Howard Tomlinson (London: Macmillan, 1983).
Amussen, Susan Dwyer, *An Ordered Society: Gender and Class in Early Modern England* (Oxford: Basil Blackwell, 1988).
Anderson, Judith H., *Biographical Truth: The Representation of Historical Persons in Tudor-Stuart Writing* (New Haven: Yale University Press, 1984).
Ashton, Robert, *The City and the Court 1603–1643* (Cambridge: Cambridge University Press, 1979).
Axton, Marie, *The Queen's Two Bodies* (London: Royal Historical Society, 1977).
Babb, Lawrence, *Sanity in Bedlam: A Study of Robert Burton's Anatomy of Melancholy* (Michigan: Michigan State University Press, 1959).
Bald, R.C., *John Donne: A Life* (Oxford: Clarendon Press, 1970).
——, *Donne and the Drurys* (Cambridge: Cambridge University Press, 1959).

Barker, Francis, The *Tremulous Private Body: Essays on Subjection* (London: Methuen, 1984).

Beal, Peter, *In Praise of Scribes* (Oxford: Oxford University Press, 1998).

Beer, Anna R., *Sir Walter Raleigh and his Readers in the Seventeenth Century* (London: Macmillan – now Palgrave Macmillan, 1997).

Beilin, Elaine, 'Writing Public Poetry: Humanism and the Woman Writer', *MLQ* 51 (1990).

——, *Redeeming Eve: Women Writers of the English Renaissance* (Princeton: Princeton University Press, 1987).

Bellany, Alastair, '"Rayling Rymes and Vaunting Verse": Libellous Politics in Early Stuart England, 1603–1628', in Kevin Sharpe and Peter Lake, eds., *Culture and Politics in Early Stuart England* ( London: Macmillan, 1994).

Bennett, H.S., *English Books and Readers 1603–1640* (Cambridge: Cambridge University Press, 1970).

Bentley, G.E., *The Jacobean and Caroline Stage* (Oxford: Clarendon Press, 1941–68).

Bergeron, David M., *English Civic Pageantry 1558–1642* (London: Edward Arnold, 1971).

——, *Royal Family, Royal Lovers* (Columbia: University of Missouri Press, 1991)

Berry, Philippa, *Of Chastity and Power: Elizabethan Literature and the Unmarried Queen* (London: Routledge, 1989).

Bevington, David and Holbrook, Peter, eds., *The Politics of The Stuart Court Masque* (Cambridge: Cambridge University Press, 1998).

Bond, W.H., 'The Reputation and Influence of Sir Philip Sidney' (unpublished PhD Dissertation, Harvard University, 1941).

Boswell, Jackson, and Woudhuysen, H.R., 'Some Unfamiliar Sidney Allusions', in Jan Van Dorsten et al., *Sir Philip Sidney: 1586 and the Creation of a Legend* (Leiden: E.J. Brill, 1986).

Breitenberg, Mark, *Anxious Masculinity in Early Modern England* (Cambridge: Cambridge University Press, 1996).

Brennan, Michael, *Literary Patronage in the English Renaissance: The Pembroke Family* (London: Routledge, 1988).

Breslow, Marvin Arthur, *A Mirror of England: English Puritan Views of Foreign Nations, 1618–1640* (Cambridge, Mass.: Harvard University Press, 1970).

Bromham, A.A. and Bruzzi, Zara. *The Changeling and the Years of Crisis* (London: Pinter, 1990).

Bromham, A.A., 'The Tragedy of Peace: Political Meaning in *Women Beware Women*', *SEL*, 26 (1986).

Burgess, Glenn, *Absolute Monarchy and the Stuart Constitution* (New Haven: Yale University Press, 1996).

——, *The Politics of the Ancient Constitution* (London: Macmillan, 1992).

Butler, Martin, 'Ben Jonson's *Pan's Anniversary* and the Politics of Early Stuart Pastoral', *ELR*, 22 (1992).

——, *Theatre and Crisis 1632–1642* (Cambridge: Cambridge University Press, 1984).

——, '"We are one mans all": Jonson's The Gipsies Metamorphosed', in Cedric Brown, ed., *Patronage, Politics and Literary Traditions in England 1558–1658* (Detroit: Wayne State University Press, 1991).

Capp, Bernard, *English Almanacs 1500–1800* (Ithaca: Cornell University Press, 1979).

——, *The World of John Taylor the Water Poet* (Oxford: Clarendon Press, 1994).

Carrithers Jr., Gale H., *Donne At Sermons: A Christian Existential World* (Albany: State University of New York Press, 1972).

Chambers, E.K., *The Elizabethan Stage* (Oxford: Clarendon Press, 1951).

Chandler, James, *England in 1819* (Chicago: University of Chicago Press, 1998).

Chapple, Anne S., 'Robert Burton's Geography of Melancholy', *SEL* 33 (1993).

Cogswell, Thomas, *The Blessed Revolution: English Politics and the Coming of War 1621–1624* (Cambridge: Cambridge University Press, 1989).

Coiro, Ann,'Milton and Class Identity', *Journal of Medieval and Renaissance Studies*, 22 (1992).

Colie, Rosalie, *Paradoxia Epidemica: The Renaissance Tradition of Paradox* (Princeton: Princeton University Press, 1966).

Collinson, Patrick, *The Birthpangs of Protestant England* (London: Macmillan, 1988).

——, *Godly People* (London: Hambledon Press, 1983).

——, *The Religion of Protestants* (Oxford: Clarendon Press, 1982).

Cook, Ann Jennalie, *The Privileged Playgoers of Shakespeare's London* (Princeton: Princeton University Press, 1981).

Cooper, Helen, *Pastoral: Medieval Into Renaissance* (Ipswich: D.S. Brewer/Rowman and Littlefield, 1977).

Coote, Stephen, *A Play of Passion: The Life of Sir Walter Ralegh* (London: Macmillan, 1993).

Corbett, Margery and Lightbown, Ronald, *The Comely Frontispiece* (London: Routledge, 1979).

Creigh, Jocelyn C., 'George Wither and the Stationers', *PBSA*, 74 (1980).

Cressy, David, *Birth, Marriage, and Death* (Oxford: Oxford University Press, 1997).

Curry, Patrick, *Prophecy and Power: Astrology in Early Modern England* (Oxford: Polity Press, 1989).

Cust, Richard, 'News and Politics in Early Seventeenth-Century England', *Past and Present*, 112 (1986).

Dahl, Folke, *A Bibliography of English Corantos and Periodical Newsbooks 1620–1642* (Stockholm: Almqvist and Wiksell, 1953).

Davies, Horton, *Like Angels from a Cloud: The English Metaphysical Preachers 1588–1645* (San Marino: Huntington Library, 1986).

Davies, Marion Wynne, '"Et in Arcadia Ego": Lady Mary Wroth's Excursion into Renaissance Pastoral', in Kate Chedgzoy et al., *Voicing Women: Gender and Sexuality in Early Modern Writing* (Keele: Keele University Press, 1996).

Davis, Lloyd, 'Redemptive Advice: Dorothy Leigh's *The Mother's Blessing'*, Jo Wallwork and Paul Salzman, eds., *Women Writing 1550–1750* (Bundoora: Meridian, 2000).

Dawson, Anthony B., 'Witchcraft/Bigamy: Cultural Conflict in *The Witch of Edmonton'*, *Renaissance Drama* n.s. 20 (1989).

Delany, Paul, *British Autobiography in the Seventeenth Century* (London: Routledge, 1969).

Doelman, James, 'George Wither, the Stationers Company and the English Psalter', *SP*, 90 (1993).

Duncan-Jones, Katherine, 'Philip Sidney's Toys', in Dennis Kay, ed., *Sir Philip Sidney: An Anthology of Modern Criticism* (Oxford: Clarendon Press, 1987), 61–80.

Eliot, T.S., *For Lancelot Andrewes* (1928: rpt. London: Faber, 1970).
Ettin, Andrew V., *Literature and the Pastoral* (New Haven: Yale University Press, 1984).
Fairholt, Frederick, *Poems and Songs Relating to George Villiers, Duke of Buckingham* (London: Percy Society, 1850).
Fincham, Kenneth and Lake, Peter, 'The Ecclesiastical Policy of King James I', *Journal of British Studies* 24 (1985).
Fincham, Kenneth, *Prelate as Pastor* (Oxford: Clarendon Press, 1990).
Finkelpearl, Philip, '"The Comedians' Liberty": Censorship of the Jacobean Stage Reconsidered', *ELR*, 16 (1986).
——, 'John Fletcher as Spenserian Playwright: *The Faithful Shepherdess* and *The Island Princess*', *SEL*, 27 (1987).
——, *Court and Country Politics in the Plays of Beaumont and Fletcher* (Princeton: Princeton University Press, 1990).
Fish, Stanley, *Self-Consuming Artifacts* (Berkeley: University of California Press, 1972).
Fox, Ruth A., *The Tangled Chain: The Structure of Disorder in the Anatomy of Melancholy* (Berkeley: University of California Press, 1976).
Frank, Joseph, *The Beginnings of the English Newspaper 1620–1660* (Cambridge, Mass.: Harvard University Press, 1961).
French, J. Milton, 'George Wither in Prison', *PMLA*, 45 (1930).
Gardiner, S.R., *History of England*, vol. 4 (London: Longman, 1883).
Goldberg, Jonathan, *James I and the Politics of Literature* (1983, rpt. Stanford: Stanford University Press, 1989).
Green, Ian, '"For Children in Yeers and Children in Understanding": The Emergence of the English Catechism under Elizabeth and the Early Stuarts', *Journal of Ecclesiastical History*, 37 (1986).
——, *The Christian's ABC* (Oxford: Clarendon Press, 1996).
Greenblatt, Stephen, *Shakespearean Negotiations* (Oxford: Clarendon Press, 1988).
——, *Sir Walter Ralegh: The Renaissance Man and his Roles* (New Haven: Yale University Press, 1973).
——, *Renaissance Self-Fashioning* (Chicago: University of Chicago Press, 1980).
Gregg, Pauline, *King Charles I* (London: Dent, 1981).
Gurr, Andrew, *Playgoing in Shakespeare's London*, 2nd edition. (Cambridge: Cambridge University Press, 1996).
——, *The Shakespearean Stage 1574–1642*, 3rd edition. (Cambridge: Cambridge University Press, 1992).
——, *The Shakespearean Playing Companies* (Oxford: Clarendon Press, 1996).
Hackett, Helen, '"Yet Tell Me Some Such Fiction"', in Clare Brant and Diane Purkiss, *Women, Texts and Histories 1575–1760* (London: Routledge, 1992).
——, *Women and Romance Fiction in the English Renaissance* (Cambridge: Cambridge University Press, 2000).
Hadfield, Andrew, *Literature, Travel and Colonial Writing in the English Renaissance 1545–1625* (Oxford: Clarendon Press, 1998).
Hannay, Margaret P., *Philip's Phoenix: Mary Sidney Countess of Pembroke* (New York: Oxford University Press, 1990).
Harbage, Alfred, rev. S. Schoenbaum, *Annals of English Drama 975–1700* (London: Routledge, 1989).

Harbage, Alfred, *Shakespeare's Audience* (New York: Columbia University Press, 1941).

Haselkorn, Anne M., and Travitsky, Betty S., eds., *The Renaissance Englishwoman In Print* (Amherst: University of Massachusetts Press, 1990).

Heinemann, Margot, 'Political Drama', in A.R. Braunmuller and Michael Hattaway, eds., *The Cambridge Companion to English Renaissance Drama* (Cambridge: Cambridge University Press, 1990).

——, *Puritanism and Theatre: Thomas Middleton and Opposition Drama Under the Stuarts* (Cambridge: Cambridge University Press, 1980).

Helgerson, Richard, *Forms of Nationhood: The Elizabethan Writing of England* (Chicago: University of Chicago Press, 1992).

Hill, Christopher, *Intellectual Origins of the English Revolution* (Oxford: Clarendon Press, 1965).

——, *Society and Puritanism in Pre-Revolutionary England* (London: Secker and Warburg, 1964).

Hobbs, Mary, *Early Seventeenth-Century Verse Miscellany Manuscripts* (Aldershot: Scolar Press, 1992).

Hodges, Devon L., *Renaissance Fictions of Anatomy* (Amherst: University of Massachusetts Press, 1985).

Holt, Mack P., *The French Wars of Religion, 1562–1629* (Cambridge: Cambridge University Press, 1995).

Hoy, Cyrus, 'Massinger as Collaborator: The Plays with Fletcher and Others', in Douglas Howard, ed., *Philip Massinger: A Critical Reassessment* (Cambridge: Cambridge University Press, 1985).

Hulme, Peter, *Colonial Encounters* (London: Methuen, 1986).

Hutchison, Margarita Patricia, 'Social and Religious Change: The Case of the English Catechism 1560–1640' (unpublished PhD Dissertation, Stanford University, 1984).

Jardine, Lisa and Stewart, Alan, *Hostage to Fortune: The Troubled Life of Francis Bacon* (London: Victor Gollancz, 1998).

John Buxton, *Sir Philip Sidney and the English Renaissance* (London, 1964).

Jones, Ann Rosalind, *The Currency of Eros: Women's Love Lyric in Europe, 1540–1620* (Bloomington: Indiana University Press, 1990).

Kantorowicz, Ernst H., *The King's Two Bodies* (Princeton: Princeton University Press, 1957).

Kawachi, Yoshiko, *Calendar of English Renaissance Drama 1558–1642* (New York: Garland, 1986).

Kiessling, Nicolas K., *The Library of Robert Burton* (Oxford: Oxford Bibliographical Society, 1988).

Kittredge, George, *Witchcraft in Old and New England* (1929: rpt. New York: Russell and Russell, 1956).

Krontiris, Tina, 'Breaking the Barriers of Genre and Gender: Margaret Tyler's Translation of *The Mirrour of Knighthood*', *English Literary Renaissance* 18 (1988).

Lake, Peter, *Moderate Puritans and the Elizabethan Church* (Cambridge: Cambridge University Press, 1982).

Lamb, Mary Ellen, *Gender and Authorship in the Sidney Circle* (Madison: University of Wisconsin Press, 1990).

Laroque, Francois, *Shakespeare's Festive World* (Cambridge: Cambridge University Press, 1991).

Leggatt, Alexander, *Jacobean Public Theatre* (London: Routledge, 1992).

Levy, F.J., 'Staging the News', in Arthur Marotti and Michael Bristol, eds., *Print, Manuscript, Performance* (Colombus: Ohio State University Press, 2000).

Lewalski, Barbara K., *Donne's Anniversaries and the Poetry of Praise* (Princeton: Princeton University Press, 1973).

——, *Writing Women in Jacobean England* (Cambridge, Mass.: Harvard University Press, 1993).

Limon, Jerzy, *Dangerous Matter: English Drama and Politics in 1623/4* (Cambridge: Cambridge University Press, 1986).

——, *The Masque of Stuart Culture* (Newark: University of Delaware Press, 1990).

Lindenbaum, Peter, 'Sidney and the Active Life', in M.J.B. Allen et al., eds., *Sir Philip Sidney's Achievements* (New York: AMS Press, 1990).

——, *Changing Landscapes: Anti-Pastoral Sentiment in The English Renaissance* (Athens: University of Georgia Pess, 1986).

Lindley, David, *The Trials of Frances Howard: Fact and Fiction at the Court of King James* (London: Routledge, 1993)

Lockyer, Roger, 'An English *Valido*? Buckingham and James I', in Richard Ollard and Pamela Tudor-Craig, *For Veronica Wedgwood These* (London: Collins, 1986).

——, *Buckingham* (London: Longman, 1981).

Love, Harold, *Scribal Publication in Seventeenth-Century England* (Oxford: Clarendon Press, 1993).

Lyons, Bridget Gellert, *Voices of Melancholy* (London: Routledge, 1971).

MacLean, Gerald, *Time's Witness: Historical Representation in English Poetry, 1603–1660* (Madison: University of Wisconsin Press, 1990).

Manley, Lawrence, *Literature and Culture in Early Modern London* (Cambridge: Cambridge University Press, 1995).

Marcus, Leah S., *Puzzling Shakespeare: Local Reading and its Discontents* (Berkeley: Univ. of California Press, 1988).

——, *The Politics of Mirth* (Chicago: University of Chicago Press, 1986).

Marotti, Arthur, *John Donne, Coterie Poet* (Madison: University of Wisconsin Press, 1986).

——, *Manuscript, Print and the English Renaissance Lyric* (Ithaca: Cornell University Press, 1995.

Martin, Christopher, 'Misdoubting His Estate: Dynastic Anxiety In Sidney's *Arcadia*', *English Literary Renaissance* 18 (1988).

Marwil, Jonathan, *The Trial of Counsel: Francis Bacon in 1621* (Detroit: Wayne State University Press, 1976).

Masten, Jeffrey *Textual Intercourse: Collaboration, Authorship, and Sexualities in Renaissance Drama* (Cambridge: Cambridge University Press, 1997).

Maus, Katherine Eisaman, *Inwardness and Theater in the English Renaissance* (Chicago: University of Chicago Press, 1995).

McCabe, Richard A., *Joseph Hall: A Study in Satire and Meditation* (Oxford: Clarendon Press, 1982).

McCoy, Richard C., *Sir Philip Sidney: Rebellion in Arcadia* (Brighton: Harvester, 1979).

McCullough, Peter, *Sermons at Court: Politics and Religion in Elizabethan and Jacobean Preaching* (Cambridge: Cambridge University Press, 1998).

McMullan, Gordon, *The Politics of Unease in the Plays of John Fletcher* (Amherst: University of Massachusetts Press, 1994).

McNulty, Robert, 'The Protestant Version of Robert Parsons' *The Firste Booke of the Christian Exercise'*, *HLQ*, 22 (1959).

McRae, Andrew, 'The Literary Culture of Early Stuart Libeling', *MP*, 97 (2000).

Miller, Naomi J. and Waller, Gary, eds., *Reading Mary Wroth: Representing Alternatives in Early Modern England* (Knoxville: University of Tennessee Press, 1992).

Miller, Naomi, '"Not much to be marked": Narrative of the Woman's Part in Lady Mary Wroth's *Urania'*, *SEL* 29 (1989).

Milton, Anthony, *Catholic and Reformed: The Roman and Protestant Churches in English Protestant Thought 1600–1640* (Cambridge: Cambridge University Press, 1995).

Montrose, Louis Adrian, '"Shaping Fantasies": Figurations of Gender and Power in Elizabethan Culture', *Representations* 1 (1983).

Mueller, William R., *The Anatomy of Robert Burton's England* (Berkeley: University of California Press, 1952).

——, *John Donne: Preacher* (Princeton: Princeton University Press, 1962).

Neely, Carol Thomas, 'Constructing the Subject: Feminist Practice and the New Renaissance Discourses', *English Literary Renaissance*, 18 (1988).

Nochimson, Richard L., 'Studies in the Life of Robert Burton', *YES*, 4 (1974).

Norbrook, David, *Poetry and Politics in the English Renaissance* (London: Routledge, 1984).

——, *Writing the English Republic: Poetry, Rhetoric and Politics 1627–1660* (Cambridge: Cambridge University Press, 1999).

Notestein, Wallace, *The House of Commons 1604–10* (New Haven: Yale University Press, 1971).

——, *A History of Witchcraft in England from 1558 to 1718* (1911: rpt. New York: Russell and Russell, 1967).

——, *Four Worthies* (London: Jonathan Cape, 1956).

O'Callaghan, Michelle, *The 'Shepheard's Nation': Jacobean Spenserians and Early Stuart Political Culture 1612–1625* (Oxford: Clarendon Press, 2000).

——, 'Three Jacobean Spenserians: William Browne, George Wither and Christopher Brooke', unpublished Oxford DPhil. Dissertation (1993).

O'Connor, John J., 'James Hay and the Countess of Montgomery's *Urania'*, *Notes and Queries* 200 (1955).

——, *Amadis de Gaule and Its Influence on Elizabethan Literature* (New Brunswick: Rutgers University Press, 1970).

Ogg, David, *Europe in the Seventeenth Century* (London: A. and C. Black, 1976).

Oldridge, Darren, *Religion and Society in Early Stuart England* (Aldershot: Ashgate Press, 1998).

Orgel, Stephen, *The Illusion of Power: Political Theatre in the English Renaissance* (Berkeley: University of California Press, 1975).

——, *The Jonsonian Masque* (Cambridge, Mass.: Harvard University Press, 1965)

——, 'To Make Boards Speak: Inigo Jones's Stage and the Jonsonian Masque', in Samuel Schoenbaum, ed., *Renaissance Drama*, 1 (1968).

Orlin, Lina, *Private Matters and Public Culture in Post-Reformation England* (Ithaca: Cornell University Press, 1994).

Parker, Patricia, *Inescapable Romance: The Poetics of a Mode* (Princeton: Princeton University Press, 1979).

——, *Literary Fat Ladies* (London: Methuen, 1987).

Parry, Graham, *The Golden Age Restor'd: The Culture of the Stuart Court 1603–1640* (Manchester: Manchester University Press, 1981).

Patrick, J. Max, 'Robert Burton's Utopianism', *PQ* 27 (1948).

Patterson, Annabel, *Censorship and Interpretation: The Conditions of Writing and Reading in Early Modern England* (Madison: University of Wisconsin Press, 1984).

——, *Reading Holinshed's Chronicles* (Chicago: University of Chicago Press, 1994).

Patterson, Lee *Negotiating the Past* (Madison: University of Wisconsin Press, 1987).

Patterson, W.B., 'King James and the Protestant Cause in the Crisis of 1618–22', *Studies in Church History* 18 (1982).

Peck, Linda Levy, *Court Patronage and Corruption in Early Stuart England* (Boston: Unwin Hyman, 1990).

Pocock, J.G.A., *The Machiavellian Moment* (Princeton: Princeton University Press, 1975).

Poole, Kristen, '"The fittest closet for all goodness": Authorial Strategies in Jacobean Mothers' Manuals', *SEL* 35 (1995).

Prest, Wilfred R., *The Inns of Court Under Elizabeth I and the Early Stuarts, 1590–1640* (London: Longman, 1972).

Purkiss, Diane, 'Material Girls: The Seventeenth-Century Woman Debate', in Clare Brant and Diane Purkiss, *Women, Texts & Histories* (London: Routledge, 1993).

——, *The Witch in History* (London: Routledge, 1996).

Quilligan, Maureen, 'Lady Mary Wroth: Female Authority and the Family Romance', in *Unfolded Tales: Essays on Renaissance Romance*, ed. George Logan and Gordon Teskey (Ithaca: Cornell University Press, 1989), 257–8.

Racin Jr, John, 'The Early Editions of Sir Walter Ralegh's *The History of the World*', *SB*, 17 (1964).

Randall, Dale B.J., *Jonson's Gypsies Unmasked: Background and Theme of The Gypsies Metamorphosed* (Durham, NC: Duke University Press, 1975).

Raylor, Timothy, 'The Design and Authorship of The Essex House Masque (1621)', *Medieval and Renaissance Drama in England*, 10 (1998).

——, 'The "Lost" Essex House Masque (1621): A Manuscript Text Discovered', *English Manuscript Studies 1100–1700*, 7 (1998).

Raymond, Joad, *The Invention of the Newspaper: English Newsbooks 1641–1649* (Oxford: Clarendon Press, 1996).

Records of Early English Drama, *Cambridge*, ed. Alan H. Nelson (Toronto: University of Toronto Press, 1989).

Records of Early English Drama, *Norwich 1540–1642*, ed. David Galloway (Toronto: University of Toronto Press, 1984).

Roberts, Josephine A., 'An Unpublished Literary Quarrel Concerning the Suppression of Mary Wroth's *Urania*', *Notes and Queries* 222 (1977).

——, 'Labyrinths of Desire: Lady Mary Wroth's Reconstruction of Romance', *Women's Studies* 19 (1991).

Rollins, Hyder E., *A Pepysian Garland* (1922: rpt. Cambridge, Mass.: Harvard University Press, 1971).

Russell, Conrad, *Parliaments and English Politics* (Oxford: Clarendon Press, 1979).

Salzman, Paul, 'Contemporary References in Mary Wroth's *Urania*', *Review of English Studies* 29 (1978).

——, *English Prose Fiction 1558–1700: A Critical History* (Oxford: Clarendon Press, 1985).

Sawday, Jonathan, *The Body Emblazoned: Dissection and the Human Body in Renaissance Culture* (London: Routledge, 1995).

——, 'Shapeless Elegance: Robert Burton's Anatomy of Knowledge', in Neil Rhodes, ed., *English Renaissance Prose: History. Language and Politics* (Tempe: MRTS, 1997), 173–202.

Schiesari, Juliana, *The Gendering of Melancholia* (Ithaca: Cornell University Press, 1992).

Schleiner, Winifried, *The Imagery of John Donne's Sermons* (Providence: Brown University Press, 1970).

Schrieber, Roy E., *The First Carlisle, Sir James Hay, First Earl of Carlisle as Courtier, Diplomat and Entrepreneur* (Philadelphia: American Philosophical Society, 1984).

Sellin, Paul R., *So Doth, So Is Religion: John Donne and Diplomatic Contexts in the Reformed Netherlands, 1619–1620* (Columbia: University of Missouri Press, 1988).

Shaaber, M.A., *Some Forerunners of the Newspaper in England 1476–1622* (1929, rpt. London: Frank Cass, 1966).

Shami, Jeanne, 'Kings and Desperate Men: John Donne Preaches at Court', *John Donne Journal* 6 (1987).

——, ed., *John Donne Journal*, 11 (1992), Nos. 1 and 2.

Sharpe, Kevin, ed., *Faction and Parliament: Essays on Early Stuart History* (Oxford: Clarendon Press, 1978).

——, *Reading Revolutions: The Politics of Reading in Early Modern England* (New Haven and London: Yale University Press, 2000).

——, *Remapping Early Modern England* (Cambridge: Cambridge University Press, 2000).

——, 'Faction at the Early Stuart Court', *History Today* 33 (1983).

Shuger, Debora Kuller, *Habits of Thought in the English Renaissance: Religion, Politics and the Dominant Culture* (Berkeley: University of California Press, 1990).

Simon, Jean Robert, *Robert Burton (1577–1640) L'Anatomie de la Mélancolie* (Paris: Didier, 1964).

Sinfield, Alan, 'Power and Ideology: An Outline Theory and Sidney's *Arcadia*', *ELH*, 52 (1985).

Smith, Nigel, *Literature and Revolution in England 1640–1660* (New Haven: Yale University Press, 1994).

Somerset, Anne, *Unnatural Murder: Passion at the Court of James I* (London: Weidenfeld and Nicolson, 1997).

Sommerville, C. John, *The News Revolution in England* (New York: Oxford University Press, 1996).

Sommerville, J.P., *Royalists and Patriots: Politics and Ideology in England 1603–1640*, 2nd edition (London: Longman, 1999).

Spufford, Margaret, *Small Books and Pleasant Histories: Popular Fiction and its Readership in Seventeenth-Century England* (London: Methuen, 1981).

Stachniewski, John, *The Persecutory Imagination: English Puritanism and the Literature of Religious Despair* (Oxford: Clarendon Press, 1991).

Strong, Roy, *Henry, Prince of Wales and England's Lost Renaissance* (London: Thames and Hudson, 1986).

Sturgess, Keith, *Jacobean Private Theatre* (London: Routledge, 1987).

Swift, Caroline Ruth, 'Female Identity in Lady Mary Wroth's Romance *Urania'*, *English Literary Renaissance* 14 (1984).

Thomas, Keith, *Religion and the Decline of Magic* (New York: Scribners, 1971).

Tricomi, Albert H., *Anticourt Drama in England 1603–1642* (Charlotteville: University Press of Virginia, 1989).

Tyacke, Nicholas, *Anti-Calvinists: The Rise of English Arminianism c. 1590–1640* (Oxford: Clarendon Press, 1987).

Veeser, H. Aram, ed., *The New Historicism* (London: Routledge, 1989).

Venuti, Lawrence, *Our Halcyon Days* (Madison: University of Wisconsin Press, 1989).

Vicari, E. Patricia, *The View From Minerva's Tower: Learning and Imagination in The Anatomy of Melancholy* (Toronto: University of Toronto Press, 1989).

Vickers, Nancy, '"The blazon of sweet beauty's best": Shakespeare's Lucrece', in Patricia Parker and Geoffrey Hartman, eds., *Shakespeare and the Question of Theory* (New York: Methuen, 1985).

——, 'Diana Described: Scattered Woman and Scattered Rhyme', *Critical Inquiry*, 8 (1981).

Wall, Wendy, *The Imprint of Gender* (Ithaca: Cornell University Press, 1993).

Waller, Gary, 'Mother/Son, Father/Daughter, Brother/Sister, Cousins: the Sidney Family Romance', *Modern Philology*, 88 (1991).

——, *The Sidney Family Romance: Mary Wroth, William Herbert and the Early Modern Construction of Gender* (Detroit: Wayne State University Press, 1993).

Walmsley, Joan M., *John Reynolds, Merchant of Exeter* (Lewiston: Edwin Mellen Press, 1991).

Walsham, Alexandra, *Providence in Early Modern England* (Oxford: Oxford University Press, 1999).

Walton, Izaak, *Lives*, ed. S.B. Carter (London: Falcon, 1951).

Watt, Tessa, *Cheap Print and Popular Piety 1550–1640* (Cambridge: Cambridge University Press, 1991).

Webber, Joan, 'Celebration of Word and World in Lancelot Andrewes' Style', *JEGP*, 64 (1965).

——, *Contrary Music: The Prose Style of John Donne* (Madison: University of Wisconsin Press, 1963).

——, *The Eloquent 'I': Style and Self in Seventeenth-Century Prose* (Madison: University of Wisconsin Press, 1968).

Weinberger, Jerry, 'The Politics of Bacon's History of Henry the Seventh', *The Review of Politics*, 52 (1990).

Welsby, Paul A., *Lancelot Andrewes 1555–1626* (London: SPCK, 1958).

White, Peter, *Predestination, Policy and Polemic: Conflict and Consensus in the English Church from the Reformation to the Civil War* (Cambridge: Cambridge University Press, 1992).

White, Stephen D., *Sir Edward Coke and 'The Grievances of the Commonwealth'* (Chapel Hill: University of North Carolina Press, 1979).

Williams, Ethel Carleton, *Anne of Denmark* (London: Longman, 1970).

Wilson, David Harris, *King James VI and I* (London: Jonathan Cape, 1956).

Woolf, D.R., *The Idea of History in Early Stuart England* (Toronto: Toronto University Press, 1990).

Worden, Blair, *The Sound of Virtue: Philip Sidney's Arcadia and Elizabethan Politics* (New Haven: Yale University Press, 1996).

Woudhuysen, Henry, *Sir Philip Sidney and the Circulation of Manuscripts* (Oxford: Oxford University Press, 1996).

Wrightson, Keith, *English Society 1580–1680* (London: Hutchinson, 1982).

Young, Michael B., *James I and the History of Homosexuality* (London: Macmillan, 2000).

Zaller, Robert, *The Parliament of 1621* (Berkeley: University of California Press, 1971).

# Index

Abbot, George (Archbishop of
    Canterbury), 61, 169, 174
Acheson, Katherine O., 212n.5
Adams, S.L., 215n.63, 232n.25,
    233n.50
Adson, John, *Courtly Masquing
    Ayres*, 205
Alexander, William, 68
*Algiers Voyage*, 145
Allstree, Richard, 155
almanacs, 154–8
*Amadis de Gaule*, 73–4
Amussen, Susan Dwyer, 222n.37
Anderson, Judith, 190, 238n.77
Anderton, James, *The Reformed
    Protestant*, 173–4
Andrewes, Lancelot, 41–7, 58, 61,
    Easter sermon, 42–4; opening of
    parliament sermon, 44–7, 80
Anne of Denmark, Queen, 67–8
Archer, Thomas, 141, 143
Armada, Spanish, 55–7, 78
Ashmore, John, 133–4
Ashton, Robert, 225n.27
Atwell, Hugh (subject of Rowley's
    'Elegy'), 138–9
Axton, Marie, 221n.33

Babb, Lawrence, 23, 213n.25
Bacon, Francis, and impeachment,
    22, 58, 107, 120, 131, 133–4,
    147, 148, 189–91; *History of
    the Reign of King Henry VII,
    The*, 189–91; *Novum
    Organum*, 9, 79
Bald, R.C., 45, 47, 48, 135, 136,
    215n.48–9, 216n.68–9, 216n.71,
    225n.26, 231n.54, 231n.56,
    231n.62, 231n.65
ballads, 6, 147, 150–54
Barclay, John, *Argenis*, 69, 75–81
Barker, Francis, 13, 211n.2
Barrington, Thomas, 146

Bayly, Lewis (Bishop of Bangor), *The
    Practise of Piety*, 162–3, 237
Beal, Peter, 130, 230n.33–4
Beaumont, Francis, 96
Beer, Anna R., 316n.68
Beeston, Christopher, 82
Beilin, Elaine, 15, 16, 212n.9–10,
    228n.5
Bellany, Alexander, 226n.45, 226n.48
Bennett, H.S., xviii, 210n.13
Bentley, G.E., 224n.2, 225n.31,
    230n.47, 231n.67, 231n.70
Bergeron, David M., 90, 211n.6,
    225n.22–3
Bernard, Richard, *The Faithful
    Shepherd*, 176
Berry, Philippa, 66, 220n.12, 221n.23,
    221n.32
Bevington, David, 227n.61
Bodleian MS Malone 23, 130–1,
    308n.37–8
Bohemia, 34–5, 45–6, 54–8, 69, 79, 89,
    99, 108, 119, 123, 125, 141–5,
    151, 171, 175, 177, 195, 196
Bolton, Edmund, (translator of Lucius
    Florus), 196; *Hypercritica, The*, 270
Bond, W.H., 220n.16
'Book of Sports, The', 57, 144, 161–2,
    166–7
Boswell, Jackson, 220n.16
Bowers, Fredson, 226n.39, 226n.41,
    227n.58
Brathwait, Richard, *Time's Curtain
    Drawn, Natures Embassie*, 229n.32
Braunmuller, A.R., 303n.8
Breitenberg, Mark, 26–7, 213n.27,
    213n.30–2
Brennan, Michael, 220n.18
Brerely, John, *see* Anderton, James
Breslow, Marvin, 216n.89
*Brief Description, A*, 144
British Library Sloane Manuscript
    542, 133

Bromham, A.A., 86, 88, 224n.1, 224n.9, 225n.14, 225n.21

Brooke Christopher, 138

Browne, Daniel, 155–7

Buckingham, George Villiers, Duke of, xx, 9–11, 36, 49, 65, 66, 70, 102, 131, 133, 153–4, 196; and Jonson's *The Gypsies Metamorphosed*, 109–11; and Massinger, 97–101, 150; and parliament, 98, 147–8, 213; and Taylor, 126; and *Urania*, 65–7, 70, 74–5; and verse libels, 130–3, 185, 204; and Wither, 120–1; and *Women Beware Women*, 86

Bunny, Edmund, *A Booke of Christian Exercise*, 164

Bunyan, John, *Grace Abounding*, 163, 235n.18

Burgess, Glen, 51, 205, 214n.41, 216n.82, 239n.85, 239n.90, 240n.4

Burton, Robert, *Anatomy of Melancholy, The*, xviii, 17–31, 275, 285; anxiety about masculinity in, 35; editions of, 25

Butler, Charles, 318n.99

Butler, Martin, 4, 6, 108–9, 110–11, 210n.8–9, 224n.1, 227n.64, 227n.70, 228n.71

Butter, Nathaniel, 141, 143, 154, 233n.36

Buxton, John, 220n.16

Cadenet, Marquis of, 2–3, 151, 196

Calvert, George, 145

Calvin, 32, 77, 164, 169, 173, 236n.21

Cambridge (and drama), 83

Camden, William, 193, 194, 195

Capp, Bernard, 125, 155, 229n.19–20, 229n.23, 229n.27, 234n.70–6

Carleton, Dudley, 1, 2, 5, 6, 7, 103–4, 141, 143, 147

Carr, Robert (Earl of Somerset), 97–8

Carrithers Jr., Gale, 214n.45–6

catechisms, 166–7

Catholicism, 39–40, 43, 49–51, 55, 58, 59–63, 77, 138, 155, 164–6, 168, 170, 173–6, 239–43

Cecil, Edward, 150

*Certain and True Newes, The*, 144

*Certain Letters*, 143

Chamberlain, John, xviii, 1–12, 50, 55, 58–9, 65, 75, 77, 80, 83, 109, 143, 147, 148, 149, 163, 204, 208, 237n.61

Chambers, E.K., 224n.2, 226n.40

Chandler, James, xviii, 209n.9

chapbooks, 209–18

Chapple, Anne S., 213n.35

characters, 168

Charles, Prince (later Charles I), 2, 31, 59–63, 149, 169, 177, 189, 194

Cleaver, Robert, *Godly Form of Household Gouernment, A*, 201

Clifford, Anne, 211n.5

Coeffeteau, F.N., *Table of Human Passions, A*, 200

Cogswell, Thomas, 206, 209n.7, 240n.5

Coiro, Ann, 230n.36

Coke, Edward, 147, 149, 161, 164–5, 192, 232n.28

Colie, Rosalie, 23, 213n.19, 213n.29

Collinson, Patrick, 31, 166, 214n.39, 214n.42, 235n.1, 235n.10–11, 236n.26

cookbooks, 199

common law, 264–5

Communion, 49–50, 68–9; kneeling to take, 176

*Contents of the Watermans Bill, The*, 149

Cook, Ann Jennalie, 112, 228n.74

Cooke, Alexander, *More Work for a Mass Priest*, 174–5, 217n.91

cooking, 273–4

Cooper, Helen, 223n.48

Coote, Stephen, 237n.63

*Copy of Two Letters Sent from Spain, The*, 145

corantos, *see also* news, 140–3

Corbett, Margery, 291n.15

Corbett, Richard, 132

Coryate, Thomas, 125

Coventry, Thomas, 167

Craigie, James, 211n.14, 211n.16

Creigh, Jocelyn C., 229n.15

Cressy, David, 160, 235n.6
Croft, P.J., 228n.3
Crowley, Robert, *Schoole of Vertue and Book of Good Nurture, The*, 201-2
Curry, Patrick, 234n.76
Cust, Richard, 140, 210n.11, 231n.2-3

Dahl, Folke, 232n.9, 232n.11, 232n.21-2
Daniel, Samuel, 191-4; *Civil Wars, The*, 263; *Collection of the Historie of England, The*, 191-4
Davies, Horton, 215n.58
Davies, John, *Antiquae linguae Britannicae*, 197-8
Davies, Marion Wynne, 221n.36
Davis, Lloyd, 171, 237n.40-1
Dawson, Anthony B., 104, 227n.56
Day, Angel, *English Secretarie, The*, 198
*Declaration of the Reformed Church, The*, 144
Dekker, Thomas, *see* Rowley, William
Delany, Paul, 212n.4
Denny, Edward, 65-7, 71, 72, 74, 115
Dent, Arthur, 235n.18
*Description of Giles Mompesson, The*, 147
*Deserved Downfall of a Corrupted Conscience, The*, 152
Dewe, Thomas, 199; *Passions of the Mind in General*, 200
D'Ewes, Simonds, 100, 138
Dod, John, (*see also* Cleaver, Robert), 201
Doelman, James, 229n.14
Donne, John, 32-41, 47, 134-8; Anniversaries/elegies, 134-8; Christmas Day sermon, 39-41; sermons, 32-41, 65; White Hall sermon, 35-9; and Countess of Bedford, 33-5
Drake, William, 204
Drayton, Michael, 177, 191, 193-4
Drury, Elizabeth, 135-8

Drury, Robert, 136-8
Duncan-Jones, Katherine, 210n.10, 220n.13

East India Company, 199-200
economics, 275
education, 272-9
Edwards, Philip, 99, 226n.47
Egerton, Stephen, *Brief Method of Catechising, A*, 166, 167
elegy, 186-91
Eliot, T.S., 41, 215n.54
Elizabeth I, 69, 77-8, 81, 123, 130-1, 144, 165, 184, 194
Elizabeth, Princess of Palatine/Bohemia, 34-5, 54, 98, 108, 123, 142, 150, 171
Englefield, Francis, 149-50
Erondelle, Pierre, *French Garden for English ladyes, A*, 198
*Essex House Masque, The*, 154-5
Ettin, Andrew V., 223n.48
Evans, John, *Palace of Profitable Pleasure, The*, 198

Fairholt, Frederick, 226n.45
Farmer, Norman K., 230n.38, 230n.40, 230n.45-6
Felton, John, 100
Finch, John, *The Worlds Great Restauration or the calling of the Jews*, 162
Fincham, Kenneth, 217n.96, 218n.105, 235n.1, 235n.16
Finkelpearl, Philip, 92, 93, 225n.32, 226n.35-6
Fish, Stanley, 23, 292n.26
Fletcher, John, 92-7; *Island Princess, The*, 92-4; (with Beaumont and Massinger), *Tragedy of Thierry and Theodoret, The*, 96-7; (with Masssinger), *Double Marriage, The*, 101-3; *Wild Goose Chase, The*, 94-6
Florus, Lucius, 196
Flower, Joan, 153-4
Ford, John, *see* Rowley, William
Fortune Theatre, 8-9, 82
fowling, 273-4

Fox, Ruth A., 23, 292n.26
France, 2
Frank, Joseph, 231n.7, 232n.10, 232n.12, 232n.21
Frederick of Bohemia, xx, 2, 34–5, 45–6, 54, 69, 79, 98, 108, 123, 142, 144, 150
French, J. Milton, 228n.8
Frewen, John, *Certain Choise Grounds*, 167
Fulwood, William, *Enemy of Idleness, The*, 198

Gainsford, Thomas, 119
*Gallants to Bohemia*, 153
Galloway, David, 224n.4
Gardiner, S.R., 150, 234n.59
Gataker, Thomas, *Sparke Towards Kindling of Sorrow, A*, 52–4
gazetto, *see* corantoes
geography, 268–9
Gil, Alexander, *Logonomia Angliae*, 198
Goldberg, Jonathan, 70, 211n.15, 222n.37, 239n.93
Gondomar, Ambassador of Spain, 3, 8, 57, 91, 119, 150
Goring, George, 233n.50
grammar, 197–8
Granger, Thomas, *A Familiar Exposition or Commentarie on Ecclesiastes*, 176
Green, Ian, 236n.25, 236n.27
Greenblatt, Stephen, 12, 13, 186–7, 211n.18, 211n.1, 238n.67, 237n.69
Greg, W.W., 227n.67
Gregg, Pauline, 218n.105
Greville, Fulke, 68, 93, 299n.28
Grimeston, Edward, 196, 200
Gunpowder Plot, 69
Gurr, Andrew, 112, 224n.2, 228n.75, 306n.76

Hackett, Helen, 218n.4, 222n.40, 222n.43, 223n.47
Hadfield, Andrew, 225n.33
Hakewill, George, 58–63; *King David's Vow*, 59–60; *Vanity of the Eye, The*, 59; *Wedding Robe, The*, 61–3, 218n.107

Hall, Joseph, 135, 168–70; *Art of Divine Meditation*, 168, 169; *Characters of Virtues and Vices*, 168; *Contemplations*, 170; *Heaven Upon Earth*, 168; *Holy Observations*, 168; *Meditations and Vows*, 168
Hannay, Margaret P., 221n.29
Harbage, Alfred, 112, 224n.3, 228n.74
Harrington, James, 190
Harrington, Lucy, Countess of Bedford, and Donne, 33–5
Hay, James, Viscount Doncaster and Earl of Carlisle, 2, 4, 36, 154, 218n.5
Healy, Tom, 288n.8
Heinemann, Margot, 85, 88, 121, 122, 220n.19, 224n.1, 224n.8, 224n.10–11, 225n.19–20
Helgerson, Richard, 191, 192, 238n.82–3, 238n.85, 239n.89
Henry, Prince of Wales, 59, 68, 108, 131, 135, 136, 162–3, 168, 169, 182, 186, 188
Herbert, Philip, 170
Herbert, William, 67, 70, 97, 111, 113–14
Heylyn, Peter, *Microcosmus*, 194–5, 197
Hill, Christopher, 161, 182, 235n.10, 237n.62
Hill, Robert (*see also* Perkins, William), 175
Hind, Arthur, 217n.93–4
history, 181–97
Hobbs, Mary, 210n.15
Hobby, Elaine, 212n.5
Hodges, Devon, 20, 23, 213n.17, 213n.26
Holland, Philemon, 196
Holt, Mack P., 233n.29
Holyday, Barton, *Technogamia*, 132–3
Horace, 'Odes', 133
Hoy, Cyrus, 226n.50, 227n.53
Hulme, Peter, 94, 226n.37
Hutchison, Margarita, 166, 236n.25, 236n.28

Ireland, 188

James I, xx, 2, 6, 133, 143, 173, 175, 196; confrontation with parliament, 206–7; Directions to Preachers, 51, 73, 106–8; Oath of Allegiance, 36, 58, 82, 175; proclamation against abuse of strangers, 91; proclamations against Mompesson and monopolies, 147–8; proclamation against speech of matters of State, 8, 102, 117, 148; *Versus*, 10–11, 32; and *Argenis*, 75–80; and Bacon, 9, 189–91, 270; and ban on corantos, 141, 207; and 'Book of Sports', 57, 161–2; and George Hakewill, 60–3; and Massinger's treatment of his relationship with Buckingham, 97–101; and parliament, 45–51, 149–50; and Ralegh, 182–8; and sermons, 32, 44–5, 60, 62, 67, 91; and *The Gypsies Metamorphosed*, 9–10, 153–4, 156; and *The Sun in Aries*, 124; and verse libels, 130–3; and witches, 104, 149; and Wither, 123; and *Women Beware Women*, 118–19; as reader, 208
Jardin, Roland du, *Discourse of the Married and Single Life, A*, 202
Jardine, Lisa, 238n.71–5
Jenison, Robert, *Height of Israel's Heathenish Idolatry*, 175, 216n.91
Johnson, John, 157
Jones, Ann Rosalind, 70, 221n.35, 228n.5
Jonson, Ben, 3; Epigrams, 134; *Gypsies Metamorphosed, The*, 6, 9–10, 108–11; *Masque of Blackness, The*, 115; *Pan's Anniversary*, 4, 6, 9, 108–9; lost *Argenis* translation 76; on Daniel, 191; on Donne, 135–6; on Ralegh, 182
Juel-Jensen, Bent, 221n.30
Juvenal, 229n.32

Kantorowitcz, Ernst, 221n.33
Kawachi, Yoshiko, 224n.3
Kay, Dennis, 220n.16

Keere, van den, Pieter, 194
Kiessling, Nicholas, 30, 214n.37–8
King, Henry, 216n.91
Kinney, Arthur, 106, 227n.59
Kittredge, George, 234n.68
Knollys, Richard, (*see also* Grimeston, Edward), *The Generall History of the Turks*, 196
Krontiris, Tina, 223n.47

La Rochelle, 144–5
Lake, Peter, 235n.1
Lamb, Mary Ellen, 212n.5, 218n.3, 219n.4, 219n.7, 222n.39, 222n.40, 222n.42
Larkin, James F., 211n.13, 304n.29
Laroque, Francois, 228n.77
*Last Summons, The*, 145
Laud, William, 162, 176, 195
Le Grys, Robert, translator of *Argenis*, 76
Lea, Richard, 169
Lee, Maurice, 289n.2
Leggatt, Alexander, 224n.2
Leigh, Dorothy, *A Mother's Blessing*, 171–3, 239n.105
letter writing, 198
*Letter Written by Captaine Edward Winne, A*, 145
*Letters Patent Made by the French King*, 144–5
Levy, F.J., 140, 231n.4
Lewalski, Barbara, 14, 15, 211n.4, 212n.6–8, 220n.22, 228n.5, 231n.61
libels, *see* verse libels
*Life, Confession and Heartie Repentance of Francis Cartwright, Gentleman, The*, 154
Lily, William, *Short Introduction of Grammar, A*, 197
Limon, Jerzey, 107, 210n.6, 224n.1, 227n.62
Lincoln's Inn, 47–9, 51
Lindenbaum, Peter, 222n.45
Lindley, David., 209n.6
Livy, 196
Lockyer, Roger, 98, 226n.43
London, and Middleton, 124–6

Long, Kingesmill, translator of *Argenis*, 76, 105
Love, Harold, 129, 146, 209n.3, 229n.33, 233n.37
Lovell, Robert, *Two Soveraigne Salves for the Souls Sicknesse*, 160–2, 235n.7
Lucas, F.L., 88, 303n.18
Lyons, Bridget Gellert, 23, 213n.26

McCabe, Richard, 168, 232, 236n.29–32, 236n.34–6, 236n.38
McClure, Norman, 289n.1
McCoy, Richard C., 221n.27
McCullough, Peter, 31, 214n.40, 214n.42, 215n.58, 217n.100
MacLean, Gerald, 230n.36
McClure, Norman, 1, 2, 210n.1
McMullan, Gordon, 101–2, 225n.32–3, 226n.52, 227n.53
McNulty, Robert, 236n.19
McRae, Andrew, 226n.45, 230n.42–3
Manley, Lawrence, 90, 225n.24–5, 228n.77
Manners, Catherine (wife of Buckingham), 10
Mansell, Robert, 145
manuscript publication, xvi, 178–84, 187
Marcus, Leah, xv, 69, 209n.2, 217n.96, 221n.32, 227n.61, 235n.9
Markham, Gervase, *Hungers Prevention*, 198–9
Marotti, Arthur, 129, 130, 137, 209n.3, 229n.33, 230n.35, 230n.44, 231n.63–4
Martial, 134
Martin, Christopher, 221n.27
Martyn, Joseph, *New Epigrams and a Satire*, 134
Marvell, Andrew, 185
Marwil, Jonathan, 217n.97
masques, 2, 4, 107–111
Massinger, Philip, 133, 97–103; *Duke of Milan, The*, 100–101; *Maid of Honour, The*, 98–100; (with Fletcher), *Double Marriage, The*, 101–3
Masten, Jeff, 69–70, 103, 221n.34, 227n.54

Maus, Katherine Eisemann, 13, 211n.3
May, Edward, 47–51
Mayer, John, *English Catechism, The*, 166–7
meditation, 167–70
Middleton, Thomas, 83, 85–92; *A Game at Chess*, 11, 85, 206; *Anything for a Quiet Life*, 88–90; *Changeling, The*, 181; *Honourable Entertainments*, 83, 90–2; *Sun in Aries, The*, 83, 90; *Triumph of Truth, The*, 90; *Women Beware Women*, 85–8; and Lord Mayor's Shows, 114, 124
Miller, Naomi J., 218n.2, 218n.4, 222n.40
Milton, Anthony, 52, 159, 166, 173, 175, 176, 214n.42, 216n.81, 216n.88, 217n.96, 218n.105, 235n.1–3, 236n.19, 236n.21, 236n.24, 237n.42–3, 237n.50, 237n.52
*Mirror of Knighthood, The*, 74
Mitchell, Francis, 152
Mompesson, Giles, 147–8, 152
monopolies, 30, 120–1, 123, 126, 131, 147
Montagu, Henry, 150
Montrose, Louis Adrian, 221n.32
Mueller, Janel, 214n.45
Mueller, William, 22, 23, 213n.20–1, 214n.45
Mulryne, J.R., 225n.12
Mun, Thomas, *Discourse of Trade, A*, 199–200
Murray, Thomas (secretary to Prince Charles), 61
Murrell, John, *Delightful Daily Exercise for Ladies and Gentlewomen, A*, 199
Musgrave, Christopher, *Musgrave's Motives*, 174

Nashe, Thomas, 128
Neely, Carol Thomas, 209n.1, 218n.2
Nelson, Alan, 224n.5
Netherlands, and corantos, 195–8
Neve, Jeffrey, 157
*New Booke of Spelling, A*, 198

*Newes from France*, 145
Newfoundland, 201
*News from Poland*, 232n.17
news, 5–7, 140–54, and Burton, 41
Nochimson, Richard, 213n.34,
    214n.36
Norbrook, David, 91, 220n.18,
    220n.19, 229n.17, 230n.50,
    239n.93
Norwich (performance at), 83
Notestein, Wallace, 1, 2, 210n.4,
    220n.20, 233n.38, 234n.68

O'Callaghan, Michelle, 117–19, 121,
    220n.18, 227n.65, 228–9n.9–13,
    229n.23, 238n.83
O'Connor, John J., 218n.5,
    223n.46
*Observations Concerning, see also*
    Rowlands, Richard, 144
Ogg, David, 232n.16
Oldridge, Darren, 313n.1
Orgel, Stephen, 107, 110, 210n.6,
    289n.12, 227n.61, 227n.68
Orlin, Lena, 227n.56
Osman II, Emperor of Turkey, 142,
    232n.17
Overbury, Thomas, xvii, 70, 79, 131,
    209n.6
Oxford, 83, 132–3

Palatine (*see also* Bohemia,
    Frederick and Elizabeth), 2, 73,
    75, 119, 143, 150, 208, 245
pamphlets, 199–202; and Burton, 41
Parker, Patricia, 222n.40, 222n.44,
    223n.49
parliament, 32, 44–6, 48–51, 110, 130;
    bills, 149–50, 180, 206; debates
    and diaries, 146–50
Parry, Graham, 221n.24
Parsons, Robert (*see also* Edmund
    Bunny), 164
pastoral poetry, 67, 101
Patrick, J. Max, 213n.22
Patterson, Annabel, xv, 67, 76, 80,
    288n.2, 220n.16, 223n.54,
    223n.57, 223n.60, 226n.46
Patterson, Lee, 209n.1

Patterson, W.B., 217n.96
Peacham, Henry, 151
Peck, Linda Levy, 220n.19, 221n.23,
    233n.42
Perkins, William, *The Golden Chain*,
    175–6
Perrot, James, 49, 50, 54, 150
Perseus, 229n.32
petitions, 149–50
Philip IV, King of Spain, 201
Philips, Samuel, 218n.104
Pocock, J.G.A., 238n.76
Poland, 142, 232n.17
Pool, Kristen, 236n.39
*Post of Ware, The*, 151–2
Prague, 142
Prest, Wilfred, 48, 210n.3, 216n.72
Prideaux, John, 216n.91
*Prince Henry's Barriers*, 68
proclamations, 10–11, 163, 147–8
Puritanism, 159–61, 166
Purkiss, Diane, 105, 225n.16,
    227n.57
Pym, John, 49, 50, 146

Quilligan, Maureen, 218n.4

Racin Jr, John, 237n.63
Ralegh, Walter, xxi, 94, 181–9;
    *History of The World*, 181–9,
    262, 279
Ramus, Petrus, *Rhetorica*, 197
Randall, Dale, 110, 227n.69
Raylor, Timothy, 108, 111,
    228n.72–3
Raymond, Joad, 140, 231n.5–7,
    232n.19–20
Reeve, Clara, 302n.53
Reynolds, John, 177–81; *Triumphs
    of God's Revenge, The*, 187–91;
    *Votivae Angliae*, 187;
    *Vox Coeli*, 187
Roberts, Josephine, 64, 69, 71,
    80, 218n.2, 218n.4, 218n.5,
    221n.33, 222n.40–1, 223n.46,
    228n.1
Rogers, Timothy, *Roman Catherist,
    The*, 217n.91
Rollins, Hyder, 151, 234n.64–5

romance, 64–81

Rosen, Barbara, 234n.68

Rowlands, Richard (aka Richard Verstegan), 144, 232n.28

Rowley, William, 'Elegy', 138–9, (with Thomas Dekker and John Ford); *Witch of Edmonton, The*, 104–7

Russell, Conrad, 205, 215n.63, 233n.41, 233n.47, 233n.50, 240n.4

Sabbath (*see also* 'Book of Sports'), 160–3, 166–7, 172

Sacharles, John de Nicholas y, *Reformed Spaniard, The*, 174

Salzman, Paul, 218n.1, 218n.5, 220n.17, 223n.54

Sawday, Jonathan, 38, 213n.24, 215n.53

Sawyer, Elizabeth (and *The Witch of Edmonton*), 104–7

Schiesari, Juliana, 213n.27

Schliener, Winifried, 214n.45

Schreiber, Roy E., 210n.5, 210n.7

Scott, Thomas, 150, 177

Sellin, Paul R., 215n.46

sermons, 31–58, 159–62

Shaaber, M.A., 231n.1

Shami, Jeanne, 214n.46

Sharpe, Kevin, 181–2, 204, 214n.41, 215n.63, 220n.19, 240n.1–2

Shepherd, Thomas, 49, 161

Shuger, Debora Kuller, 35, 44, 47, 215n.47, 215n.60–1, 216n.66

Sidney, Mary, 68, 121

Sidney, Philip, 6, 114, 121, 135; *Arcadia*, 64, 67–9, 73; *Defence of Poetry*, 73–4, 158; and Mary Sidney, psalms, 121

Sidney, Robert, 64, 114

Simon, Jean Robert, 213n.34

Simpson, Evelyn, 34, 36

Sinfield, Alan, 221n.27

Slatyer, William, *Historie of Great Britanie, The*, 193–4

Smith, Nigel, xvi, 209n.4

Smyth, John, 146

Somerset, Anne, 209n.6

Sommerville, C. John, 142, 232n.18

Sommerville, J.P., 51, 187, 205, 214n.41, 216n.8, 187n.70, 239n.85, 239n.90, 240n.4

Spain, 2, 55, 60, 123, 169, 173, 177, 182, 184–6, 255–6

*Speech Made in the Lower House of Parliament, A*, 150

Speght, Rachel, 89; *Mortalities Memorandum*, 14–17; *Mouzell for Melastomus, A*, 15

Spufford, Margaret, 150, 234n.60–1, St Omer, 144

Stachniewski, John, 23, 213n.26

Steen, Sara Jayne, 212n.5

Stewart, Alan, 238n.71–5

Story, G.M., 44, 215n.56, 215n.59

Stringer, Gary, 230n.53

Strong, Roy, 92, 221n.24–5

Sturgess, Keith, 224n.2

Swetnam, Joseph, *Arraigment*, 15

Swift, Caroline Ruth, 222n.40

Synod of Dort, 176

Tacitus, 239n.96

Tanner, J.R., 295n.85

Taylor, John, 123–9, 196–7; *Brief Remembrance of All the English Monarchs, A*, 196–7; *Praise, Antiquity and Commodity of Beggery, Beggers and Begging, The*, 127–8; *Shilling, A*, 129; *Subject's Joy, for the Parliament, The*, 123; *Superbiae Flagellum*, 126–7; *Taylor's Goose*, 128–9; *Taylor's Motto*, 124–6

*Tempest, The*, 94

Theophrastus, 168

Thomas, Keith, 154, 234n.69

Traske, John, 162

Tricomi, Albert, 87, 225n.15

*True Copies of the Insolent, Cruell, Barbarous and Blasphemous Letter*, 232n.17

*True Copy of the Latin Oration of . . . Ossolinski, A*, 232n.17

*True Relation of a Wonderfull Sea Fight, A*, 145–6

Tyacke, Nicholas, 214n.42, 216n.86, 235n.1, 236n.21
Tyler, Margaret, 74
Tymme, Thomas, *A Silver Watchbell*, 164–5

Ussher, James (Bishop of Meath), 48–51, 59

Van den Keere, Pieter, 141–3
Veeser, H. A., 209n.1
Venner, Tobias, 239n.100
Venuti, Lawrence, 227n.61
Vere, Horace, 143, 150
verse libels, 98–100, 178–84, 226n.45
Veseler, George, 141–3
Vicari, Patricia, 23, 30, 213n.26
Vickers, Brain, 238n.75
Vickers, Nancy, 222n.44
Villiers, Edward, 147
Villiers, George, *see* Buckingham
Virgil, 134

Wall, Wendy, 209n.3, 229n.33
Waller, Gary, 218n.3, 297n.3
Walmsley, Joan M., 237n.53–4
Walsham, Alexandra, 180, 237n.56–8
Walton, Izaak, 33, 214n.44
Ward, Samuel, 54–8, 162, 177, 223, 245; Engaving 'To God', 55–7; *Happiness of Practice, The*, 55, 57–8; *Jethro's Justice of the Peace*, 58; *Life of Faith, The*, 57
Warre, James, *Touchstone of Truth, The*, 165–6
Wats, James, 176
Watt, Tessa, 151, 160, 234n.62–3, 235n.5
Webber, Joan, 20, 23, 28, 33, 213n.18, 213n.28, 214n.45, 215n.57
Webster, John, 85, 88
Weinberger, Jerry, 238n.76
Welsby, Paul, 44, 215n.62
White, John, 157
White, Peter, 214n.42, 236n.21, 237n.48

White, Stephen D., 236n.23
Williams, Ethel Carleton, 220n.22
Willis, John, *Art of Memory, The*, 200
Wilson, David H., 226n.42, 226n.49
Winwood, Ralph, 2
witches, 104–7
Wither, George, 117–23, 152; *Abuses Stripped and Whipped*, 117, 174; *Songs of the old Testament*, 121–3, 212; *Wither's Motto*, 117–21, 173
women, and advice, 171–3; and catechisms, 167; and Middleton, 87–8; and Fletcher, 94–6; and Taylor, 127
women writers, 14–17, 64–75, 114–17, 171–3; as monstrous, 65–7, 115–16
*Wonderfull discouerie of the witchcrafts of Margaret and Phillip Flower, A*, 153–4
Wood, Anthony a, 132
Woolf, D.R., 181–2, 191, 192, 237n.59–60, 238n.78, 238n.80, 238n.84, 239n.87, 239n.90, 239n.94–7
Worden, Blair, 221n.27
Woudhuysen, Henry, 220n.16, 230n.33
Wright, Thomas, (*see also* Dewe, Thomas), 276
Wrightson, Keith, 235n.4
Wroth, Mary, xxi , 87–112, 113–17; 'Pamphilia to Amphilanthus', 113–17; *Urania*, xvii, 64–75, 285; publication of, 65–7
Wynne, Edward, 145

Yelverton, Henry, 148–9
Young, Michael B., 209n.6

Zaller, Robert, 45, 161, 215n.63–5, 216n.74–6, 216n.90, 217n.99, 226n.44, 233n.41, 233n.43, 233n.50, 234n.51–2, 235n.12–14, 236n.23

Printed in the United States
25275LVS00001B/91

9 781403 900739